THE ZONDERVAN 2006
PASTOR'S ANNUAL

AN IDEA & RESOURCE BOOK

T. T. CRABTREE

D1481425

ZONDERVAN™

GRAND RAPIDS, MICHIGAN 49530 USA

ZONDERVAN™

The Zondervan 2006 Pastor's Annual
Copyright © 1985, 2005 by the Zondervan Corporation

Requests for information should be addressed to:

Zondervan, Grand Rapids, Michigan 49530

Much of the contents of this book was previously published in Pastor's Annual 1986.

ISBN-10: 0-310-24365-3
ISBN-13: 978-0-310-24365-6

Printed in the United States of America

05 06 07 08 09 10 11 12 /❖ DCI/ 10 9 8 7 6 5 4 3 2 1

CONTENTS

Preface 9
Acknowledgments 10
Contributing Authors 11

SERMONS

Jan 1   Sun AM Necessities *(1 Corinthians 13)* 13
Jan 1   Sun PM Lost Things *(Luke 15:1–32)* 16
Jan 4   Wed PM What Is Happiness? *(Psalm 1:1–6)* 18
Jan 8   Sun AM God Can Use You *(Matthew 9:36–10:7)* 20
Jan 8   Sun PM The Great Discovery *(Matthew 13:44–46)* 23
Jan 11 Wed PM What Is Man? *(Psalm 8:1–9)* 25
Jan 15 Sun AM Things Truly Christian *(James 1:19–27)* 27
Jan 15 Sun PM Laying Foundations *(Matthew 7:24–29)* 30
Jan 18 Wed PM What Is the Bible? *(Psalm 19:7–11)* 32
Jan 22 Sun AM What Jesus Does for Sinners *(Revelation 1:4–7)* 34
Jan 22 Sun PM The Prayer God Hears *(Luke 18:9–14)* 36
Jan 25 Wed PM Is Self-Inventory Possible? *(Psalm 19:12–14)* 39
Jan 29 Sun AM Things Still Sacred *(Genesis 2:21–25;* 41
                 Matthew 16:13–19; 2 Timothy 3:16–17)
Jan 29 Sun PM Love and Forgiveness *(Luke 7:36–50)* 43
Feb 1   Wed PM Do We Need Religion? *(Psalm 37:1–22)* 46
Feb 5   Sun AM What Jesus Refuses to Do *(Matthew 12:14–21)* 48
Feb 5   Sun PM The Fate of God's Word *(Luke 8:4–15)* 50
Feb 8   Wed PM What Can We Do When Troubles Come? 52
                 (Psalm 121:1–8)
Feb 12 Sun AM What the Church Must Remember *(Matthew 28:16–20)* . . .53
Feb 12 Sun PM The Pretenders *(Matthew 13:24–30, 36–43)* 55
Feb 15 Wed PM How Does One Psalmist Picture Salvation? 58
                 (Psalm 40:1–10)
Feb 19 Sun AM Things Most Precious *(1 Peter 1:1–8)* 59
Feb 19 Sun PM The Persistent Host *(Luke 14:15–24)* 61
Feb 22 Wed PM What Does It Mean to Know God? *(Psalm 46:1–11)* 63
Feb 26 Sun AM Things Mercifully Simple *(Acts 16:25–40)* 65
Feb 26 Sun PM When Forgiveness Is Hard *(Matthew 18:21–35)* 67
Mar 1   Wed PM How Do Our Sins Get the Best of Us? *(Psalm 65:1–13)* . . .71
Mar 5   Sun AM Faith: A Theology of the Cross *(1 Corinthians 1:18–25)* 73
Mar 5   Sun PM The Winners *(Luke 11:5–13)* 75

Mar 8 Wed PM What Kind of World Is This? *(Psalm 115:1–18)* 77

Mar 12 Sun AM Hope: A Theology of the Resurrection 79
(1 Corinthians 15:1–8, 12–25, 35–58)

Mar 12 Sun PM The High Cost of Commitment *(Luke 14:25–35)* 82

Mar 15 Wed PM Is Revival Coming? *(Psalm 85:1–13)* 84

Mar 19 Sun AM Love: A Visible Ethic *(1 Corinthians 13)* 86

Mar 19 Sun PM A Way of Showing Mercy *(Luke 10:25–37)* 89

Mar 22 Wed PM When May We Expect the Harvest? *(Psalm 126:1–6)* 91

Mar 26 Sun AM The Certainty of the Resurrection 93
(1 Corinthians 15:1–19)

Mar 26 Sun PM The Deciding Factor *(Matthew 25:1–13)* 95

Mar 29 Wed PM What Is It Like to Die? *(Psalm 17:1–15)* 98

Apr 2 Sun AM If There Had Been No Resurrection 100
(1 Corinthians 15:12–19)

Apr 2 Sun PM When God Speaks, People Should Listen 102
(Hebrews 1:1–3; 2:1–4; 3:7–8; 4:12–16)

Apr 5 Wed PM Barriers to Blessings *(Luke 16:10–13)* 105

Apr 9 Sun AM Blessed Is He Who Comes in the Name of the Lord 106
(Isaiah 44:21–25; Philippians 2:5–11)

Apr 9 Sun PM The Incomparable Christ *(Hebrews 2:2–14)* 108

Apr 12 Wed PM Foundations for Stewardship: The Grace of Christ 110
(2 Corinthians 8:7–15)

Apr 16 Sun AM The Meaning of the Resurrection 111
(1 Corinthians 15:29–33)

Apr 16 Sun PM The Danger of Drifting *(Hebrews 2:1–4)* 113

Apr 19 Wed PM Thanks Be to God *(2 Corinthians 9:1–15)* 115

Apr 23 Sun AM The Order of the Resurrection *(1 Corinthians 15:20–28)* . .117

Apr 23 Sun PM Take Me to Your Leader *(Hebrews 2:5–13)* 119

Apr 26 Wed PM The Criterion for Stewardship: Faithfulness 121
(1 Corinthians 4:1–2)

Apr 30 Sun AM The Nature of Our Resurrection Bodies 122
(1 Corinthians 15:35–49)

Apr 30 Sun PM Liberation from Life's Greatest Enemies 124
(Hebrews 2:14–18)

May 3 Wed PM The Profit in Trials *(James 1:1–5)* 127

May 7 Sun AM The Challenge of the Resurrection 129
(1 Corinthians 15:50–58)

May 7 Sun PM The Kind of Priest You Need *(Hebrews 4:14–5:10)* 131

May 10 Wed PM Resources for Bad Times *(James 1:5–8)* 133

May 14 Sun AM An Exciting Discovery for Mother's Day 135
               (Galatians 3:26–29)
May 14 Sun PM An Old Testament History Lesson (Hebrews 5:11–6:8) 137
May 17 Wed PM Putting Tests into Perspective (James 1:9–12) 139
May 21 Sun AM The Witnessing Woman (1 Peter 3:1–6) 141
May 21 Sun PM Jesus Is Better (Hebrews 8:1–9:14) 143
May 24 Wed PM God's Part in Temptation (James 1:13–18) 145
May 28 Sun AM The News We Want to Hear (2 Samuel 18:1–5, 24–33) . . .147
May 28 Sun PM The Supreme Sacrifice (Hebrews 9:23–10:18) 149
May 31 Wed PM I Believe the Bible (James 1:19–27) 152
Jun 4 Sun AM Living in a Haunted House (Matthew 12:43–45) 154
Jun 4 Sun PM Challenge to Discipleship (Hebrews 10:19–39) 157
Jun 7 Wed PM The Problems with Partiality (James 2:1–13) 159
Jun 11 Sun AM What Is the Foundation of Your Home? 161
               (Matthew 7:24–27)
Jun 11 Sun PM The Faith of Our Father (Hebrews 11:8–19) 163
Jun 14 Wed PM A Faith That Is Alive (James 2:14–26) 166
Jun 18 Sun AM Duties of a Daddy (1 Timothy 6:11–16) 167
Jun 18 Sun PM Living by Faith (Hebrews 11:23–29) 169
Jun 21 Wed PM The Powerful Tongue (James 3:1–8) 172
Jun 25 Sun AM The Recovery of Family Life (Hosea 1:2–9; 3:1–3) 173
Jun 25 Sun PM Getting Ready to Race (Hebrews 12:1–2) 176
Jun 28 Wed PM Consistency (James 3:9–12) 178
Jul 2 Sun AM When Christ Comes to Your House (Mark 1:29–31) 181
Jul 2 Sun PM Responding to God's Discipline (Hebrews 12:5–11) 184
Jul 5 Wed PM To Be Wise (James 3:13–18) 186
Jul 9 Sun AM The Great Invitation (Isaiah 1:1–20) 188
Jul 9 Sun PM Compelled to Excel (2 Corinthians 8:1–15) 191
Jul 12 Wed PM Self-gratification (James 4:1–10) 193
Jul 16 Sun AM The Great Encounter (Isaiah 6:1–13) 195
Jul 16 Sun PM The Impulse to Give (2 Corinthians 8:8–12) 198
Jul 19 Wed PM To Criticize Is to Crucify (James 4:11–12) 200
Jul 23 Sun AM The Great Promises of Peace (Isaiah 26:1–4) 201
Jul 23 Sun PM The Meaning of Stewardship (2 Corinthians 8:1–5) 204
Jul 26 Wed PM The Self-made Man (James 4:13–17) 206
Jul 30 Sun AM A Great Call (Isaiah 55:1–7) 208
Jul 30 Sun PM A New Day in Giving (2 Corinthians 9:1–7) 210
Aug 2 Wed PM Man, That's Living! (James 5:1–6) 213
Aug 6 Sun AM How Do You Describe an Elephant? 215
               (1 Corinthians 1:1–19)

Aug 6 Sun PM The Biblical Perspective on Bitterness *(Luke 17:3–10)* . . .218
Aug 9 Wed PM Precious Patience *(James 5:7–11)* 220
Aug 13 Sun AM The Church in Unity and Diversity 222
(1 Corinthians 1:10–17)
Aug 13 Sun PM The Biblical Perspective on Anxiety *(2 Timothy 1:7–13)* . . .224
Aug 16 Wed PM Taking Oaths *(James 5:12)* 226
Aug 20 Sun AM The Ties That Bind *(1 Corinthians 3:1–23)* 228
Aug 20 Sun PM The Biblical Perspective on Worrying 231
(Matthew 6:25–34; Philippians 3:13–14)
Aug 23 Wed PM Proper Prayer *(James 5:13–18)* 232
Aug 27 Sun AM What about Church Discipline? *(1 Corinthians 5:1–13)* . . .234
Aug 27 Sun PM The Biblical Perspective on Depression 236
(1 Kings 19:1–13)
Aug 30 Wed PM Bringing Back Backsliders *(James 5:19–20)* 239
Sep 3 Sun AM Conversations of Jesus: Nicodemus *(John 3:1–12)* 241
Sep 3 Sun PM Saved and Sure of It! *(1 John 5:13–15)* 244
Sep 6 Wed PM What Kind of Christian? *(1 Thessalonians 1:1–4)* 247
Sep 10 Sun AM Conversations of Jesus: The Woman at the Well 249
(John 4:7–14)
Sep 10 Sun PM An Old Man's Love Letter *(2 John 1–6)* 251
Sep 13 Wed PM What Kind of Gospel? *(1 Thessalonians 1:5)* 254
Sep 17 Sun AM Conversations of Jesus: Paul *(Acts 9:1–9)* 256
Sep 17 Sun PM The Many Faces of Love *(3 John 1–7)* 258
Sep 20 Wed PM What Kind of Church? *(1 Thessalonians 1:6–10)* 261
Sep 24 Sun AM Conversations of Jesus: Mary Magdalene 262
(John 20:11–18)
Sep 24 Sun PM The Faith Once Delivered *(Jude)* 265
Sep 27 Wed PM What Kind of Preaching? *(1 Thessalonians 2:1–6)* 267
Oct 1 Sun AM The Grace of Salvation *(Ephesians 2:8–10)* 270
Oct 1 Sun PM Facets of the Stewardship Gem *(1 Peter 4:7–11)* 273
Oct 4 Wed PM What Kind of Ministry? *(1 Thessalonians 2:7–12)* 275
Oct 8 Sun AM The Grace of Serving *(Romans 15:14–19)* 276
Oct 8 Sun PM From Heart to Hand *(Exodus 35:20–29)* 278
Oct 11 Wed PM A Spiritual Checkup *(1 Thessalonians 3:1–5)* 280
Oct 15 Sun AM The Grace of Growing *(2 Peter 3:17–18)* 281
Oct 15 Sun PM God's Plan of Giving *(Matthew 23:23–24;* 283
1 Corinthians 16:1–2)
Oct 18 Wed PM A Good Report *(1 Thessalonians 3:6)* 285
Oct 22 Sun AM The Grace of Giving *(2 Corinthians 8:1–7; 9:6–8)* 286
Oct 22 Sun PM Dead but Still Speaking *(Psalm 49:10–11, 16–17;* 289
Hebrews 11:4)

Oct 25 Wed PM   An Earnest Prayer *(1 Thessalonians 3:11–13)* 291
Oct 29 Sun AM   The Grace of Sufficiency *(2 Corinthians 12:7–10)* 292
Oct 29 Sun PM   Sacrificial Giving *(Mark 12:41–42; 2 Corinthians 8:1–9)* . . .294
Nov 1   Wed PM   A Wholesome Life *(1 Thessalonians 4:1–8)* 297
Nov 5   Sun AM   Guidelines for Investing in Eternity *(Luke 16:1–9)* 298
Nov 5   Sun PM   Life after Death *(1 Peter 1:3–4)* 301
Nov 8   Wed PM   Death and Grief *(1 Thessalonians 4:13–18)* 304
Nov 12 Sun AM   The Great Impossibility *(Luke 16:9–13)* 305
Nov 12 Sun PM   Heaven: What Will It Be Like? *(John 14:1–2)* 308
Nov 15 Wed PM   The Season of His Coming *(1 Thessalonians 5:1–3)* 311
Nov 19 Sun AM   Thankful for God's Best *(Luke 1:57–64)* 312
Nov 19 Sun PM   Heaven: Will You Be There? *(Matthew 8:11–12)* 314
Nov 22 Wed PM   Contrasting Children *(1 Thessalonians 4:4–10)* 317
Nov 26 Sun AM   God Holds the Deed *(Psalm 24:1–5)* 318
Nov 26 Sun PM   Heaven: Be Prepared *(Revelation 21:19–27)* 320
Nov 29 Wed PM   Final Instructions to the Church 323
                  (1 Thessalonians 5:11–22)
Dec 3   Sun AM   Jesus' View of Money *(Luke 16:1–2)* 325
Dec 3   Sun PM   Jesus, the Light of the World *(Isa. 9:2–7; John 8:12–30)* . . .328
Dec 6   Wed PM   The Calling of Andrew *(John 1:35–42)* 330
Dec 10 Sun AM   Where Is Christmas? *(Galatians 4:4–5; Luke 2:8–14)* 331
Dec 10 Sun PM   Crowded Rooms and Empty Lives *(Luke 2:1–7)* 333
Dec 13 Wed PM   The Winning of Nathanael *(John 1:43–51)* 335
Dec 17 Sun AM   Your King Comes to You *(Zechariah 9:9–16)* 337
Dec 17 Sun PM   Missing the Main Event *(Mark 11:1–11)* 340
Dec 20 Wed PM   Nicodemus *(John 3:1–22; 7:45–53; 19:38–42)* 342
Dec 24 Sun AM   Immanuel—God with Us *(Matthew 1:21–25)* 344
Dec 24 Sun PM   Home for Christmas *(Luke 2:1–7)* 346
Dec 27 Wed PM   The Samaritan Woman *(John 4:3–42)* 348
Dec 31 Sun AM   God Is Able *(1 John 5:1–21)* 350
Dec 31 Sun PM   He Cared Enough to Send the Very Best *(Luke 2:1–20;* . . .352
                  John 3:16)

MISCELLANEOUS HELPS

Message on the Lord's Supper

The Lord's Presence—In Crisis (Psalm 139:7–12) 355

Messages for Children and Young People

Keeping Our Appointments with God (Matthew 28:16) 357
The Best News (Luke 2:10) 358
Learning to Have Faith in God (Hebrews 11:6) 359

Funeral Meditations

Sorrow Not as the Hopeless (1 Thessalonians 4:13) 361
"Death Be Not Proud, Thou Too Shalt Die" 362
     (1 Corinthians 15:19–22, 51–52, 54, 56)
Salt of the Earth (Matthew 5:13) 363
The Shepherd Psalm (Psalm 23) 364

Weddings

A Simple Marriage Ceremony 365
A Marriage Ceremony 366

Sentence Sermonettes
. 368

Indexes

Subject Index 371
Index of Scripture Texts 373

PREFACE

Favorable comments from ministers who serve in many different types of churches suggest that the *Pastor's Annual* provides valuable assistance to many busy pastors as they seek to improve the quality, freshness, and variety of their pulpit ministry. To be of service to fellow pastors in their continuing quest to obey our Lord's command to Peter, "Feed my sheep," is a calling to which I respond with gratitude.

I pray that this issue of the *Pastor's Annual* will be blessed by our Lord in helping each pastor to plan and produce a preaching program that will better meet the spiritual needs of his or her congregation.

This issue contains series of sermons by several contributing authors who have been effective contemporary preachers and successful pastors. Each author is listed with his sermons by date in the section titled "Contributing Authors." I accept responsibility for those sermons not listed there.

This issue of the *Pastor's Annual* is dedicated to the Lord with a prayer that he will bless these efforts to let the Holy Spirit lead pastors in preparing a planned preaching program for the year.

ACKNOWLEDGMENTS

All Scripture quotations, unless otherwise noted, are taken from the *King James Version*. Additional translations used are the following:

The Holy Bible, New International Version®. NIV®. Copyright © 1973, 1978, 1984 by International Bible Society. Used by permission of Zondervan. All rights reserved.

The Living Bible. Copyright © 1971 by Tyndale House Publishers, Wheaton, Illinois.

The New American Standard Bible. © Copyright 1960, 1962, 1963, 1968, 1971, 1972, 1973, 1975, 1977 by The Lockman Foundation. Used by permission.

The New English Bible, copyright © 1970 by Oxford University Press.

Revised Standard Version of the Bible, copyright 1946, 1952, 1971 by the Division of Christian Education of the National Council of Churches of Christ in the USA. Used by permission.

CONTRIBUTING AUTHORS

Tom S. Brandon . . . . .AM   October 1, 8, 15, 22, 29
Mark Brister . . . . .PM   July 9, 16, 23, 30
Harold T. Bryson . . . . . . .PM   April 2, 9, 16, 23, 30
     May 7, 14, 21, 28
     June 4, 11, 18, 25
     July 2
James E. Carter . . . . .AM   May 14, 21, 28
     June 4, 11, 18, 25
     July 2
Bennie Cole Crabtree . . . . . .   Sentence Sermonettes
T. T. Crabtree . . . .   Messages for Children and Young People
J. B. Fowler . . . . .AM   January 1, 15, 22, 29
     February 5, 12, 19, 26
Michael C. Fuhrman . . . . .AM   August 6, 13, 20, 27
Clyde Glazener . . . . .PM   April 5, 12, 19, 26
W. T. Holland . . . . .PM   January 4, 11, 18, 25
     February 1, 8, 15, 22
     March 1, 8, 15, 22, 29
David L. Jenkins . . . . . . .PM   January 1, 8, 15, 22, 29
     February 5, 12, 19, 26
     March 5, 12, 19, 26
J. Estill Jones . . . . .AM   December 17, 24, 31
Howard S. Kolb . . . . .AM   December 10
               PM   December 10, 17, 31
D. Terry Land . . . . .PM   May 3, 10, 17, 24, 31
     June 7, 14, 21, 28
     July 5, 12, 19, 26
     August 2, 9, 16, 23, 30
D. L. Lowrie . . . . .AM   November 5, 12, 19, 26
     December 3
Jerold McBride . . . . . . .AM   January 8
               PM   September 3, 10, 17, 24
     December 6, 13, 20, 24, 27
Dale McConnell . . . . . . .AM   March 5, 12, 19
     April 9
               PM   December 3
Alton H. McEachern . . . .   Funeral Meditations
     Message on the Lord's Supper
     Weddings

Robert L. Perry	.PM	August 6, 13, 20, 27
		September 6, 13, 20, 27
		October 4, 11, 18, 25
		November 1, 8, 15, 22, 29
Paul W. Powell	.AM	March 26
		April 2, 16, 23, 30
		May 7
Allen Reed	.AM	July 9, 16, 23, 30
Dan Vestal	.AM	September 3, 10, 17, 24
	PM	November 5, 12, 19, 26
Bill Whittaker	.PM	October 1, 8, 15, 22, 29

JANUARY

■ Sunday Mornings

The beginning of a new year offers hope for the future. It is a time when we renew our commitments to the basics. "Things Worth Remembering" is the suggested theme for the morning sermons in January.

■ Sunday Evenings

In the parables, Jesus Christ spoke about God as no person had ever before spoken. Through the parables, he continues to speak to us with penetrating insight. "Patterns for Pilgrims" is the theme for a series of messages based on the parables of our Lord.

■ Wednesday Evenings

The Psalms pose questions about life that are relevant regardless of the time or place in which someone lives. "Questions by the Psalmist" is the theme for the Wednesday evening meditations for the month.

SUNDAY MORNING, JANUARY 1

Title: Necessities

Text: "So faith, hope, love abide, these three; but the greatest of these is love" *(1 Cor. 13:13 RSV).*

Scripture Reading: 1 Corinthians 13

Hymns: "How Firm a Foundation," Rippon

"The Solid Rock," Mote

"To God Be the Glory," Crosby

Offertory Prayer: Heavenly Father, we come to you through Jesus Christ our Lord. With appreciative hearts we thank you for what you have done and promise to do for us. Now out of gratitude for all our blessings, we bring our tithes and offerings into your storehouse for your kingdom's work. Bless them that they may lift burdens and advance your kingdom, through Christ our Lord. Amen.

Introduction

Michelangelo and Raphael were great Italian Renaissance painters. The story is told that Michelangelo, eight years older than Raphael, came into Raphael's studio and examined one of Raphael's early drawings. Picking up a piece of chalk,

Michelangelo scrawled across the painting the Latin word *Amplius*, which means "greater" or "larger."

To the older master's trained eye, Raphael's painting demonstrated too little vision. Michelangelo insisted that Raphael think bigger and paint better. Surely this is what almighty God thinks of most of our plans and efforts. The God who thinks big wants us to live greater, nobler lives.

If we are to live 2006 magnificently and gloriously, there are some things we can't do without. Paul lists three of them.

I. We can't do without faith.

In his book *The Gift of Love*, R. L. Middleton tells about an experience that A. J. Cronin, a British physician turned author, had in the venerable city of Vienna shortly after World War I.

Cronin had looked forward to revisiting the city he had known and loved. But when he finally reached Vienna, he was deeply distressed as he saw how the city had been destroyed by the Germans. Walking amid the ruins of the once beautiful city, he grew furious as he witnessed the ravages of war.

As the cold night fell, he sought shelter in a small, dimly lit church. Sitting down to wait out the winter rainstorm, he turned to see an old man coming into the sanctuary. Clad only in an old suit but standing painfully erect, the old man walked down the aisle carrying a little girl in his arms.

When the old man put down the cold, poorly dressed little girl, Cronin saw that she was paralyzed. But as the old man supported her, she knelt at the altar, clinging to the rail.

After a few minutes of prayer, the little girl placed a candle on the small stand adjacent to the altar. Then the old man picked her up and started up the aisle with his precious burden.

Cronin followed them out of the church and watched as the man gently placed the girl on a dilapidated wagon and pulled a potato sack over her twisted limbs. Unable to hold his silence, Cronin asked the old man if the war had maimed the child. He answered that she was crippled by the same bomb that had killed her mother and father.

When Cronin asked if they came to the church often, the old man replied that they came daily to pray. Then he added, "We come to show the good God that we're not angry with him."

Doesn't that show you the necessity of faith better than I ever could? Faith is something we can't do without if we are to make 2006 rich and meaningful for us.

Paul tells us that though faith is essential, there is a second attribute we must possess if 2006 is to mean all it ought to mean for us.

II. We can't do without hope.

The late Dr. G. Campbell Morgan tells about a man whose shop was among the buildings destroyed in the Chicago fire of 1871. The next morning, arriving at what had once been his place of business, the man set up a table in the midst of the charred debris. Above the table he placed a sign that read, "Everything lost except wife, children, and hope. Business will be resumed as usual tomorrow morning."

Hope is something we can't do without in 2006. Life will test us and try us. If we lose hope, we will never survive.

George Frederick Watts, a nineteenth-century British painter, has poignantly pictured hope in one of his works. The scene is of a woman sitting on a globe of the world playing her harp; every string, except one, broken. One could easily title the picture *Despair*. But Watts titled the picture *Hope*, because he knew that as long as one string remained, there was still hope of making music from it.

Christian hope is a two-pronged thing: not only does hope give us victory in life's current crises, but it also gives us assurance of rest and peace with God when this life is over. The hope written of in the Bible is a confident expectation; hope is an assurance that is absolute. Paul writes in Romans 5:2: "[We] rejoice in hope of the glory of God." We live in hope that tomorrow will be better, that life will be sweeter, that we shall become better. Hope is as natural to believers as the beating of our hearts. It is within us because God has put it there. It is something we can't do without in 2006.

Finally, let's consider the last of Paul's essentials of life.

III. We can't do without love.

The largest art museum in the world is the Louvre. Among its five thousand paintings are two that are particularly relevant to the necessity of love. In the first painting, an indignant, angry father is ordering his son out of the house. The father's finger is raised in anger against the wicked son. The weeping mother and sisters and brothers cower in the background.

In the second picture, the same members of the family are shown, but the scene has changed drastically. The father lies lifeless on his bed. His family kneels by the side of his bed. The wife's face is buried in her hands.

The door to the little cottage is open. The rebellious son stands with his hand on the door latch and his foot on the doorstep. Grief is written across his face. He has come home, but it is too late—too late for the boy to confess to his father that he is sorry and wants forgiveness; too late for the father to speak the words of forgiveness and reconciling love the boy longs to hear. For both it is too late. They have learned in an agonizing way that love is one thing we can't do without.

Love's healing touch is desperately needed in our homes, businesses, schools, churches, and the government. Therefore, we need to let God fill our hearts with his love. Then we need to share that love with others. Love is life's most precious gift; in the new year we can't do without it.

Conclusion

As we begin this new year, more than anything God wants to write *Amplius* across our lives. He wants to make them bigger and better. He who put the stars in the heavens and raised the rocky mountains above the flat plains can do it—will do it—if we will let him.

SUNDAY EVENING, JANUARY 1

Title: Lost Things

Text: "'I tell you . . . there will be more rejoicing in heaven over one sinner who repents than over ninety-nine righteous persons who do not need to repent'" (*Luke 15:7 NIV*).

Scripture Reading: Luke 15:1–32

Introduction

There is no more life-suffocating experience in the world than to feel unloved, to feel that no one cares. Even though we occasionally encounter people who declare that they don't need anyone, that they can "make it alone," we know that even as they utter those words they are crying out to be recognized and appreciated.

This need to feel loved is not a human weakness—God made us this way. Loving and caressing are equally important to a child's well-being as nutritional nourishment. A child who grows up in a home with argumentative, negligent parents usually shows evidence of personality scars—insecurity, hostility, and other severe problems.

During his time on earth, Jesus was especially sensitive to emotionally and spiritually hurting people. One way he effectively described God's love for all people is in beautiful and winsome parables. In Luke 15 Jesus weaves three simple but poignant scenes into one parable of "lost things." In each instance he depicts the incalculable value of that which was lost. The thrust of his message is how much God loves us regardless of where we are or what condition we are in at the moment. Jesus graphically portrays a shepherd who braves imminent danger to search for his lost sheep, a woman who is distraught because she has lost a prized and precious coin, and a heartbroken father who spends his time waiting expectantly for the return of his wayward son. The three stories all support the overall theme of Luke's gospel: "The Son of Man came to seek and to save what was lost" (19:10 NIV).

I. First, Jesus told the story of a lost sheep (vv. 3–7).

A. *The Shepherd, not the sheep, is the important figure in the parable.* Jesus knew well the relationship that existed between a true shepherd and his sheep: any shepherd worthy of the name would not rest until the last one of his flock was secure in the fold. The emphasis in this parable is not on what caused the sheep to be lost. Indeed, by nature the sheep has a poor sense of direction and needs to be able to see its shepherd at all times. The meaning of the parable, however, is drawn by understanding the nature of the shepherd.

B. *The emphasis in Jesus' story is on the attitude of the shepherd.* He was deeply distressed over the one lost sheep. Are we that concerned about the "one lost wanderer" from our fold? Do we tend to say instead, "Well, here are the faithful ones who appreciate what we are doing and who deserve our best attention"? Or "The wanderer is always a problem. He doesn't deserve our time."

The shepherd was not passive. He did not let the sheep disappear into the enveloping wilderness. Rather, the shepherd actively pursued the sheep. Jesus portrayed the shepherd as saying, "I will go myself, and I will seek until I find, and bring the lost one back!"

C. *Just as the shepherd left the security of the ninety-nine to seek the one poor sheep who was lost, so did the Son of God come from the glory of heaven to seek out his lost people.* This is the heart of the Bible; it is the reason behind Bethlehem's manger and Calvary's cross. Jesus didn't have to pursue us actively. But he chose, out of his boundless mercy, to make himself a desolate, empty, suffering man—a man of sorrows yearning for fellowship, a man crying, "I thirst!" while hanging on a cross. The message of the gospel—and of this story—is that there was no sacrifice too great for God to make to bring us back to himself.

II. The second story is about a lost coin (vv. 8–10).

A. *Again, as with the lost sheep, note that it is the owner who suffers, not the object lost.* Although opinions differ as to the worth of this coin, it seems most likely that the coin was of relatively small monetary value. The women of those days, however, often wore on their brow a frontlet called a *semedi.* A *semedi* was made up of coins and was given to a woman by her husband on their wedding day. Thus it would be comparable to the wedding band a married woman wears today. It was of priceless value to this woman because her husband had given it to her. She suffered much by her loss of it.

B. *Diligence was a characteristic of the woman.* We have no idea how long this woman searched for the lost coin. No doubt she explored every nook and cranny, every crack in the earthen floor. Her diligence was fruitful. She found the coin, and she did what the shepherd did when he brought home his lost sheep: she called all of her friends and neighbors together to rejoice with her.

C. *Note the application Jesus makes (v. 10): imagine the scene in heaven when a person is rescued from his or her hopeless, sinful state and brought into the fold of God.* Apparently spontaneous cheers break forth from the innumerable hosts of angelic beings throughout the celestial domain of God. We know that great value is placed on one repenting sinner.

D. *Jesus clarified his mission in these two stories.* He came to seek and to save sinners. Thus he explained the reason why he had fellowship with them. This speaks eloquently to the church, for traditionally we are much more comfortable with our "secure ninety-and-nine" than we are with the truant individual who seems to have a fight on his or her hands in living the Christian life.

Jesus is saying to us in these stories that the greatest joy to the church is not its secure financial standing or beautiful buildings, but the realization of its mission—the seeking and saving of the lost. Spontaneous joy should break out from the church, not only when we retire a building debt, but when a lost soul is redeemed by the grace of God.

III. The last of this trilogy of parables deals with a lost son (vv. 11–32).

A. *The story of the prodigal son has been called "the paragon of the parables."* It is the story of a common, heartbreaking experience—a beloved child chooses to leave home and go his own way, refusing to incorporate into his decisions the faithful and consistent teachings he received in childhood.

B. *The beautiful part of the story, of course, is that the young man did come to himself.* His pain was creative. He "came to his senses," and in a very touching soliloquy, he "talked to himself" with both shame and realism. He took full responsibility for his sins, resolved to make a full confession of them, and returned to his father's house as a hired servant.

C. *More compelling than the story of the repenting boy is that of the waiting father, who never forgot his wandering son while he was away.* It was undignified for the old man to break his stride and run, but this father forgot himself and ran all the way to meet his returning son!

Immediately the father set plans in motion to celebrate his son's return. His actions parallel those of the rejoicing shepherd and woman in the two previous stories. But there is an added dimension to God's love in this third story: we see how sensitive God's love is, especially when we need it most. Augustine said, "God loves each one of us as if there were only one of us to love."

Conclusion

Even though it is dangerous to compare a human reaction with God's reaction, we can say that in these three stories Jesus has presented the Father as loving us all—especially when we are hurting from the results of our sin. With amazing grace he pursues that which is lost.

WEDNESDAY EVENING, JANUARY 4

Title: What Is Happiness?

Text: "Happy is the man" *(Ps. 1:1 NEB).*

Scripture Reading: Psalm 1:1–6

Introduction

In the 1920s William Lyon Phelps published a little book entitled *Happiness.* That many wish either to become or remain happy is evidenced by the popularity of this book: not only was it reprinted thirty times during the eight years following publication, but it was still in print nearly fifty years later.

The writer of Psalm 1 does not attempt to define happiness; he illustrates it. He shows us that happiness is not in our circumstances; it is in ourselves. Happiness primarily concerns not the externals of life, but the condition of our spiritual health and the degree of our intimacy with God.

What is happiness? Four affirmations will help us toward an understanding.

Happiness is a matter of proper balance.

Not only does all work and no play make Jack a dull boy; it is also apt to develop him into a neurotic, cross-grained man. People who enjoy being sad are not saintly; they are sick. Piety does not manifest itself in a sigh any more than in a smile. A hearty laugh is a truer mark of nobility than a cynical sneer.

On the other hand, pursuing pleasure for pleasure's sake is equally harmful. To make the quest of pleasure the whole end of living is to court disillusionment. Modern socialites slave to have a good time; in fact, they are slaves to their good times. They are merry, but they are also tired, nervous, and bored.

The point of these examples is that one's life must have balance if he or she is to be happy.

II. Happiness is a matter of a true sense of values.

Happiness is the ability to appreciate the best things, the highest values. Happiness depends on other factors besides merely having a good time. That happiness can be bought by those who have the price is a popular heresy today, but it *is* a heresy. The truth is that it can be gained only by those who live by God's principles. The unhappiest people in the world are those who can pay the price of everything and know the value of nothing.

III. Happiness is a matter of outgoing interests.

A. *We must be interested in other people.* To eat and drink may make one merry, but it is more fun if one eats and drinks with someone else. Oliver Wendell Holmes once described happiness as "four feet on a fireplace fender." Happiness is a product of relationships. No individual can attain real happiness alone. In our relationships with others, however, we must have their welfare in mind. To be happy we must consider the other person's right to be happy. No one can build happiness on someone else's unhappiness.

B. *We must be dedicated to a cause worthy to claim our best.* The happiest people are those who are so immersed in some great cause that they don't notice if they are happy or not. These are the people with singing hearts. When you get to the heart of the religion, you will find a song. True happiness is the most persuasive herald the gospel has in the world. Millions live unhappily because, while they have something to live *on*, they lack the supreme condition of a happy life, something to life *for*.

IV. Happiness is a matter of Christian hope for the future.

If we are to be happy, our lives must be pointed in the right direction. Deep down in our hearts, we know that we are immortal. English philosopher James Martineau once said, "We do not believe in immortality because we can prove it; we try to prove it because we believe in it." Everywhere and in every culture the faith in an eternal tomorrow exists. The universal verdict of humankind is that this life is not all there is. For the Christian the rainbow of a larger hope rims the horizon of eternity.

Conclusion

"Blessed [or happy] are those who hunger and thirst for righteousness, for they will be filled" (Matt. 5:6 NIV). All other quests end in futility. Those who are hungry for pleasure become disenchanted and bored. Those who are hungry for possessions drop the keys to their safe-deposit boxes when they die. Those who lust for power, even if they gain it, are robbed of their scepters and shorn of their royal purple when "the night cometh." But those who are hungry and thirsty for righteousness will be fully satisfied—not once, but again and again as spiritual appetite returns.

SUNDAY MORNING, JANUARY 8

Title: God Can Use You

Text: "And as ye go, preach, saying, The kingdom of heaven is at hand" *(Matt. 10:7)*.

Scripture Reading: Matthew 9:36–10:7

Hymns: "Make Me a Blessing," Wilson

"Lord, Lay Some Soul upon My Heart," McKinney

"I Love to Tell the Story," Hankey

Offertory Prayer: For life, for health, for family for friends, and most of all for Jesus Christ, we thank you today, heavenly Father. As we commit our gifts to you, we also place ourselves and this hour of worship in your hands. May your will be done and your kingdom come into the life of every person gathered here today, through Jesus Christ our Lord. Amen.

Introduction

Allegheny ants, a common species in the eastern United States, help enrich forest areas by carrying tons of soil from below ground to the surface. A three-year study by the University of Wisconsin revealed that one colony of ants moved fifteen tons of subsoil, building clusters of large mounds and burrowing five and a half feet below the surface. This "deep plowing" increases the nutrients, clay, and organic matter of the surface soil in the forest. No wonder the writer of Proverbs said, "Go to the ant . . . consider her ways, and be wise" (6:6).

If God can use Allegheny ants to move fifteen tons of subsoil to the surface, surely God can use you in 2006!

I. God can use you when you see others compassionately.

Jesus remained consistently compassionate. From the time he sent his disciples on their first witnessing mission until his death, Jesus was "moved with compassion" (Matt. 9:36).

A.   *Because of the power of Christian love, God can use you in 2006.* This is a reason from within. The compassion of Matthew 9:36 and the love of 1 Corinthians 13:7 are inseparable. The latter reminds us that love "beareth all things, believeth all things, hopeth all things, endureth all things." Christian love enables us to accept and love people who are different from us. It reaches out in compassionate tenderness to people in need.

B. *Because of the desperate condition of the lost, God can use you in 2006.* This is a reason from without. Some are moved to fear, some to contempt, and others to outright rejection by the desperate needs of people, but Christians should be moved to compassion.

Billy Graham arrived at Sir Winston Churchill's residence in 1954 to find the great statesman looking pale and frightened. As the evangelist entered, Churchill looked up and asked, "Young man, do you have any hope?" This is the question asked by every person in the face of desperation.

The lost have no purpose in life. Jesus saw them "scattered abroad, as sheep having no shepherd" (Matt. 9:36). Nothing is as tragic as a soul who has no purpose in life.

II. God can use you when you respond to a challenge enthusiastically (Matt. 9:37).

Christ faced squarely the challenge of evangelizing his people—the task was overwhelming, and few were willing to become involved. Nevertheless, he responded to the challenge not with despair or defeatism but with enthusiasm.

As long as your response to a challenge is that of doubt, fear, and despair—as long as you pose as an expert who knows all the reasons why the church must fail, the lost cannot be reached, and the cause of Christ must be content with mediocre accomplishments—you will never be anything but an obstacle to the progress of God's work. Squarely face a challenge with enthusiasm.

A. *Because of the tremendous job to be done, you must face the challenge enthusiastically (Matt. 9:37).* The passage is saying, "There is much to be done, many to be won. This is a real challenge!"

Helping people who are trying to escape the boredom of life turn to Christ is a tremendous job indeed. Consider the ancient Roman society. A society that pours out money on pleasures is a decadent society. Suetonius tells us that Emperor Vitellius set on the table at one banquet two thousand fish and seven thousand birds. There is no doubt about what the Roman world was trying to do: it was trying to escape boredom. Extravagance is always a sign of the desire to escape.

We are living in an age of decadence and escapism, and as Christians, there lies our challenge. Sir John Reith once said, "I do not like crises, but I like the opportunities they bring." The church has the challenge today to lead people to life in Jesus Christ. You must respond to this challenge enthusiastically!

B. *Because so few are willing to become involved, you must face the challenge enthusiastically (Matt. 9:36).*

The church staff, a handful of Sunday school workers, and a few dedicated deacons are not enough in the face of the tremendous harvest of souls for which God holds the church responsible. The fact that so few are willing to get involved should move you to new heights of enthusiasm as you give this task your all. If only a few are willing to respond, there is no time to waste.

III. God can use you when you come to him prayerfully (Matt. 9:38).

In the face of an overwhelming challenge, we are tempted to come to God mournfully, complaining about the heavy burden he has placed on us. But Christ says we should come to God prayerfully.

A. *Come to him prayerfully, acknowledging that this is* his *harvest.* Verse 38 reminds us that Jesus is the "Lord" of the harvest—that is, he is the one to whom the harvest belongs. Therefore, God has more at stake and thus more interest in the success of this battle for souls than we do. We are only his reapers, but we must enter the fields if the harvest is to be gathered.

B. *Come prayerfully, believing that more people will get involved (Matt. 9:36).* We must not wait until others get involved before we enter the fields—we must get involved, praying and believing that others will join us.

IV. God can use you when you accept his power trustingly (Matt. 10:1).

The Twelve responded to Christ's call and in simple trust accepted the power required for their task of witnessing.

A. *Because of the source of that power, you can accept it trustingly.* "He gave them power" (Matt. 10:1). Now that Christ is physically absent, the Holy Spirit serves as the source of our power. Acts 1:8 assures us, "You will receive power when the Holy Spirit comes on you; and you will be my witnesses" (NIV). But we must accept this power trustingly. Jesus did not save us until we *recognized* him as the Savior and *put our trust in him* for salvation. Just so, the Holy Spirit does not control us in the sense of permeating our will, reason, and emotions until we recognize him as the one who was sent by the Father to sanctify our lives and *trust* him to perform his ministry in and through us.

B. *Because of the purpose of that power, you can accept it trustingly (Matt. 10:1; Acts 1:8).* God does not grant power without a purpose. But once we are sincere in our desire to be used by God, we can trust him to impart the power to accomplish his purpose.

V. God can use you when you share the gospel joyfully (Matt. 10:7).

Wherever the disciples went, there was joy and excitement—the long-awaited Messiah had come, the kingdom of heaven was at hand!

A. *You can share the gospel joyfully because of the power of the gospel.* Verse 6 says that these people were "lost," yet the gospel has the power to save them. You can share the gospel with the same joy that Paul did when he said, "I am not ashamed of the gospel, because it is the power of God for the salvation of everyone who believes: first for the Jew, then for the Gentile" (Rom. 1:16 NIV). Remember that there is never a person whom the gospel cannot change.

B. *You can share the gospel joyfully because of the availability of salvation (Matt. 10:7).* You do not have to wait on the kingdom of heaven—it is at hand. You can enter it now!

Conclusion

God can use you in 2006 when (1) you see others compassionately, (2) you respond to a challenge enthusiastically, (3) you come to him prayerfully, (4) you accept his power trustingly, (5) you share the gospel joyfully. If you are not yet a Christian, as you come to accept him, God can use you to influence others to know him in 2006.

SUNDAY EVENING, JANUARY 8

Title: The Great Discovery

Text: "'The kingdom of heaven is like treasure hidden in a field'" *(Matt. 13:44 NIV).*

Scripture Reading: Matthew 13:44–46

Introduction

Matthew 13 is a chapter filled with parables Jesus told, and most of them are very brief. The two we will study tonight provide deeper insight into the love of God for sinful humans, a theme we saw in three Luke 15 stories that we explored last week.

After Jesus related the parables of the sower sowing his seed, of the tiny mustard seed growing into a sprawling tree, and of the leaven raising the whole lump of dough, he dismissed the crowd. He had been sitting beside the Sea of Galilee when he told these stories. Verse 36 says that Jesus "sent the multitude away, and went into the house," which undoubtedly was the house of Simon Peter in Capernaum. His disciples came in with him and immediately asked him to explain one of his parables. After Jesus gave the explanation of that parable, the one about the wheat and tares growing together in the field, he gave them several more short parables in rapid-fire order.

The first two of these were the parables of the hidden treasure and the pearl of great price, both of which underscore God's love for all humankind. These two parables are similar, yet each gives a slightly different perspective from which to view God's remarkable love for a sinful, rejecting world.

I. The parable of the hidden treasure (v. 44).

A. *We must identify the three elements of this parable—the field, the man, the treasure—to catch the glory and wonder of its meaning.*

    1. There is no doubt that the field is the world. The scope of this world is not just this physical world in which we live; it also includes the mental and spiritual realms. When God looks at the world, he doesn't see it fragmented

into physical, social, cultural, intellectual, and spiritual levels. He sees one great, all-inclusive world containing people of all backgrounds, of all levels of mental comprehension and spiritual condition. He sees people as products of his creation, fallen and gone astray, and now objects of his love. Then, when Jesus died on the cross, the sin burden that pressed on him included the sins of all the world, not just of a select few. On the cross, provision was made for every soul to be redeemed, even though not all would receive him.

2. The man represents the Lord Jesus, who came into this world, this field, and recognized it as the original joy and delight of the Creator. In the person of his Son, God entered the world and identified with humankind by taking on human flesh with all of its limitations except sin. This is the way that a perfect, holy, sovereign God drew close to sinful humankind. Not only did the God-man Jesus come close to humans, he made it possible for them to come close to God.

3. What is the treasure found in the field? When the Lord Jesus came into this world and mingled with the people in it—the sinners, the religious, the righteous, the immoral, the decent—he discovered something that set his sinless soul afire. Hidden beneath the veneer of sin and deception placed in the world by Satan, the god of this world, was the *potential* for growing God's kingdom—the kingdom of heaven. But here is a mystery: after Jesus made this discovery, he hid the treasure again. Why?

    During the brief three and a half years of our Lord's earthly ministry, he revealed much of the kingdom of heaven in his conduct as well as his teachings. The glory of this coming kingdom projected from his very being. Despite this, the majority of the people ignored him, passed him by, or considered him a momentary sensation. So he hid his treasure again. Then he set about to buy this field, the world. The price was astronomical: to purchase it, he had to sell all he had. He emptied out his heavenly glory and humbled himself by taking on the form of a servant, making himself obedient unto death (Phil. 2:6–11).

B. *The paradox in what Jesus did is that there was joy in his mission that overrode the sorrow of the world's rejection.* But where was the fountain from which this joy flowed? The joy of our Lord's heart was to do God's will. He knew the ultimate goodness of God's will; he knew its perfection. The joy in the heart of Jesus was the accomplishing of God's will in the world.

    This joy was his strength, the power enabling him to endure the cross. This should be our pattern. How often have we chafed in trial and temptation, tragedy and heartache, so certain that there could be no design for good in what was happening to us. Yet as we walked through that fire, we saw the Son rise "with healing in his wings." Truly "for the joy that was set before him" Jesus endured the cross, despising the shame.

II. The pearl of great price (vv. 45–46).

The focus of this parable is the love of God for sinful humans. To understand this more fully, we need to examine the two key elements of the parable: the merchant and the pearl.

A. *The merchant represents the Lord Jesus, who has left heaven to come to earth to seek one pearl of great price.* With his omniscience the Lord saw the church, composed of all those—past, present, and future—who would repent of their sins and receive him as Savior. With great joy he gave all that he had to purchase that pearl. Christ "loved the church, and gave himself for it," says the Scripture (Eph. 5:25).

B. *The pearl represents the sinner.* The origin of the pearl is illuminating. A pearl is the product of a living organism, an oyster. When a grain of sand gets within the shell of an oyster, injury is done to the organism. The oyster, the victim of the injury, covers over that which injures it with *nacre,* layer after layer of it, until the pearl is formed.

The grain of sand—the core or beginning of the pearl—represents the "sinners, saved by God's grace," who make up the church. Because of their sinful lifestyle, they were a disappointment to their Creator. They were aliens to the plan and purpose of God for humankind. But they responded to God's call to repentance, and God began to cover them with layer after layer of his grace—like the nacre from the oyster. That is what he is doing today; that is the process that is going on in the church right now.

Conclusion

God is covering us with layer after layer of his grace each day of our lives, making us more and more like his Son. One day he will present us, his church, in heaven as the trophies of his grace—complete, perfected, righteous before God. Thus, in the first parable we have God searching in the world for those who will make up his kingdom. In the second parable we see the outcome—what will happen to those who belong to God's family. Where do you fit into these matchless expressions of God's love?

WEDNESDAY EVENING, JANUARY 11

Title: What Is Man?

Text: "What is man?" *(Ps. 8:4 NIV).*

Scripture Reading: Psalm 8:1–9

Introduction

Centuries ago the psalmist asked, "What is man" (Ps. 8:4). He shows us that while man may be of little significance quantitatively, he is of great significance spiritually.

What is man? The question is still relevant today. To answer it, let us apply four tests to understand and evaluate man.

I. Man is to be understood, and his worth is to be judged, by his origin.

Controversy rages in this arena. The physiologist, the negative naturalist says, "Man is an accident in a world that is foreign to him; he is abortively, purposelessly produced by processes over which he has no capacity to be responsible." (See Carlyle Marney, *Structures of Prejudice* [New York and Nashville: Abingdon, 1961], 49). One philosopher says, "Man is little more than a chance deposit on the surface of the world, carelessly thrown up between ice ages by the same forces that rust iron and ripen corn" (Carl L. Becker, *The Heavenly City of the Eighteenth Century Philosophers* [publisher unknown], 14). Another description—the only reliable one—tells us, "God said, 'Let us make man in our image, in our likeness'. . . . So God created man in his own image, in the image of God he created him; male and female he created them" (Gen. 1:26–27 NIV).

The Genesis account, then, establishes a number of significant facts: (1) Man is a created being, not a created thing. (2) Man is an end, not a means to an end, and is never to be so used. (3) Man is a spiritual being, and this dimension distinguishes him from the animals. (4) Man is more than a bundler of instincts responding to sense stimuli. Man's origin is in God by a special act of creation, the crown of all his works.

II. Man is to be understood, and his worth is to be judged, by the pattern by which he was cut, the design by which he was created.

In Australia lives a strange animal called a platypus. Although a warm-blooded mammal, the platypus has some reptilian features. It also has fur like a beaver, feet like a mole, and a bill like a duck. It can swim like a fish and lays eggs like a chicken. The platypus is definitely of mixed design.

Man is like that. On the physical side, man is not very different from the other animals. He has, however, a spiritual and rational nature like that of his Maker. "God created man in his own image" (Gen. 1:26 NIV). It is this dimension that makes man different from the other animals.

III. Man is to be understood, and his worth is to be judged, by the relationships for which he was created.

The first chapters of Genesis are not scientific accounts, nor are they entertaining myths. Here in simple form is the most beautiful story of what happened and why. A significant detail of this story is God's walking in the garden in the cool of the day with the man and his wife. Man was created for fellowship with his Maker, whose image he bears. Another important part of the story is the creation of woman and the reason for it. "The LORD God said, "It is not good for the man to be alone. I will make a helper suitable for him" (Gen. 2:18 NIV). Man was also created for fellowship with others of his own kind. Thus God laid the foundation for the human family. Man was created for these relationships.

Man's ability to fellowship with God and his fellow humans is God's gift, but we know that man's ability to pursue evil thoughts is not God's gift. Evil thoughts and actions, which destroy relationships, have another source altogether. Sin diminishes man's worth. Not only does he lose the integrity of his relationship, but he also loses fellowship with God. If we acknowledge this, isn't it reasonable to agree with Nietzsche that man is "vermin on the crust of the earth"?

The Christian believes in the infinite worth of every individual because God has not surrendered him to the powers of evil. God loves him. Life's true dimensions are in this relationship. A man's life reaches its maximum in its relation to God through Jesus Christ, and after that, to other people.

IV. Man is to be understood, and his worth is to be judged, by the destiny God purposed for him when he created him.

We ought to see ourselves in Abraham's experience. It is written of him, "He ... obeyed and went, even though he did not know where he was going" (Heb. 11:8 NIV). No road maps, no charted course, no detailed knowledge, but with a sense of mission burning in his soul. Though Abraham did not know where he was going, he knew who controlled his travels.

We need to be more like Abraham. As God's redeemed children, we move toward the destination God has chosen for us. Though man has lost the way, he may find it again through accepting God's way—Jesus Christ.

Conclusion

It is now appropriate to flesh out in practical terms the applications of these principles.

Any service that improves man is a service to God, because man is a child of God. We serve God as we serve our fellow humans.

Any ministry that helps man to fulfill the relationships for which he was created is in line with the will of God. Man is God's child, God created man as his child, but man is an estranged child who needs to be redeemed.

Since man is estranged, he must trust in Christ. When he does this, he is in step with his Creator. Time, tide, and the universe are on the side of the Christian because his "life is now hidden with Christ in God" (Col. 3:3 NIV).

SUNDAY MORNING, JANUARY 15

Title: Things Truly Christian

Text: "If anyone considers himself religious and yet does not keep a tight rein on his tongue, he deceives himself and his religion is worthless. Religion that God our Father accepts as pure and faultless is this: to look after orphans and widows in their distress and to keep oneself from being polluted by the world" *(James 1:26–27 NIV).*

Scripture Reading: James 1:19–27

Hymns: "What a Friend We Have in Jesus," Scriven

"Make Me a Channel of Blessing," Smyth

"Take My Life, and Let It Be," Havergal

Offertory Prayer: Heavenly Father, we come before you humbly, not on our own merits, but in the name and on the merits of Jesus Christ our Lord. But we do not come empty-handed. Remembering in gratitude what you have freely given to us, we gladly give back our tithes and offerings to you. Accept and use them to further your kingdom's work through Christ our Lord. Amen.

Introduction

Gustave Doré, a well-known nineteenth-century French painter, was traveling in Europe when he lost his passport. The customs official insisted on Doré's showing the document to identify himself.

"But," he said, "I am Doré the artist."

The officer didn't believe him. Explaining that a lot of people who lose their passports claim to be someone they are not, the officer gave Doré a pencil and a piece of paper and told him to prove it.

Taking the pencil, Doré quickly sketched scenes of the immediate area and handed the paper back to the officer.

The official was convinced with just one glance at the picture. He let Doré pass by. "No one else can draw like that," he said.

It's easy for one to say, "I am a Christian. I am a follower of Jesus." But that isn't enough. If we are truly Christians, our lives and actions must show it. According to the teachings of the New Testament, a genuine Christian will produce Christ-like fruit.

In today's text James lists three things that must be an integral part of every Christian's life.

I. A controlled tongue.

James says that mere conformity to a Christian code does not necessarily mean that one is a true Christian. To illustrate, he pictures a person who gives the outward appearance of being a believer, giving scrupulous attention to the externals of the Christian faith. A modern example of this type of person would be as follows. He is careful to be in church on Sunday morning. He judiciously figures his tithe on Saturday night and pompously places it in the collection plate on Sunday morning. He sings the hymns loudly and closes his eyes during the prayers. Looking at him, other believers would say, "My, my! Isn't he a fine Christian!"

But James says a true Christian is very different from this type of person. James writes that genuine Christianity expresses itself in some simple, down-to-earth ways. One of those ways is controlling the tongue (James 1:26). If one fails to do that, James sternly warns, "this man's religion is vain."

A. *Though the tongue is small, it is powerful (James 3:3–5).* It is analogous to a small match that starts a fire that may destroy thousands of acres of timber.

B. *Though the tongue can do well, it can also do much evil (James 3:6, 9–11).* "Blessing and cursing" both are products of the tongue (v. 10).

C. *Though the tongue is in man, man alone can tame it (James 3:7–8).* Only the Holy Spirit can ultimately control the tongue.

Henry Van Dyke gives two rules we should put into practice. First, he says we should never believe a bad report about anybody unless we positively know it to be true. Second, we should never give a bad report to anybody unless we feel it is absolutely necessary. If we do tell it, we must remember that God is listening.

II. A compassionate spirit.

James states that genuine Christianity is more than words: it reaches out in love to those who are in need—"the orphans and widows" (1:27).

A. *True Christians will be concerned for others.* This is the attitude of Jesus; he was always concerned about people in need. It is not enough to say simply to the hungry, "Go and be fed." We have to help feed them.

B. *True Christians will respond to the needs of others.* James writes that true Christianity expresses itself by visiting the fatherless and widows. Dr. Harold S. Songer says in *The Broadman Commentary* that this means "to look after" them. Just giving a turkey at Christmas is not "looking after" their needs. Looking after these people involves continual sacrifice. Genuine Christianity has eyes that see, arms that embrace, and a purse that opens.

In his book *Love's Meaning*, Archibald Rutledge wrote about attending a worship service in which everything was proper. The singing was contagious. The prayers were "splendid." The minister read the Scriptures with "unusual sonority," Rutledge related. As the worshipers left the service, they saw an unkempt woman weeping by the churchyard fence.

Only one of the worshipers paid any attention to the poor woman. Kneeling beside her, the church lady dried the tears of the desperate individual. Rutledge's conclusion was simple yet profound: "The only one of all of us who really knew how to worship God" was the woman who did something to help.

III. A clean life.

In the last part of verse 27, James declares that a genuine Christian will "keep ... from being polluted by the world." In other words, one who is a true follower of Jesus will live a clean life. Christians are people whose lives have been purified.

A. *Christians will live in the world.* We are to be salt and light to the world, Jesus says. Our purity needs to be seen by the world. A monastic type of life is contrary to Scripture. We are to be like yeast that leavens the whole lump of dough.

B. *Christians will not let the world live in them.* Although we are all sinners, Christians are commanded to live upright moral lives. We can do this only through the strength the indwelling Holy Spirit gives (Gal. 5:22–26; Eph. 5:15–20).

Conclusion

How are we to define Christianity? The meaning is obvious only in the charitable words from our mouths and in the loving acts done from our hearts.

SUNDAY EVENING, JANUARY 15

Title: Laying Foundations

Text: "'Everyone who hears these words of mine and puts them into practice is like a wise man who built his house on the rock'" *(Matt. 7:24 NIV)*.

Scripture Reading: Matthew 7:24–29

Introduction

The word *foundation* applies to both tangible and intangible things. Serious parents are interested in seeing that their children get a "good foundation" in school. They know that their children's education and the application of that education will spell the difference between success and failure in developing working skills.

Furthermore, Christian parents are eager that their children receive a good *spiritual* foundation. Much of this is done at home on a day-to-day basis as children observe the attitudes and reactions of their parents toward life situations: their responses to crises, their handling of situations that could compromise their Christian convictions, their dealing with temptation.

Tonight's parable speaks of two kinds of foundations.

I. The setting of the parable (vv. 24–25).

As Jesus established the setting for his story, he spoke of certain *circumstances* that were very familiar to the people who were listening to him (v. 25). Those who have traveled in the Middle East, particularly in the southern part of Israel and Jordan, know about the *wadis*, the dry stream beds that crisscross the Judean wilderness. They knife their way between limestone hills, creating stark, awesome valleys. But then come the spring rains and the flash floods. Within minutes those dry, desolate wadis flood with raging torrents of water and turn into mighty, rushing rivers. Surely it would be ludicrous to build a residence on such a piece of land.

II. The characters.

A. *The wise man dug through the sand until he came to the rock shelf.* In many areas of Palestine the sandy soil is quite shallow. A person does not have to dig very far until he comes to a shelf of rock. So the wise builder in Jesus' story had moved away from the dry bed of the stream and had leveled another, stabler area. There he had carefully laid the foundation for his house.

B. *The foolish man was impatient to see immediate results.* Here was a man who lived for the day. He operated on whim and impulse. He knew nothing of perseverance. Let's use our imagination a bit to describe the scenario of these two builders.

   One day the foolish builder built a house. He might have noted his neighbor who also was building, and he might have said to himself, "Look at that silly

30

man! There he is in this hot sun, digging down in the sand. Down and down he digs, before he even begins to build his house. And see how far he has to carry his materials! Look at this wide, flat area. The ground is level and smooth, the sands are packed and hard. With all of the wadis in this area, the chances that the water would come here are remote."

He wasn't concerned about tomorrow; he thought only about today. He wanted what he wanted *now*, so he rushed headlong into a project for which he was not prepared.

C. *Today's world is filled with people who live only for the present.* The most important thing in life for them is to have what they want when they want it. "Patience" and "waiting" and "listening" are foreign ideas to them. Instead, they push their way through life, doing things their way, satisfying their selfish egos, and never stopping to count the cost.

III. The summary of the parable (vv. 28–29).

A. *The stability and strength of a person's life cannot be truly determined until the floods and storms come.* Some Christians have only a shallow, fair-weather relationship with God. They have acknowledged Jesus Christ as Savior; they have repented of their sins. But then immediately they have pushed their relationship with God to the back of their lives.

B. *There are two levels on which one relates to his Christianity; one is a surface level, where a person "speaks the language" and "goes through the ritual" of religion; the other is a deeper level where commitment and dedication are needed.* This is what spells the difference between these two men Jesus used as the main characters of his parable. So when the real testing times of life come—and they will come—they come with fury and force! Those whose relationship with God is at surface level will experience catastrophe. Those who have struggled to see God as their rock shelf will weather the storm victoriously. They will emerge even stronger and more confident of the power and sustaining grace of God.

C. *The word* obedience *summarizes the difference between hearing and doing.* Jesus demands our implicit obedience. Learning to obey is the most important lesson in life.

Conclusion

Christ's claim is that obedience to him is the only sure foundation for life. Furthermore, it is his unfailing promise that the life that is founded on obedience to him and to his Word is safe, regardless of how vicious the storm, how menacing the winds, or how high the floodwaters.

What is the foundation for your life?

WEDNESDAY EVENING, JANUARY 18

Title: What Is the Bible?

Text: "The law of the LORD is perfect, converting the soul: the testimony of the LORD is sure, making wise the simple" *(Ps. 19:7).*

Scripture Reading: Psalm 19:7–11

Introduction

Because the wisdom of God is multifaceted and fathomless, it is difficult to answer the question, What is the Bible? The apostle James describes the Bible as a mirror (James 1:23–24). Paul describes the Bible as food, as milk for spiritual babies, as meat for the spiritually mature (1 Cor. 3:2–3). In his first epistle, Peter describes it as "incorruptible seed" for producing a spiritual crop. One psalmist describes God's Word as gold to enrich and as honey to sweeten (19:10).

What is the Bible? Let's note six metaphors that clarify the answer in a practical way.

I. The Bible is a judge or critic.

The writer of Hebrews tells us that "the word of God is living and active.... it judges the thoughts and attitudes of the heart" (4:12 NIV). As Christians we need a divinely provided critic to judge us for our own good and for the glory of God. Often we resent the criticism of others, but we have no cause for resentment when God, through his Word, points out our sins and shortcomings.

Who can deny the reliability of the Bible as a judge, a critic? The playwright might question the judgment of the critics; the prisoner might feel that the sentence imposed by the judge is unfair; the politician might question the decision of the voters: every person, however, must bow before the verdict of the Bible. When our thoughts are revealed as impure and our motives as selfish, we need to accept the judgment of God's Word and turn to Christ for forgiveness, cleansing, and victory.

II. The Bible is a lamp and a light

The psalmist states this beautifully: "Thy word is a lamp unto my feet, and a light unto my path" (119:105). How blessed to know that we have in our hands a never-failing lamp whose light shines forth in the darkness.

While he was on the earth, Jesus boldly proclaimed, "I am the light of the world. Whoever follows me will never walk in darkness, but will have the light of life" (John 8:12 NIV). The Bible is like the star of Bethlehem leading to the person of Christ himself. It is like the fiery pillar that led the children of Israel by night through the wilderness. No wonder the psalmist said, "The entrance of thy words giveth light" (119:130).

32

III. The Bible is a burning fire.

There was a time in his ministry when Jeremiah despaired utterly and tried to quit but at last had to declare, "But if I say, 'I will not mention him or speak any more in his name,' his word is in my heart like a fire, a fire shut up in my bones. I am weary of holding it in; indeed, I cannot" (20:9 NIV). His heart was warmed to a spiritual fervor and he could not keep still. If our hearts have grown cold and we lack enthusiasm for God's work, the probability is that we have gotten too far away from the fire of divine truth. Fire warms. As a living fire, the Bible warms our hearts.

But it is also the function of fire to refine and purify, to burn away the dross. One psalmist said, "The law of his God is in his heart; none of his steps shall slide" (37:31). The real cure for backsliding is the Word of God. The psalmist wrote, "Thy word have I hid in mine heart, that I might not sin against thee" (119:11). This psalmist had learned of the refining and cleansing quality of God's Word. We all have in our lives impurities that need to be cleaned out and dross that needs to be consumed. The Bible is a burning fire.

IV. The Bible is the hand of God.

In a great penitential psalm, Psalm 32, David says, "For day and night thy hand was heavy upon me" (v. 4). Conviction for sin because of our guilt is nothing less than the hand of God on us. God touches our lives through his Word.

The Bible as a whole is like the hand. Each book of the Bible, like each finger of the hand, serves a special purpose. No other creature has an appendage like the human hand. It is not a hoof or paw. How skillfully trained surgeons use their hands to operate. How skillfully God uses the Bible to lead us into his will. The Bible is as different from any other book as the human hand is different from the appendages of any other creature. Other books are like a paw; the Bible is like a hand.

V. The Bible is a hammer.

The prophet Jeremiah records God as saying, "Is not my word . . . like a hammer that breaks a rock in pieces?" (23:29 NIV). Who has not used a hammer to crush some hard substance? This is exactly what the Word of God does to the hearts of people. Sin hardens human hearts as hard as flint, and only the hammer blows of the Word of God can crush them. God honors his Word.

We need to remember, however, that a hammer is useless unless it is used in a human hand. So it is with the Word of God. We need to take it and use it. If we fail to use this tool he has given us, we fail indeed.

VI. The Bible is a sword.

In Ephesians 6, where the Ephesians are told to put on the whole armor of God, Paul reminds them that their only effective weapon is "the sword of the Spirit, which is the word of God" (6:17 NIV). This is to be our weapon. We must never forget that our adversary, the Devil, is resourceful and powerful; no weapon forged by man can prevail against him. We must use "the sword of the Spirit, which is the word of God."

Conclusion

The Bible is a judge and critic, a lamp and light, a burning fire, the hand of God, the hammer of God, and the sword of the Spirit. Let us seek to know it, to reverence it, and to use it for his glory and for the winning of the lost everywhere.

SUNDAY MORNING, JANUARY 22

Title: What Jesus Does for Sinners

Text: "From Jesus Christ, who is the faithful witness, and the first begotten of the dead, and the prince of the kings of the earth. Unto him that loved us, and washed us from our sins in his own blood, and hath made us kings and priests unto God and his Father; to him be glory and dominion forever and ever. Amen" *(Rev. 1:5–6)*.

Scripture Reading: Revelation 1:4–7

Hymns: "Crown Him with Many Crowns," Bridges

"Love Divine, All Loves Excelling," Wesley

"When I Survey the Wondrous Cross," Montgomery

Offertory Prayer: Father, for every expression of your love to us, we give thanks today. Forgive us for taking our blessings for granted, and give us sensitive, grateful hearts. Accept now these tithes and offerings we joyously give to you this morning. Even as Jesus blessed and multiplied the bread by Galilee, bless and multiply these gifts that the workers in your kingdom may be strengthened around the world. For Jesus' sake. Amen.

Introduction

John Francis Perring says the Bank of England owes him more than $1 trillion. He claims that his great-grandfather Perring invested more than $100,000 in the bank many years ago. The younger Perring, a Chicago musician, asserts that the bank paid interest to his great-grandfather until 1846. Since that time, Perring says no interest has been paid, and he wants the Bank of England to rectify the account. Although Perring has been pursuing the claim against the bank for a number of years, the bank has not shelled out a dime. And in all likelihood it won't.

In contrast to this, think about the inexhaustible resources that belong to Jesus Christ and are freely available to us by faith. For these spiritual riches to be ours, we have only to receive him as our Savior and confess him as our Lord. Then all that Jesus possesses and all that he does for sinners will be credited to our account.

The text for our message this morning focuses on three things Jesus does for sinners.

I. Jesus loves us in our sins.

This marvelous truth is expressed in the last part of verse 5 ("Unto him that loved us"). But Christ's love for us is not a past tense thing. His love is always current, and a literal translation of the meaning is "is loving us." How can we describe that love?

A. *Jesus loves us as we are.* There is nothing we can do to make God love us. There is nothing we can do to make God stop loving us, because "God is love." God loves us in Jesus Christ, just as we are.

Oliver Cromwell once told his portrait painter to paint him "warts and all." Cromwell wanted the people to remember him as he was. Similarly, Jesus loves us warts and all. We don't have to "clean up our act" before Jesus can love us. He loves us as we are.

B. *Jesus loves us sacrificially.* The word that is here translated "love" is the strongest word for love in the Greek New Testament. The late Kenneth S. Wuest said that "God's love for a sinful and lost race . . . springs from his heart in response to the high value he places upon each human soul. Every sinner is exceedingly precious in his sight" (Kenneth Wuest, *Golden Nuggets in the Greek New Testament* [Grand Rapids: Eerdmans, 1955], 60–61). This sacrificial love of Jesus for sinners is displayed in the cross (Rom. 5:8).

II. Jesus frees us from our sins.

John wrote that Christ "washed us from our sins in his own blood" (v. 5). According to Dr. Morris Ashcraft in *The Broadman Bible Commentary,* "freed, or loosed, is preferable to the variant reading 'washed.'" Through his death, burial, and resurrection, Jesus is able to free sinners—those who will receive him—from the control of the sinful nature (John 1:12–13).

A. *He looses us from our sins by giving himself.* Martin Leu, in a four-and-one-half-year period, gave two hundred pints of blood to the Norfolk, Nebraska, Lutheran blood bank. There is no way to know how many lives Leu's blood saved. We are saved from our sins because Jesus shed his blood for us (1 Peter 1:18–19).

B. *He looses us from our sins as we accept him.* The word translated "washed" or "loosed" is in a tense that indicates a completed experience. It points to a definite time when the loosing took place. Jesus called it the new birth when he talked to Nicodemus about his greatest need (John 3:1–12). The loosing from sin that Jesus gives the repentant sinner is an experience we call conversion (Acts 9:1–22).

III. Jesus lifts us out of our sins.

The lifting grace of Jesus is stated in verse 6: "And hath made us kings and priests unto God and his Father." The Revised Standard Version translates it, He has "made us a kingdom, priests to his God and Father." Regardless of how one reads the verse, the meaning is the same: Jesus lifts us out of our sins to a new dimension of living.

35

Jesus said to his disciples: "I, if I be lifted up from the earth, will draw all men unto me" (John 12:32). Jesus was lifted up on the cross (John 3:14) to lift sinners out of their sins. Everywhere the gospel of Christ has been preached, it has lifted sinners out of degradation and blackness into God's glorious forgiveness and love.

Jesus lifted the immoral woman of Sychar and made her the great Samaritan evangelist. He lifted Saul of Tarsus and made him the great apostle to the Gentiles. He lifted Simon Peter and made him the great preacher to the Jewish world. He lifted William Booth and made him the great founder of the Salvation Army. He lifted Billy Sunday out of his drunkenness and made him a great evangelist.

In his hymn "He Lifted Me," Charles H. Gabriel wrote of the lifting grace of Jesus:

> *In loving-kindness Jesus came*
> *My soul in mercy to reclaim,*
> *And from the depths of sin and shame*
> *Thro' grace he lifted me.*
>
> *From sinking sand he lifted me,*
> *With tender hand he lifted me,*
> *From shades of night to plains of light,*
> *Oh praise his name, he lifted me!*

Conclusion

Author John Masefield, a sixteenth-century poet laureate of England, wrote a drama titled *The Trial of Jesus*. In the drama Procula, the wife of Pontius Pilate, receives the news that Jesus has been raised from the dead. Addressing Longinus, Procula asks if he thinks Jesus is still dead. Longinus replies that he doesn't think so.

Troubled, Procula asks Longinus where he thinks Jesus is. He replies, "Loose in the world, Lady, where neither Jew nor Roman nor anyone else can stop him" (James Hefley, *A Dictionary of Illustrations* [Grand Rapids: Zondervan, n.d.], 50).

Indeed, Jesus is alive and loose in the world, and he lives to set sinners loose from their sins that they too might live eternally.

SUNDAY EVENING, JANUARY 22

Title: The Prayer God Hears

Text: "'For everyone who exalts himself will be humbled, and he who humbles himself will be exalted'" *(Luke 18:14 NIV)*.

Scripture Reading: Luke 18:9–14

Introduction

In this brief and well-known parable, Jesus describes men who went to church. Their motives were poles apart. Equally extreme were the results of their church-going efforts on this particular Sabbath.

It is expedient to examine the parable from four different angles. First, we will look at the audience for this parable. Second, we will examine the main characters. Third, we will analyze the prayers these men prayed in the temple. Finally, we will listen to the assessment Jesus made of these men's actions.

I. The immediate audience (v. 9).

A. *Jesus had in his congregations those who considered themselves so good that they could hardly stand it.* Yet there were also those who were painfully honest, and they considered themselves so bad they could hardly stand it! The latter had come face-to-face with the sin in their lives—with the infinite distance that existed between them and God, and they were repulsed by what they saw.

B. *This self-righteous, holier-than-thou attitude in Jesus' day was found largely in a religious party called the Pharisees.* Now, not all members of the brotherhood of Pharisees were guilty of this attitude. So it was the satanic spirit of pharisaism that Jesus was condemning, and in his story he personified pharisaism in one man, one Pharisee.

C. *The spirit of pharisaism is still with us.* We all have a tendency to exalt ourselves. We all have instances in our lives when we measure the deeds of others by the ruler of our own actions; it affords us a perfect opportunity to look down patronizingly on those who do not reach our standards of holiness. Jesus is showing us that this is the sin of self-worship.

II. The main characters (v. 10).

The Pharisee and the tax collector have been oversimplified into stereotypes, and for this reason we may have missed some very important facts about them.

A. *Basically, there was something quite sad about the Pharisee.* He was generally very serious about his service to God. Some Christians are in earnest about their relationship with God until it touches their pocketbooks or interferes with their plans and selfish desires. But not the Pharisee: he fasted and sacrificed for God. He was highly respected in his society.

He did not merely encourage people to give go some worthy cause—he set the pattern. He was the first to give. Whereas the publican, or tax collector, had a corrupting influence on the community, the Pharisee worked faithfully and sacrificially to preserve its holy traditions and faith. He loved the temple and all of its sacred precincts.

B. *By nature the publican was a tough, calloused fellow who had turned against his own people, entering the employ of the Roman Empire, the pagan force that ruled the world.* He had agreed to bleed his people of every cent of taxes he possibly could. This reality is in sharp contrast to the sentimental picture we traditionally have of the contrite, penitent publican.

Jesus was not overlooking this man's past. Whereas the Pharisee had made an obvious contribution to the religious life of the people, the publican had done just the opposite. Because of the exorbitant taxes he demanded from the people, he had taken away their pleasure in living and had turned life into a burdensome existence.

37

C. *Jesus was looking beyond the individuals represented in this story and dealing with the spirit that controlled them.* This is why he praised the publican and condemned the Pharisee. This same spirit can control every person who lives contrary to God's commandments. Christ also proved here how a person's judgments can be so overwhelmingly wrong when he or she condemns or praises another. God looks past the veneer with which we cover ourselves and looks deeply into the heart.

D. *We must admit that there is something of both of these men in all of us.* There are those who, like the Pharisee, are judged by others as being shining examples of what a person should really be. They seem to do all of the "right things" in life. They are "religious," in the sense that they support the church and religion in general. But what of the deep, inner motives that lurk inside that private room in their hearts where no person ever goes?

There may well be something of the publican in each of us too. There are those heavily burdened in their consciences because of past deeds and wrong choices. Because of this, they have come to be disgusted with themselves, and they can no longer cope with what has happened or is happening in their lives.

III. The prayers of the men (vv. 11–13).

A. *The Pharisee's prayer was self-centered.* The Pharisee likely chose a prominent place in the temple. He stood when he prayed, for that was the general posture for praying among the Jews. He began his prayer in the typical Hebrew fashion, with the *berakah*, or thanksgiving. But quickly his thanksgiving became a praise directed toward himself rather than toward God. His prayer rapidly degenerated into self-congratulation and a pompous comparison of himself with the publican.

B. *The publican's prayer was God-centered.* The publican "stood at a distance." Both men were "standing," but the words Luke used were different. The word he used to describe the Pharisee indicated his standing tall and proud, showing total security and self-satisfaction. The word describing the posture of the publican suggests humility and a recognition of his unworthiness, or standing with a bowed head. The publican's prayer struck the right note with God as he recognized his true state as a sinner needing mercy. It was the key that opened the door to salvation and raised the gates through which flowed the unending mercy and grace of God.

IV. The assessment of men's actions (v. 14).

A. *Jesus showed the need for confession of guilt.* Certainly the lifestyle of a publican was as despicable to Jesus as it was to any Jew in Palestine. But the reason this man went to his home justified was that he had repented of his sin; he was willing to forsake his sinful lifestyle. On the other hand, the Pharisee, who was so religiously correct in his attention to rituals, went to his home not justified before God, but condemned; he had not repented nor recognized his need for divine mercy.

B. *Jesus' message in this parable is that God is not interested primarily in our good deeds, but in our willingness to let him do the work of grace in us.* Many people are crippled today by an overwhelming sense of guilt for wrongs they have done. They do not feel "good enough" to go to church, convinced that the church is for "good people." God alone can form us into vessels of honor to be used for his glory.

Conclusion

The prayer God hears is the completely earnest recognition of our total unworthiness before God. We need to realize fully that we don't depend on God for his admiration of us. We depend on God for his grace to us.

WEDNESDAY EVENING, JANUARY 25

Title: Is Self-Inventory Possible?

Text: "Who can discern his errors? Forgive my hidden faults" *(Ps. 19:12 NIV).*

Scripture Reading: Psalm 19:12–14

Introduction

There is no doubt that the psalmist is talking to us in his cry, "Who can discern his errors?" He is one with us and we with him. We too know the impossibility of self-inventory. We don't possess the fine art of accurate self-scrutiny, of an exact personal inventory. Why is this true? There are four practical reasons that explain the phenomenon.

I. Self-inventory is impossible because of the growing complexity of the modern world about us.

Our interests are complicated and worldwide. We know infinitely more about this world than we do about ourselves. We know more about the United Kingdom of Great Britain than we do about the kingdom of heaven within us. We know more about the conflicts in the Middle East than we do about the conflict between heaven and hell raging within us.

II. Self-inventory is impossible because of the silent, unconscious growth of sin within our hearts.

As day creeps into night, so do our besetting sins come upon us. If we have rooted in our hearts some sin, perhaps one little sin, that sin will grow silently, slowly, and unknown to us until we have lost control. When did we cease to possess the sin and when did the sin begin to possess us? Who can say? It is impossible to tell.

III. Self-inventory is impossible because good and bad are fighting within us.

Paul told the Galatians, "For the sinful nature desires what is contrary to the Spirit, and the Spirit what is contrary to the sinful nature. They are in conflict with each other, so that you do not do what you want" (5:17 NIV). If we are Christians, the Holy Spirit dwells within us, but the old man, Adam, still strives for mastery. The good and the bad are warring within us. This has been true of the greatest of God's saints, people such as Job, David, Peter, John the Baptist, and John the apostle. The good and bad are hopelessly mixed up in all of us. As an unknown writer has put it:

> *There is so much good in the worst of us,*
> *And so much bad in the best of us,*
> *It ill behooves any of us*
> *To talk about the rest of us.*

IV. Self-inventory is impossible because of the low standard of our moral judgment.

How prone we are to kid ourselves into thinking that our own conscience is an infallible guide. History records the tragic stories of people who thought they were doing right when actually they were fighting against God. Saul of Tarsus is a case in point. Why should this be so? Why should the standard of our moral judgment be low?

A. *It is a matter of background.* Our early training and education, the mores of our group—our background—all enter into our way of looking at things. The part early training and education play cannot be overestimated.

B. *It is a matter of spiritual maturity.* Paul wrote to the Corinthians, "The spiritual man makes judgments about all things, but he himself is not subject to any man's judgment" (1 Cor. 2:15 NIV). It is true that guilt may be shoved so deep into the unconscious that we are not even aware of its existence, but it is not true that a trained psychiatrist's help is needed to ferret it out. Though we would not belittle the good a psychiatrist can do, the Holy Spirit of God can search out our guilt, bring it to the surface, and bring us to repentance.

C. *It is because some pet sin has taken root in our hearts.* Sin, like some cancerous growth, cuts the optic nerve of the soul and we cannot see. In one of his great wartime poems, "Searchlights," Alfred Noyes depicts the probing rays of those powerful lights as they seek enemy ships and planes. Then he has this startling line: "Search for the foe in thine own soul." So should we all.

Conclusion

True, we cannot discern all our errors. But we can pray with David, "Create in me a pure heart, O God, and renew a steadfast spirit within me" (51:10 NIV). God will hear that prayer. An unknown poet has stated the matter well:

> *For who can all his errors tell,*
> *Or count the thoughts by which he fell?*
> *Omniscient God, to Thee alone*
> *My sin's infinity is known!*
> *Do Thou my secret faults efface,*
> *And show forth all Thy cleansing grace.*

SUNDAY MORNING, JANUARY 29

Title: Things Still Sacred

Text: "Remove not the ancient landmark, which thy fathers have set" *(Prov. 22:28).*

Scripture Reading: Genesis 2:21–25; Matthew 16:13–19; 2 Timothy 3:16–17

Hymns: "Wonderful Words of Life," Bliss

        "Jesus Paid It All," Hall

        "God, Give Us Christian Homes," McKinney

Offertory Prayer: Father, we thank you for the covenant you have made with us that you will supply our needs. Therefore, bless these tithes and offerings we now give to you, and supply our daily needs according to your riches in Christ Jesus our Lord. Amen.

Introduction

Although we have thrown out many of our sacred things, some are still hallowed even in this superficial age.

The late Clarence W. Cranford, pastor of Calvary Baptist Church, Washington, D.C., once told of a girl visiting a Vienna museum. Upon seeing a priceless piano that once belonged to Beethoven, she asked the guide if she might play it. He reluctantly said yes. As she hammered out a senseless ditty, the guide told the assembled tourists that Paderewski had once traveled to Vienna just to see that piano.

When the girl heard Paderewski's name mentioned, she stopped playing and asked the guide if Paderewski had played Beethoven's piano.

"No," the guide replied. "We wanted him to, but he said he wasn't worthy."

Is this not a parable of our decade? Things long held sacred are profaned and ridiculed.

Some things are still sacred. Surely, therefore, we ought to heed the admonition of Solomon: "Remove not the ancient landmark, which thy fathers have set" (Prov. 22:28). As we look at this passage this morning, let it become a mirror in which we see reflected some things that are still sacred.

I. The Word of God is still sacred.

Ignorance today about the Bible is appalling. Upon being asked about Golgotha, a Yale University student said that was who slew David. Among 18,000 Bible Belt high school students answering a questionnaire on the Bible, 16,000 of them couldn't name three Old Testament prophets; 12,000 didn't know the names of the four Gospels; and 10,000 couldn't name three of the twelve disciples.

One influential modern-day scholar took it upon himself to separate "myth" from "truth" in the Scriptures. In the myth column, he listed the preexistence of Christ; his virgin birth, deity, miracles, death for sinners, resurrection, ascension, and second coming; the last judgment; the personality and power of the Holy Spirit; the doctrine of the Trinity; and the doctrine of original sin.

41

In spite of this rampant ignorance and skepticism, the Word of God is still sacred. Why?

A. *The Word of God is sacred because God authored it (2 Tim. 3:16)*. It is not the type of book a man would write if he could or could write if he would.

B. *The Word of God is sacred because divinely inspired men wrote it (2 Peter 1:20–21)*. God "breathed" on those who wrote. Common men wrote under divine inspiration.

C. *The Word of God is sacred because it is eternal (2 Peter 1:23–24)*. A novel might last for a generation. A poem might last half a millennium. But the Bible will last forever because truth is eternal (Matt. 24:35).

II. The home is still sacred.

Regardless of the way moderns may treat the home, it is still sacred.

A. *The home is sacred because God created it (Gen. 2:21–25)*. The home was the first institution created by God. No modern-day human plan to bypass or subvert the home will succeed.

B. *The home is sacred because God blesses it (Gen. 1:25)*. God blesses only what is good. And all God blesses is sacred.

III. The church is still sacred.

William Barclay, in his book *A Spiritual Autobiography*, says, "Maybe it is fitting that I who have served the Church for more than forty years should end by saying, 'I believe in the Church'" ([Grand Rapids: Eerdmans, 1975], 117).

Norman Vincent Peale's statement about the church has been proved true in my own experience: "The church is where all our hopes come true!" What a strange, perplexing, but blessed thing is the church. It is still sacred two thousand years after it was founded by Jesus.

A. *The church is sacred because God conceived it (Eph. 1:4–6)*.

B. *The church is sacred because Christ founded it (Matt. 16:13–19)*.

C. *The church is sacred because the Holy Spirit fills it (Acts 2:1–4)*.

Conclusion

A striking memorial containing two statues sits in front of Boston's Trinity Church. One is of Phillips Brooks who became pastor of the church in 1869; the other is of Jesus who stands behind Brooks. The Savior's hands rest on Brooks's shoulders.

There are some things in this pagan world that are still sacred because the hand of the Savior rests on them.

SUNDAY EVENING, JANUARY 29

Title: Love and Forgiveness

Text: "'Two men owed money to a certain moneylender. One owed him five hundred denarii, and the other fifty. Neither of them had the money to pay him back, so he canceled the debts of both. Now which of them will love him more?'

"Simon replied, 'I suppose the one who had the bigger debt canceled.'

"'You have judged correctly,' Jesus said" *(Luke 7:41–43 NIV).*

Scripture Reading: Luke 7:36–50

Introduction

Probably no two emotions common to human beings are more closely related than love and forgiveness. When these emotions are experienced together, they take on a certain unselfishness that is inexpressibly beautiful in its manifestation.

Perhaps the chief reason why the result of the expression of love and forgiveness is so winsome in a person is that it is the chief characteristic of God in his attitude toward humans. Love and forgiveness radiated from Jesus Christ constantly.

Tonight's parable is one that, in spite of its brevity, contains a piercingly plain but accurately attractive description of God's love and forgiveness toward sinful humankind. To understand fully Jesus' purpose for and meaning of the story, the event eliciting this parable will be studied.

I. The audience.

Three persons are involved: Simon (a Pharisee), who had invited Jesus into his house for dinner; the woman, who, as Simon would have said, brazenly invaded the privacy of his home; and Jesus.

A. *To Simon the Pharisee, Jesus was an enigma.* To get a firsthand opportunity to observe Jesus, and perhaps even to find a means whereby he could gain a theological advantage over Jesus, Simon decided to prepare a dinner and invite Jesus to come. There, at close range, he could watch Jesus' every move; he could analyze every word Jesus spoke.

B. *The woman had been a prostitute.* The King James Version has Luke introducing the woman as one who was "a sinner." The word used is synonymous with "harlot." Simon knew immediately who she was. In utter horror, this fastidious Pharisee watched this unclean woman cross his threshold and defile his home. No doubt stunned speechless, he and his dinner guests watched as the woman came to where Jesus reclined on one of the couches arranged around the low table. She stooped down beside Jesus while tears flowed freely onto his feet. Then she loosened the tresses of her hair and wiped Jesus' feet dry. From the folds of her robe, she took a vial of precious ointment and poured its contents on Jesus' feet.

C. *Significant to understanding the audience is the contrast in the ways Simon and Jesus saw this woman.* Simon thought he knew who this woman was, but he knew only what she had been. He drew his conclusions about her on the basis of his own inadequate human judgment. This is typical of human nature. But how did Jesus see her? He knew this woman in a way Simon never could have known her, and he saw her as Simon never could have seen her. Jesus showed the woman to Simon by comparing her with him. Christ showed Simon that his boasted morality was as coarse as sackcloth and that the woman's adoration was as fine as fine-spun silk.

II. The symbolism.

Jesus was pleading earnestly for the soul of Simon. But he knew that he had to pierce through a gross misunderstanding of what God wanted from an individual.

A. *The meaning is in the attitude of the moneylender, in relation to the proportion of the debt.* One debtor owed 500 pence (roughly one and a half years' wages) and 50 pence (two months' wages). The extraordinary element is that the moneylender forgave them both. He canceled both debts! There, in the moneylender's mercy, flashes a picture of the grace of a forgiving God. The man saw the bankruptcy of both debtors. According to the laws of the day, they were both totally at his mercy. But in a sweep of unbelievable forgiveness, he wiped out the debt of both men.

B. *Jesus dealt with Simon at the point of his understanding.* Simon would have admitted that he was imperfect, all right; but at the same time he would have thanked God that he was not such a sinner as the woman was. Actually, Simon's sin was the sin of the spirit—and sins of the spirit are always worse than sins of the flesh.

1. The symbolism Jesus was teaching, then, was that everybody is spiritually bankrupt in the presence of God.

2. He taught that there is forgiveness for all. Mel Trotter, a great nineteenth-century preacher of the gospel, used to say, "We are all *redeemed*, but we are not all *saved*."

III. The application.

A. *Simon saw himself as easy to forgive.* Christ reminded Simon that when he entered the house, he was not even given the most common courtesies that were always extended in Palestinian homes. No servant waited at the door with a basin of water to wash his feet. Simon, the host, didn't give Jesus the customary kiss of greeting, nor did he practice the Eastern custom of placing a drop of fragrant perfume on Christ's forehead.

B. *The woman saw herself as unworthy of forgiveness.* She washed Jesus' feet with her tears and lovingly dried them with her hair. She kissed his feet, and she poured the entire contents of a costly bottle of perfume on him. All this she did, not in payment for her forgiveness, but in a natural outflow of her love and gratitude for what he had done for her.

C. *The saving faith of the woman was a gift from God.* Note what Jesus then said to the woman in Simon's presence: "Your faith has saved you; go in peace" (v. 50). God gives us saving faith when we repent of our sins, and it becomes our means of entrance into the kingdom of God.

Conclusion

The most important thing that happened to this woman was the change that came to her. Her sins were forgiven; she was given a new nature and was born into the family of God. But something else happened that we cannot overlook: she outwardly expressed her new relationship with God. She could not hide how she felt about the love and forgiveness she had received from the Lord. What she did for him was a spontaneous outpouring of her love and gratitude. Have you experienced the love and forgiveness of God in your life? If so, does the world know it?

FEBRUARY

■ Sunday Mornings

Examine the spiritual basics by continuing with the theme "Things Worth Remembering."

■ Sunday Evenings

Continue focusing on the parables with the theme "Patterns for Pilgrims."

■ Wednesday Evenings

Continue to pursue the Psalms with the topic "Questions by the Psalmist."

WEDNESDAY EVENING, FEBRUARY 1

Title: Do We Need Religion?

Text: "The wicked borroweth, and payeth not again: but the righteous showeth mercy, and giveth. For such as be blessed of him shall inherit the earth; and they that be cursed of him shall be cut off" *(Ps. 37:21–22).*

Scripture Reading: Psalm 37:1–22

Introduction

A factory chaplain in England addressed a large crowd of workers as they were gathered in their canteen; he then asked for questions or comments. One worker stood and said, "We don't want religion! We have everything we want. We have plenty of money. The company furnishes recreation. Food is put before us free; and we don't even have to clear away and wash the dishes. *What do we need religion for?*" For an answer the chaplain simply pointed to a poster prominently displayed in the canteen. It read, "During the past month, 1,200 knives and forks have been stolen from this canteen. In the future those using the canteen must bring their own cutlery." What an overwhelming answer.

All over the world, thousands are asking this question, if not by their words, then by their deeds, their interests, their attitudes, their neglect. Do we need religion? Our text gives an answer clearly and concisely. Here is the contrast between the wicked and the righteous, those who have religion in their hearts and those who don't.

I. We need religion to change the essential quality of our lives, to change our very natures.

Wicked versus righteous—the contrast is obvious. We need religion to change from wicked to righteous, from lost to saved, from unsaved to Christian. The Bible

46

recognizes only two kinds of people: the righteous or the person who is "like the chaff which the wind driveth away."

We need religion to change our very natures. We need to be born again, to be made alive in Christ, to be made new creatures in him. How can any observant person doubt that people are sinners? Look at the vast armies of law enforcement officers and the tremendous outlay for penal institutions. Look at the unbroken sway of godless materialism, the greed, the selfishness, the self-seeking. Human nature is sinful. Sinfulness, evil, and wickedness are the native qualities of the human heart. Our hearts, or nature, need to be changed.

II. We need religion to change the ruling spirit of our lives.

We need to be changed from one that "borroweth, and payeth not again," to one that "showeth mercy, and giveth."

The Spirit of Christ and the spirit of the world are at exactly opposite poles. The spirit of the world is to hate; the Spirit of Christ is to love. The spirit of the world is to grab, to acquire, to possess; the Spirit of Christ is to give, to suffer, to die. The spirit of the world is selfishness; the Spirit of Christ is altruism. As Paul urges the Philippians, "Do nothing out of selfish ambition or vain conceit, but in humility consider others better than yourselves. Each of you should look not only to your own interests, but also to the interests of others" (2:3–4 NIV). Until Christ saves us from our sins, and until we grow in his grace, the spirit of the world is the spirit of our lives. We need the religion of Christ to change the ruling spirit of our lives from the spirit of the world to the Spirit of Christ. Let this be our prayer:

Holy Spirit, all divine,
Dwell within this heart of mine;
Cast down every idol throne;
Reign supreme, and reign alone.
—Andrew Reed

III. We need religion to change the ultimate destiny of our lives.

Listen to the last part of the text: "For such as be blessed of him shall inherit the earth; and they that be cursed of him shall be cut off" (Ps. 37:22). The wicked and the righteous contrast not only in nature and spirit, but also in their ultimate destiny. They are not going to the same place. Those dressed in their sins will be damned to hell. Those clothed in the righteousness of the Son of God will first inherit the earth (Matt. 5:5) and ultimately the kingdom of heaven.

Conclusion

We need religion because we need to be changed. Nothing except the blood of Christ shed for our sake can do that. We must never trifle with the serious questions of life. None is more serious or more sober than "What shall I do then with Jesus which is called Christ?" (Matt. 27:22). What will you do with him?

SUNDAY MORNING, FEBRUARY 5

Title: What Jesus Refuses to Do

Text: "He shall not strive, nor cry; neither shall any man hear his voice in the streets. A bruised reed shall he not break, and smoking flax shall he not quench, till he send forth judgment unto victory" *(Matt. 12:19–20).*

Scripture Reading: Matthew 12:14–21

Hymns: "All Hail the Power of Jesus' Name," Perronet

          "Jesus Shall Reign Where'er the Sun," Watts

          "Crown Him with Many Crowns," Bridges

Offertory Prayer: Our Father, all we are and have is due to your loving-kindness. As we pause quietly to worship in your presence this morning, speak to our hearts and reveal yourself to us. As we hold up our empty cups, fill them with your grace. Bless now these tithes and offerings we lay on your altar and grant that they may be used to bring to others the blessings we know in Christ. Amen.

Introduction

In the Alpine Mountains of Switzerland, there is a place where a traveler can throw a piece of wood in one direction, and it will float into the Danube River and on into the Black Sea. A piece of wood thrown in another direction will travel into the Rhine River and on into the North Sea. Thrown in yet another direction, a piece of wood will travel into the Rhone River and out into the Mediterranean Sea. Although these three pieces of wood are thrown from the same place, they eventually reach three different seas, many miles apart. Their final destination is determined by the direction in which they are originally thrown.

Life is like that. What we will be tomorrow is being determined by the choices we make today. Character doesn't bloom suddenly.

This was even true of our Lord Jesus. Day by day he made choices; day by day his character developed. Some things he chose to do. Others he refused to do. By his choices, his life's path was determined.

As we look in the Gospels, we are thrilled by the things Jesus willingly did. Willingly he raised dead Lazarus. Willingly he healed the man with the withered arm. Willingly he raised the dead son of the widow at Nain.

But there is another side to Jesus' ministry. He steadfastly refused to do some things when he was on earth, and he refuses to do certain things today. Matthew, quoting Isaiah, refers to some of those things in our text.

I. Jesus refuses to be impatient with sinners.

Once in a fit of temper, Martin Luther shouted, "If I were God and the world had treated me as it has treated him, I would have kicked the wretched thing to pieces long ago." This may often be our attitude. But it isn't the attitude of Jesus.

Jesus was mercifully patient with sinners. This is seen in his every word and action. When the adulterous woman was brought to Jesus, she was met with divine patience. When Peter grievously failed his Master, Peter was encouraged by Jesus' patience.

Quoting from Isaiah 42:3, Matthew pictures Jesus' patience in verse 20: "A bruised reed shall he not break." Consider the scene Matthew depicts. A reed had been stepped on by some heavy-footed animal. Bruised, almost broken, the slightest wind or touch would finish what the heavy-footed animal had begun.

But Matthew is not talking about reeds and animals; rather, he is talking about the gentleness of Jesus with bruised and broken humankind. It is a beautiful picture of the Savior who refused to be impatient with sinners.

II. Jesus refuses to discourage those who are weary.

Jesus is the great encourager. It is not his desire to discourage us along life's way. We get enough of that from others. His common greeting to his followers was, "Be of good cheer!" His common message was, "Blessed are you!" His common benediction was, "Peace I leave with you!"

Echoing Isaiah, Matthew pictures Jesus' refusal to discourage those who are weary: "Smoking flax shall he not quench" (Matt. 12:20). First-century people illumined their homes with a linen wick that smoked only when about out of oil. Here Matthew describes a light that is almost extinguished. It futilely struggles for existence. The slightest breath will put it out.

The application of the metaphor is clear. The flickering light represents people who are overwhelmed by life's burdens and are about to succumb to life's unbearable loads. Jesus will not strike us further to crush us. He strengthens; he does not tear down. He blesses; he does not curse. He cheers us; he does not chide. He lifts burdens, he does not compound them. All of this shows that Jesus refuses to discourage those who are weary.

III. Jesus refuses to enter where he is uninvited.

Jesus is not an intruder. If you want Christ and the joy he brings, then you must invite him to enter your life. The text of Matthew's quotation indicates this. Matthew shows that the blessings the Savior brings are available to each of us, but the one who "hears his voice in the streets" (v. 19) must open the door to him.

Conclusion

Holman Hunt's painting of Christ is deeply moving. He pictures the Savior knocking at the vine-covered door; there is no knob on the outside of the door—it must be opened from within. Far up in the corner of the picture, Hunt has written in Latin, "O do not pass me by."

Jesus pleads with us. He invites us and urges us to receive him. But he will do no more. Jesus never enters where he is not invited.

SUNDAY EVENING, FEBRUARY 5

Title: The Fate of God's Word

Text: "But the seed on good soil stands for those with a noble and good heart, who hear the word, retain it, and by persevering produce a crop" *(Luke 8:15 NIV)*.

Scripture Reading: Luke 8:4–15

Introduction

In ancient Palestine there were no massive fields to cultivate. Rather, because of the mountains and valleys of Galilee, the only arable section of Palestine, a farmer was forced to cultivate his soil wherever he could. The presence of the black, volcanic basalt rock was an interminable menace to the farmer. To clear a plot of ground completely from those ever-present stones was an almost impossible task. So the farmer cultivated small patches of land here and there as best he could.

When Jesus told his parable, he and his disciples were traveling throughout the villages and towns of Galilee. Apparently a farmer was sowing seed on a nearby hillside. It was such a familiar sight to the people that they would hardly have noticed it. So, very carefully, Jesus pointed out the obvious to the crowd. He showed them exactly what the sower was doing.

I. The pathway (v. 5).

From the beginning of this parable there is an underlying sadness, a sense of tragedy. Jesus was talking about people who were receiving his message, the gospel seed he was sowing in their midst. In spite of the outward indication of success because of the large crowds, Jesus was sorrowfully aware of the fate of his words. Actually, according to Jesus' parable, a piddling 25 percent of his words were finding a home in interested, serious hearts!

A. *Seed cannot take root on a much-traveled and smooth pathway.* The point is that people who are only "paths" over which daily traffic passes will hardly provide soil into which the eternal seed can be deposited. People who are always busy may be those who are most in danger of being hardened pathways on which the eternal seed falls to no avail.

B. *People who cannot be receptive soil for at least fifteen minutes a day—who never allows themselves to be plowed and who never wait for what God would drop into the furrows of their hearts—are like the hardened pathway.* These busy people have lives that are major highways but hearts that are deserted.

C. *The birds in the parable represent the countless forces and temptations to which we submit our minds.* They seek to dominate us, and sadly they often do. We can name them many things: unchecked ambition, immorality, the craving for power, the quest for recognition and praise. How do we combat these predatory fowls that attack us daily? We meditate daily on the Scriptures and converse with God in prayer. This regular exercise serves to break up the hardened soil on the pathway.

II. The rocky soil (v. 6).

It would appear that things are improving a bit, for, instead of a hardened path, there is at least a thin layer of soil in which the seed can germinate. It actually begins to take root. Here we have the symbol of those who receive the seed of God's Word with some kind of enthusiasm. They take notice; they appear to listen with interest and concern. But one day it's all over. The heart that for a while was a glowing coal of fire suddenly becomes a cold black lump. What has happened?

A. *In many cases, it was simply an emotional Christianity, a spiritual "high" that was no more than that.* Some people are inspired by the Bible as they would be by some moving patriotic speech.

B. *This "shallow soil" Christianity happens when people are interested not in Christ, but in some preacher, or hallowed surroundings, or the "good feeling" they get from starting their week in church.* Theirs is a sad fate: their dry intellect and their superficial emotionalism do not endure.

III. The thorny ground (v. 7).

A. *Here again is some good soil dominated by weeds, thorns, and thistles.* Jesus likens these things to the cares, riches, and pleasures of life. People with such hearts are sad, for somewhere in the tangled frustration of their lives is the fleeting taste of what is genuine. They have encountered the penetrating goodness of God's Word, but these encounters have been dulled by other interests, or "thorns," in their lives. The thorns then start to choke out what is meaningful and good and lasting.

B. *We need to examine what demands our time, our priorities, and our interests.* When we are approached to perform a task in the Lord's work, is our answer usually that we have too many obligations already? Be careful. These attractive weeds can grow tall around us. They can successfully blind us to what is important in our lives from God's standpoint.

IV. The good soil (v. 8).

The good soil symbolizes the hearts of people who not only hear the Word, but also hold fast to it. To take the Word of God seriously means to see my neighbor as my brother or sister in Christ, to see myself as accountable before God every day of the week. It is to realize that I am his, and therefore he has a right to do with my life what he wills.

Conclusion

God's grace is not a cheap grace. It costs all that we have. People can loaf their way into hell; but the kingdom of God is seized by force. In the quiet fields where the seed is being sown, far more is happening than at the crossroads where traffic lights flash their busy signals.

WEDNESDAY EVENING, FEBRUARY 8

Title: What Can We Do When Troubles Come?

Text: "I will lift up mine eyes unto the hills, from whence cometh my help. My help cometh from the LORD, which made heaven and earth" *(Ps. 121:1–2)*.

Scripture Reading: Psalm 121:1–8

Introduction

"Grit your teeth and bear it" is the philosophy many would suggest when troubles come. For trivial matters, especially troubles of our own making, this might work. But the psalmist's example is much more effective. Psalm 121 belongs to a group known as the Pilgrim Psalms. It was written to be sung antiphonally as a group of pilgrims sang in unison while walking toward Jerusalem (v. 8).

What can we do when troubles come? Here are four suggestions to allow God's help to reach us.

I. We must try to view trouble objectively.

Establishing a proper perspective is a difficult task indeed. Yet it is essential. Learn to gauge your own perspective by asking these questions of yourself.

A. *What about the troubles of a minor nature we have brought on ourselves?* God has equipped us with a sense of humor. In this case, we ought to use this and have a good laugh at ourselves.

B. *What about those troubles that confuse us by their proximity?* Look at what the psalmist did. He took a long look at distant hills then turned back to analyze his problems. His perception of his problems changed when he took his eyes off of them.

C. *What about those troubles that have meant the wreck of all our cherished plans?* Acts 16:6–8 tells us of the wreckage of one mission initiative after another. Then follow two of the most thrilling verses in the New Testament (vv. 9–10), where Paul receives the call to cross over into the continent of Europe with the gospel. The most strategic move in Paul's career arose out of the ashes of ruined plans.

II. When troubles come, we must see them as God's opportunities.

We must not wallow in self-pity, asking, "Why did this have to happen to me?" We ought not to bristle in resentment, nor brood over our troubles, nor complain. We should ask, "What blessing in somber hue is this? God didn't send it, but he can use it for my good if I have faith."

A. *Our troubles can be God's opportunity to make something out of us.* Our God is a sovereign God. He overrules all things for the ultimate good of those who love him (Rom. 8:28).

B. *Our troubles can be God's opportunity to spread the gospel.* This was Paul's interpretation of his first imprisonment in Rome (Phil. 1:12).

C. *Our troubles can be an opportunity to develop our moral and spiritual muscles.* Hit by a car, a young dog suffered two broken hind legs. The veterinarian put the dog's entire hindquarters in a cast for some weeks. During this period, the dog dragged himself around the house with his two front legs. When he had completely recovered, he was a full-chested dog! If God can do that for a dog, he surely can do as much for us.

D. *Our troubles can be our opportunity for promotion to higher things.* Joseph's career in Pharaoh's court is a classic example of this.

III. When troubles come, we must allow them to elicit inner strength.

A. *Inner reserves must be stored before troubles come if they are to be called forth in crisis.* We must learn to walk with God while the sun is shining if we are going to stand with him in the storm. Daniel's life demonstrates this (Dan. 6:10).

B. *Troubles will call out our inner reserves of strength.* More than 1,800 years ago, the Stoic philosopher and Roman emperor Marcus Aurelius said, "Men must be arched and buttressed from within, else the temple wavers to dust." Troubles not only develop character, they reveal it.

IV. When troubles come, we must look outside ourselves to God, the source of all our strength.

When the psalmist asks, "From whence cometh my help?" (v. 1), his answer is "My help cometh from the LORD" (v. 2). How is this help mediated to a person?

A. *By prayer.* "I will left up mine eyes unto the hills" (v. 1). Of course this means prayer.

B. *By Bible study.* Growth in grace and in knowledge of the Lord can be obtained only through in-depth Bible study.

C. *By exercising faith.* Christians know that faith is the means by which they live daily. The unsaved must realize that faith in Christ is their only hope.

Conclusion

Let no person think that he or she will not experience trouble. There are no exceptions. When troubles come, we must view them correctly, respond to them directly, and look with confidence to God, from whom our help comes.

SUNDAY MORNING, FEBRUARY 12

Title: What the Church Must Remember

Text: "Go ye therefore, and teach all nations, baptizing them in the name of the Father, and of the Son, and of the Holy Ghost: teaching them to observe all things whatsoever I have commanded you: and, lo, I am with you always, even unto the end of the world. Amen" *(Matt. 28:19–20).*

Scripture Reading: Matthew 28:16–20

Hymns: "The Church's One Foundation," Stone

"Lead Me to Calvary," Hussey

"O Happy Day That Fixed My Choice," Doddridge

Offertory Prayer: Heavenly Father, for all your blessings bestowed on us, we lift grateful hearts of thanksgiving. And now as we bring our tithes and offerings to you as an expression of our love and obedience, bless the gift and the giver to further your kingdom's work, through Christ our Lord. Amen.

Introduction

A person's last words are immeasurably valuable. The words before death are significant because often they crystallize the actions of the individual's life. They can also reflect the priorities of that person's life. Here are some examples of the last words of famous people. Beethoven's last words were "Too bad! It's too late." St. Francis of Assisi's last words were "Welcome, Sister Death." Knowing death was imminent, John Wesley said, "The best part is God is with us." When Woodrow Wilson's physician told him he was dying, President Wilson replied, "I am ready."

This morning we look at the last words of our Savior. Jesus talks to the church about his work in the world. He reminds the church of its task to do his work. He wants the church to remember some important things.

I. The church must make disciples.

In the first part of verse 19, our Lord says just before he ascends, "Go ye therefore, and teach all nations." The imperative verb "teach" expresses the command "Go, make disciples." This needs further study.

A. *Who is to be discipled?* Jesus says that all nations are to be discipled. The gospel is for the whole world.

B. *How are we to disciple?* It is to be done by evangelism—by sharing the Good News with others.

A tender story about John A. Broadus, former president of Southern Baptist Theological Seminary, illustrates the point. When Broadus was only sixteen, he became a Christian. Encouraged to talk to his unsaved friends about Jesus, young Broadus spoke to a mentally retarded friend named Sandy about his need to be saved. Sandy made a profession of faith. Whenever they met after that, Sandy would smile and say, "Howdy, John? Thankee, John."

Broadus later related, "And if ever I reach the heavenly home and walk the golden streets, I know the first person to meet me will be Sandy, coming and saying again: 'Howdy, John? Thankee, John.'"

It is our business to make disciples.

II. The church must mark disciples.

When persons enter military service, they swear allegiance to the constitution of the United States. That *makes* them soldiers. When they are assigned to a base, they are given uniforms. That *marks* them as soldiers.

Baptism is that initial act in the life of new believers that marks them as believers. Jesus is referring to this in verse 19: ". . . baptizing them in the name of the Father, and of the Son, and of the Holy Ghost."

A. *Who is to be baptized?* The answer is clear: those who have been taught.

B. *Why are they to be baptized?* Jesus commands it. Cornelius, Lydia, and the Ethiopian eunuch all responded to the teachings about Christ with baptism.

C. *How is it to be done?* It is to be done publicly, "in the name of the Father, and of the Son, and of the Holy Ghost," and preferably by immersion, for that is what the word means in the original Greek.

III. The church must strengthen its disciples.

Verse 20 mandates that the church strengthen its disciples: ". . . teaching them to observe all things whatsoever I have commanded you." Too many of our churches are strong in making and marking disciples but weak in maturing them. The neglect is tragic.

A. *What needs to be taught to strengthen disciples?* Jesus gives us the answer: "All things whatsoever I have commanded you." These precepts are found in the New Testament.

B. *Why are these things to be taught?* Jesus has commanded believers to "observe all things." More than the sacrifice of fatted rams, the Lord God wants the obedience of his people.

Conclusion

When Pompeii was destroyed by the eruption of Mount Vesuvius in AD 79, the heat and ashes suddenly overwhelmed many of the citizens of the city. They were killed instantly—while even in motion—and were preserved in their activity. Among those suddenly turned to stone was a Roman soldier. When excavated centuries later, he was standing at his post guarding the doomed city. We must not be dead, frozen soldiers who only stand mechanically at our posts. Rather, we must be alive and vigorous, remembering those things Christ told us to do.

SUNDAY EVENING, FEBRUARY 12

Title: The Pretenders

Text: " 'The harvest is the end of the age, and the harvesters are angels' " *(Matt. 13:39 NIV).*

Scripture Reading: Matthew 13:24–30, 36–43

Introduction

In none of Jesus' parables do we find a clearer picture of the true purpose and tactics of the Devil than in this parable of the wheat and the tares. Here we see plainly that the Devil is committed to the destruction of anyone and everything that has the stamp of God's goodness on it.

Therefore, in this solemn and almost frightening parable, Jesus was trying to impress three things on his followers: First, he underscored the validity of *the owner* of the field in which the seed was sown; second, he introduced *the invader*, who planned and calculated to undermine the work of the owner; and finally, undoubtedly with sadness, he described *the pretenders,* the offspring of the invader's work.

I. The owner (vv. 24, 37–38).

A. *The field in this parable belonged to this man.* It had its boundaries; it was identifiable. This man took great pride in his field. He had cultivated it and prepared it for sowing. He was a conscientious, purposeful farmer. He intended to raise wheat, and he marshaled all of his agricultural skills to do the very best he could.

B. *This is still God's property on which we live!* Sometimes we forget that fact because of the blatant evil around us. At no time has God relinquished his proprietorship. The Devil has been described as "a squatter" in this world. A squatter is one who settles on land he has no right to and works it for his own advantage. This is what lies behind Christ's speaking of the sower sowing the seed in his field. The world, ultimately, is not the property of the one who is forever sowing evil seed in it.

C. *No part of this world has the Lord forfeited to the Devil.* This is why Jesus commissioned his followers to "go into all the world and preach the gospel to every creature." In Paul's epistle to the Romans, he wrote, "The whole creation groaneth and travaileth in pain together until now," waiting for the revealing of the sons of God (8:22). When Adam and Eve sinned, this world was cursed; since that day it has borne the stigma of that divine displeasure. Still the world writhes and heaves in spiritual agony.

D. *The owner represents the Lord Jesus, fulfilling his mission.* While he was on earth, he did the sowing personally. Then, before he was crucified and ascended to the Father in heaven, he commissioned his followers to carry on his work of sowing. And what is the "seed" he is sowing? It represents the sons and daughters of the kingdom of God.

How can we summarize what Jesus tells us about the owner of the field? He is the Son of God. He is also the one who "sows the seed" from which grow believers in the Lord Jesus Christ. He sows in all the field. The whole world is his, and he longs to save those in every corner of his world.

II. The invader (vv. 25, 39).

We are not to misunderstand the phrase "while everyone was sleeping" to suggest carelessness or irresponsibility. Rather, it means that the farmer and his hands had done all they could. They had prepared the field and had carefully sown the seed. There was nothing more they could do at that point. This is an accurate picture of the sensitive work of the Holy Spirit in convicting sinners of their sins and planting in their heart the gospel seed.

Jesus was specific about the enemy: he was the avowed, particular enemy of the sower. He said, "His enemy came." That which the Devil hates about Christians is *Christ in them.* Thus, when Christ is truly being honored in our lives, we are more than ever the targets of the Devil's attacks.

III. The pretenders (vv. 26, 38).

What of the fruit of this seed sown secretly in the nighttime? (vv. 28–30). The servants wanted desperately to fan out through that field and pull up every tiny blade of the tares, which had begun to grown. But they received this astonishing advice from the owner of the field: "Let both grow together until the harvest." In other words, there was no way they could get every single blade of the choking tares that had begun to spring up. Furthermore, in their indignant zeal, the servants would have pulled up many blades of the wheat.

In these words Christ counseled his disciples to have patience in the face of all the havoc that evil seems to be creating in the midst of God's working. It is a great temptation to wade into a situation in our indignation and straighten out the problem once and for all!

A. *Jesus' solution was to "let both grow together until the harvest."* Sometimes in our zeal to have a "holy church," we only make it easier for self-righteousness to flourish in the midst of the holiness. It is often the case that when we root up all the "sins" in the church, we do little more than leave room for the subtle and even more destructive "sins of the spirit"—the holier-than-thou attitude, the spiritual snobbery, the "supersaints," the "supercritics" who, armed with their Bibles, have the last word on what is wrong with everyone who doesn't agree with their interpretation of Christianity.

B. *This does not mean that we are not to battle against evil when we see it clearly.* Jesus said that persons who are unrepentant of their blatant and open sin are to be excluded from the fellowship of the church. In spite of these rare and exceptional cases, Jesus is saying in this parable that, for the most part, it is hard to wait, lest in our haste we bruise the tender wheat, the young, sensitive, impressionable Christians who inevitably get hurt in such situations.

Conclusion

The final judgment is going to be full of surprises. When the time comes for the separation of the goats from the sheep, the wheat from the tares, we most likely will see how distorted our best judgment was in many situations. For in that day, Jesus, our Lord and King, will come with his sickle and reap his wheat. Then all of our sickles of judgment will fall to the ground, along with all of the illegitimate "crowns of righteousness" we have put on our heads! We must never forget that God can find, bring home, and set at his table even the worst who have repented of their sins and called him their Savior and Lord.

WEDNESDAY EVENING, FEBRUARY 15

Title: How Does One Psalmist Picture Salvation?

Text: "I waited patiently for the LORD; and he inclined unto me, and heard my cry. He brought me up also out of an horrible pit, out of the miry clay, and set my feet upon a rock, and established my goings. And he hath put a new song in my mouth, even praise unto our God: many shall see it, and fear, and shall trust in the LORD" *(Ps. 40:1–3).*

Scripture Reading: Psalm 40:1–10

Introduction

A young evangelist tells of preaching in an isolated community. Twenty-two men were converted in that revival, and a new church was later organized. Most remarkable was the work of an enthusiastic new Christian named Hervie. Hervie had a zeal for God. When the evangelist pursued a non-Christian in the community, the man remarked, "I'm glad you came. Hervie was here talking to me. He sure is proud of what the Lord has done for him."

Hervie simply told those men what Christ had done for him and reasoned, "If he did that for me, he will do the same for you." And he would invariably add, "It's been almost a year since I made a change; and I've been praising the Lord ever since." That was what cut these sincere but simple men to the heart. They knew Hervie. Something had happened to this man. Something had changed him.

This was also true of the psalmist. Something had happened to him. His patient waiting for the Lord was rewarded; for the pit was exchanged for the rock, the miry clay for security. He had been wonderfully delivered by the grace of God. The psalmist had something to tell; and in the language of grateful remembrance, he told it. In three clear pictures he describes his experience.

I. The psalmist pictures his former condition.

"He brought me up also out of an horrible pit, out of the miry clay" (v. 2). What a graphic picture of a lost soul in his utter helplessness! The dungeon of that day was shaped like a bottle buried in the ground. The sides were slick and perpendicular. The only opening and hope of rescue was at the top. The prophet Jeremiah was incarcerated in such a place (Jer. 38:7–13) and was rescued by an officer in the mercenary bodyguard of the king. Using ropes, the officer released the prisoner. The psalmist is saying, "That was my plight in the horrible pit in the miry clay of sin. Only the Lord could hear my cry, and only the Lord could lift me out." People are helpless in their sin. God's grace reaches down and lifts us out of the depths.

II. The psalmist pictures God's great deliverance.

A. *This was a divine deliverance.*
B. *This was a personal deliverance.*
C. *This was a deliverance in response to a sinner's cry.*

58

III. The psalmist pictures the blessedness of his present estate.

As a result of God's great deliverance, four things are true of this psalmist.

A. *He is secure.* "He . . . set my feet upon a rock, and established my goings" (v. 2). The believer is secure. God did not lift us up out of the horrible pit of sin only to let us fall back in again (see John 10:27–29).

B. *He is happy.* "And he hath put a new song in my mouth" (v. 3). Joyless religion is suspect. Religion that weighs us down instead of lifting us up is not true religion.

C. *He is thankful.* "And he hath put a new song in my mouth, even praise unto our God" (v. 3). Our gratitude for saving grace should deepen, resulting in greater and greater love and loyalty to him.

D. *He will be useful.* "Many shall see it, and fear, and shall trust in the LORD" (v. 3). No one can deny the power in the testimony of a changed life.

Conclusion

How long has it been since the Lord brought you up out of a horrible pit? Are your feet on the rock or still in the miry clay? Are many seeing and fearing and trusting in the Lord because of you?

SUNDAY MORNING, FEBRUARY 19

Title: Things Most Precious

Text: "Blessed be the God and Father of our Lord Jesus Christ, which according to his abundant mercy hath begotten us again unto a lively hope by the resurrection of Jesus Christ from the dead, to an inheritance incorruptible, and undefiled, and that fadeth not away, reserved in heaven for you, who are kept by the power of God through faith unto salvation ready to be revealed in the last time" (*1 Peter 1:3–5*).

Scripture Reading: 1 Peter 1:1–8

Hymns: "Are You Washed in the Blood?" Hoffman

"Blessed Assurance, Jesus Is Mine," Crosby

"When We All Get to Heaven," Hewitt

Offertory Prayer: Heavenly Father, as you have given us our daily bread, supplying all our needs, we now return to you these tithes and offerings in gratitude. For life's provisions, we give thanks. For the privilege of helping expand the work of your kingdom, we also give thanks. As we give these tithes and offerings in love, accept them and use them for your glory, in Jesus' name. Amen.

Introduction

An American minister visiting Paris wanted to attend church, so seeing a large cathedral on one of the main avenues, he went inside. He was late and the cathedral was packed, so he had to stand against the back wall with the other latecomers.

As the choir sang the anthem for the morning, the preacher noticed a shabbily dressed elderly man standing near. His clothes were tattered and worn, his hair was disheveled, and he held an old hat that looked as though it had been reclaimed from a trash barrel.

As the choir came to the closing refrain of the anthem, the preacher spoke: "O Lamb of God who takes away the sin of the world, have mercy on us, have mercy on us." The American's worship reverie was broken by the audible whisper of the old man. With a pained look on his face, the man sobbed aloud, "O God, what a dream, what a dream! If only he could! If only he could!" Then he turned around and rushed from the sanctuary.

Are the blessings we have in Jesus Christ only a dream? Are they real or are they only the figments of a warped imagination?

These are some of the questions Peter's readers were asking. Suffering for their faith, they were wondering if serving Jesus was worth the cost. But Peter wrote to assure them that their blessings in Christ were most precious. It would be worth it all when they met Jesus.

I. We have a new birth.

Our new birth is declared in verse 3: "Blessed be the God and Father of our Lord Jesus Christ, which according to his abundant mercy hath begotten us again unto a lively hope by the resurrection of Jesus Christ from the dead." Peter is talking about the new birth. This joyful concept that a person can begin life again was hinted at by the Old Testament prophets, but it was only clearly revealed in the earthly ministry of Jesus.

Peter is also writing out of his own experience. Remembering the day when he first met Jesus, Peter calls his readers to their initial encounter with Jesus, the time when they were born again.

A. *The new birth is provided by God's abundant mercy.* It does not come from our goodness or our obedience to the law or our adherence to church rituals. Rather, as Peter says, it comes to us "according to his abundant mercy." Mercy is God's compassion toward sinners.

B. *The new birth is an experience.* Peter says that he "hath begotten us again," and the tense of the verb shows that it is a definite experience that takes place at a definite time in our lives.

II. We have a new hope.

Verse 3 speaks of being born to a "lively hope by the resurrection." When Jesus was crucified, the world collapsed on the apostles. They cowered behind bolted windows and locked doors in their upper room in Jerusalem. But Easter morning changed everything for them. What changed them and gave them new courage? Peter declares that it was "the resurrection of Jesus Christ from the dead." Seeing their resurrected, living Lord so transformed the apostles that by AD 65 there may have been as many as 20,000 believing Jews in Jerusalem.

III. We have a new heritage.

Our new heritage is made clear in verse 4: "To an inheritance incorruptible, and undefiled, and that fadeth not away, reserved in heaven for you." Peter is discussing our heavenly home—our holy inheritance.

A. *It is incorruptible.* It won't perish. Jesus warned about gold and silver and earthly possessions that will perish.

B. *It is undefiled.* There is no blemish on it. It is perfect.

C. *It will never fade.* A beautiful rose will fade. The face of the most beautiful woman will wrinkle. But our heavenly inheritance will endure.

D. *It is reserved in heaven.* The Greek word translated "reserved" means "kept." Our heavenly reward is safely guarded by our heavenly Father.

Conclusion

Edinburgh physician Sir James Simpson found in 1847 that chloroform was a good substitute for ether in relieving the pain of childbirth. Simpson's theory was proved true when Queen Victoria gave birth to Prince Leopold under chloroform. The great importance of this discovery is obvious. Yet when asked what he considered to be his greatest discovery, Simpson replied, "That Jesus has saved me, a poor sinner!"

SUNDAY EVENING, FEBRUARY 19

Title: The Persistent Host

Text: "Then the master told his servant, 'Go out to the roads and country lanes and make them come in, so that my house will be full. I tell you, not one of those men who were invited will get a taste of my banquet'" (*Luke 14:23–24 NIV*).

Scripture Reading: Luke 14:15–24

Introduction

One of the most poignant and compassionate of all of Jesus' parables is "the Great Supper." In this touching story, Jesus is asserting clearly that the kingdom of God is not some distant "pie in the sky" situation, but is here and now! Because of the awareness that God's kingdom is here, right now, you can come to understand what kind of God loves you and desires to have daily contact with you.

The action in the story is fast-paced. The emotions that surface are strong and positive. First, we find an amazing *free offer* from the host, who has prepared this sumptuous banquet. Second, we see an inconceivable *indifferent response* from those who are invited. Finally, we are surprised by a *compassionate invitation* extended by this remarkable host.

I. The free offer (vv. 15–17).

How many times during any given week do you receive in the mail some third-class advertisement with a "fabulous *free offer*" inside "if you act at once"? You find yourself wanting to fill out the order blank and cash in on that fantastic windfall.

But a bit of cautious wisdom tells you to read the fine print. When you do, you discover that the offer is not really "free" at all.

A. *When Jesus came with his offer of free grace, a salvation that does not have to be "worked for," the people found it hard to accept.* They were accustomed to a religion that demanded works.

B. *The setting of this parable was in the home of a prominent Pharisee in Jerusalem where Jesus had been invited for a Sabbath meal.* While Jesus was eating, a man suffering from dropsy came in. Before Jesus healed him, he asked the guests, "Is it lawful to heal on the sabbath or not?" When they did not answer him, he used the proverb concerning the ox that had fallen into a well on the Sabbath. While he had them on the defensive, Jesus battered their selfish pride and hypocrisy by telling them how they invited only their special friends and relatives to their banquets so that those people would reciprocate.

C. *Jesus took advantage of this situation to tell this searching parable of a benevolent host who prepared a banquet and extended an invitation with no strings attached: "Come, for everything is now ready" (v. 17).* Since the supper represented, in the symbolism of the parable, the kingdom of God, Jesus was saying that God's kingdom is ready right now for all who accept his invitation to come and enter it! There is no waiting until after death to enter and enjoy this kingdom.

The kingdom of God has been compared to a great city hospital, whose doors are never closed. However late the sick or the injured may arrive, they will find that preparations have been made to receive them and to minister to their needs.

II. The indifferent response (vv. 18–20).

What is obvious from the reaction of these people who had already been invited and who knew ahead of time about the banquet? They simply did not want to come! They were more interested in going on with business as usual. Jesus did not call their responses "reasons," but "excuses." And judging by what each of these men said, we must know that on the level of common sense, either they were liars or fools.

A. *What are the three excuses offered?* We are preoccupied with our *possessions*, represented by the man who had bought the field. Many people are outside the kingdom today because possessions are an all-important obsession in their lives. Second, we are *busy*, illustrated by the man with his oxen. To some, work is their god. But again, the end result is to secure for themselves what this world has to offer. The third man represented *human affection*. It is praiseworthy for a man to love his wife and family, to desire to be with them. But when that human affection turns to worship, when people place their love for their family above their love for God, they are making a tragic mistake.

B. *There is something else about this banquet we must not overlook: it was a gift—a free offer of the master's grace.*

III. The compassionate invitation (vv. 21–24).

A. *Note the reaction of those approached this time by the servant.* When they received the invitation, there is no indication that they hesitated at all. Apparently no coercion was necessary. No material possessions, obsession with work, or human affection stood in the way.

B. *Still the word went out, "Yet there is room!"* During this time, those previously invited guests with all of the excuses were going about their business. They didn't know the glory of the feast they were missing; they didn't realize that those enjoying that feast were their desperate, outcast brothers.

C. *The tragedy is that they had been invited too, but they considered it unimportant, an interference with their lifestyle.* Can't you see the parallel with what happens in our day as well? Countless scores of people receive the invitation; they may listen to it every Sunday in church. But other things are far more important to them.

D. *Furthermore, an element of faith was involved here.* The invited guests had to have faith that the promise involved in the invitation was genuine, that a feast was indeed prepared. They could not see the feast until they took "the step of faith" and entered the banquet hall. So it is when one accepts God's offer of salvation.

Conclusion

Notice how eager the host of the feast was to fill his banquet hall. He was prepared to use every legitimate means at his disposal to get the people in. Still he shut out those who showed no desire or appreciation for his hospitality.

"Compel them to come in, that my house may be filled!" was the order he gave his servant. This host displayed a humility that attracted the poor and the humble; yet at the same time, he had a lordliness about him that resisted the haughty and self-satisfied.

The beautiful word of hope, of eternal encouragement, is this: "And yet there is room!" Until Jesus comes and declares that the opportunity to be saved is ended, there is room at the Master's table.

There is a place set for you, my friend. Have you accepted the invitation?

WEDNESDAY EVENING, FEBRUARY 22

Title: What Does It Mean to Know God?

Text: "'Be still, and know that I am God; I will be exalted among the nations, I will be exalted in the earth'" *(Ps. 46:10 NIV).*

Scripture Reading: Psalm 46:1–11

Introduction

Psalm 46 refers to some great catastrophe (v. 6). It tells us also that God has delivered his people (vv. 8–9). The psalm is filled with thunder and lightning—a tumultuous scene. It does not have a quiet message. We need to read verse 10 in its entirety if we are to get its full impact. Moffatt translates this verse, "Give in, he cries, admit that I am God, high over the nations, high above the earth."

Against the background of catastrophe and divine deliverance, the psalmist is telling us what it means to know God. In the very eye of the social hurricane, in the very citadel of history, God reigns; and man may know this sovereign God. What does it mean to know God? Three words summarize this text: *surrender, experience*, and *sovereignty*. There is, then, a threefold answer to our question.

I. To know God means surrendering to him completely.

There is a surrender that saves us; and it is this that God, through the psalmist, is urging us to do: "Be still," "give in," "surrender," "know that I am God."

When powerful enemies came against Jehoshaphat, king of Judah, he met the crisis through the surrender of prayer, "O our God, will you not judge them? For we have no power to face this vast army that is attacking us. We do not know what to do, but our eyes are upon you" (2 Chron. 20:12 NIV). Jehoshaphat evaluated his armies: "We have no power to face this vast army." He judged his own leadership, "We do not know what to do." And he appraised his God, "Our eyes are upon you." He is saying, "We throw ourselves on your mercy, for we have no other hope." That is surrender. Jehoshaphat could have continued groping blindly; he could have surrendered to the situation. Instead, he surrendered to God in a complete commitment.

Our extremity is God's opportunity. Our weakness is the opportunity for God's strength. We come to know God when we surrender completely to his will. This is the first step toward a knowledge of God; and the second step stems from the first.

II. To know God means experiencing him personally.

"Surrender, and know that I am God." The psalmist's expression means "to know God intimately." It means to know by experience, to make the pragmatic test. God is available to his people. He is invincible against his enemies.

Everyone is challenged to experience God personally. No vicarious experience will do. It is a great thing to be the heir of a great tradition, but it is a tragic thing to suppose that we can substitute tradition for personal experience.

Jacob, returning from his twenty-year sojourn in Padan-aram, met God on the banks of the Jabbok River. In his prayer he said, "O God of my father Abraham, God of my father Isaac, O LORD who said to me, 'Go back to your country and your relatives" (Gen. 32:9 NIV). "Who said to me" is the key phrase in Jacob's prayer. The God who had been the God of his grandfather, Abraham, and of his father, Isaac, was now his God also. He had come to know him for himself, to know him by personal experience.

Are we founding our hope on a Christ who has spoken to us and to whom we speak daily, face-to-face and heart-to-heart? Is our religion firsthand, personal experience? At the end of his ordeal, after talking with God face-to-face, Job said, "My ears had heard of you but now my eyes have seen you. Therefore I despise myself and repent in dust and ashes" (Job 42:5–6 NIV).

III. To know God means recognizing his sovereignty.

Our text also says, "I will be exalted among the nations, I will be exalted in the earth" (Ps. 46:10 NIV). In any true sense, we do not know God until we recognize his sovereignty, his rule over all the earth.

A. *This was the faith of Israel in the Old Testament.* "The Old Testament expresses the sovereignty of God in many ways: He rides upon the clouds (Ps. 68:4). He scatters the hoarfrost like ashes (Ps. 147:16). He calls out the stars by number (Isa. 40:26). The most crucial area of His sovereignty is not in nature but in the movement of historical events. He overrules Pharaoh (Ex. 6:1), uses the Assyrian as the rod of His anger (Isa. 10:5), and anoints Cyrus, king of Persia, to do His will" (Isa. 44:28) (Lawrence E. Toombs, *The Old Testament in Christian Preaching* [Philadelphia: Westminster, 1961], 64–65).

B. *This was the faith of Jesus.* He was nurtured in Israel's faith in God's majestic sovereignty, but to that he added the quality of God's seeking love, which is able to triumph over every conceivable experience of humankind.

C. *This was the faith of our fathers.* An astonishing aspect of the Bible is how seldom any word such as *chance* or *luck* or *fortune* occurs. The Bible is concerned with the kingdom of God, and in that kingdom there is neither accident nor luck. Our fathers believed this. The ultimate control was always God's.

D. *This must be our faith today.* It must be if we are to know God as he is. Do we believe that Jesus is King of Kings and Lord of Lords? Do we believe that all authority and power, all dominion and rule are in his hands? As Christians do we glory in the fact that we are children of the King?

Conclusion

We can know God; and all who know him are secure. This world belongs to God and not to any of its leaders or inhabitants. God cannot be defeated. Neither evil nor the designs of evil people can ultimately triumph.

SUNDAY MORNING, FEBRUARY 26

Title: Things Mercifully Simple

Text: "[He] brought them out, and said, Sirs what must I do to be saved? And they said, Believe on the Lord Jesus Christ and thou shalt be saved, and thy house" *(Acts 16:30–31).*

Scripture Reading: Acts 16:25–40

Hymns: "At the Cross," Watts

        "Ye Must Be Born Again," Sleeper

        "We Have Heard the Joyful Sound," Owen

Offertory Prayer: Great and gracious heavenly Father, the giver of both physical and spiritual life, we pause to thank you for all your blessings. Out of gratitude for your blessings, and in obedience to your teachings, we now bring our tithes and offerings to you. Bless these gifts to the winning of the lost and the strengthening of your kingdom. We pray in the name of Christ our Lord. Amen.

Introduction

While Benjamin Franklin was living in Philadelphia, George Whitefield, a young and notable evangelist was preaching there. Whitefield was such a godly man that one of his biographers wrote that he lived more in heaven than on earth.

Franklin was a great admirer of the English evangelist. Whitefield was very eager to lead Franklin to know the Savior. Thus, he wrote to Franklin, urging him to take seriously his need for salvation. Adding a personal note, Whitefield wrote something like this: "You will excuse this freedom. I must have something about Christ in all my letters."

It was this kind of earnest concern for people's salvation that motivated Paul. The passage read this morning was taken from Paul's second missionary journey. He and his company had crossed the Aegean Sea from Asia Minor into Macedonia. Pushing westward with the gospel, they came to the ancient city of Philippi, named for the father of Alexander the Great.

Having been cast into prison at Philippi for their strong witness, God sent an earthquake at midnight that opened the jail and liberated all the prisoners. But Paul and Silas didn't flee.

Knowing that his life would be taken by his superiors for having let his prisoners escape, the Philippian jailer pulled out his sword and was about to fall on it when a voice rang out of the darkness, "Do thyself no harm, for we are all here!" Frightened and bewildered, the jailer rushed up to Paul and Silas and fell down before them and cried out, "Sirs, what must I do to be saved?"

Paul didn't complicate this with a long theological answer. The man asked a simple question: Paul gave a simple answer.

This morning as we look at this marvelous experience from the life of the great apostle, let me talk to you about a simple question with a simple answer. This passage deals with simple things that each of us can understand.

I. The simple question.

The asking of this simple question, "What must I do to be saved?" has been the key that has unlocked grace's door for millions of people. In a garden of Milan, Italy, in the fourth century, a brilliant young scholar, weary of an empty life, wept a prayer to God: "O Lord, how long? How long? Tomorrow and tomorrow and tomorrow? Why not now? Why not this hour make an end of my weakness? The scholar Saint Augustine wrote that he heard a voice speaking in Latin, "Take up and read." Reaching for one of Paul's letters, Augustine obeyed, and a spiritual renewal took place.

A. *It is a personal question.* No one can ask the question for you. Jesus stands ready to save you, but the question, "What must I do to be saved?" is one you must ask for yourself.

B. *It is an imperative question.* There is no other way to be saved except by the asking of this question. Peter told his hearers at Pentecost, "And it shall come to pass, that whosoever shall call on the name of the Lord shall be saved" (Acts 2:21).

II. The simple answer.

Plato had inscribed over the door to his academy at Athens, "Let no one enter here who is ignorant of geometry." That demand kept many people out of Plato's classroom. There are certain doors we can enter only when we have received a high degree of knowledge or have attained to a certain position in the community. But God will have none of this. The doorway that leads to eternal life is cluttered with nothing complex or difficult that would keep the simplest searcher out of the kingdom. The things a person must know to be saved are mercifully few and simple. The door to eternal life stands wide open.

When the pale, trembling jailer fell down before Paul and asked his simple question, he received an equally simple answer: "Believe on the Lord Jesus Christ and thou shalt be saved!"

Chrysostom, another fourth-century believer, wrote that since the way to eternal life is so simple, we have it within our power to be saved while sitting at home. And I might add, we have it in our power to be saved while we are at work, driving a car, cooking a meal, or lying sick in bed.

A. *What this simple answer doesn't say.* Although the passage speaks of our "believing on the Lord Jesus Christ," this is not just intellectual belief (see James 2:19).

B. *What it does say.* Paul said to "believe on the Lord Jesus Christ." To believe on Jesus means to trust him, to rely on him alone, to commit oneself to him.

Conclusion

The best-known verse in the New Testament clearly shows us the simple way to be saved: "For God so loved the world, that he gave his only begotten Son, that whosoever believeth in him should not perish, but have everlasting life" (John 3:16).

SUNDAY EVENING, FEBRUARY 26

Title: When Forgiveness Is Hard

Text: "Then came Peter to him, and said, Lord, how oft shall my brother sin against me, and I forgive him? till seven times? Jesus saith unto him, I say not unto thee, Until seven times: but, Until seventy times seven" (Matt. 18:21–22).

Scripture Reading: Matthew 18:21–35

Introduction

If we were to search the New Testament for the person who seemed most human—more like we are than any other—it would most likely be Simon Peter.

"Simon bar Jonah," as he was known when Christ called him to be one of his disciples, is known for experiencing and expressing great extremes in his emotions. Often his desire to be spiritually strong and dependable exceeded his depth of commitment. Consequently, he seemed to show his weakness more often than the other disciples.

For example, the parable Jesus related in tonight's text was prompted by one of Peter's emotion-charged questions for Christ. We do not know the details behind the question. But it is likely that Peter's problem was more serious than just a disagreement with one of the other disciples. It may be that Jesus' piercing words in the Sermon on the Mount about forgiving, loving, and praying for one's enemies were causing Peter to have some agonizing bouts with his conscience.

The Jewish rabbis had laid down a guideline by which to deal with these situations. They said that to forgive a person *three times* was adequate. Peter knew that Jesus' teachings went beyond that, but how far he was not sure. So, in making an effort to be benevolent, he *exceeded* the requirement of the rabbis. Implicit in his question is the notion that to forgive one's offending brother *seven times* surely would be enough. Knowing Peter's nature, we can imagine that, having asked the question, he waited to hear Jesus commend him for his generosity in having such great patience toward his enemy. Therefore he was not prepared at all for Jesus' answer.

Jesus answered Peter with a story. It was a challenge addressed to Peter—and to each one of us. It probes deeply into our hearts and consciences and makes us face the stabbing truth about this business of forgiveness.

I. Forgiveness is revealing.

A. *Forgiveness is never easy.* This is true because forgiveness means the forgiving person—the innocent party—fully acknowledges the wrongdoing of the offending one and lets the guilty one go free! Forgiveness means that one is able to *love genuinely* with a love that is able to go beyond the problem and extend to the person involved. This truth mirrors *God's* forgiveness toward us.

B. *Jesus set the story in the context of God's grace when he began with the statement, "The kingdom of heaven is like. . . ."* Purposely, Jesus made the debt the servant owed the king a staggering one; 10,000 talents would amount to about $12 million in our money. The point Jesus was making, of course, is that our debt to God is totally and forever beyond the possibility of payment. When the king demanded that the man and his family be sold into slavery as payment on the debt, the man fell on his face and begged the king for patience. The king had compassion on the man and canceled his debt.

C. *The king's forgiveness was based on the man's attitude, not his ability to pay the debt.* The king freed this man of his debt by *paying it himself,* which he did when he crossed it off the books. The king forfeited $12 million—money that was due him. Jesus describes the magnitude of God's forgiveness toward us in this. He wanted to impress on Peter that when we stand before God, there is no way we can pay our sin debt. Therefore, God's forgiveness reveals not only his immeasurable grace, but our total hopelessness without it.

II. Forgiveness is demanding.

A. *The next scene in this story focuses on the human nature of man, set in contrast to the nature of God.* The servant who had been so marvelously forgiven left the king's presence and went out into the streets where he was no longer in the overwhelming atmosphere of the king's grace and forgiveness. He was forced to rub shoulders with ordinary people, to reckon with his own kind. We see then how quickly he forgot mercy and how easily he remembered his grudges. This man changed when he left the king's presence; he wasn't the same man at all.

He met a man who owed him 100 denarii, or about $20 in our money: 500,000 times less than the amount *he* had owed the king! In spite of this, the servant demanded that his debtor repay the money. The poor man begged for mercy and patience, promising that he would repay all. But the servant refused to show patience and forgiveness; he threw his debtor into prison until he could pay the debt.

B. *What does God's forgiveness demand of us?* It insists that we look at others through the eyes of *mercy* and not justice. The principle of justice said that *both* of these man owed honest debts and that those debts should be collected. But the principle of *mercy* looks at the debtor instead of at the debt. Mercy tempers cold justice with compassion.

III. Forgiveness is liberating.

A. *In forgiving the offender, the innocent party liberates him, lets him go free; this is what God does in regard to our sins.* Humankind had offended God; deliberately, with eyes wide open, they had stepped across God's boundary and broken his law. Then, through the sacrifice of his Son, God's wrath and anger were dissolved, and he freed the offender from the curse of eternal death. Through Christ, God extended to sinful people this magnificent gift of forgiveness.

B. *But what happens when we have difficulty forgiving one who has hurt or wronged us?* When we refuse to forgive someone or when we limit our forgiveness, we are exercising a sinister power play to keep that offending one in our debt. We may sadistically enjoy this feeling of being able to keep this person under a dark cloud of guilt. But in doing so, we are exposing ourselves to a deadly spiritual radiation that attacks peace and joy and contentment. It will eventually turn one into a critical, negative person who manifests everything *but* a Christian spirit. It can even have physiological repercussions and make us physically or mentally ill.

C. *What does it mean when we do forgive someone who has wronged us, and by so doing, set that person free?* True forgiveness is experienced only in relationship and is known only in reconciliation. When God forgives us, his forgiveness brings about an amazing and unutterably wonderful relationship. We are reconciled to God, and we begin to enjoy a fellowship with him that the world can never know nor take away. Consequently, when true forgiveness is expressed, reconciliation is brought about.

Conclusion

The bottom line of this story Jesus told is that God expects us to manifest the same spirit of forgiveness toward others that he has shown toward us. The genuine forgiveness that we extend to one who has offended us is, in reality, God's forgiveness extended through us. The poet said so accurately, "To err is human; to forgive, divine. Forgiveness is hard, yes; but the harvest it produces in the life of the one who practices it fills countless silos.

MARCH

■ **Sunday Mornings**

"Redemption through the Cross of Christ" is a relevant theme any time of the year. It is particularly appropriate, however, as we approach the celebration of Christ's resurrection. This series will enhance your appreciation of Easter's meaning.

■ **Sunday Evenings**

Continue the series on the parables entitled "Patterns for Pilgrims."

■ **Wednesday Evenings**

Continue the series "Questions Asked by the Psalmist."

WEDNESDAY EVENING, MARCH 1

Title: How Do Our Sins Get the Best of Us?

Text: "When we were overwhelmed by sins, you forgave our transgressions" *(Ps. 65:3 NIV).*

Scripture Reading: Psalm 65:1–13

Introduction

Sin is not just rhetoric in preaching. It is the cause of the deepest woes of the human race. There is ample testimony to this fact outside religious circles. When governments try to build a just and righteous society, their prisons, criminal codes, and courts of law advertise the grim presence of sin. Sin is our greatest problem, and, as this psalmist confessed, we are not equal to it.

I. Our sins are stronger than we are in their power to fasten on us a sense of guilt we cannot shake off.

Sin is not, and has never been, something on the surface to be easily cleared away. Sin has its seat in the human heart. Sinful pleasures lure us in anticipation. When they pass from acts anticipated to acts committed, something happens in our souls as automatic as an apple falling from a tree. All the moral laws of the universe conspire to further the process; no natural force can prevent it.

II. Our sins are stronger than we are in their power to become habitual.

If a man contemplating stepping out of a tenth-story window had only that single act to consider, his problem would be simple. He is free to step out or not to step out as he chooses. But after he steps out, a power that he cannot control takes over—the law of gravity. Master of the single act, he is not master of the pull of gravitation that follows.

Many people blithely play with sin, supposing that separate acts that they may do or refrain from doing, as they choose, make up the problem. Sooner or later they discover to their sorrow that they are dealing with moral laws built into the structure of the universe as surely as the law of gravitation. Sin always parades itself as liberty; it always ends up as slavery. We are free to begin an evil habit; we are not always free to stop.

III. Our sins are stronger than we are in their power to make us tempt others to sin.

We are tempted. We fall into sin. We pity ourselves because the outward pressures were too strong for the inward braces. But we quite forget that we are not simply the passive objects of temptation. Sin always makes us active tempters of others. No drug fiend is ever content until he wins a partner in his vice. A thief recruits other thieves. A gossip is not satisfied until other lips are tearing reputations to shreds. A drunkard is not content to drink alone. Sin is contagious. The tempted becomes the tempter as soon as she falls into sin. Thus when sincere persons truly repent, they abhor themselves, not only because they are sinners, but also because they have tempted others to sin.

IV. Our sins are stronger than we are in their power to bring their natural consequences upon others.

Even though sin is intensely personal, there never is a private sin. Our sins always spill over the boundaries of our own lives to envelop the lives of others. You could never build around your sin a wall high enough or thick enough to contain all of your sin's consequences. They always spill over or seep through. They often fall in cruel disaster on those who love us best. Sinning, even in its most private forms, is like putting poison into the public reservoir. Sooner or later it will have its lethal effect.

V. Our sins are stronger than we are in their power to find us out.

The request of the tribes of Reuben, Gad, and part of Manasseh was at first misunderstood by Moses, who supposed that they were seeking to shirk their share of the conquest of western Palestine. When they had convinced him that such was not the case, he gave them his blessing but added this solemn warning, "But if you fail to do this, you will be sinning against the LORD; and you may be sure that your sin will find you out" (Num. 32:23 NIV). "You may be sure your sin will find you out." These words mean exactly what they say. Your sin will track you down, spoil your character, ruin your happiness, destroy your influence, and perhaps drag others down with you.

Conclusion

Sin brings people into the debt of a great guilt they cannot pay and into the bondage of habits they cannot break. It makes people tempters to others; it hurls its results like vitriol across the faces of loved ones and friends. There is no need to deal delicately with sin or to speak apologetically concerning it.

SUNDAY MORNING, MARCH 5

Title: Faith: A Theology of the Cross

Text: "Jews demand miraculous signs and Greeks look for wisdom, but we preach Christ crucified: a stumbling block to Jews and foolishness to Gentiles, but to those whom God has called, both Jew and Greeks, Christ the power of God and the wisdom of God" *(1 Cor. 1:22–24 NIV)*.

Scripture Reading: 1 Corinthians 1:18–25

Hymns: "We Praise Thee, O God, Our Redeemer," Cory

"Man of Sorrows, What a Name," Bliss

"Alas, and Did My Saviour Bleed," Watts

Offertory Prayer: Father, grant us now the faith to transform our allegiances from material things to spiritual realities so that we may give a gift to you that is worthy and noble. We ask this in the name of the one who had enough faith to give his very life. Amen.

Introduction

In our text this morning, the great apostle affirms the uniqueness of the cross of Jesus Christ. Here Paul strips his message of fancy rhetoric; here he proclaims Christ crucified as the essence of the Christian faith (v. 23).

I. The preaching of the cross rejected.

To the Jew the cross was a scandal; to the Greek it was an absurdity (v. 23). For both the Jew and the Greek, a false understanding of God precipitated the rejection.

A. *The Jew could not see how the Chosen One of God could be destined for a cross.* The preaching of the cross did not square with the announcement that Jesus was the Messiah. Conversely, to the Jew, it proved definitively that Jesus could not possibly be the Promised One of God. You see, their law was perfectly clear: "Anyone who is hung on a tree is under God's curse" (Deut. 21:23 NIV).

Now Paul clearly reminded the Corinthians that he had only one message, namely, "Jesus Christ and him crucified" (2:2). The apostle even asserted that he glories in the cross (Gal. 6:14). This was difficult for pious Jews to embrace because from birth they had always been taught that anyone who hangs on a cross is cursed of God. To the Jew this theology of the cross was a scandal (Gr. *skandalon*), a stumbling block.

73

B. *For the Greek, God was distant, aloof, unconcerned, apathetic about humankind's plight and the world's problems.* God could not and would not bother himself with humankind's welfare. For the Greek it was insane to think that God would be so filled with love that he would "become flesh." It was equally preposterous to think that God could not only care but also hurt and die. In addition, pivotal doctrines such as creation, incarnation, crucifixion, and resurrection were judged to be absurd.

The Greeks made a methodological mistake: they presupposed that a person's thoughts could define God, rather than God's actions defining himself. The cross was pivotal to Paul because it teaches what God is like. He is a foolish God who doesn't do things the way we would expect: he dirties his hands by forming us out of the dirt of the ground, and he takes on the same flesh made from dirt; he believes in us and thinks that we are worth loving, caring, and dying for ("While we were still sinners, Christ died for us"). God is very lavish indeed in his love for us and extravagant with his forgiveness. He is a gracious God who doesn't deal with us as our sins deserve, and he will not allow our sin to destroy creation. Rather, as Creator-Redeemer, he destroys our sin on a Roman cross.

II. The results of preaching the cross.

In the cross of Christ, God accomplishes at least two things.

A. *First, he reveals.* Christ is the "wisdom of God" (v. 24); that is, he is the Word of God. In Jesus Christ we know what God is like. To see the Father, we look at the Son. He is the image of God, a snapshot into the reality of God. Through the cross we learn that God is love and that he will go to any length to show us that love. The cross of Christ proclaims God's willingness to forgive our sin and his desire to be united with us. The cross rectifies our mistakes and shows God's forgiveness for deeds we deem unforgivable. As the apostle John wrote, "This is how God showed his love among us: He sent his one and only Son into the world" (1 John 4:9 NIV).

B. *Second, he redeems.* Christ is the power of God unto salvation (v. 24). God is not preached as one who became angry at man for his sin and abandoned him. On the contrary, God wants to win back the rebellious. We can't be so loathsome that he can't love us. Again, as the apostle John wrote, "This is love: not that we loved God, but that he loved us and sent his Son as an atoning sacrifice for our sins" (1 John 4:10 NIV).

Conclusion

Sergeant Joe Friday used to say in *Dragnet,* "Just the facts, ma'am, just the facts." Here is Paul's proclamation of the facts—the bare facts. Here is Paul's message of salvation stripped to its core: Christ crucified.

What is your theology of the cross? Is it a stumbling block for you? Do you see it as foolishness? Or do you believe God when he declares the cross to be the power of God for salvation?

SUNDAY EVENING, MARCH 5

Title: The Winners

Text: "I say to you: Ask and it will be given to you; seek and you will find; knock and the door will be opened to you. For everyone who asks receives; he who seeks finds; and to him who knocks, the door will be opened" *(Luke 11:9–10 NIV).*

Scripture Reading: Luke 11:5–13

Introduction

We hear a lot today about "the survivors"—those who by dogged determination or brute force make it through some soul-crushing, heart-wrenching experience. Bloody and battle-scarred, perhaps a bit bitter, they emerge "the survivors."

On the other hand are "the winners." These people encounter the same dragons, the same hot, burning sands, the same immovable objects and irresistible forces. Yet they emerge from the traps of life sure of step and sound of heart. They are not just "survivors," tattered and torn. They have survived, all right, but as *winners*! They have an attitude of triumph about them.

This is what God wants for Christians. One of the most damaging advertisements for the kingdom of God is a battered Christian who portrays the Christian life as an endless stretch of trouble and persecution. In this parable Jesus was dealing with just such an issue. This man faced a real crisis in his life and family. He knew something was available to help him overcome his dilemma. He never entertained the idea of quitting.

The resource Jesus underscores with this story is the untapped privilege of prayer, which belongs to every member of God's family. Thus in this parable we have a panoramic view of prayer—its mystery, its meaning, its malfunction, and the marvel of its potential.

I. The mystery of prayer.

A. *The timing of Jesus' telling of this story is not mere coincidence.* The disciples had been observing Jesus' prayer life. On this particular day, they had had opportunity to watch him. They saw the transformation that came over him when he prayed. They could sense the power and authority radiating through his personality. One of the disciples asked Jesus to teach them to pray, as John the Baptist had taught his disciples. Jesus responded first by giving them a model prayer that outlined the areas of life a petitionary prayer should cover. After giving them the model, Jesus told this story about a man who found himself one day at the end of his resources.

B. *Prayer has an element of mystery.* Knowing what prayer is *not* is important. It is not a means of informing God about something he doesn't know. He knows all things fully and completely. Neither is prayer a means of manipulating God, an attempt to change his mind or maneuver him to act favorably toward us in a particular matter. Prayer is not coercing God into doing something he is reluctant to do.

C. *There are different kinds of prayers.* In petitionary prayers we place our needs before God. In intercessory prayer we function as our brother or sister's keeper and intercede for that person. In prayers of pure praise to God we do nothing but thank him for his wonders.

At times our most effective praying is done when we are silent before God and let him speak to us by his Spirit. At other times, we pour out our hearts to God, relating our frustrations, hurts, and hostility. These cleansing experiences are always effective. Indeed, because of its diversity, prayer as communication with God is a mystery—but a delightful one.

II. The meaning of prayer.

A. *Praying is not an optional activity of the Christian life.* It is not a recreational game. It is born when a person realizes the urgency of his or her situation. The man in Jesus' parable became a man of persistent, incessant prayer because he was desperate. The man understood he had no alternatives, no secondary approach. We need to apply that to our own attitude toward prayer.

When you and I dare to accomplish tasks for God, we invariably find that our resources are inadequate, and we are driven to God in prayer. We may be in a position where other people are depending on us. They look our way; they take their cues from our reactions. This forces us to live by faith in Christ, surrendering pride and self-sufficiency.

B. *The meaning of prayer then is simply the realization that we exist in a state of total dependence on God.* We come to realize how helpless we are without this communication line open between God and us.

III. The malfunction of prayer.

Is it possible to misunderstand prayer to the point that we fail to practice it as God intended?

A. *James said yes.* In his probing little epistle, he writes that we "do not have" either because "do not ask"—we don't pray at all—or because we "ask with wrong motives"—we pray wrongly, and thus prayer malfunctions for us (James 4:3). Some think of prayer as simply quiet, peaceful, serene meditation. There may well be those times when prayer *is* a quiet, meditative, calm experience. Most of the time, however, prayer involves a violent conflict within the will. Even Jesus experienced this element of conflict in his prayers—for example, he wept at the graveside of Lazarus and he sweat drops of blood in Gethsemane.

B. *In a very real sense, prayers are battlefields on which victories are won in Christians' lives.* Again in the life of Jesus, we have no way of knowing all that transpired when he prayed. But the writer of Hebrews states, "During the days of Jesus' life on earth, he offered up prayers and petitions with loud cries and tears to the one who could save him from death, and he was heard because of his reverent submission" (Heb. 5:7 NIV).

76

IV. The marvel of prayer.

A.   *Verses 9–10 are God's incredible guarantee concerning prayer.* Sometimes we fret and chafe when prayers are not answered. There are several reasons for God's delays.

   1.   We may have asked outside of his will for something that is wrong for us, however "right" it may have seemed at the time.

   2.   God may be using that prayer experience to bend our wills to his will.

B.   *The very privilege of prayer, of actual communication with God, is a marvel of God's grace and goodness to his people.*

Conclusion

   David, in Psalm 18, tells us that God once upset the whole universe in order to answer his prayer. For some untold reason, David was distressed almost to the point of death. God moved dramatically, cataclysmically in nature to answer the prayer of one of his faithful servants: the heavens parted, the mountains shook, the lightning flashed. This is the confidence you and I, as children of this great God, can have in this privilege of prayer. We can be confident that our loving God will, if necessary, upset the whole universe to answer the cry from one poor child of his who calls on him for deliverance.

WEDNESDAY EVENING, MARCH 8

Title: What Kind of World Is This?

Text: "The heaven, even the heavens, are the LORD's: but the earth hath he given to the children of men" *(Ps. 115:16).*

Scripture Reading: Psalm 115:1–18

Introduction

   Certainly you have heard someone comment, "It's a crazy world." There are some merits to the remark. Indeed, what kind of a world is it that will take its finest young men from their homes and send them out to kill one another? To say that ours is a crazy, confused world is to cite effects, not causes. This is God's world. It was originally a good world. He created it that way (Gen. 1:31).

   What has happened? Some primitive tribes in Africa explain it through a legend: God has a half-witted brother who often causes God's plans to miscarry. God has no half-witted brother of course, but he does have some children who are not smart. By their selfishness and sin, they are continually destroying God's best for the world. Humankind's ability to reject God's best shows an important point. God had a choice: to create puppets who couldn't choose except as God pulled the strings or to create beings with the power to choose, even perversely. God did the latter. Humankind then made a perverse choice to sin, and God has purposed throughout history to win humankind back to himself. This is what our text is telling us: that humans are free moral beings even though God is sovereign. It also has some pointed contemporary suggestions.

I. This is a world of failed stewardship to God.

"But the earth hath he given to the children of men" (v. 16). This does not mean a quitclaim deed, but it does mean that humans have been entrusted with the management of certain things (Gen. 1:28). The children of men are stewards entrusted with the management and use of that which is another's. We are stewards—stewards of our possessions, stewards of the years God gives us, stewards of our physical bodies, stewards of our minds, and stewards of our souls.

But humans, for the most part, refuse to recognize the true owner and their own stewardship to God. As Paul says in that dark passage in Romans 1: "They did not think it worthwhile to retain the knowledge of God" (v. 28 NIV). This helps explain this world of ours.

II. This is a world of unbridled freedom.

Freedom is always within limits or it is not freedom at all. Instead, it is anarchy, the worst form of slavery (Gen. 2:16–17; 3:2–3). What are these limits of our freedom? We did not choose our heredity, but we are free to make the best or the worst of it. We did not choose our native ability, but we are free to double our talent or to bury it. We are not always free to select our vineyard of service, but we are free to make it produce or to surrender it to the weeds.

People have mutilated their God-given freedom by choosing to sin. They have overstepped their freedom, abused their privileges, and prostituted their kinship to God for wickedness and perversity. They have chosen rebellion rather than obedience. That's the kind of world we are living in.

III. This is a world of transgressed law.

Laws of God are compelled to operate. They never fail. Humans have transgressed God's law, and judgment is therefore inevitable.

A. *There is a paradoxical law about selfishness and preservation.* "Whoever wants to save his life will lose it, but whoever loses his life for me will find it" (Matt. 16:25 NIV). Yet many suppose that ultimate security lies in selfishness. They live by the creed of self first. In this, however, is death.

B. *There is a law of retribution, the law of the harvest.* "Do not be deceived: God cannot be mocked. A man reaps what he sows" (Gal. 6:7 NIV). This law is repeated in various forms throughout the Bible (Gen. 9:6; Ex. 21:23–25; Est. 7:10; Prov. 26:27; Matt. 7:1–2). The law of the harvest inevitably reflects the planting season. This carries over into every realm, but we have ignored it and transgressed it. In the end we receive what we plant.

C. *There is a law about sin.* "The soul that sinneth, it shall die" (Ezek. 18:4). "The wages of sin is death" (Rom. 6:23). Sin means death, eternal and spiritual. Our sins will find us out in this life and in the life hereafter.

Conclusion

What kind of world is this? It is a world brutalized by the sins of humans. Sin has marred the beauty and goodness of the world God created, sometimes beyond recognition. Let us hold fast to God's righteousness, repenting of our sins, so the wonder of God's creation can be seen in us.

SUNDAY MORNING, MARCH 12

Title: Hope: A Theology of the Resurrection

Text: "And if Christ has not been raised, our preaching is useless and so is your faith" *(1 Cor. 15:14 NIV).*

Scripture Reading: 1 Corinthians 15:1–8, 12–25, 35–58

Hymns: "All Hail the Power of Jesus' Name," Perronet

"O God, Our Help in Ages Past," Watts

"The Church's One Foundation," Stone

Offertory Prayer: Father, grant that this day we will allow you to live through us and give through us. Our hope is Christ in us. In the name of Jesus, our blessed hope. Amen.

Introduction

Christian proclamation knows only one Lord—Jesus, the crucified and resurrected Lord. All that the Christian church knows, believes, and preaches depends on faith in the resurrection. As Paul, the first to tell of the resurrection, writes, "If Christ has not been raised, your faith is futile; you are still in your sins" (v. 17 NIV).

The disciples had confessed Jesus as the Messiah before the resurrection, but the catastrophe of the crucifixion shattered their confessions, and we see them betraying, deserting, and denying Jesus. Without Easter there is no message from or for the Christian church. It was the risen Lord who rescued the disciples from their aimless wanderings, who restored their crushed faith, and who rejuvenated their hopeless spirits.

I. A faith with a future.

The resurrection of Christ means that we have a faith that is not futile, but rather *a faith with a future.* Remember Friday: it seemed then that all was lost. Consider the specifics of that day. We hear crowds crying out, "Crucify!" and soldiers mocking, "He saved others but he can't save himself." We hear a prisoner jeering, "Save yourself—and us!" and an innocent, loving man saying that he is thirsty. He questions why God has forsaken him at a time like this, and then he finally declares that his work is finished. A couple of friends bury the lifeless body of the one who had taught about life, love, truth, and goodness. It did, in fact, seem finished. Life had no meaning or justice. Death had overcome life, darkness had overwhelmed

79

the light, the lie had eclipsed the truth, hate had overthrown love, evil had vanquished goodness. There was no hope in that kind of world.

But Christian faith proclaims that that is not the final reality. Hear the lyrics of a song written by Darrel Adams:

> *It once was an age of sin and death,*
> *And the hissing snake of pride*
> *Was wrapped around the world so tight,*
> *It seemed all good had died.*
>
> *And when they strung up Jesus,*
> *The venom killed Him dead.*
> *But come next Sunday morning,*
> *He crushed the serpent's head.*

That is the truth; that is the gospel proclamation; that is the difference Easter makes. We have a faith with a future.

A. *We have a faith with a future because life has overcome death.* The apostle Paul then quotes from the Old Testament: "'Death has been swallowed up in victory. Where, O death, is your victory? Where, O death, is your sting? . . .' Thanks be to God! He gives us the victory through our Lord Jesus Christ" (1 Cor. 15:54–57).

Thus the resurrection vindicates Jesus' message. Death cannot defeat life. The serpent has struck the Son's heel, but the Son has crushed its head. We need no longer fear the serpent's venom, for it is powerless and impotent to hurt those who are in Christ Jesus. He lives! Thanks be to God!

B. *We have a faith with a future because the Light shines in the darkness.* The Light came into the world, and the powers of darkness neither understood nor appreciated the Light, and they tried to extinguish the Light. Religious zealots tried to keep Jesus from teaching and loving, and they tried to keep the people from listening and responding, but they could not. So they played their trump and got the Light nailed to a tree, and darkness covered the earth for three hours. For three hours the world was left to itself. Evil, hate, death, and the lie held sway.

But now the Light shines brighter than ever. The powers of darkness cannot keep the witnesses from shouting, "He lives! He lives!" Nor will they be able to keep every knee from bowing and every tongue from confessing that "Jesus is Lord" to the glory of God the Father. The Light shines! Thanks be to God!

C. *We have a faith with a future because love has overthrown hate.* The Evil One tries to make light of a loving lifestyle. Love is portrayed as sissyish and weak. To open yourself up to love is to make yourself vulnerable. You might get hurt if you live the risky way love calls you to live. Isn't "turning the other cheek" and "loving your enemies" silly and dangerous in the real world?

Yes and no. Yes, if we see things before the resurrection. Yes, if we see things through our physical eyes only. But no, if we see the reality of the empty tomb; no, if we look at life through the eyes of faith. God has vindicated his Son. In the resurrection God is saying that we all should live like Jesus. Yes, his loving put him on a Roman cross, but the God who is life and love raised him on the third day. In the end, love is the final reality. Thanks be to God!

D. *We have a faith with a future because the Truth has conquered the lie.* The liars of the world could not be bothered with truth in their quest to get rid of Jesus. They promised what they could not deliver; they corrupted the facts when the facts proved him innocent; they blasphemed their God to crush his Son.

But the resurrection vindicates Jesus and affirms that the way he lived is the way we should live also. His integrity and honesty can be ours. The Truth has defeated the lie. Thanks be to God!

E. *We have a faith with a future because goodness has vanquished evil.* Leo Dyrocher made "good guys finish last" a national maxim. Mark Twain lulled us into believing that "the Lord helps those who help themselves." But a resurrection faith says that at the center of existence is goodness: God himself. Goodness has vanquished evil. Resurrected living means a commitment to goodness in relationships, even when nice guys seem to finish last.

We are not crazy when we commit ourselves to ultimate realities such as life, light, love, truth, and goodness. When you are drowning in a sea of despair, pick up your spirits because Jesus lives! That is the basis of hope. Thanks be to God!

II. We have a future.

The resurrection of Christ means, first, that we possess a faith with a future; and second, it guarantees that we have a future. Christ's resurrection is the first-fruits of the believer's resurrection. Here Paul provides the Christian with a sense of hope in his or her salvation. The firstfruits from a harvest are a promise of more harvest yet to come, and the resurrection of Christ is the assurance that we too shall rise at the sound of the trumpet.

Christ inaugurates a new covenant in which the cycle of sin and death, begun in the old Adam, is broken. In the old Adam all seemed desolate and hopeless, but in the new Adam there is redemption and hope. Jesus defeated sin and death, thereby liberating those who believe in him.

Our hope is not just that Jesus has overcome our ultimate foes. Our hope is also the assurance that in Jesus we too shall overcome our foes and that we will participate in the harvest of the resurrection.

Conclusion

When you read the newspaper and hear the news on TV, do you ever want to give up? Does it seem that the "bad guys" are winning? Do vice and murder and crime and indecency seem to know no boundaries? Remember, "greater is he that is in you than he that is in the world" (1 John 4:4). The resurrection means that. Remember "Christ in you, the hope of glory" (Col. 1:27). He is our hope. We will overcome because he lives.

SUNDAY EVENING, MARCH 12

Title: The High Cost of Commitment

Text: "'Anyone who does not carry his cross and follow me cannot be my disciple'" *(Luke 14:27 NIV).*

Scripture Reading: Luke 14:25–35

Introduction

Numerous motivations prompt commitment. People are committed to movements designed to save our national forests or protect our wildlife. Other worthy causes in most recent years have been designed to stop abortion, the spread of HIV/AIDS, child abuse, and illegal drug use. The list of worthy causes is long.

At the time of Christ, however, there was often one motivation for commitment: life or death. In Palestine the Jews were feeling the grinding pressure of the Roman Empire. They had lost their pride as a nation, a people "chosen of God." Consequently, they were always looking for a leader to be committed to, one who would rescue them from their national dilemma.

Many would-be messiahs and saviors came and gathered their disciples around them. But sooner or later, they were discovered to be weak pretenders or even psychotic madmen. Disillusioned, the people recovered but still waited for some leader who would give them hope.

Then Jesus came. Never had the people experienced anyone like him. He was like no so-called messiah. He was the essence of kindness and humility, yet he had a commanding authority. Most of the time he spoke quietly, unpretentiously, yet his words pierced the heart.

We come tonight to study two brief parabolic illustrations Jesus gave. These eleven verses easily fall into three sections.

I. The setting (vv. 25–27).

A. *The time was the last days of our Lord's earthly ministry.* It may have been the weekend before his crucifixion. He had been invited to a meal in the home of a Pharisee somewhere in the vicinity of Jerusalem, where he had healed a man on the Sabbath, thereby incurring the Pharisees' hostility. He explained his actions with the illustration of the ox or donkey that had fallen into a pit on the Sabbath. The implication was that human needs were far more important than the life of an animal.

B. *Jesus confronted his audience with their snobbery.* He did so by relating the parable of the great supper, in which the master of the house had instructed his servants to go into "streets and alleys" and invite "the poor, the crippled, the blind and the lame" into his banquet room (v. 21 NIV).

C. *Jesus declared for the first time the terms of discipleship (v. 25).* His words had a winnowing effect, and many of the people left. He made this declaration after he

82

left the Pharisee's house and while he was traveling and speaking to large crowds.

D. *A phrase Jesus spoke three times during this brief address to the people is significant: "cannot be my disciple" (vv. 26–27, 33).* He was referring to those who refused to put their loyalty to him above their other loyalties, however noble. He summarized with this statement: "Anyone who does not carry his cross and follow me cannot be my disciple" (NIV).

II. The illustrations.

Through two parables Jesus gave the reason for his demanding terms of discipleship.

A. *The first illustration (v. 28) concerned the building of a tower and the need to first count the cost.* Then, without a break, he gave the second illustration, that of the king who had to consider the number of his troops before going to battle with another king (vv. 31ff.). In both illustrations Jesus was referring metaphorically to discipleship and not salvation. Sadly, there are those who are truly born again who never become dedicated, committed, and loyal disciples of Christ. They are in the circle of his redeeming love and grace, but they remain on the periphery.

B. *The first parable centered on construction.* There is something about building that stirs the creative urges in us. The architect sits at the drawing board and dreams, assimilating all of the skills of his or her professional training. Then the architect meets with a builder, and in time they determine a projected cost for the project. Next, land is cleared, foundations are poured, and the framework starts to rise. In the story Jesus told, the builder was so obsessed with a desire to translate his dream into reality that he neglected a most important step in the project—he failed to sit down with his builders and count the cost. True assessments had to be made.

C. *Many Christian lives are like that of the builder.* A marvelous foundation is laid. A set of plans for a new life provides the guidelines for that building. But somewhere somehow someone refuses to count the cost of building a Christian life. The result is that a shabby tent is created instead of a sturdy house. Refusing to see the cost of discipleship ensures a pitiful substitute for what God intends in our lives.

D. *The second illustration Jesus gave had the same theme.* In this story a king was challenged in battle by another king and his army. Jesus asked whether the first king would consider whether to go to war with his 10,000 men against the other king's 20,000 men. If he were wise, he would send a delegation of his men to meet the other king long before they arrived at the battleground to ask for terms of peace. In other words, the king should assess the situation, explore all the possibilities, and then draw upon his resources of wisdom. He should count the cost of the battle, and seeing that he does not have the necessary resources to win, use his ingenuity to bring about peace without the loss of a single man.

III. The application.

A. *In effect, Jesus was saying that if our purpose is to be his disciple, we must build and we must battle.* Both actions require counting the cost—preparation. Always there have been those, like the rich young ruler, who have liked the thought of following Jesus but have not been willing to count the cost.

B. *These people live in spiritual tents instead of in the spiritual mansions God would have them build for him.* They win no battles against temptation and sin; instead, they lie wounded on the battlefield because they did not assess the strength of their enemy and prepare themselves to wage war against him. When you and I start to build our lives for God, we will be attacked on every hand. We need both the trowel and the sword. They go together; they are inseparable. Recall the story of Nehemiah rebuilding the walls of Jerusalem. The people were told to have a trowel in one hand for laying the stones and a sword in the other hand to battle against the enemy.

Conclusion

Hymnwriter Reginald Heber penned:

The Son of God goes forth to war,
A kingly crown to gain.
His blood-red banner streams afar,
Who follows in His train?

Commitment to Christ, to his cause, to his church, to his people, is not cheap. But the reward is the product—our view of Christ! When we see him in his full glory, we will be like him. The last, finishing touches on our lives will have been made.

WEDNESDAY EVENING, MARCH 15

Title: Is Revival Coming?

Text: "Wilt thou not revive us again: that thy people may rejoice in thee?" *(Ps. 85:6)*.

Scripture Reading: Psalm 85:1–13

Introduction

Psalm 85 pictures conditions in Judah shortly after the return from the Babylonian captivity. The people had expected great things from their deliverance, but the harsh realities of their return brought bitter disappointment. Only a small percentage of the captives had returned, and these returned to a scene of complete desolation and not a little opposition. Their great hopes reflected in Isaiah 40–66 had not been realized. This accounts for the extremes of emotion exhibited in the psalm. The psalmist moves from gratitude (vv. 1–3) through disappointment (vv. 4–7) to a conditioned but glad assurance (vv. 8–13). In the second section (vv. 4–7) he appeals earnestly with a fervent prayer. This is capsulized in our text: "Wilt thou not revive us again: that thy people may rejoice in thee?" (v. 6).

People ask the same question today, only rephrased: Is revival coming? Religious books and articles are very much occupied with this vital question. Is it appropriate to expect a revival?

The answer cannot be yes or no, because the coming of revival will be of God. Nonetheless, there are certain earmarks in God's people that show revival.

I. We must have information.

A. *We must know what revival is.* "Revival is a work of the Spirit among God's own people whereby they get right with God and with each other" (Vance Havner, *Repent or Else!* [Westwood, N.J.: Revell, 1958], 14). To revive a fire on the hearth, you don't start a new fire; you simply stir up the live coals already there. You free them from the smothering ashes, add fuel, and fan them into flame. It has been said that revival is not a thing, it is a person. When we pray for revival, we are not pleading for a thing, but for the Lord. We need him!

B. *We must know that God is at the door.* He is ready to send revival. Why doesn't he? Second Chronicles 7:14 gives us the reason: we have not humbled ourselves, prayed, sought his face, or turned from our wicked ways. The church in Laodicea needed a revival, but they didn't know it. The Spirit sternly but tenderly rebuked them and reminded them that the Lord was at the door (Rev. 3:20). He is at the door of his churches today.

III. We must have a realization.

Before revival comes, God's people must have a clear perception of two things.

A. *It is God's people who need to be revived.* The psalmist prays, "Wilt thou not revive *us* again: that *thy people* may rejoice in thee?" (v. 6). The very word *revive* presupposes the presence of life. We do not speak of reviving a dead man. We revive those who are alive but appear to be dead. It is God's people who need to be revived. Two qualities of the early church, which was living in the power of the Holy Spirit demonstrate this.

1. Their vigorous corporate prayer life. They believed in the shared prayer of God's people. When Peter and John were arrested in the temple and were subsequently tried, threatened, and released, they reported to the assembled church what had happened. The church immediately engaged in prayer, not to be kept safe, but to be given the power to "speak [God's] word with great boldness" (Acts 4:29 NIV). The first organization within the church came into being to relieve the leaders of administrative details so that they might have time to pray (Acts 6:1–7). Is our church more of an organization than a praying community?

2. Its fearless and faithful witness. The Savior was preached and the faith propagated. Every member was a missionary and an evangelist. They witnessed to the risen Christ.

B. *It is God who does the reviving.* "Wilt *thou* not revive us again?" the psalmist prays. We are agreed, formally at least, that revival must come from God. But is that

85

the presupposition in *all* our plans and preparation? Is not our emphasis largely on people? Do we not feel that the moment the church decides to snap out of it, revival will come? To meet the conditions for revival's coming is vital, but remember it is God and only God who sends it.

III. We must have an expectation.

Before revival comes God's people must have faith to believe that revival will come. They must have a sense of expectation. When we plan revival meetings, do we expect anything to happen?

When the foundation for the restored temple was laid after the return from Babylon, the youth who had been born in Babylon shouted jubilantly, but many of the old men who had seen the temple of Solomon in all its glory wept (Ezra 3:10–13). Any true Christian who has ever seen a real, Spirit-blessed revival among God's people is hungry to experience another. Do we expect it to come?

Conclusion

Do we pray for the day when sinners will weep with conviction? Do we pray for the day when believers will seek to be reconciled to one another? Do we pray for the day members of churches will be mightily filled with the Holy Spirit and will go out in the Spirit's power seeking to witness to lost neighbors and friends? If we do this—when we do this—God will answer our prayers, and revival will come.

SUNDAY MORNING, MARCH 19

Title: Love: A Visible Ethic

Text: "Love is patient, love is kind. It does not envy, it does not boast, it is not proud. It is not rude, it is not self-seeking, it is not easily angered, it keeps no record of wrongs. Love does not delight in evil but rejoices with the truth. It always protects, always trusts, always hopes, always perseveres" *(1 Cor. 13:4–7 NIV)*.

Scripture Reading: 1 Corinthians 13

Hymns: "Love Is the Theme," Fisher

"At Calvary," Newell

"I Love Thee," Anonymous

Offertory Prayer: Father, we say with our mouths that we love you. We do indeed. But it is our actions in addition to our words that demonstrate our love for you. May our actions at this time of offering demonstrate for all to see that we love you and your church. In the name of your gift to us. Amen.

Introduction

In this magnificent love chapter, the apostle Paul calls us as followers of Christ to a life of giving. Love is something we do. Our problem with this passage is not that it is difficult to understand; quite the opposite, it is too easy to know exactly what is being asked of us. Our problem is being willing to do it. These verses are amazing both in their simplicity (they are easy to understand) and in their profundity (demonstrating them would revolutionize our relationships in our homes, churches, and society). Fifteen verbs of the passage reveal what it would mean to make our faith and hope tangible. In them we see both what love does do and what love does not do.

I. What love does do.

A. *Love suffers long.* How does this description translate into actions? Look at a small part of Abraham Lincoln's life. No one treated him with more contempt that a man named Stanton. Stanton cruelly maligned Lincoln's name, yet Lincoln made Stanton the minister of war because he was the most qualified. Not only that, but Lincoln always extended Stanton every possible courtesy. After an assassin's bullet prematurely ended the president's life, Stanton said, "There lies the greatest ruler of men the world has ever seen." Suffering long had revealed Lincoln's strength.

B. *Love acts kindly (v. 4).* Once a layman decided that a seminary professor was a heretic. The layman conscientiously tried to get the professor fired. However, the layman explained to the professor that his actions were motivated by a love for him. Needless to say, most of us hope that we never have a "friend" like that. Love acts kindly; it doesn't work for the detriment of another.

C. *Love rejoices in the truth (v. 6).* Have you noticed that arguments often have little to do with veracity and more to do with sinning? There are usually three sides to every story: your side, my side, and the right side! As Christians, we need to seek that third side—the truth.

D. *Love bears all things (v. 7).* No insult can sidetrack love from the pursuit of its end. Hosea pictures God as faithful to Israel, yet Israel turned to other loves. In chapter 11 God asks rhetorically if he should allow Assyria to rule over Israel. Then he answers his own question: "How can I give up on Ephraim?" God's heart only knows how to love and to continue loving despite rejections, trouble, and heartaches.

E. *Love also believes all things (v. 7).* Love creates a climate of trust. Some people are very suspicious because they have never learned to trust. Love prefers to be overly generous rather than overly suspicious.

F. *Love hopes all things (v. 7).* Christians believe that sin, death, and evil have ultimately been swallowed up; it follows that we believe that the sin and evil of an individual can be transformed by a saving encounter with the Lord Jesus Christ. The gospel is the good news of a second chance, a third chance, ad infinitum, and thus we believe that the last word has not been spoken yet about individuals. Even in depravity there is hope.

G. *Love also endures all things (v. 7).* The verb means to conquer, and it is well illustrated in the story of George Mattheson, who had lost both his sight and the woman he loved. Yet he still wrote in one of his prayers that he hoped that he might accept the hand that he had been dealt "not with dumb resignation but with holy joy; not only with the absence of murmur but with a song of praise." Love can wait through the stillness of silence, the darkness of night, the coldness of death. This is a palpable love.

II. What love does not do.

Sometimes we learn what something is by understanding what it is not.

A. *Love does not envy (v. 4).* Often we want the belongings of another. Sometimes we even resent others for having something we want; worse, we resent God for what others have. Envy points to someone who is more concerned about the well-being of self than the well-being of others. Love does not envy.

B. *Love does not boast (v. 4).* To boast is to lose one's perspective. We brag when we think that we have accomplished something unique. We brag when we assume we accomplished it on our own. The self-made man syndrome is a laughable fallacy. There is no place for boasting in a loving life.

C. *Love does not puff itself up (v. 4).* The Corinthians were so esteemed in their own eyes that they had become like an inflated balloon. Love does not puff itself up; rather, it builds others up. Have you affirmed anyone recently? Have you told anyone that you like or appreciate him or her?

D. *Love does not behave rudely (v. 5).* Love is sensitive. Rudeness displays a lack of regard for the other person's feelings. Speaking the truth is never an excuse to criticize; we are to "speak the truth in love" (Eph. 4:25).

E. *Love does not seek its own advantage (v. 5).* Love focuses on responsibilities rather than privileges. In love we think more about our duty than what we are owed. Rather than selfishness, love is selflessness. It is a quality of love characterized by a bigness of spirit.

F. *Love does not lose its temper (v. 5).* Love does not make life miserable for others. Anger is devastating. Children have been psychologically mutilated because of their parents' wrath. Lives must be cushioned in love.

G. *Love does not keep a record of wrongs (v. 5).* Have you ever been in a discussion and asked someone what you did wrong and they hit you with a list of eighteen things? They kept a mental record! Part of the great art of living is to learn what to forget.

H. *Love does not delight in evil (v. 6).* Some of us just love to hear about others' troubles and shortcomings. A gossip does not have to enjoy telling information: a gossip may be one who enjoys hearing it. Additionally, gossip is not defined by its truthfulness; gossip is defined by its negative effect on others. We should feel free to talk about other persons as long as we say good things.

Conclusion

There is not a person here who is too uneducated, too poor, or too simple to perform the greatest work in the world—to love. We all can make love visible.

A preacher was famous for his eloquent sermons on love. He spoke of the brotherhood of humanity. One day he poured wet cement in his driveway, and after smoothing it out, he went inside for a cold drink. While he was inside some neighborhood children wrote in the cement. When the parson went back outside to view his handiwork, he saw the imprints and was furious. He ranted and raved. A neighbor was taken aback and asked, "What happened to all of that talk of love?" The preacher responded, "I love children in the abstract but not in the concrete!" Now admittedly that is a bad pun, but it does make the point that it is in the concrete where we must do our loving!

The apostle John lived to an old age, and toward the end of his life he had lost his strength. He had to be carried back and forth to church meetings. He was thoroughly drained and had the energy to say only one thing, which he repeated over and over: "Love one another." Finally, some of the members of the congregation grew tired of hearing the same message reiterated, and they asked him why he repeated that one phrase. John replied, "If that alone is done, if you love one another, that is enough."

Let us love one another!

SUNDAY EVENING, MARCH 19

Title: A Way of Showing Mercy

Text: "Behold, a certain lawyer stood up, and tempted him, saying, Master, what shall I do to inherit eternal life? He said unto him, What is written in the law? how readest thou? And he answering said, Thou shalt love the Lord thy God with all thy heart, and with all thy soul, and with all thy strength, and with all thy mind; and thy neighbor as thyself. And he said unto him, Thou hast answered right: this do, and thou shalt live. But he, willing to justify himself, said unto Jesus, And who is my neighbor?" *(Luke 10:25–29).*

Scripture Reading: Luke 10:25–37

Introduction

Probably no story from Jesus is more familiar to us than the parable of the good Samaritan. The downside of that, however, is that the story contains so much emotion and drama that we tend to get carried away with its beauty and warmth and fail to allow its probing truth to enter our hearts.

Jesus' purpose in relating this parable was not just to tell a pretty story. Rather, he told it in response to a question from a lawyer who had already interrupted Jesus twice during the course of his teaching session. The lawyer was a member of a professional segment of Jewish society that loved discussion and debate. They relished the opportunity to articulate the social problems of the day. One of the problems they especially enjoyed discussing was this question, "Who is my neighbor?"

Probably this lawyer had been among those who had justified themselves for ignoring the full force of Jesus' statement about loving one's neighbor by saying that "neighbor" meant only a fellow Jew, and even then he was a neighbor only under restricted conditions. This selective definition prevented them from confronting certain unpleasant people or situations.

Rather than debate the question with the man, Jesus simply told a story that answered the question so definitively that there was nothing more to be said.

I. The authentic situation (v. 30).

A. *This lawyer had been accustomed to considering who was really needy from a safe, removed environment of his professional colleagues.* We do this sometimes in our comfortable, congenial committee meetings or in our sacred, stained-glass gatherings. We consider our needy world, and with a pious "Be ye clothed" or "Be ye fed," we toss our token sop to the spurned of society. The very fact that these people could be our neighbors is beyond comprehension!

B. *So Jesus verbally thrust the lawyer into the real world of murderous strife and ugly reality.* Jesus knew the roadway of life is strewn with those whose bodies and souls are maimed and bleeding because of ruthless sin. He put the lawyer on the Jericho Road, so dangerous and infested with robbers that a part of it was called "The Way of Blood." Then Jesus showed him a mutilated body lying beside the roadway, as if to say, "Here is your neighbor!"

C. *What about this man lying by the roadside?* It is hard to even *like* a person in that condition, much less love him. Furthermore, to get involved with him would interfere with our plans and, heaven forbid, spoil our pleasure. Then Jesus told the lawyer how he was to care for this neighbor. He showed the depths that his compassion and concern had to plumb: "Thou shalt love thy neighbor as thyself."

D. *Jesus then followed that repulsive picture of life with a still more unpleasant one.* He gave the lawyer a picture of how people generally act in such situations. He used a priest and a Levite as the antagonists in the story. In contrast, Jesus said very little about the robbers who committed the dastardly deed.

Why? The thieves did what was expected of them, what was the result of their degenerate, evil nature. But the priest and Levite failed to do what they should have done by their very profession.

II. The unexpected traveler (vv. 33–34).

A. *In a masterfully skillful twist, Jesus chose the "hero" to be a Samaritan.* Why a Samaritan? Why couldn't the protagonist in this story have been another Jew, a good Jew, a benevolent Jew? Why couldn't he have been a Nicodemus, a Joseph of Arimathea, a Saul of Tarsus, a Barnabas? Why a despised Samaritan? Perhaps it was simply to show that when God's Spirit controls the heart and soul of a person, that person can be utterly transformed.

B. *The Samaritan, when he saw the wounded man, "had compassion on him, and went to him."* This was Jesus' way whenever a need presented itself: he was drawn to it like metal to a magnet—whether it was a fallen woman at Jacob's well, or blind Bartimaeus in Jericho, or the synagogue ruler Jairus, or a hungry multitude on a mountainside. Jesus strode right into the midst of the need or the scene of tragedy.

C. *In this short sentence, "And when he saw him, he had compassion on him, and went to him," is the very reason for the Son of Man's coming into this world.* This helpless, mutilated man by the roadside is humanity, sick in sin and moral corruption, doomed to death. The act of the Samaritan can be compared with God's stooping in Christ to rescue us and raise us up to moral and spiritual health.

III. The unqualified responsibility (vv. 36–37).

A. *The tender beauty of this simple story, the plain and piercing lesson in it, forced the proud Jewish lawyer to admit the obvious: the real neighbor in the story was "he that showed mercy."* Jesus then dismissed him with an exhortation that could not be debated or questioned. The lawyer had to acknowledge that his neighbor was not just a small, appealing segment of society, but any hurting, wounded human being. This was the broad sector to whom he was responsible to minister.

B. *Likewise, Jesus says to us, "I have been a neighbor to you. I have shown you what love is like. I have picked you up out of your lost, wretched condition and made a new person of you. Go, and do thou likewise."* This parable gives us a pattern for a life of love lived out of gratitude to God in this world; the pattern is plain and clear.

C. *Such is love; it draws no boundaries.* It never asks, "Who is my neighbor?" We must make no excuses and ask no questions. Love makes no excuses.

Conclusion

We cannot force ourselves to do something like this by merely saying, "I will do as the Samaritan did." We cannot will ourselves to practice this kind of love. Instead, we let the love of God come into our own hearts as a permanent part of our being, and it will prompt us, at any moment, at any turn in the road, to meet human needs as God places them in our pathway.

WEDNESDAY EVENING, MARCH 22

Title: When May We Expect the Harvest?

Text: "They that sow in tears shall reap in joy. He that goeth forth and weepeth, bearing precious seed, shall doubtless come again with rejoicing, bringing his sheaves with him" *(Ps. 126:5–6).*

Scripture Reading: Psalm 126:1–6

Introduction

Three notes are sounded in Psalm 126: the note of *praise* (vv. 1–3), the note of *prayer* (v. 4), and the note of *expectancy* (vv. 5–6). This psalmist, who likely was a returned exile himself, captured the emotions of the first wave of returning exiles. Their feelings were mixed: they had great joy at their own release but great sorrow for their brethren who, by their own choice, were still captives in a foreign land. They gave themselves to burdened prayer. They took refuge in their faith that God would be true to himself, that the harvest would yet come.

These same feelings ought to run in deeper channels through every Christian's heart. We were once captives in sin's bondage. Others of our brethren are still not released. But God's harvest, if the conditions are fulfilled, is still sure. What are these conditions? When may we expect the harvest?

I. We may expect to reap in joy when we sow in tears.

What kind of tears are these? Consider this question from two opposing vantage points.

A. *A negative view.*
1. These are not tears of despair over world conditions. The only harvest these tears will produce is more despair, and you do not reap that harvest with joy.
2. These are not tears of pessimism over the prospects of defeat. These are easily seen, but no farmer reaps a harvest when he or she fails to sow because of unfavorable weather. So it is with spiritual things.
3. These are not tears of discouragement over the difficulties to be encountered. In producing any crop—spiritual, mental, or physical—there are always weeds, blight, and insects between the time of sowing and the harvest. Problems are inevitable.

B. *A positive view.*
1. These are tears of sorrow. Some soil, like the wayside hearers, will not receive the seed. Neither the soil nor the listeners will bear fruit.
2. These are tears of urgency. The field is large and the laborers few. Jesus never hurried, but he was always urgent.
3. These are tears of concern. Jesus cried for the unredeemed. When Jesus was coming to make his last entry into Jerusalem, he saw the city and wept over it (Luke 19:41). These were tears caused by his burden for the people, their blindness, their sins, and their rejection of their God. Such were the tears of Moses, of Jeremiah, of Ezekiel, and of Paul. Why does it take so many so long to win so few? Because of our lack of concern. Because of our eyes are dry.

II. We may expect to reap in joy when we go forth to sow the seed.

Our task as Christians is twofold.

A. *Our task includes going forth.* We must cover our territory, our field, as we go forth. And how wide is that? Jesus answered this in explaining his parable of the tares. He said simply, "The field is the world" (Matt. 13:38). We dare not limit that.

B. *Our task includes sowing.* "As ye go, preach," the Lord said (Matt. 10:7). "A sower went forth to sow" (Matt. 13:3). Many church members go forth but do not sow. They participate in community activities but fail to present the gospel. We may not expect a harvest unless we sow as we go.

III. We may expect to reap in joy when the seed we sow is the Word of God.

A. *The seed must be the very living, saving gospel of the Son of God, which the Spirit can bless in people's hearts.* The expectation of the harvest is based on principles that are fixed and sure. If we sow in tears, if we go and sow where the soil has been prepared, and if the seed is the Word of God, we "shall doubtless come again with rejoicing, bringing our sheaves with us."

B. *Isaiah represents God as saying of his Word, "It will not return to me empty, but will accomplish what I desire and achieve the purpose for which I sent it" (Isa. 55:11 NIV).* Paul tells the Galatians that the harvest is sure. As we sow we reap (Gal. 6:7).

Conclusion

This message ends with a question we cannot elude: Are we expecting a harvest of people won to our Lord, a harvest for a quality of life that will influence people for God? Let it be so!

SUNDAY MORNING, MARCH 26

Title: The Certainty of the Resurrection

Text: "For I delivered to you as of first importance what I also received, that Christ died for our sins according to the Scriptures; and that He was buried, and that He was raised again the third day according to the Scriptures" *(1 Cor. 15:3–4 NASB).*

Scripture Reading: 1 Corinthians 15:1–19

Hymns: "Because He Lives," Gaither

"How Great Thou Art," Boberg

"At Calvary," Newell

Offertory Prayer: Our Father, it is with joy and gratitude that we come into your presence today. You are so good to us. For your Spirit that dwells in us, for your love that overshadows us, for your hand that upholds us, we offer thanks. Accept now our gifts as an expression of our heartfelt appreciation for all you are and all you do. In Christ's name. Amen.

Introduction

In one of Plato's dialogues, there is an account of Socrates' last day on earth. As he awaited execution, a group of his followers came to visit.

Naturally the discussion turned to the subject of immortality. Where would the philosopher go after death? What lies beyond the grave? Could Socrates shed any light on these questions?

They talked all day, examining the questions from every angle they could. They concluded that it was almost impossible to attain any certainty about such questions in this present life. All people can do, they reasoned, is take the best of human notions and let that be a raft on which they sail through life. Furthermore, they considered, this voyage is risky, but it is the only alternative, unless people could find some word from God to more surely and safely carry them.

These friends who assembled in the jail in Athens never found that sure word of God. But we have it. It is given to us in 1 Corinthians 15.

Clearly, according to verse 12, some in Corinth doubted the resurrection of the dead and said so. Paul begins this chapter by giving proofs of Christ's resurrection because his and ours rise and fall together.

Paul begins with the gospel that Christ died, was buried, and rose again on the third day. But can we justify such a contention? He lived; no intelligent being can deny that. He died; that fact nobody needs to deny. He died quivering on a cross after about six hours of agony and suffering. To be sure of his death, one of the soldiers pierced his side with a spear, and the last remaining drops of his blood were poured out to prove that he had, in fact, died. They soldiers didn't even take the trouble to break his legs, for he was clearly dead.

That is all well—but what about his resurrection? What are the proofs of that? Paul gives us three solid proofs in the text.

I. The testimony of Scripture (vv. 3–4).

The resurrection of Christ should not have been a surprise. Jesus often spoke of it (Mark 9:10, 31). But before Jesus spoke of it, it had been prophesied in the Old Testament. He referred to these prophecies on the road to Emmaus (Luke 24:25–27). The Scriptures Jesus used were Psalms 16:10 and 68:18.

What shall we say of this kind of evidence? Fulfilled prophecy is the greatest and highest of all the attestations that Christ is truly the Son of God and was raised from the dead.

A. *It is the evidence cited again and again in the first apostolic sermons in the early chapters of Acts.* The apostles kept quoting fulfilled prophecy to prove that Jesus is the Messiah.

B. *It is the evidence that led to the conversion of the learned Greek rhetorician Justin Martyr.* He said, "To declare that a thing shall come to pass long before it is in being, and then to bring it to pass, this is nothing but the work of God."

C. *It is the evidence that convinced Pascal, one of the greatest scientific minds of all times.* He wrote, "The greatest of the proofs of Jesus Christ are the prophecies."

II. The testimony of eyewitnesses (vv. 5–8).

Paul next relates a list of those who had seen Christ. The word *seen* refers to seeing with the eye as opposed to a vision or a hallucination. This is also strong evidence. How do you prove anything? In a court of law, we determine the credibility of a case by the number, agreement, and reliability of witnesses.

A. *The resurrected Christ was seen by Peter and then by the rest of the Twelve (v. 5).*

B. *The resurrected Christ was seen by five hundred brethren at one time.* When Paul wrote this, most of these people were still alive and could have been questioned if his readers had desired to do so (v. 6).

If one man told you that he saw something, you may or may not believe it. If ten people told you that they all saw the same thing, you would have to be impressed. If five hundred people told you that they saw the same thing at the same time, you could not doubt the veracity of their statements.

94

C. *The resurrected Christ was seen by James.* James was the half brother of our Lord. At the time he saw Jesus, he would have been classified as a hostile witness. He and his family did not believe Jesus was the Messiah until after the resurrection.
D. *The resurrected Christ was seen by the apostle Paul himself on the road to Damascus.* Paul would certainly be classified as a hostile witness. He was devoting his life to destroying Christianity at that time.

III. The testimony of a changed life (vv. 8–10).

Paul's last, and perhaps strongest, argument is a personal testimony of the change Christ had made in his life. Paul's words here have all the ingredients of a good testimony.
A. *He tells about his past life: "I persecuted the church of God" (v. 9).*
B. *He tells what made the difference in his life: "But by the grace of God I am what I am" (v. 10).*
C. *He tells about his changed life: "I labored more abundantly than they all" (v. 10).*
    In essence, Paul says, "You know what I used to be, you know what I am now: meeting the resurrected Christ is what made the difference."

Conclusion

G. Campbell Morgan once said that some people say the true account of what happened to Saul of Tarsus was that he had an epileptic seizure in a thunderstorm. "If that is true," said Morgan, "men ought always to pray for a multiplication of thunderstorms and an epidemic of epilepsy."

Here are the convincing evidences of the resurrection: the testimony of Scripture, the testimony of eyewitnesses, and the testimony of a changed life. You need to believe it today and act on it by following the risen Christ.

SUNDAY EVENING, MARCH 26

Title: The Deciding Factor

Text: "Watch therefore, for ye know neither the day nor the hour wherein the Son of man cometh" *(Matt. 25:13).*

Scripture Reading: Matthew 25:1–13

Introduction

The fact that time does not stand still, that all of life is moving toward a climax, a consummation, is nowhere more clearly illustrated than in Jesus' parable of the ten virgins. In this parable the sense of urgency is evident. Everything hinges on preparation—preparation before a great event takes place.

In this instance, Jesus compares the kingdom of God to a wedding, specifically the elaborate procedure in a Jewish wedding. A Jewish marriage had three stages: the engagement, the betrothal, and the marriage itself. This parable is set during the third stage of marriage, when the bridegroom goes to the house of the bride to bring her in marriage to his own home. It is this event that takes place in the parable, and the ten virgins are friends who have joined the celebration.

It was customary for girls to keep the bride company as she waited for the bridegroom and to celebrate by dancing along the road with their lamps or torches. In this story of Jesus, the ten virgins are of two types: five were wise and brought lamps and oil for the lamps; five were foolish and brought their lamps but were without oil. From all outward appearances the ten young women were alike. When the story is over, however, we discover that five of them were really impostors. They had not been serious about attending the bride and waiting for the bridegroom. Let's examine the hoax more closely.

I. The cover-up (vv. 1–5).

Here we see the tactics used by these five foolish young women, who, for whatever reasons, wanted to participate in the wedding without making the proper preparation.

A. *All of these ten young women looked alike.* Each had a lamp, each was dressed in such a way that her attire would pass for that of one who was part of an Eastern wedding party. Each claimed to have been invited to be a participant.

B. *To be a part of such a wedding party was an honor indeed.* Why? When the bridegroom came, these young women would be in the social limelight for at least one week. Note the expertise of the foolish young women's devious plan. The imitation was perfect; they had dressed themselves like the true bridesmaids and had trimmed their lamps like the others. After a while, when everyone grew weary, they lay down to sleep just as the five wise young women did. What a deceptive sight they made! No one could tell them apart.

C. *There are many ways in which persons can hide their unrepentant souls and appear to be devoted believers in Christ.* The simplest and most popular way to do this is through local church membership. Some do not join a church to declare their personal faith in Christ and to be in an atmosphere where they can grow in grace and in the knowledge of the Lord Jesus Christ. Instead, some join for social reasons, for business reasons, or to gain a sense of security or belonging.

II. The exposure (vv. 6–9).

A. *The moment of truth had come when the five foolish young women could no longer keep up their false appearance.* Suddenly, without warning, their cover-up was exposed; they could no longer maintain their deception. The bridegroom came at midnight, and the wise bridesmaids, who were ready for him, calmly trimmed their lamps, which burned brightly.

B. *The foolish virgins looked at their lamps, and they could pretend no longer.* They knew they had no oil. Frantically they cried out to the wise young women, "Give us some of your oil!" But they replied, "No! Go and buy some for yourselves!" While the foolish ones rushed madly to purchase oil for their lamps and thereby prepare for the feast, the door was shut.

C. *The remarkable aspect of this parable is the ease with which, almost up to the very end, the foolish young women were able to keep the appearance of being thoroughly prepared and genuine as invited bridesmaids.* Some borrowed clothes and a little clever acting and everyone seemed convinced—even the other bridesmaids. The folly of pretense is that every time one is successful in effecting a ploy, her confidence increases. Soon she is sure that nothing can keep her from fooling everybody—even God.

III. The dismissal.

A. *This is the tragic, horrible moment when the bridegroom revealed to the five foolish virgins their true state (vv. 11–12).* At this point the women scurried desperately for oil. But it was too late. Their lamps were dry.

B. *The great crisis that will reveal all false imitation in the midst of the church and society is the coming of Jesus Christ.* That day will be a day of revelation. How will you stand when that day comes? The Christian will always pray the prayer of the psalmist: "Search me, O God, and know my heart: try me, and know my thoughts: and see if there be any wicked way in me, and lead me in the way everlasting."

Conclusion

The picture Jesus paints in this parable is that there may come a time when it is impossible for people to repent. In the two descriptions of the day of judgment given in the New Testament, it is clear that the judged have no recourse to last-minute pleadings or sudden changing of mind. Jesus speaks here of a door that closes, separating the true from the false and separating them forever.

We must face the fact that one day it might indeed be too late to do what we might have done to find eternal salvation. I have heard some people say in all sincerity, "Well, it's never too late to repent and to mend one's ways!" Jesus says here, very plainly, that one day it will be too late to do so!

"Watch, therefore, for ye know neither the day nor the hour when the Son of Man cometh."

WEDNESDAY EVENING, MARCH 29

Title: What Is It Like to Die?

Text: "As for me, I will behold thy face in righteousness: I shall be satisfied, when I awake, with thy likeness" *(Ps. 17:15).*

Scripture Reading: Psalm 17:1–15

Introduction

Several times a ten-year-old boy had asked his mother, "What is it like to die?" She prayed to have wisdom to give her son the right answer to this important query; one day the answer came.

The next time he asked, she replied, "Do you remember when you were very small that we would visit at your grandmother's house until late in the evening? We would put you to bed at Grandmother's, but you would awake at home the next morning in your own bed. Your father had picked you up in his arms, placed you in the car, and put you in your own bed when we reached home. You didn't even know until you awakened.

"This is what it is like to die. One day we will go to sleep down here, Jesus will take us in his strong arms to our real home, and we will awaken in the Father's house." The boy was satisfied with that answer. We should be too.

"What is it like to die?" Here are three descriptions.

I. The transition from this life to the next will be made in the arms of Jesus.

Not believing in the return of Jesus to this earth denies the promises of Scripture and robs the Christian of great hope. Jesus' return is assured, bringing with it comfort for every Christian. That last night with his disciples, Jesus said, "And if I go and prepare a place for you, I will come back and take you to be with me that you also may be where I am" (John 14:3 NIV). When Christians die, they die knowing that Jesus will conduct them safely into the land of the beyond. Only the love and power of God could and would do this.

II. The awakening will be to a conscious existence.

"Just as we have borne the likeness of the earthly man," Paul tells the Corinthians, "so shall we bear the likeness of the man from heaven" (1 Cor. 15:49 NIV). This echoes the creation story, where we are told that God created man in his own image (Gen. 1:26–27). This means that the essential elements of personality will survive the transition. Our rational nature, our spiritual kinship to our Maker, and our moral nature as a responsible being—all of these will enhance the unmarred fellowship we will have with our Redeemer and with the redeemed saints, giving us a glorious eternity.

III. This existence will be eternally satisfying.

A. *We will be with him.* Jesus reassured his disciples by saying, "that you also may be where I am" (John 14:3 NIV). We don't know much about heaven, but we do know that Jesus will be there, and that is enough.

B. *We will be like him.* John says in his first epistle, "We know that when he shall appear, we shall be like him; for we shall see him even as he is" (3:2). Then Paul's dream, shared with the Ephesians, of coming "unto the measure of the stature of the fullness of Christ" (Eph. 4:13), will come to fruition.

C. *We will be at home.* "In my Father's house are many rooms," Jesus said (John 14:2 NIV). Christ has prepared a home for us. Home is the fulfilling place on earth; it is also in heaven.

Conclusion

We have a secure position under the auspices of a powerful King who loves us and has given us a piece of his kingdom. When we die we will go to our place in his kingdom; this will be our home. There is nothing to fear in this destination.

APRIL

■ Sunday Mornings

Messages on the significance of the resurrection can strengthen the faith and motivate believers to give themselves in service to Christ. "The Relevance of the Resurrection for the Present Day" is the suggested theme for the weeks surrounding Easter.

■ Sunday Evenings

The book of Hebrews exalts Christ as the ultimate—and most intimate—portrayal of God. Christ's coming gave more knowledge of God than all the previous information the Jews had about God. A series of expository messages examining "The Superlative Christ" is suggested.

■ Wednesday Evenings

"The Basics of Stewardship" is the theme for this month's messages.

SUNDAY MORNING, APRIL 2

Title: If There Had Been No Resurrection

Text: "If Christ be not raised, your faith is vain; ye are yet in your sins. Then they also which are fallen asleep in Christ are perished" *(1 Cor. 15:17–18).*

Scripture Reading: 1 Corinthians 15:12–19

Hymns: "He Lives," Ackley

        "I Stand Amazed," Gabriel

        "All Hail the Power of Jesus' Name," Perronet

Offertory Prayer: Our Father, thank you for the bountiful way you have blessed us individually and collectively as your church. Help us now to give joyfully and generously. We ask you to bless both the gift and the giver for your glory. And bless also those who would like to give but simply do not have the means. For Christ's sake and in Christ's name. Amen.

Introduction

Periodically books and magazine articles question the resurrection of Jesus. Several years ago one such book suggested that Jesus, believing himself to be the promised Messiah, schemed throughout his life to manipulate people and events so that the Old Testament prophecies would be fulfilled and people would believe he was the Son of God. The book asserted that the vinegar passed to Jesus on the sponge was really a drug passed on by an accomplice, enabling him to simulate death. He afterwards revived and claimed to have been resurrected. Another "example" given was that Christ's body was secretly taken away and buried, leaving the mystery of the empty tomb.

Such conjectures are not new. During the first century in Corinth there were those who questioned the resurrection. They stated flatly, "Dead men do not rise again."

Paul's response was, "If you take that position, then you are saying that Jesus has not risen again; and if that be so, the whole Christian faith is ruined." Seven times in eight verses he uses the word "if" to show the consequences of no resurrection. The inevitable conclusion of those who deny Jesus' resurrection is that the Christian faith is phony, the dead have indeed perished, and we are pitiful people.

The most important events in human history are the death and resurrection of Christ. The cross and the resurrection are inseparably linked together. Without the resurrection the cross is meaningless. Apart from the resurrection the cross was a tragedy and a defeat. If Christ's bones decayed in the ground, that is not good news. Without the resurrection we would have no faith, no forgiveness, and no future.

I. If Christ is not risen, then we have no faith (vv. 13–15).

Paul uses the word "vain" three times in this passage. It means "empty" or "hollow." Paul is saying, "If there is no resurrection, then the Christian faith is an empty, hollow shell. I preached nothing, and you believed nothing."

But is the gospel an empty shell? No! Look at the changes the gospel has brought about in the world.

A. *The gospel helped children.* Before the gospel came infanticide was common. The lives of children were of little value. Jesus changed all of that when he said, "Suffer the little children to come unto me."

B. *The gospel condemned slavery.* Christianity was born in an economy when slavery was accepted as an essential social institution. Humans bought and sold other humans. Slavery as it was traditionally practiced was condemned by one phrase: "for whom Christ died."

C. *The gospel elevated women.* Women had been pawns of men. Jesus came and gave them new dignity and worth.

D. *The gospel fostered education.* At first all education was Christian education. Even today 763 of the 1,937 colleges and universities in America are church related.

E. *The gospel spawned democracy.* Thomas Paine said, "Democracy is nothing but a political name for the ideals which Christians brought into the world as religion."

Quite an impressive record, isn't it? Could Christianity be vain and empty?

II. If Christ is not risen, then we have no forgiveness (vv. 16–18).

Paul says that without the resurrection those who have died with faith in Christ have "perished." The word "perished" means destroyed. It refers to the eternal death or ruin that is the result of sin.

A. *The greatest of all tragedies is for the soul to perish.* Billions of dollars are spent on paint to keep wood from perishing, on sprays to keep plants from perishing, on monuments to keep memories from perishing. But God paid the ultimate price when he gave Jesus Christ to keep you from perishing.

B. *Death is not the end of being.* Our choice is not between resurrection and annihilation. It is between resurrection and hell. Without the resurrection of Christ, we would still be in our sins and condemned.

III. If Christ is not risen, then we have no future (v. 19).

Finally, Paul says that if there is no resurrection, then Christians are the most miserable of all people in the world. We will have denied ourselves for nothing and dedicated ourselves to nothing.

A. *We live in a world of misery.* We read about it in the newspaper, see it on television, and hear of it on the street corner. It is everywhere.

B. *Christ gives comfort to the world's sorrow, hope to the world's despair, and life to the world's death.*

Conclusion

A French philosopher once told Thomas Carlyle of his intention to start a new religion that would supplant the religion of Christ. It was to have no mysteries, and it was to be as plain as the multiplication table. Its name would be Positivism.

Reportedly Carlyle commended him. Then he told the philosopher that all he needed to do was speak as never a man spoke, live as never a man lived, be crucified and raised again on the third day, and get the world to believe he was still alive. Then his religion would have a chance to flourish.

Carlyle was right. Everything rises and falls with the resurrection of Christ. Without it, we have no faith, no forgiveness, and no future.

Will you follow the risen Christ today?

SUNDAY EVENING, APRIL 2

Title: When God Speaks, People Should Listen

Text: "In the past God spoke to our forefathers through the prophets at many times and in various ways, but in these last days he has spoken to us by his Son" *(Heb. 1:1–2 NIV).*

Scripture Reading: Hebrews 1:1–3; 2:1–4; 3:7–8; 4:12–16

Introduction

Perhaps the most compelling part of television programming is the commercials. Advertisers have inserted "hidden persuaders" within interesting television advertisements. One of my favorite commercials was from E. F. Hutton. The commercial pictured people in a busy airport terminal. Two men talked amid the noisy chaos of bustling humanity. One man said to the other, "My broker is E. F. Hutton, and E. F. Hutton says, . . ." With the mention of the name, people froze in their tracks, stopped talking, and leaned in to hear what E. F. Hutton said. The commercial closed with the axiom, "When E. F. Hutton talks, people listen."

The author of Hebrews starts with the idea that when God speaks, people should listen. In the first two verses alone, the author uses the words "spoke" (v. 1) and "spoken" (v. 2) in reference to God. God has spoken. People should listen. In fact, people should push aside every other voice to hear what God is saying. Let us stop for a few moments and listen while God speaks through his Word.

I. God speaks in a progressive manner (vv. 1–2).

A. *God spoke to people in ancient times.* "In the past God spoke to our forefathers through the prophets at many times and in various ways, but in these last days he has spoken to us by his Son" (Heb. 1:1 NIV). The emphasis in verse 1 is on how God spoke in ancient times. The Lord spoke at "many times" and in "various ways." The expression "many times" depicts God's progressive revelation of himself through the years. The Bible records God speaking to the patriarchs, to Moses, and to the apostles.

God not only spoke at various times. He also spoke in "various ways." God spoke in dreams and visions and through miracles, prophets, and priests.

B. *God is speaking to people in the present time.* "In these last days he has spoken to us by his Son" (Heb. 1:2 NIV). When Jesus came to earth, God spoke his ultimate Word.

The opening statement of the book of Hebrews presents the uniqueness and the supremacy of Jesus Christ. In times past God's speaking was not complete, but in these last days, God's full, completed word is spoken through his Son.

II. God speaks in a crucial manner (Heb. 2:1–4).

A. *God's Word is an important word.* "We must pay more careful attention, therefore, to what we have heard, so that we do not drift away" (Heb. 2:1 NIV). God's eternal message is so important that it cannot be ignored, dismissed, or forgotten. The author pleads for close attention to God's Word because of its great importance.

B. *God's Word is a certain word.* "For if the message spoken by angels was binding, and every violation and disobedience received its just punishment, how shall we escape if we ignore such a great salvation?" (Heb. 2:2–3 NIV). When God spoke in ancient days by angels, the words were certain. When God told the angels to announce good news, good news came. When God told the angels to announce judgment, judgment came. God's Word was certain. Surely if the word through angels was certain, there would be a greater note of certainty with God's Son.

III. God speaks in an entreating manner (Heb. 3:7–8, 12–13).

A. *God compassionately speaks to the people about having hard hearts.* "So, as the Holy Spirit says: 'Today, if you hear his voice, do not harden your hearts as you did in the rebellion, during the time of testing in the desert'" (Heb. 3:7–8 NIV).

The Holy Spirit exhorts through Psalm 95 not to develop a hard heart. The psalmist reflects on the unhappy incidents recorded in Exodus 17:1–7 and Numbers 20. These passages record how the Israelites developed a negative spirit in the wilderness about their leader, their diet, and the way they traveled. In English, the name given to the place of revolt was "Provocation." God was deeply grieved over Israel's attitude; and because of this, the psalmist pled earnestly for the people not to develop a hard heart (v. 8).

B. *God compassionately speaks to the people about having unbelieving hearts.* Listen to God's warning: "See to it, brothers, that none of you has a sinful, unbelieving heart that turns away from the living God" (Heb. 3:12 NIV). God's Word has no "take it or leave it" clause. God's Word is not harsh; rather, we find in it tender compassion.

God wants believing hearts. He earnestly appeals for belief. "Encourage one another daily, as long as it is called Today, so that none of you may be hardened by sin's deceitfulness" (Heb. 3:13 NIV). Sin's deceitfulness prevents belief, so earnestly and tenderly Jesus speaks words of warning against refusing to open one's life to the Lord.

IV. God speaks in a powerful manner (Heb. 4:12–16).

A. *God's Word has the ability to show the inner life of a person.* God's Word has the power of a double-edged sword. "It penetrates even to dividing soul and spirit, joints and marrow; it judges the thoughts and attitudes of the heart" (Heb. 4:12 NIV). God's Word has the power to effect the innermost part of a person. It makes us see ourselves as we are. It condemns and convicts us until we acknowledge the seriousness of our sin.

B. *God's Word has the power to point us to Jesus Christ.* God calls attention to his Son: "Therefore, since we have a great high priest. . ." (Heb. 4:14 NIV). Human beings are not left in condemnation. Instead, God gives us a great high priest who knows our problems and can help with them. Therefore, people can come boldly and confidently to the Lord to find help. The power of God's Word is to introduce people to the mercy found in Jesus Christ.

Conclusion

Many voices are speaking in today's world; it is a noisy world. In the letter to the Hebrews, God is speaking. And, when God speaks, you should listen.

WEDNESDAY EVENING, APRIL 5

Title: Barriers to Blessings

Text: "'Whoever can be trusted with very little can also be trusted with much, and whoever is dishonest with very little will also be dishonest with much. So if you have not been trustworthy in handling worldly wealth, who will trust you with true riches?'" *(Luke 16:10–11 NIV)*.

Scripture Reading: Luke 16:10–13

Introduction

A college football coach said after a mid-season game that the next week his team would practice the basic skills of blocking and tackling again. He was suggesting that until the fundamentals were mastered, the team could not reap the benefits from complex football strategy. The Bible clearly tells us that the same principle is true in the Christian life. Failure to give attention to the fundamentals in the Christian walk—such as stewardship—presents a barrier to blessings.

I. Unfaithfulness with material things is a barrier to faithfulness in more important things.

A. *Our Lord's statement in Luke 16:10 tells us that little things provide a measuring device for faithfulness to God.* By the sense of stewardship we show as we use what we see as small gifts of God, we demonstrate our trustworthiness and indicate the kind of stewards we would be with greater gifts.

B. *Many talk of their willingness to go the second mile, as Jesus exhorted us, but they have never been willing to go the first mile.* The first mile in Christian stewardship involves faithfulness in using material blessings for God's glory. Tithing is just the beginning point of stewardship.

II. Unfaithfulness with material things is a barrier to growth.

A. *Many college classes have what we call prerequisites.* That term simply means that certain courses must be completed before the student may take a desired class. Consider the person who enrolled in a class called "Stoichiometry," assuming that a decent mathematics background would be sufficient. One class period convinced him that the suggested prerequisites were truly necessary, and he dropped the class.

B. *The Christian doesn't grow in Christ beyond an elementary experience until the fundamentals of stewardship are mastered.* For many who would grow in Christ, the greatest need is to go back to the basics. Part of that process involves the stewardship of one's material possessions.

III. Unfaithfulness with material things is a barrier to spiritual blessings.

A. *Our Lord's statement in verse 11 tells us that we cannot expect God to trust us with true riches if we fail to prove trustworthy with things that do not have spiritual significance.*

Jesus' statement can be taken to mean that poor stewardship precludes the possibility of enjoying an abundant life. People who talk about "going deeper with the Lord" while refusing to tithe are involved in futile rhetoric. They will never know all the joys and challenges God wants to grant them in their Christian walk until they become willing to be faithful stewards of their material blessings.

B. *Perhaps most churches should have a stewardship emphasis preceding any revival effort.* A successful stewardship revival may well remove some of the barriers that preclude the possibility of a great spiritual revival.

Conclusion

Have you learned the fundamentals of the Christian walk? Do you need to go back to the basics? You can remove one barrier to spiritual blessings by committing yourself to Christian stewardship. As you do, you open the possibility of knowing more abundantly God's true riches.

SUNDAY MORNING, APRIL 9

Title: Blessed Is He Who Comes in the Name of the Lord

Text: Matthew 21:1–11

Scripture Reading: Isaiah 44:21–25; Philippians 2:5–11

Hymns: "Blessed Be the Name," Wesley

        "I Will Sing of My Redeemer," Bliss

        "Joy to the World! The Lord Is Come," Watts

Offertory Prayer: Father, as we celebrate your Son's coming into Jerusalem to begin that final, climactic week, we welcome you to come into our presence even now as we give these offerings. In the name of our Savior. Amen.

Introduction

Palm Sunday is a time of Christian celebration. On this Sunday Jesus was received the way we think he ought to have been received: disciples placed their garments on the donkey for a saddle, and people spread their coats on the road while others waved palm branches to prepare the way for Jesus' arrival in Jerusalem. Not only that, but the crowds shouted, "Hosanna," which means "Save now." This is exactly what we want Jesus to do.

The crowds also cheered, "Blessed is he who comes in the name of the Lord!" Jesus comes in the name of the Lord, but what does it mean to come in the name of the Lord? How did he come then and how does he come to us today?

I. How he came then.

That day Jesus was the right kind of Savior. That day he was living up to expectations. This royal, triumphal entry into Jerusalem near the time of the Passover feast was ideal. The people wanted a Jew to ride into Jerusalem and overthrow Rome. The Passover recalled a time when God had delivered Israel from bondage in Egypt. The great prophet Isaiah (chap. 44) reminded the Jews of a time when God delivered Israel from exile in Babylon. Now Jesus' kingly processional into Jerusalem rekindled hopes that God would deliver Israel from Roman occupation.

But Jesus didn't accomplish what the people expected of him, so their cheers turned to jeers, "Hosanna" became "Crucify," and blessing became cursing.

A. *The crowds thought that the side with the strength was the side with the stronger God.* That's why bondage in Egypt, exile in Babylon, and occupation by Rome became theological crises and tests. The ruling country had the ruling god. We often fall into the same trap. Strength can be the Devil's illusion. Consider the strength—and the concomitant errors and evil—of Adolf Hitler.

In the Bible God is revealed best not in strength but in silence. You remember that scene in Gethsemane when Jesus fell on his knees and pleaded with the Father: "If it is possible, may this cup be taken from me." Not once but twice and even three times the Son prayed from the depths of his being, "If it is possible. . . ."

How did the loving Father respond to his beloved Son? With stony silence. No ministering angels. No voice from the blue. Stark silence! In dark Gethsemane Jesus would have to lean on conviction, not display; on faith, not sight.

That's the way it was with Jesus—and that's the way it must be with us. Be leery of those who so glibly and confidently say, "God told me, God led me. God taught me." Have they been to Gethsemane? Have they seen Jesus' faith? My friend, God most often comes to us, not in strength but in silence.

B. *The crowds that day wanted God to come in power—to overthrow Rome—but instead Jesus came in peace—to teach them to live with Rome and each other.* Jesus did not ride a white steed into Jerusalem like a conquering military hero. Rather, he rode a donkey, a symbol of peace at that time.

The Garden of Gethsemane shows the contrast of power and peace. Peter understood power. When the arresting party came to cuff Jesus, Peter drew his sword and cut off a man's ear; but Jesus wouldn't tolerate that. Jesus came not to bear arms but to so change us that we would beat our arms into plowshares. Where the Spirit of Christ is, there is peace; where there is peace, there is the Spirit of Christ.

II. How he comes now.

How can Jesus come into our midst this day? How can that Palm Sunday so many years ago inform and energize our living now?

A. *Palm Sunday means that we can experience the presence of God.* The Bible is essentially the story of God coming to humans: he came to us in a manger in Bethlehem and on a donkey in Jerusalem. He is Immanuel, "God with us." The angel announced the glad tidings of Christ's birth with the declaration. "He shall be called Jesus for he will save his people from their sins"; at the sight of Jesus that first Palm Sunday, the crowds spontaneously broke into shouts of exclamation, "Hosanna!" "Save now!" To save is why he left heaven for Bethlehem; to save is why he left Bethany for Jerusalem; and to save is why he wants to come into your life.

B. *Palm Sunday means that we can know the love and acceptance of God.* In a fragmented, competitive world, we need to hear that word of wholeness and of the brotherhood of love. To live in times such as these, we need the security of knowing that our Creator loves us and takes great delight in us; as Redeemer he has not given up on us but still seeks us; as Consummator he plans to bring us into his joy.

God loves you. God accepts you. Jesus rode a donkey into Jerusalem announcing the good news that God loves you.

Conclusion

Are you ready for his coming? Are you ready for Palm Sunday? Are you ready to receive Jesus? Are you ready for our Savior? Are you ready to shout, "Hosanna! Blessed is he who comes in the name of the Lord"?

SUNDAY EVENING, APRIL 9

Title: The Incomparable Christ

Text: "In these last days [God] has spoken to us by his Son" *(Heb. 1:2 NIV).*

Scripture Reading: Hebrews 2:2–14

Introduction

No hero of history can even begin to compare with Jesus Christ. No one's character can compare to Christ's. No one's ministry can compare to Christ's.

The author of Hebrews affirmed the incomparable nature of Jesus Christ. Throughout the epistle Christ is seen to be above the angels, superior to Moses, better than Old Testament priests, and the ultimate sacrifice for sin. The author began the epistle to Hebrews by affirming the absolute supremacy of Jesus Christ.

Today's world needs to examine closely the life and ministry of Jesus Christ. In only two short Bible verses one may see four traits in which he is incomparable.

I. Jesus is the creator of the world.

A. *Many ideas have been proposed about the creation of the world.* People have always pondered the question, "How did the world begin?" Various answers have been given. Some say the world and the human race evolved over billions of years. Others say that the world and the human race came as a result of a gigantic cosmic explosion. But no idea has surpassed God's answer: "In the beginning God..." (Gen. 1:1).

B. *The Bible teaches clearly that Jesus is the creator of the world: "... through whom he made the universe" (Heb. 1:2 NIV).* The use of "universe" implies everything in time and space. Every single part of the created order has been designed by Jesus Christ—whether atoms, rivers, lakes, mountains, sun, moon, stars, or human bodies. There is nothing created that has not been the handiwork of God.

Human beings have constructed great buildings. They have designed sculptures and painted pictures. Human beings have made great works of human ingenuity, but none compares to Christ's creation of the world. He is the incomparable Creator.

II. Jesus is the revealer of the Father.

A. *Many false portraits of God have been drawn by people's imaginations.* Another query of the human race is, "What is God like?" Instead of looking at the biblical revelation of God, human beings have used their own speculation to think of God. Consequently, such erroneous ideas of God as a raging tyrant, a benevolent grandfather, and a capricious deity have emerged. These human speculations have not given a true picture of what God is like.

B. *The Bible teaches plainly that Jesus is the revealer of the Father's nature: "The Son is the radiance of God's glory and the exact representation of his being" (Heb. 1:3 NIV).* These words tell much about the Christ. The word "being" expresses essential being. Jesus Christ is of the essential being of the Father. And "exact representation" refers to his character. The Son's character is exactly like that of his Father. If you wish to know what God is like, look at Jesus. He is the revealer of the Father.

III. Jesus Christ is the sustainer of creation.

A. *Numerous theories exist about how affairs on earth proceed.* Some think there is a predetermination in the ways of the earth; that is, human choice has little to do with the outcomes of life. Others think there is a fortuitous chance about life, that events and affairs of human beings exist and happen without the control of anyone. The question, "Who is in control of this earth?" is a legitimate one.

B. *The Bible says that Jesus Christ is the sustainer of the human existence: ". . . sustaining all things by his powerful word" (Heb. 1:3 NIV).* The word "sustaining" has a twofold usage. On the one hand, Jesus upholds the world by his great sovereignty. If it were not for the sustaining providence of God, everything would collapse into nonexistence. On the other hand, "sustaining" may be used in the context of movement; he moves the world to its logical conclusion. The words of an old folk song express the idea of God's sovereignty: "He's got the whole wide world in his hands." While world affairs might seem at times to be out of control, the Bible teaches that Jesus Christ is the sustainer of creation.

IV. Jesus Christ is the purger of sins.

A. *Many attempts have been made to dispense with the guilt of sins.* The history of the human race is the history of an attempt to eradicate guilt. Some seek to eliminate guilt by rationalizing. They explain away the reality of sin by making it a "social disease" or a "psychological maladjustment." Others try to cover their sins by performing good deeds. Even religious people will perform religious acts to purge their sins.

Macbeth in William Shakespeare's play of the same name saw the effects of guilt in his wife Lady Macbeth. In tones of despair he spoke to the court physician:

> *Cure her of that.*
> *Canst thou not minister to a mind distressed,*
> *Pluck from the memory a rooted sorrow,*
> *Raze out the written troubles of the brain*
> *And with some sweet oblivious antidote*
> *Cleanse the stuffed bosom of that perilous stuff*
> *Which weighs upon the heart?*

B. *Only Jesus can rid a person of guilt: "After he had provided purification for sins, he sat down at the right hand of the Majesty in heaven" (Heb. 1:3 NIV).* Through his atoning death on the cross, Jesus did what no priest or sacrifice could do. He made the absolute, unique offering for sin. He is the incomparable Christ.

Conclusion

People are always comparing one person with another. They say one quarterback or running back is better than another. People even compare preachers. Try to compare Christ with someone: the writer of Hebrews did. He compared Jesus with Moses, the Old Testament priests, and the angels. The conclusion was that no one and no thing compares to Jesus Christ. He is incomparable.

WEDNESDAY EVENING, APRIL 12

Title: Foundations for Stewardship: The Grace of Christ

Text: "For ye know the grace of our Lord Jesus Christ, that, though he was rich, yet for your sakes he became poor, that ye through his poverty might be rich" *(2 Cor. 8:9).*

Scripture Reading: 2 Corinthians 8:7–15

Introduction

Our society is tremendously influenced by heroes who provide models for us. For this reason, advertising firms pay enormous sums of money to movie stars, athletes, and popular singers to market certain products. Many Americans will be influenced to use a product their heroes use.

Jesus is far more than just another hero. He is the perfect model of what God's people should be. The apostle Paul exhorted the Corinthian Christians to follow Jesus' example in their attitude toward Christian stewardship.

I. Jesus was rich.

When Paul here refers to the wealth of Jesus in the preincarnation state, he is talking of wealth beyond description. All the attendant circumstances of being God were his. The glorious riches of being face-to-face with the Father are beyond our comprehension. The richest people on earth are paupers when their holdings are compared to the riches of the preincarnate Son.

II. Jesus became poor.

"Though he was rich, yet . . . he became poor," is a very restrained way to speak of the voluntary impoverishment of Jesus. The christological hymn in Philippians says he "emptied himself" (2:7), and the expression suggests accurately that Jesus chose to surrender the riches that were attendant to his deity.

However, Jesus did more than simply renounce heavenly treasures, for he divested himself of everything on earth as he went to the cross. He gave up all possessions including his very clothes, his support group, and the fellowship of his followers when he gave his life at Calvary. His poverty became as absolute as his wealth had been.

III. His motivation was that we might be rich.

The reason Jesus left the attendant circumstances of deity and came to earth to know total impoverishment was that he knew of our bankruptcy and wanted us to share in his wealth. When we become partakers of the grace of Jesus Christ, we become heirs of the riches of the Father. Without Jesus as our Savior, we are absolutely spiritually bankrupt.

Conclusion

If you are a disciple of Jesus Christ, you will seek to be like him. His relationship with us is characterized by giving—a giving that is almost incomprehensible. His example in selflessness and stewardship compels us to be faithful in our own stewardship. Can you be miserly in sharing material blessings for God's service when Jesus left heaven for you? Commitment to Christ brings you into special relationship with the world's greatest giver. Go imitate your Savior!

SUNDAY MORNING, APRIL 16

Title: The Meaning of the Resurrection

Text: "If I fought wild beasts in Ephesus for merely human reasons, what have I gained? If the dead are not raised, 'Let us eat and drink, for tomorrow we die'" *(1 Cor. 15:32 NIV).*

Scripture Reading: 1 Corinthians 15:29–33

Hymns: "Christ the Lord Is Risen Today," Wesley

        "There Is a Fountain Filled with Blood," Cowper

        "The Solid Rock," Mote

Offertory Prayer: Our Lord, in these days of moral compromise and spiritual weakness, help us to stand for something lest we fall for anything. May we ever and always stand on the great and eternal principles of your Word. Teach us to rejoice in you. Remind us that all we have comes from your grace and that all we are is due to your grace. Help us to be cheerful givers. Accept these gifts as a humble expression of our gratitude. In Christ's name. Amen.

Introduction

We all have strolled through a cemetery and read the epitaphs on the tombstones. The graves have been marked and kept through the years because of what they contain—the bodies of loved ones.

How different from the tomb of Jesus. It is famous, not for what it contains, but for what it does not contain—it is empty! The best news the world has ever received was spoken by the angel on the first Easter morning when he said concerning Jesus, "He is not here: for he is risen" (Matt. 28:6).

What does the resurrection mean to you and me? It gives meaning to all of the Christian life. If Christ is not risen, then we will not be raised. And if we will not be raised, all is lost.

In this difficult passage, Paul declares that without the resurrection, baptism is meaningless, sacrifices for the cause of Christ are meaningless, and moral restraint is meaningless.

This means that the resurrection not only has eternal significance but also practical application to our lives. These practical meanings of the resurrection can be seen in the series of four questions that Paul asked in these verses.

I. Without the resurrection our baptism is meaningless.

Verse 29 is one of the most disputed passages in all the Bible. There are more than fifty different interpretations of it.

A. *Some say that it refers to baptism by proxy; that is, one person can be baptized for another.* This is the belief and the practice of Mormons today.

B. *Some say that it refers to being baptized "because of" someone else.* For example, a loved one's death may cause another to repent and follow the Lord in baptism.

C. *The correct meaning is that baptism symbolizes the death, burial, and resurrection of Christ (Rom. 6:1–5).* If there is no resurrection, then baptism is a meaningless ritual.

II. Without the resurrection our sacrifices are useless.

Paul then speaks of the dangers, hardships, and sacrifices he made for the cause of Christ. He speaks of "fighting wild beasts" and then says, "I die daily." This is a strong expression of the danger of death he daily encountered.

Paul's argument was this: hardships, dangers, and sacrifices are meaningless if there is no resurrection.

A. *Being a Christian was risky.* In fact, the Christians were the only people in the first century outside the praetorian guard who believed in anything strongly enough to die for it. That's why the gospel swept the world.

B. *Christ still calls on us to sacrifice for him.* Missionaries must leave home for foreign countries. Christians in countries like India, Sudan, and China are often killed or imprisoned for their faith. Businessmen often suffer when they stand for what is right. It is without apology that we ask people to sacrifice for Christ. But these sacrifices have no meaning if there is no resurrection.

III. Without the resurrection our morals are groundless.

Paul continues his argument: Not only are baptism and sacrifices meaningless, but so is moral restraint if there is no resurrection.

A. *Some people have always lived without restraint.* The philosophy of the Epicureans was, "Let us eat, drink, and be merry, for tomorrow we die." Many live by this hedonistic philosophy today.

B. *The man who lives without restraint is a fool.* Jesus told the story about such a man in Luke 12:13–21.

C. *We must watch our company if we want to live the right kind of life.* Paul warns that wrong companions corrupt a person's morality (1 Cor. 15:33).

D. *The call for moral restraint and holy living is meaningless if there is no resurrection.*

Conclusion

The poignant message of Paul in this passage is that without the resurrection, baptism is meaningless, our sacrifices are meaningless, and our moral restraint is meaningless.

An old Indian chief heard the gospel story for the first time. He said, "The Jesus road is good, but I have followed the Indian road all of my life and I will follow it to the end."

One year later he was close to death. At this point he said to the missionary who stood by his bed, "Can I take the Jesus road now? My road ends here!"

All other roads "dead end" at the grave. The way of Christ is the way of life.

SUNDAY EVENING, APRIL 16

Title: The Danger of Drifting

Text: "We must pay more careful attention, therefore, to what we have heard, so that we do not drift away" *(Heb. 2:1 NIV).*

Scripture Reading: Hebrews 2:1–4

Introduction

Far up the Niagara River, boaters begin to see signs of warning of the impending falls. Some have not heeded the warning signs and have gone to their death over the 167-foot drop.

The writer of the letter to the Hebrews posted warnings throughout his letter. He has warnings to believers about negligence (2:1–4), disobedience (3:7–19), desertion (5:11–6:20), rebellion (10:19–39), worldliness (12:14–17), and unwillingness to listen to God (12:25–29). In the first warning, the writer of Hebrews warned about drifting away from the Lord. The Greek verb used here means to "drift or flow alongside or by." The metaphor in mind seems to be that of allowing the current to carry one away from a fixed point through carelessness and unconcern. Instead of keeping a firm grip on the truth, the person drifts. Using the metaphor of drifting lets us gain insights about moving away from the fixed point of the gospel.

I. The reality of drifting.

The writer of Hebrews began with the possibility of God's people drifting: "...so that we do not drift away." The expression indicates that the possibility of drifting is present.

A. *The possibility of drifting may be seen in Bible characters.* Lot pitched his tent toward Sodom. He allowed the secularity of Sodom to influence him and his family. Samson drifted in his relations with Delilah. He allowed himself to drift gradually into the thought patterns of the pagans. David was "a man after God's own heart," but in a moment of leisure, his heart drifted with lust toward Bathsheba. Peter did not mean to deny the Lord. His denial of Jesus came as a result of drifting away from commitment to Christ.

B. *Drifting is a possibility in any Christian's life.* No Christian has the premeditated intention of going away from the Lord. It sneaks up on a person covertly.

II. The reason for drifting.

The writer of the letter to the Hebrews diagnosed the cause of drifting as neglect. The believers were neglecting their great salvation experience in Christ, and this neglect caused them to drift.

A. *Neglecting comes through inattention.* The readers of the letter to the Hebrews were not giving attention to their salvation experience in Jesus Christ. They had joined life with Christ, but they had failed to open more of life to the Lord. This inattention caused drifting.

Suppose you do not give attention to an important relationship such as marriage. Before long you will notice that you have drifted apart. Just as marriages require attention, so a believer's relationship with the Lord requires attention.

B. *Drifting comes through lack of discipline.* Paul wrote to Timothy, "Do not neglect your gift" (1 Tim. 4:14 NIV). Becoming a better Christian involves spiritual discipline. Unless a Christian resists the Devil, studies God's Word, engages in prayer daily, and applies faith to life, drifting is inevitable.

III. The result of drifting.

The writer of the letter to the Hebrews examined the possibility and cause of drifting. He then listed the tragic result of drifting—punishment: "every violation and disobedience received its just punishment" (Heb. 2:2 NIV).

A. *Drifting inevitably led to punishment for God's people in Old Testament times.* The writer of Hebrews referred to an Old Testament incident in which the Israelites drifted away from the Lord. The expression "if the message spoken by angels" probably refers to the revelation of Moses at Sinai. This word that God gave was binding on his chosen people.

God's people let these commands of God slip or drift. Consequently, God punished the people. Throughout Israel's history the Lord fit punishments to the crime. Drifting away from the Lord always leads to punishment.

B. *Drifting always leads to punishment for God's people in the present.* The writer of Hebrews asked a poignant question: "How shall we escape if we ignore such a great salvation?" (Heb. 2:3 NIV). The pronoun "we" refers to believers. The writer uses it twice for emphasis.

IV. The remedy for drifting.

The biblical writer was not content to tell about the reality, the reason, and the results. He wanted the readers to apply the remedy for drifting. He wrote, "We must pay more careful attention, therefore, to what we have heard, so that we do not drift away" (Heb. 2:1 NIV). The remedy for drifting is obvious—give heed to what you have heard.

A. *Look to the initial experience with Christ.* The writer's expression "what we have heard" refers back to the initial experience of salvation, the time when Christ was invited into a person's life. God's ultimate word was spoken in Jesus Christ, and believers responded by opening their lives to him.

B. *Take seriously the relationship with Jesus Christ:* "We must pay more careful attention." Hearing and receiving Christ is not enough. Believers need to be concerned about developing their relationship with Christ and sharing it. It is the remedy for drifting.

Conclusion

Can you see some signs of warning? The world has swift currents. The possibility that you could drift in your relationship with Jesus Christ is real. Make up your mind now to develop your relationship with him.

WEDNESDAY EVENING, APRIL 19

Title: Thanks Be to God

Text: Thanks be to God for his indescribable gift!" *(2 Cor. 9:15 NIV).*

Scripture Reading: 2 Corinthians 9:1–15

Introduction

Have you ever wanted to express deep joy and celebration but could not find words to articulate your feelings? One gets the impression that Paul experienced that sensation after writing two great chapters about giving. He seems to sing the words of the text as one last expression of motivation that undergirds all of Christian living: gratitude to God for his indescribable gift.

I. The grounds for gratitude is God's indescribable gift.

A. *The identity of that gift is Jesus.* The Bible declares the central purpose of God's love to be "that whosoever believeth in him should not perish, but have everlasting life" (John 3:16). God has graced our lives with bountiful blessings, but the gift that gives meaning to life itself is God's indescribable gift, Christ Jesus.

B. *The motivation for that gift is love.* The apostle Paul writes that "God commendeth his love toward us, in that, while we were yet sinners, Christ died for us" (Rom. 5:8). Clearly God sent Jesus because God's love for each person is vast enough to move God to give his very best for us. Only love is adequate motivation to explain God's gift to us.

C. *The result of that gift is reconciliation.* Paul reminds us that when Jesus came, "God was in Christ, reconciling the world unto himself" (2 Cor. 5:19). A remarkable gift is made more remarkable if it improves the circumstances of the recipient. God's indescribable gift involves not only indescribable sacrifice on God's part but also indescribable impact upon us. His gift of Jesus provides us opportunity to be reconciled to God. It meets our greatest need, redemption from sin.

II. The response to such an indescribable gift is gratitude.

That Paul exulted with this expression of thanksgiving for God's gift indicates our need to exult in gratitude toward God. We need to express our thanksgiving for Jesus.

A. *We should express our thanks verbally.* As did Paul, we need to say, "Thank you, Lord!" Common courtesy demands that our gratitude be spoken.

B. *We should express our thanks with our behavior.* We normally seek to show our appreciation if it is real. We should relate to others and to life in a way that indicates our gratitude to God.

C. *We should express our thanks with our stewardship.* A grateful heart will find expression in tithing. We have the privilege of saying thank you with good stewardship of our resources.

Conclusion

How are your manners? Do you think of yourself as one who is mannerly and courteous toward others? Would you be discourteous toward God? You have been the recipient of the greatest of gifts by God. How do you say, "Thank you"? With lips and lifestyle and your usage of resources for God, you can express gratitude. Isn't it time for you to thank him?

SUNDAY MORNING, APRIL 23

Title: The Order of the Resurrection

Text: "But every man in his own order: Christ the first fruits; afterward they that are Christ's at his coming. Then cometh the end" *(1 Cor. 15:23–24).*

Scripture Reading: 1 Corinthians 15:20–28

Hymns: "One Day," Chapman

"The Old Rugged Cross," Bennard

"When We All Get to Heaven," Hewitt

Offertory Prayer: O Lord, our Lord, how excellent is your name in all the earth. When we consider the heavens, the work of your hands, the wonder of the earth, and the vastness of space, we are amazed that you know even us.

Thank you for making us in your image. Thank you for loving us with an everlasting love. Thank you for providing for every need of our lives. Thank you for our wonderful and complete redemption in Jesus Christ.

When we think of these things, we delight to confess, "O Lord, our Lord, how excellent is your name in all the earth!" Accept now this offering as an expression of our wonder, gratitude, and thanksgiving. In Jesus' name. Amen.

Introduction

One of the great Christians was William Booth, founder and first general of the Salvation Army. For forty-seven years he trudged through the slums of London preaching the gospel to the outcasts of society.

Through all of his heartaches and spiritual struggles, William Booth's constant companion and helper was his wife, Catherine. She was "the army's mother." The last two years of her life she was sick. Yet through all of her illness her faith remained unshaken. She wrote to a friend, "Don't be concerned about your dying. Only go on living well, and the dying will be all right." On October 4, 1890, she died in the arms of her husband.

At the funeral service white streamers fluttered from flagpoles, and white badges gleamed on every soldier's arm. For this was the army's way; they did not mourn in black. Catherine was in heaven, and white was the sign of rejoicing, a symbol of her promotion to glory.

This has always been the way God's people face death. Paul speaks of this hope in this morning's text. There we are told of some Christians in Corinth who were saying plainly, "Dead men do not rise." Paul responded in essence, "If you take this petition, then you are saying that Jesus did not rise. And if that is true, then we have no faith, no forgiveness, and no future."

But there is no "if" about it, says Paul. Christ is risen. That is simple truth. Then Paul proceeds to give the order of events surrounding the resurrection.

117

I. Christ was the beginning of the resurrection.

Paul begins by saying that Christ *is* risen from the dead. The resurrection of Christ is finished work.

As a result of his resurrection, Christ has become the "first fruits" of the dead. This is an agricultural term that refers to the firstfruits of the harvest. In the late spring or the early summer, the people gathered in the first heads of ripened grain and offered them as a sacrifice of thanksgiving to God according to the law of Moses (Lev. 2:10ff.). The firstfruits represented both the beginning of the harvest and a promise of a forthcoming general harvest. Paul saw Christ as both the beginning and the promise of the resurrection of believers.

A. *Death came into the world as a result of one man's sin (v. 21).* Through the disobedience of Adam, sin and death passed to all people (Rom. 5:12).

B. *Through Jesus Christ the resurrection is available to all.* Christ became sin for us, and thus we have life in him (2 Cor. 5:21).

C. *God has made a beginning and a pledge to us.* That pledge is an empty tomb. It is God's promise. Christ is the beginning.

II. We will be raised at his coming (v. 23).

Paul then declares, "But every man in his own order: Christ the first fruits; afterward they that are Christ's at his coming." The word "order" is a military term that describes troops arranged in ranks or companies. The "coming" describes the arrival of a king. Paul says that Christ our King will return and will arrange his soldiers into ranks as military troops behind him; and like a mighty army, they will march out of the grave into glory.

A. *Christ, the captain of our salvation has led the conquest.* He marched out of the grave.

B. *When Christ returns, we will follow him.* We can now die in assurance and confidence.

The ancient Egyptians, Greeks, Norsemen, American Indians, and other people groups have all believed in a life hereafter. This belief is written into our very nature. Even Mark Twain said, "I have successfully exploded every possible argument for an afterlife—but after all that, I fully expect there will be one." In Christ assurance has come.

III. The kingdom shall be given over to God (vv. 24–28).

Today people are asking, "Where is history going?" The answer is in this passage; let all speculation cease: everything is coming under the control of God.

A. *God is the ultimate sovereign of this universe.* The time will come when all things will be put under him. The universe will be lined up like troops in subordination to God (v. 28).

B. *Christ is God's agent to bring this about.* Christ will reign in heaven until all the forces that oppose God are subdued. Death will be the final enemy defeated, and then all things and all people will bow before God (vv. 25–28).

Conclusion

Jesus' life, death, and resurrection were the beginning of the end. The fact that he is reigning is proof of his victory over death. The victory is not yet complete, but it is certain. The Nazi forces did not surrender on D-Day, but from that hour on the ultimate outcome was inevitable.

So it is with Christ's death and resurrection. The victory is already won. One day he will return, and then the task will be fully and finally accomplished.

SUNDAY EVENING, APRIL 23

Title: Take Me to Your Leader

Text: "In bringing many sons to glory, it was fitting that God, for whom and through whom everything exists, should make the author of their salvation perfect through suffering" *(Heb. 2:10 NIV).*

Scripture Reading: Hebrews 2:5–13

Introduction

Science fiction often depicts creatures from other worlds landing on earth. The typical request of these alien creatures to people on earth is, "Take me to your leader."

The writer of Hebrews wanted the believers to keep their leader, Jesus Christ, in mind. In Hebrews 2:10 he is described as the "author [captain, KJV] of their salvation." The Greek word here is used to describe the leader of a group of people, the founder of a school of thought, or a pioneer who blazes trails for others to follow. Let us as believers take a close look at our leader, Jesus Christ.

I. The Leader's example (vv. 5–9).

A. *The writer of Hebrews used a quotation from the Psalms to depict what God intended human beings to be.* God made the human race "a little lower than the angels." The expression depicts the dignity of the human race. God crowned the human race with "glory and honor." Human beings were the recipients of God's special favor. In addition to the human race's special dignity and special favor, God also placed in the human race's hand a special dominion. "[Thou] didst set him over the works of thy hands: Thou hast put all things in subjection under his feet" (Heb. 2:7–8).

With the aid of Psalm 8, the author of Hebrews emphasized the ideal person. Ideally, God created human beings with a unique dignity and a special dominion. Only a casual look at the human race will disclose that people are not what God intended them to be.

B. *We see Jesus become what God intends a person to be.* "But we see Jesus, who was made a little lower than the angels for the suffering of death, crowned with glory and honor; that he by the grace of God should taste death for every man" (v. 9).

Though the human race is not what God intends, one can see what God intends in a person through Jesus Christ. Through Christ, the complete person, human beings can be restored to the place of glory, honor, and responsibility for which God created the human race.

II. The Leader's desire (v. 10).

A. *The Leader has a desire to bring fallen humanity into God's family.* The author writes, "In bringing many sons to glory, it was fitting that God, for whom and through whom everything exists, should make the author of their salvation perfect through suffering" (v. 10 NIV). It was appropriate for God to send his Son. Human beings were caught in the tenacious hold of sin, and God's desire was to rescue them from this bondage. The desire of Jesus is to "bring many sons" into God's family.

B. *The Leader has a desire for God's children to reflect God's character.* The purpose of the Son was not just to bring many sons but to bring many sons into *glory*. The word "glory" was used to describe God's character (John 1:14). Also, the word "glory" was used to describe a future completion of the believers (Rev. 21:26). The purpose of Jesus in bringing people into God's family is to reflect God's character now and later.

III. The Leader's life (vv. 11–13).

A. *The Leader helps his people by setting them aside for a holy purpose.* Consider verse 11: "Both the one who makes men holy and those who are made holy are of the same family" (NIV). Sanctification is a dominant theme in the letter to the Hebrews (cf. Heb. 10:14, 29; 13:12). In Old Testament times certain people, selected vessels, and appointed days were "sanctified" or "set apart" for God's use. God helps people by setting them apart to accomplish his mission. The Leader made it possible for believers to be equipped to help God with his mission.

B. *The Leader helps believers grow and develop.* The writer of Hebrews was concerned that some professing believers were simply maintaining the status quo. They were seemingly inert and needed to develop and to serve their Lord in their state of sanctification. Jesus can help move his people from where they are to where they need to be.

The author of Hebrews supported the idea that Christ helps his people develop. In Hebrews 2:12–13, three Old Testament verses are cited: Psalm 22:22 and Isaiah 8:17–18. These quotations substantiate the reality that Jesus not only has redeemed sinners but is also continuing to help them grow and develop.

Conclusion

Let me take you to the leader of Christianity: Jesus Christ. He gives us an excellent example of what a human being can be. He expressed his desire that people come into God's family to reflect God's character. He helps us become what God wants us to be. Let's follow the Leader.

WEDNESDAY EVENING, APRIL 26

Title: The Criterion for Stewardship: Faithfulness

Text: "Moreover it is required in stewards that a man be found faithful" *(1 Cor. 4:2).*

Scripture Reading: 1 Corinthians 4:1–2

Introduction

To evaluate the effectiveness of a person's efforts in a given field, judges establish criteria. The earned run average of a relief pitcher in baseball, the percentage of passes completed by a quarterback in football, or the average number of yards gained per carry by a running back are typical types of criteria. Many other factors are considered in the evaluation of pitchers and quarterbacks and running backs, but the aforementioned are the primary ones.

Paul declares in the text that a key criterion for evaluating a steward is faithfulness. Other things may be taken into account, but the key requisite for good stewardship is faithfulness. One may draw two very clear conclusions from Paul's declaration.

I. A poor steward is unfaithful.

Whatever else one may say about a steward, if he is not a good steward, he is unfaithful, for faithfulness is a key criterion by which stewardship is judged. Nobody wants to say he or she is willfully unfaithful to his or her commitment to the living Christ: "I received Christ as my Savior and Lord, but I've decided not to keep my commitment to him." Those words are horrifying to the believer, but our text teaches that our actions declare them for us if we are poor stewards.

A. *God judges faithfulness rather than just the harvest.* Stewards are not required to out-produce or out-perform others. Their evaluation will not be based on the number of people they brought to Christ, but they will give an account for their faithfulness in sharing the gospel. They will not be evaluated on the beauty of their singing, but they will give an account for their faithfulness in singing the Lord's song.

B. *Stewards can be encouraged because they are not judged in comparison to another's gifts.* Paul wrote in another letter to the saints at Corinth, "If there be first a willing mind, it is accepted according to that a man hath, and not according to that he hath not" (2 Cor. 8:12). Apparently some in that day were guilty of "subjunctive mood stewardship": "I would give liberally if I were rich, or I could tithe if I had another's circumstances." The stewardship of each person is seen by God in relation to that person's blessings.

II. A good steward is faithful.

A. *One obvious area in which stewards will be faithful to the Master is in the use of their material possessions.* They will recognize that they are trustees and God is the owner. Then they will return at least a tithe to be used in the cause of Christ through his church and will also recognize they are trustees as they use the remainder.

B. *Believers also hold the gospel in trust.* All believers are responsible to be good trustees of God's message to the world. This is the thrust of Jesus' declaration to Peter in Matthew 16:19. The gospel is the key to the kingdom. Those who know it are responsible to unlock the gates for others.

Paul obviously understood this concept. When he wrote to the church at Rome, he declared himself to be "obligated both to Greeks and non-Greeks, both to the wise and the foolish" (Rom. 1:14). His indebtedness to them is not a result of what they had done but was rather a result of what God had done for Paul. God had saved him and entrusted the gospel to him. A believer who is a good steward will be faithful to share the good news entrusted to him.

Conclusion

Are you a good steward for God? You can be. The criterion for good stewardship is faithfulness in obedience to him. You don't have to be talented or rich, but you must be faithful.

SUNDAY MORNING, APRIL 30

Title: The Nature of Our Resurrection Bodies

Text: "As we have borne the image of the earthly, we shall also bear the image of the heavenly" *(1 Cor. 15:49).*

Scripture Reading: 1 Corinthians 15:35–49

Hymns: "Crown Him with Many Crowns," Bridges

"Were You There?" Spiritual

"Blessed Assurance, Jesus Is Mine," Crosby

Offertory Prayer: Our heavenly Father, when we behold the birds of the air and the lilies of the field, we are reminded of the constancy of your love and the bounty of your provision. Teach us to live by faith. Teach us to seek first the kingdom of God. Teach us to give as you give. We pray this is Christ's name. Amen.

Introduction

One of the most forlorn places on earth is a cemetery of the unclaimed dead, New York City's Potter's Field. This cemetery receives about four thousand such bodies annually.

When people are buried there, there are no funeral rites, no flags, no flowers, no markers on the graves. The pallbearers are prisoners from the city's workhouse. The bodies arrive at the burial place in pine coffins. The prisoners chisel a number on each box. Then the coffins are placed in a common trench.

The only marker at Potter's Field is a single monument, erected there about fifty years ago, bearing the one word "Peace." It is somewhat misleading. Few of those buried there ever found peace on earth. Whatever reward there may be for them will have to be in the life to come.

While all cemeteries are places of sadness, defeat, and despair, the Bible says that one day the cemetery will be the most lively place on earth. When Christ returns, the graves will open and the dead in them will be raised. That is the great theme of Paul in 1 Corinthians 15.

In this passage Paul answers two pertinent questions: "How is the resurrection possible?" and "What kind of body will we have in the resurrection?"

Paul's answer to the first question is simple. He points to agriculture to show that it is natural for life to come from death. A seed is planted in the ground, decays in death, then blossoms a new and more glorious plant. All of this is possible by God's power. He alone can bring life out of death. The same power that operates in the farmer's field will operate in the cemetery. It is the power of God.

The more important question is, "What kind of bodies will we have in the resurrection?" Paul gives us a lengthy answer to that question.

I. We will have a suitable body (vv. 38–42).

A. *God gives to each creature a body suitable for its existence.* Birds, fish, and humans all have bodies perfectly adapted to their environments.
B. *Our resurrection body will be suitable for the resurrected life.* Our bodies will be adapted to the conditions of eternal life.

II. We will have a superior body (vv. 42–44).

In these verses Paul uses the metaphor of seeds and plants again. He suggests that if you want to know what our resurrection bodies will be like, you should go to a garden. Seeds are sown in the ground, and from their decay comes a plant far more superior to that which was placed in the ground.

The analogy is our bodies are the seeds, our burial is the planting, our resurrection is the harvest.

A. *Our resurrection body will be incorruptible, that is, not subject to decay.*
B. *Our resurrection body will be glorious, that is, not subject to sin.*
C. *Our resurrection body will be powerful, that is, not subject to the limitations and handicaps of this life.*
D. *Our resurrection body will be spiritual, that is, not mere flesh and blood.*

III. We will have a Christlike body (vv. 45–49).

The clearest picture of what our resurrection body will be like is that of Jesus Christ. The apostle John concurs in 1 John 3:2. What kind of body did Jesus have when he was resurrected?

A. *Jesus had a transcendent body.* Throughout his ministry he was subject to the laws of time and space and matter. He could be in only one place at one time. To go from one place to another required that he move in time and in space. But after his resurrection, he was no longer limited to time and space. His body transcended former limitations.

His resurrected body showed no ill effects from the mortal wounds he had recently received. So our resurrection bodies will not be limited by the afflictions, infirmities, and handicaps that we have experienced on this earth.

B. *Jesus had a recognizable body.* When he appeared to his disciples, they recognized him; he looked essentially the same. He also spoke with them, walked with them, and allowed them to physically inspect his scars. In like manner, we will know each other in the resurrection.

Conclusion

Joseph Forte Newton wrote a beautiful statement about the death of his father. When Newton was just a boy, he looked for the first time into an open grave; it was a strange and terrifying experience for him. He listened as the old country minister adjusted his glasses and read the words of Jesus, "I am the resurrection and the life. . . . Let not your heart be troubled."

Newton said he would never forget the power of those words. It was as if a powerful but gentle hand had been put forth from the unseen to caress and heal his spirit. Then he said, "From that day to this I have loved Jesus beyond the power of words to tell."

I hope it is the same with you.

SUNDAY EVENING, APRIL 30

Title: Liberation from Life's Greatest Enemies

Text: "Since the children have flesh and blood, he too shared in their humanity so that by his death he might destroy him who holds the power of death—that is, the devil—and free those who all their lives were held in slavery by their fear of death" *(Heb. 2:14–15 NIV).*

Scripture Reading: Hebrews 2:14–18

Introduction

One of the most moving moments in American history was the release of prisoners from North Vietnam war camps. The prisoners had been captured by the enemy and housed in atrocious conditions, subjected to unjust treatment, and brainwashed about American ideas. Politicians negotiated for the release of the prisoners. Christians prayed for their release. Finally, the prisoners were actually released from the terrible tyranny of the enemy.

The writer of Hebrews portrays helpless human beings crying for release from the bondage of life's greatest enemies: sin, death, and the Devil. He asserts that Jesus Christ, the Christians' leader, encountered these sinister forces to deliver people from them. Let us examine these enemies and celebrate Christ's deliverance from them.

I. Christ delivers from the tyranny of sin.

Sin is an ugly reality in the experience of human beings. It is a hostile, destructive, inward power that will destroy unless one gets deliverance. Jesus can deliver us from the binding tyranny of sin. But how can he do this?

A. *Jesus delivers from the penalty of sin.* Throughout the book of Hebrews, sin is portrayed as an ugly stain that must be eradicated if we are to be purified. To remove the ugly stain of sin, Christ came as a priest to offer the sacrifice of himself.

"He had to be made like his brothers in every way, in order that he might become a merciful and faithful high priest in service to God, and that he might make atonement for the sins of the people" (Heb. 2:17 NIV). Jesus ministered before God to make atonement for sin. The verse is a picture of the Jewish high priest's work on the Day of Atonement. The priest made sacrifices to deliver people from the penalty of sin. Jesus is the Great High Priest who alone is capable of delivering people from the penalty of sin.

B. *Jesus delivers from the power of sin.* Although people may be delivered from the penalty of sin, they still have to deal with the sinister power of sin. Jesus helps people live victoriously over that power: "Because he himself suffered when he was tempted, he is able to help those who are being tempted" (Heb. 2:18 NIV).

The problem of temptation and sin is ever-present, but Jesus can help us because he knows what it is like to be human. He sympathizes because he knows the torture of temptation. And because Jesus went through temptations without yielding, he can deliver us from the power of sin.

II. Christ delivers from the dread of death.

Death is an awesome reality that every person faces. Death is the direct result and inevitable fruit of sin. Only Jesus has the power to deliver a person from the dread of death.

A. *Jesus is able to deliver from the dreaded enemy of death.* "He too shared in their humanity so that by his death he might destroy him who holds the power of death—that is, the devil" (Heb. 2:14 NIV). Jesus' death was more powerful than the deaths of other persons. Other people have died unusual deaths, but they have remained dead. Jesus died, and he rose triumphantly over the grave. He defeated life's greatest enemy.

Jesus alone is capable of giving a person victory over death. To defeat an enemy one has to be more powerful than the enemy. No other person has ever been able to defeat death. Jesus tasted the experience of death, and God raised him from the dead. Through Jesus' death and resurrection, a person's ultimate enemy has been defeated.

B. *Jesus is able to deliver from the dreadful result of death.* Many people fear that death will be the end of their existence. Unbelievers have no hope for the future. They can live only for the present. Their greatest hope is to live on in the minds of other people.

Jesus Christ liberated people from the dread of nonexistence. He taught that his followers will continue to exist in a qualitative life. "I am the resurrection, and the life: he that believeth in me, though he were dead, yet shall he live" (John 11:25).

III. Christ delivers from the power of the Devil.

The Devil is just as much a reality as sin and death. Biblical writers wrote with certainty about the reality of the Devil. Jesus identified the reality of the Devil and accused him of being a murderer, a liar, and a thief.

A. *Jesus has deprived the Devil of his ultimate power.* According to the writer of Hebrews, Jesus destroyed the one who had the power of death. The word "destroy" in Hebrews 2:14 means to "render impotent." At the cross Jesus fought with Satan and all his sinister forces. He defeated the Devil in his ultimate power.

B. *Jesus is helping win battles against the Devil's limited power.* Many people question the fact that Jesus defeated the Devil. They see signs that the Devil is still active in the world. Christ's death did deprive the Devil of his ultimate power. In the future the Devil will be destroyed completely. Yet until that day believers have to recognize that the Devil has limited power.

The war with evil is over. Battles will continue to be fought. During the time of the Devil's limited power, Jesus is able to help one to be delivered from the Devil. "And they overcame him by the blood of the Lamb, and by the word of their testimony; and they loved not their lives unto the death" (Rev. 12:11).

Conclusion

The greatest enemies of the human race are sin, death, and the Devil. You can try to deliver yourself. But Jesus alone can give deliverance from life's greatest enemies.

MAY

■ Sunday Mornings

A twofold plan unfolds for the month: first, we will conclude the series on the significance of Christ's resurrection; then, with a series entitled "Enriching Marriage and Family Relationships," we will delve into the needs of families.

■ Sunday Evenings

Continue with the series based on the book of Hebrews using the theme "The Superlative Christ."

■ Wednesday Evenings

We will examine our day-to-day behavior in light of the principles delineated in the book of James with a series called The Practice of Genuine Religion."

WEDNESDAY EVENING, MAY 3

Title: The Profit in Trials

Text: "Consider it pure joy, my brothers, whenever you face trials of many kinds, because you know that the testing of your faith develops perseverance. Perseverance must finish its work so that you may be mature and complete, not lacking anything" *(James 1:2–4 NIV).*

Scripture Reading: James 1:1–5

Introduction

Something that has irked me throughout all my years as a student is tests. Teachers used to infuriate me by coming to class, tests in hand, and say with a smile, "This is not intended to discourage you or to make you nervous—it is simply to see what you know. It is a learning experience." Actually, the only questions I remember are those that I then missed.

James draws a close parallel to this illustration with his view of spiritual tests. James does not say we should seek out trials. Knowing our weaknesses, we may fervently and appropriately pray that God may be pleased to exempt us from them. Regardless, Christians should know that trials are a spiritual discipline essential to the maturing of the Christian life. They are designed to purify our faith, produce patience, and perfect our character.

I. Testing purifies faith.

A. *James begins with a vivid picture in verse 3 to describe a purification process.* Metal in those days was purified by heat. The metal would melt and impurities would float to the surface. Our faith, according to James, undergoes much the same process under the heat of testing. The test may be painful, but impurities are removed. Our profit is that we learn in whom to believe.

B. *In the late 1960s, one of the women nominated for an Academy Award was Patricia Neal, for her performance in* The Subject Was Roses. It was thought to be the high point in movie history when the spotlight focused on her, for her history was so moving. In 1960 she was wheeling her baby son in a carriage across a New York City street when a car slammed into the carriage. The baby lived but endured several operations and months of hospitalizations. Two years later Patricia's daughter got the measles and died unexpectedly. Then in February 1965 Patricia herself almost died of massive hemorrhages. Her speech, vision, and mind were impaired, but she fought back. As if to culminate her victories in these tragedies, she won the Oscar. One press writer asked her the key to her courage. She pointed to a plaque that read: "Fear knocked at the door. Faith in God answered. No one was there." Fear is dissipated by faith when put to the test.

II. Testing produces patience.

A. *A major problem we all have with testing is dealing with the time factor.* We know good will come of an unpleasant circumstance—we just wish it would hurry up. For this we need patience.

B. *Patience is the second result of testing.* But patience is not simply the ability to endure until our hopes are fulfilled. It is that steadfastness, that endurance, that fortitude that *conquers* the problem. It does not just wait for something else to happen.

C. *Patience is what gave life to the testimony of the martyrs.* Some Christian martyrs have died with smiles on their faces—smiles that reflected the words of one martyr who said, "When I looked into the fire, I saw the glory of the Lord." This is not a shallow victory; it is a meaningful victory in the most profound sense. Spiritual trials become spiritual victories in just that same way when patience is allowed to have its perfect work in us.

III. Testing perfects character.

Patience is sometimes hindered from exercising its influence and achieving its crowning triumphs in our lives. This happens when we grow weary of trials and resort to questionable ways of extricating ourselves. But if permitted to run its full course, patience, through the trials of life, will do two things for a person.

A. *First, it will make a person perfect.* James does not use the word to imply sinlessness. The thought is one of maturity, or of being fully developed. It is reaching the end for which one is created. For Christians it refers to a spirit mature in judgment and in understanding.

B.   *Second, patience will make the person complete.* This completion refers to being perfectly equipped. The same words are used in the Old Testament of an animal completely fit to be sacrificed. It was blemish-free. Such constancy gives us a growing strength that we might conquer old sins. We become entirely fit to serve—fully grown, fully equipped, deficient in nothing.

Conclusion

By our persevering in trials, God completes a remarkable work in our lives. If through these trials we depend on the grace of God, we become entirely fit to serve, fully grown, fully equipped, and deficient in nothing. Let us then turn to him as our source of strength.

SUNDAY MORNING, MAY 7

Title: The Challenge of the Resurrection

Text: "Therefore, my beloved brethren, be ye steadfast, unmovable, always abounding in the work of the Lord, forasmuch as ye know that your labor is not in vain in the Lord" *(1 Cor. 15:58)*.

Scripture Reading: 1 Corinthians 15:50–58

Hymns: "Low in the Grave He Lay," Lowry

"When I Survey the Wondrous Cross," Montgomery

"Victory in Jesus," Bartlett

Offertory Prayer: Our loving Father, you have taught us to pray, "Give us this day our daily bread." But in your gracious way, you have provided so much more than just bread. And you have given it to us even when we did not ask. With grateful hearts we now return to you that which you have already shared with us. In Jesus' name we pray. Amen.

Introduction

In his journal John Wesley tells of his mother's death. "We stood around the bed and fulfilled her last request: 'Children, as soon as I am released, sing a psalm of praise to God.'"

How powerful our lives would be if we would radiate such hope and faith in the hour of our death. Actually, there is no reason why we can't; we are all partakers of the same hope.

Throughout this chapter Paul seeks to prove and to explain the resurrection. Now in these closing verses he presents the challenge of the resurrection.

The word "therefore" introduces our practical duty. Great truths ought to lead always to noble living. Paul tells us here that the resurrection should challenge us to three things.

I. The resurrection should challenge us to faithfulness (v. 58).

Paul's words are, "Be ye steadfast, unmovable." These words exhort us to have a firmness, a stability in faith. The resurrection should cause us to remain loyal to Jesus regardless of our circumstances.

A. *Corinth was a hard place to live the Christian life.* In this seaport town and center of pagan worship, temptations and trials constantly confronted the Christians. However, Paul still asserted that the resurrection was motivation enough to keep the Corinthians true to Christ.

B. *Just as the Corinthians were barraged with temptations, so are we.* It is not easy for us to live a consistent Christian life in our town. But we must stay true to Christ. A very simple and perhaps overworked illustration of how we need to act is that of a postage stamp. It takes a licking every time it goes to work. It may be pounded, crushed, and hidden under a pile of other mail with none to see or care. Yet it sticks to its task until the work is done. Dare to be a "postage stamp" Christian. Through fair weather and foul, through lickings, poundings, and obscurity, stick to your faith.

II. The resurrection should challenge us to diligence (v. 58).

Paul says we should be "always abounding in the work of the Lord."

A. *What is the work of the Lord?* It is doing good to others in the name of Jesus Christ. Jesus went about doing good. He fed the hungry, helped the sick, befriended the outcasts, and sought the lost. We should follow his pattern.

B. *To what extent are we to be involved in the work of the Lord?* We are to "abound" in his work. This word describes a river that runs over its banks. It has flooded the countryside. The resurrection should challenge us to work diligently for the Lord. Some people abound in the work of their political party, civic club, or fraternal order. God should have first claim on us.

III. The resurrection should challenge us to confidence (v. 58).

Paul motivates us to persevere when he says, "You know that your labor in the Lord is not in vain." We need such a reminder that our work is not wasted when we work for him.

A. *Many lives are empty and meaningless.* People continually give their first-rate loyalty to second-rate causes. Their priorities are out of order with their values.

B. *The resurrection guarantees that our labor for the Lord is never wasted.* The view of life of the writer of the book of Ecclesiastes was this: "Vanity, vanity, all is vanity." In contrast is the view of the apostle Paul, who stands on this side of the cross and the empty tomb and says, "Our labor in the Lord is not in vain." The difference between an empty life and a fulfilled one is serving the Lord in the certainty of the resurrection.

Conclusion

When Dr. W. E. Sangster, England's great Methodist preacher, lay dying with muscular atrophy, he reminded a friend that all his life he had preached that Jesus was adequate for every crisis. Now that he had only a few days to live, he wanted his friend to know that Christ was indeed adequate in the hour of death. He said to him, "Tell everyone it is true; tell them for me that God is wonderfully near his children when they come to the end of life's road."

Do you know Christ? Have you received him as your Lord and Savior? If not, do it today. He is the one who lived, who died, and who rose again. He lives evermore as both Lord and Savior.

SUNDAY EVENING, MAY 7

Title: The Kind of Priest You Need

Text: "Therefore, since we have a great high priest who has gone through the heavens, Jesus the Son of God, let us hold firmly to the faith we profess" *(Heb. 4:14 NIV)*.

Scripture Reading: Hebrews 4:14–5:10

Introduction

A priest's task is like that of a bridge builder. The writer of Hebrews writes of Jesus as the Great High Priest. He is the perfect bridge builder. A chasm existed between a holy God and sinful people. A bridge touching both banks had to be built—that is, to fulfill the office of Great High Priest, Jesus had to be fully in touch with God and fully in touch with the people. Let us notice the basic qualifications for a bridge builder or Great High Priest.

I. Jesus has a unique relationship with the Father.

According to the Old Testament qualification, one must have a unique relationship with God to be a priest. The writer of Hebrews gives us some insights about the unique relationship of Jesus to God, the heavenly Father.

A. *Jesus possesses the nature of God. Jesus can be the supreme High Priest, for he and the Father are one.* Notice the title of Jesus in Hebrews 4:14: "Son of God." The expression "son of" was used to describe the nature of a person. The nature of Jesus is that of God. Jesus is able to represent God to humans, for he has the same nature as the Father.

B. *Jesus receives his appointment from the Father (cf. Heb. 5:1, 4, 10).* The real priest does not choose to enter the priesthood. The authentic priest receives the call and ordination from the Father. Throughout Jesus' life and ministry he was constantly aware that his appointment was by the Father.

C. *Jesus obeys the Father.* In his divine appointment Jesus fulfilled one requirement for the high priesthood: he remained faithful to the Father. Jesus is the perfect High Priest in that he always does the will of the Father. The consuming passion of Jesus was to obey the Father's desire.

II. Jesus has an amazing identity with human nature.

To be a priest according to the Old Testament qualification, one must be sympathetic with human beings. The writer of Hebrews gives several insights about how Jesus amazingly identifies with human beings.

A. *Jesus identifies with the human race by becoming like them.* The priest must have a perfect identity with the human race. "For we do not have a high priest who is unable to sympathize with our weaknesses" (Heb. 4:15 NIV). The greatest truth about God is that he chose to become a human being. He identified with his creation by becoming like them and experiencing life as they experienced it.

B. *Jesus understands human temptations because he was tempted himself.* Jesus was not content just to become a human being. He allowed himself to be tempted as human beings are. He was "tempted in every way, just as we are—yet was without sin" describes the victory of Jesus over temptation. He fought the same battles we fight, and he won.

C. *Jesus bestows mercy to helpless human beings.* "Let us then approach the throne of grace with confidence, so that we may receive mercy and find grace to help us in our time of need" (Heb. 4:16 NIV). Since Jesus identified with the human race and engaged in the same kind of battles, he has mercy and gives grace to those who have fallen. "He is able to deal gently with those who are ignorant and are going astray, since he himself is subject to weakness" (Heb. 5:2 NIV). Jesus is eminently qualified to be our High Priest, for he has an amazing identity with human beings.

III. Jesus has a distinctive capability for the work.

Old Testament priests were required to learn the skills of performance. They had to learn the methods of making sacrifices and of performing the rituals involved. The writer of Hebrews makes clear that Jesus was qualified to be the kind of priest we need because of his distinctive capacity for priestly work.

A. *Jesus is able to enter into the presence of God.* The author of Hebrews uses the Old Testament imagery of the high priest. In Hebrews 4:14 Jesus is said to have "gone through the heavens" (NIV). Under the old covenant the high priest went once a year into the Holy of Holies. This was the place in the temple where God was said to dwell in mercy with his people. The high priest went inside to make atonement for the people. Only he was qualified to enter. Jesus is uniquely capable of going into the presence of the Father to make atonement for sins.

B. *Jesus is able to offer an adequate sacrifice for sins.* "Every high priest is selected from among men and is appointed to represent them in matters related to God, to offer gifts and sacrifices for sins" (Heb. 5:1 NIV). The expressions "gifts and sacrifices" suggest the entire sacrificial system. The sacrifices were offered as a substitute for sins of his people. Jesus as our Great High Priest offered the only adequate sacrifice for sin—his life.

C. *Jesus is able to be our Savior.* Because the work of Jesus as High Priest was adequate, he became our eternal Savior. "And, once made perfect, he became the source of eternal salvation for all who obey him" (Heb. 5:9 NIV). Jesus alone is capable of providing eternal salvation.

Conclusion

Human beings need a bridge to get to God. They need one who knows their plight and knows God. Jesus is just the priest people need. He knows them fully, and he knows God fully. Let him be your priest.

WEDNESDAY EVENING, MAY 10

Title: Resources for Bad Times

Text: "If any of you lacks wisdom, he should ask God, who gives generously to all without finding fault, and it will be given to him. But when he asks, he must believe and not doubt, because he who doubts is like a wave of the sea, blown and tossed by the wind. That man should not think he will receive anything from the Lord; he is a double-minded man, unstable in all he does" *(James 1:5–8 NIV).*

Scripture Reading: James 1:5–8

Introduction

Have you ever had days when you simply could not win? One fellow was driving home from work one evening and heard a radio announcer suggest to his listeners that they surprise their mates when they got home. "When you arrive for dinner," he said, "instead of growling something like 'When will dinner be ready?' why not surprise your wife with a little gift?" The man thought that sounded like a good idea, so he stopped along the way for a bouquet of flowers and a box of candy.

Instead of driving into the garage, he went up to the front door and rang the bell. His wife opened the door, saw him standing there with a radiant smile, holding out his gifts to her and declared crankily to him, "Well if this doesn't beat all! Listen, buster, the baby has colic. The washing machine is broken again. Junior got into a fight at school today and got expelled. Now, as I might have expected, you make my day perfect by coming home drunk!"

Trouble comes to us all. But there are certain resources that are universal to all Christians to help us cope with our difficulties. The emphasis of this passage is not only the need we each have for these things, but the availability of them.

I. Wisdom.

One thing this poor housewife could have used for sure was a little bit of wisdom. We all need wisdom to see our problems in their truest light and to see how to make the best use of them.

A.   *We need to understand what James means by wisdom.* It is obviously more than just intelligence. Wisdom includes a moral and spiritual quality. It is based on a healthy fear of the Lord. It is the sum of practical religion.

B. *James elaborates on two kinds of wisdom in other passages.*

    1.   One is from God. It is pure, peaceable, gentle, and easy to control.

    2.   The other is not from God. It is earthy, sensual, and demonic. James speaks here of the former.

II. Prayer.

In a cotton factory, cards on the walls of the workrooms read: "If your threads get tangled, send for the foreman." One day a new worker got her threads tangled. She tried to disentangle them but only made them worse. Then she sent for the foreman. He came and looked. Then he asked her, "You have been doing this by yourself?"

"Yes," she said.

"Why did you not send for me according to the instructions?"

"I did my best," she said.

"No, you did not," said the foreman. "Remember that doing your best is sending for me."

A. *This is what James says: to do your best in bad times you need to send for help—ask for God's wisdom.* Without this attitude, wisdom is impossible.

B. *In verse 5 James offers four different assurances to encourage us to pray.*

    1.   The basis of prayer is not the character of man but the character of God. Prayer is based on God's disposition to give to all people.

    2.   James calls attention to the generosity of God. God gives liberally.

    3.   When God gives he does not upbraid the one he gives to. That is to say, God does not grant one's request and then reproach that person for it afterwards. God might well say when we come to him, "What use have you made of the last gift I gave you?" But he doesn't. He might remind us of our unworthiness to appear before him. But he doesn't. He might turn us away by declaring, "I know that you will misuse what I give to you." But he doesn't.

    4.   James encourages us with a reminder that "it will be given to him." There is not the slightest suggestion of mere chance or probability of success. What strong encouragement we have to go to God in prayer with a bold expectancy!

III. Faith.

A. *Prayer is effective only when it is done with faith.* We are to pray believing God will answer the request.

B. *James says to pray without doubting—suggesting a continuing spirit of doubt.* He encourages us to pray without vacillating from trust to distrust, from pleading with boldness on one hand but thinking all the while it's a useless exercise. The wavering petitioner dishonors God by doubting his Word and treating God as unworthy of confidence.

Conclusion

James encourages us to pray for wisdom and to have the faith that expects that wisdom from God.

SUNDAY MORNING, MAY 14

Title: An Exciting Discovery for Mother's Day

Text: "There is neither Jew nor Greek, there is neither bond nor free, there is neither male nor female: for ye are all one in Christ Jesus" *(Gal. 3:28).*

Scripture Reading: Galatians 3:26–29

Hymns: "It Is Well with My Soul," Spafford

         "I Am Thine, O Lord," Crosby

         "O God, Who to a Loyal Home," Fosdick

Offertory Prayer: Our Father, we are grateful for this day and its special emphasis. We thank you for your blessings. We thank you for the mothers who are special blessings from you. We are grateful for their love, their compassion, their tenderness, their acceptance of us. We are aware that these characteristics mirror your love, compassion, tenderness, and acceptance of us. Please take the gifts we give with love this day and use them to extend your love throughout the world. This we pray in Jesus' name and for his sake. Amen.

Introduction

In *Reader's Digest* some years ago there was a story of a man who wanted to give his wife a special gift on Mother's Day. He wanted the gift to be unique, something he had discovered himself. In an antique store he found a pair of hames tips, those devices that look rather like a parenthesis that fit on a horse collar to hold the reins. He took them home, polished them up, filled them with flowers, and presented them to his wife on Mother's Day. He *had* made a great discovery. The key is that he made his discovery his gift to her.

Here is another exciting discovery for Mother's Day: a mother is a person. Mothers are often viewed primarily according to their function as family members. But mothers are persons—persons with feelings, rights, and privileges.

This should not be such a revolutionary discovery. Paul made the same observation a long time ago. He was arguing for spiritual unity. The Greeks divided all people into two classes: Greeks and barbarians. The Jews did the same thing as they divided the whole world into Jews and Gentiles.

Then there was the category of women. A wife was the property of her husband. Her status ranked with slaves and children. In every respect a woman was inferior to a man. But Christ changed that.

Becoming a Christian, of course, does not mean that one ceases to be a male or female. It does mean, however, that gender does not alter one's relationship to

Christ in any way. Each one of us, male or female, father or mother, boy or girl, stands in a relationship to Christ by faith, and we have a unity through our faith.

This discovery helps in preaching a Mother's Day sermon. It is hard to be realistic in a Mother's Day sermon. If a preacher is not careful, it may sound as though he or she is talking about Superwoman. Mothers leave discouraged because they know they are not like that.

But if we accept the exciting discovery that mothers are persons, a Mother's Day sermon need not be sentimental and idealistic. The sermon can inspire rather than idealize. This is what this Mother's Day sermon is designed to do.

In *Heaven in My Hand*, a delightful book describing her teaching experiences, Alice Lee Humphries tells of a visit to the home of a very poor student. In an effort to divert attention from the poor surroundings of which the student seemed conscious, she mentioned the smells coming from the kitchen and asked if her mother was the cook. The little girl replied that she was "the lady what cooks." Her mother was a lady. What she did was cook. That little girl was able to separate the person from the function.

Taking this exciting discovery for Mother's Day—that a mother is a person who functions in the family as a mother—notice some of the positive things a mother can do for her family.

I. A mother gives affirmation.

A. *She can affirm each person as an individual.* Asserting her own individuality, a mother can help others affirm and assert their individuality. This can have a life-changing effect on persons. Jesus showed the veracity of this in his encounter with the woman at the well in John 4. He treated the woman as an individual, and in this she found peace and real life.

B. *Each person is unique and irreplaceable.* A mother can affirm that truth. Halford Luccock reminds us that the mother of John Wesley, the founder of the Methodist church, had nineteen children. That was a large family even in those days and even for a competent mother such as Susanna Wesley. He humorously suggested that she got their clothes mixed on occasion but asked more seriously, "Do you imagine she ever got *them* mixed? Did Samuel sort of fade into John, and was Charles a misty blending of both? Would she have cared little if one had slipped out of her life, finding ready comfort in the fact she had eighteen left? If you have any doubt about it, read her letters to her children. Each one held his [or her] own individual place that none of the others, not all eighteen together, could fill."

II. A mother gives inspiration.

A. *She can give inspiration for spiritual development.* A Christian mother can be an inspiration to others in their spiritual development. Mothers, of course, have done this for years. Ian MacClaren reported that before his first sermon, his mother handed him her watch. She told him that whenever he looked at it he should remember that every hour of the day she would be praying for him. She added, "And son, when you preach your first sermon in your first kirk [church], say something good for Jesus." He testified that his mother shaped his ministry with that sentence, plus her beautiful life.

B. *She can give inspiration for Christian service.* By their very examples, mothers have served as an inspiration for Christian service. A minister told of coming home from college feeling rather skeptical about religion. He noticed that his mother looked tired and worried. She asked him if he would take a meal she had cooked to a man dying of tuberculosis. She also asked him to take a Bible, as she was not sure the man was a Christian. The college son asked her what he should read. She suggested John 3. After spending half the afternoon with the dying man, he told his mother, "He accepted Christ." Then he added that he had given his heart to God too.

III. A mother can give expectation.

A. *A mother expects the best for her children.* Sometimes this runs in material or social ways. But should it not also run in spiritual ways? A mother should expect the very best for her family spiritually.

B. *The greatest expectation is that each member of the family knows Christ as Savior.*

Conclusion

A mother is a person who can find full personhood in Jesus Christ. As a person who has found new life and strength through faith in Christ, she can then affirm her family, inspire her family, and expect the very best of Christian growth in them.

SUNDAY EVENING, MAY 14

Title: An Old Testament History Lesson

Text: "It is impossible for those who have once been enlightened, who have tasted the heavenly gift, who have shared in the Holy Spirit, who have tasted the goodness of the word of God and the powers of the coming age, if they fall away, to be brought back to repentance, because to their loss they are crucifying the Son of God all over again and subjecting him to public disgrace" *(Heb. 6:4–6 NIV).*

Scripture Reading: Hebrews 5:11–6:8

Introduction

When I was in seminary, some of my favorite classes were Old Testament classes. I was fortunate to have professors who were skilled in relating the narratives of the Old Testament and drawing lessons from them.

The author of Hebrews, whoever he might have been, was a master in using the Old Testament. You cannot understand Hebrews without seeing how the author compared Old Testament ideas with Christian experiences. He spoke of the character of Christ by using the figure of the Old Testament high priest. He used the Jewish sacrifices to compare with Christ's death. In Hebrews 3:12 one sees "the exodus motif" used in the letter. The exodus motif is a comparison of redemption in Christ with Israel's redemption from Egyptian bondage.

In Hebrews 6:4–6 the author seems to compare an Old Testament lesson with a situation he observed in the first-century churches. The Old Testament comparison is from the book of Numbers, which contains the report of Israel's rebellion at Kadesh-barnea. Using this rebellion at Kadesh-barnea, one may draw some vital lessons.

I. People may have glorious experiences with God.

A. *Israel had a great experience with God at Kadesh-barnea.* The experience was the time the spies returned from Canaan, the Promised Land, with glowing reports. Twelve spies returned to the Israelites to give a report of their experiences in Canaan (cf. Num. 13:26–27; 14:7). The spies were informed about the condition of Canaan. They brought back sample fruit to taste. They recognized that God wanted Israel to go to the land so they could fulfill his purpose. Although the spies came to two opposing recommendations—two wanting to go and ten not wanting to go—the experience of *all* the spies in Canaan was a glorious one.

B. *The Hebrew Christians also had a glorious experience with God.* Several words and phrases describe their experience with the Lord: "enlightened," "tasted the heavenly gift," "shared in the Holy Spirit." These describe people who had had some type of experience with the Lord.

But a glorious experience is not adequate. Some Christians seem to be satisfied with their initial conversion experience, but God wants his people to go on in many subsequent experiences with him. Evidently the author of Hebrews addressed people who had a glorious experience with God but refused to go on to maturity.

II. People may rebel against God's will.

A. *Israel chose to rebel against God's will at Kadesh-barnea.* God had delivered the Israelites out of the land of Egypt and led them to Kadesh-barnea. He wanted them to "go" from there to conquer the Canaanites, but they rebelled against the challenge of Joshua to persevere in capturing Canaan. The lesson is plain: God can deliver us from the enemy, but there is still the possibility of rebelling against God's will.

B. *The Hebrew Christians rebelled against God's challenge of development.* According to the New Testament, salvation is threefold: it refers to the experience of regeneration, to the present experience of sanctification, and to the future experience of glorification. The author of Hebrews seems to compare Kadesh-barnea to the Hebrews' experiences of sanctification.

"If they fall away" is an expression that compares with Israel's action at Kadesh-barnea. They rebelled against God's desire to conquer Canaan. Likewise, Christians may rebel against God's will to be a priest for God and to fulfill God's mission.

III. People may suffer from the results of rebellion.

A. *Israel suffered the tragic consequences of rebellion.* What happened to the Israelites at Kadesh-barnea? God made a decree that none of the generation of Israelites above nineteen years of age, except Caleb and Joshua, would enter the land of Canaan (cf. Num. 14:23ff.). The people had not kept the contract with God, so they had to suffer the consequences. They were not sent back to Egypt. They wandered and died in the wilderness. Another generation would be used to fulfill God's purpose.

Afterward, Israel wanted to repent of their mistake (cf. Num. 14:40–45). Moses told them that repentance was impossible. They had made their way, and they had to walk in it.

B. *The Hebrew Christians suffered the results of rebellion.* "It is impossible . . . if they fall away, to be brought back to repentance, because to their loss they are crucifying the Son of God all over again and subjecting him to public disgrace" (Heb. 6:6 NIV). Christians can rebel so much against God's purpose that they lose their opportunity of being sanctified. Look around and you will see many Christians and many churches wandering in the wilderness.

Conclusion

The Old Testament has many valuable lessons for believers. One important lesson is to be careful to fulfill your obligation to grow in the Lord. Not doing so could lead to arrested growth and meaningless wandering.

WEDNESDAY EVENING, MAY 17

Title: Putting Tests into Perspective

Text: "Happy is the man who remains steadfast under trial, for having passed that test he will reserve for his prize the gift of life promised to those who love God" *(James 1:12 NEB).*

Scripture Reading: James 1:9–12

Introduction

To a student, *test* is a dirty word. Most students think of tests as the sadistic tools teachers use to illustrate their superior knowledge. They think teachers delight in this exercise of torment. As the husband of a teacher, I can say without reservation that that is not the case at all. Most teachers dread tests as much as students do. In fact, no one more than the teacher wishes the students to do well.

So the issue is how to test students accurately and fairly. Teachers would love to know that. When students are so diverse—different backgrounds, different languages, different interests—how do you devise a test that is fair to each? The answer is that you don't. You simply can't.

139

Often I hear students say, "Oh, I can't wait until I graduate so I won't have to take any more tests." I regret to disappoint these expectant individuals. Tests don't end with a graduation ceremony. Life is a test. Tests will be taken every day. The tests often get *much harder* and the stakes *much higher!*

Testing may take many forms, but James mentions two of the most prevalent forms: both pertain to money.

I. Poverty is a test.

A. *The first test is designed specifically for the poor.* Most of us think we belong in this category. This group includes the "brothers of lower degree or humble circumstances." Yet despite their lowly circumstances, James tells them to rejoice. They are to rise above their outward poverty and depression and look at life from a different perspective.

B. *Christians are given a new sense of what really matters.* Because of their relationship with Christ, they come to know that they matter in the church. And they matter in the world because in Christ they have purpose. They matter to God. Because they matter, possessions matter less.

II. Riches are a test.

A. *James continues to say that the glory for the poor is the same for the rich.* Obviously, then, the source of joy is not money for both cases. For the poor man, his poverty is a test; for the wealthy man, his riches are a test. His joy, according to James, is in his humiliation.

B. *Several options might explain this humiliation in question.* It may be that his greater wealth brings to him a greater responsibility for financially backing the Lord's work.

   1. The great Southern Baptist preacher John H. Broadus once demonstrated this humbling responsibility by leaving his pulpit during the collection of the offering and looking carefully at every cent that went into the plate. When the collection was over, Broadus went back to the pulpit and said to the congregation, "My people, if you take it to heart that I have seen your offerings this day and know what sacrifices you have made or not made, remember that the Son of God, your Savior, goes about the aisles with every usher every service and with his sleepless eye sees every cent put into his plate by his people." What a humbling thought!

   2. It could be that the humiliation is the potential threat of financial disaster that always looms like a dark cloud over wealthy people. That's a humbling thought.

C. *But if the exaltation of poor people is spiritual in nature, it only stands to reason that the humiliation of the wealthy is also spiritual in nature.*

III. Rewards are for all.

Those are the tests, adapted to each as God sees fit. Passing the tests brings great rewards. James says that once the test is over and we have been approved, our reward is twofold.

A. *First, we will receive an inner blessedness.*
B. *Second, we will receive the crown of life.*

Conclusion

What fitting rewards! A crown of laurel leaves was put on the head of a champion athlete in ancient times. A crown of flowers was worn at weddings. A crown of gold marked royalty. A crown was a mark of dignity and honor. To the genuine Christian a crown is given, but this is not just any crown—it is the crown of life.

SUNDAY MORNING, MAY 21

Title: The Witnessing Woman

Text: "Wives, in the same way be submissive to your husbands so that, if any of them do not believe the word, they may be won over without words by the behavior of their wives, when they see the purity and reverence of your lives" *(1 Peter 3:1–2 NIV).*

Scripture Reading: 1 Peter 3:1–6

Hymns: "God, Give Us Christian Homes," McKinney

"Teach Me to Pray," Reitz

"O Perfect Love," Gurney

Offertory Prayer: Dear God, on this day we thank you for the love that you have shown to us. We are grateful to be constantly surrounded by the warmth of your love. One of the manifestations of your love has been the women in our lives who have witnessed to us of Christ, principally our mothers. We thank you for them. We can never repay these witnessing women for their love and care; and we can never repay you for your expressions of love. But out of a heart of love, we can give to you and to your causes. We give from love. Take these offerings, bless them, and use them for your glory. We pray in Jesus' name. Amen.

Introduction

The noted singer Marion Talley was a woman who witnessed. Marion and her mother were visiting at a mountain resort in Colorado on a Sunday. Marion asked if there were any religious services in the village. She was told all the people would meet the train and spend the remainder of the day at a rooster fight. There would be no need to try to have a service until these events were over, and even then only a few people ever attended a religious service.

When the rooster fight commenced, Marion found the little church, sat down at the organ, and began to play and sing. People heard her beautiful music. They slowly began coming in; after a while the church was packed.

Someone asked her if she would talk to them. She said: "I am Marion Talley, and I am a Christian. If you would know the reason, there she sits before you. I cannot preach a sermon, but I can point you to one. My mother's beautiful life is the greatest sermon I have ever heard and accounts for what I am as a Christian.

This was a witnessing woman.

Peter describes a witnessing woman to us as well. This section in 1 Peter deals with relationships. It deals with relationships between citizens and governmental authorities, slaves and masters, husbands and wives. The particular problem Peter tackles is that of a Christian wife with an unbelieving husband. Peter asserts that a witnessing woman can lead her husband to Christ by the quality of her life.

Many of us are Christians today because of a witnessing woman: mother, grandmother, aunt, Sunday school teacher, neighbor. On this Sunday following Mother's Day, let us broaden our focus a little. Consider the Christian woman, a mother perhaps, who functions as a witnessing woman not only to her husband but also to her family and to the larger community.

I. The witnessing woman accepts a principle.

A. *A principle of submission.* The passage begins with the words, "Wives, in the same way be submissive to your husbands." "In the same way" refers back to 1 Peter 2:13, "Submit yourselves for the Lord's sake to every authority instituted among men" (NIV). This is the Christian principle of submission, the willingness to put oneself second. "Voluntary selflessness" is what William Barclay called it.

Remember where Peter's first readers were in Christian development. In Roman practice the wife was a possession. In Hebrew thought she had a slightly higher status, but not much. Christianity then taught that in Christ there is no male or female, bond or free, Jew or Greek. That was heady stuff.

But with these new rights and privileges came Christian freedom. This liberty included the Christian's freedom to forgo all rights. Notice, too, that Peter spoke of principles and responsibilities rather than "rights."

What this means, then, is that submission is the liberating response to serve. It means that a spirit of selflessness should pervade the marriage relationship. Submission does not mean submersion.

B. *A principle that works.* Does it work? Can a witnessing woman win others by the quality of her life and the willingness to submit herself to others?

Listen to the testimony of Augustine about his mother, Monica: "When she came to marriageable age, she was bestowed upon a husband and served him as her lord, and she did all she could to win him to Thee, speaking to him of Thee by her deportment, whereby Thou madest her beautiful and reverently lovable and admirable to her husband. . . . Finally, when her husband was now at the very end of his earthly life she won him unto Thee."

II. The witnessing woman adopts a practice.

The burden of this passage has to do with the conduct and the character of the Christian woman. By these twin approaches, conduct and character, she adopts a practice that attracts people to Christ.

A. *Conduct.* "They may be won over without words by the behavior of their wives." Their very conduct will point to Christ.

B. *Character.* Character is emphasized. What makes a woman attractive? In the end it is character. Christlike character attracts people to Christ.

III. The witnessing woman avows a purpose.

A. *The purpose is to make the home Christian.* Sam Shoemaker once observed that a Christian home is not one in which the relationships are perfect. Rather, it is one in which the imperfections and failures are acknowledged and where problems are worked out in prayer and obedience to the light God sends.

B. *The purpose is to make the home a base for Christian witness and a means for witness.*

Conclusion

The witnessing woman seeks to make Christ known to others. A mother has this opportunity to witness for Christ as she makes her home Christian.

SUNDAY EVENING, MAY 21

Title: Jesus Is Better

Text: "But the ministry Jesus has received is as superior to theirs as the covenant of which he is mediator is superior to the old one, and it is founded on better promises" *(Heb. 8:6 NIV).*

Scripture Reading: Hebrews 8:1–9:14

Introduction

One of the prominent words in the letter to the Hebrews is *superior.* The author compares Jesus Christ's character with the character of angels and Old Testament heroes and with the nature of the sacrificial system. He affirms, "Jesus is better." He is better than the prophets (1:1–4); he is better than the angels (1:5–2:18); he is better than Moses (chaps. 3–4); and Jesus' work on the cross is better than the Old Testament sacrificial system of the sanctuary (8:1–10:18).

I. Jesus is better than the old sanctuary.

The author of Hebrews starts (in 8:1) to use figures from Jewish worship. He begins with the sanctuary of the tabernacle and the temple. He acknowledges the great majesty and the great purpose of the sanctuary yet affirms that Jesus is better.

A. *Jesus is the reality behind the shadow.* The tabernacle and the temple were constructed according to a great architectural plan. The design of the temple had significance in the worship of God.

We must keep in mind that the tabernacle and the temple represented a greater reality. "They serve at a sanctuary that is a copy and shadow of what is in heaven. This is why Moses was warned when he was about to build the tabernacle: 'See to it that you make everything according to the pattern shown you on the mountain'" (Heb. 8:5 NIV). The writer of Hebrews says the layout of the sanctuary and the ministries conducted there were designed according to the real but unseen world.

B. *Jesus is the remover of barriers.* In the temple and the tabernacle the ordinary Israelite could come only to the gate of the tabernacle court. The priests could go farther, and only the high priest could go into the Holy of Holies. This hierarchy of barriers portrays the reality that ordinary people were barred from the presence of God. Jesus took away the barriers. He is a better sanctuary.

II. Jesus is better than the old priesthood.

The author of Hebrews chooses another factor in the Jewish religion. Not only is Jesus seen as superior to the sanctuary, but he is also shown to be better than the Old Testament priesthood.

A. *Jesus is the master in majesty.* No one can compare to the majestic character of Jesus. Jesus belongs to a priesthood founded on personal greatness rather than human appointment. He is a priest who offers sacrifice for sins, but he does not have to offer sacrifice for his sins, for he has none. Only Jesus is able to offer a sacrifice that never has to be repeated. "We do have such a high priest, who sat down at the right hand of the throne of the Majesty in heaven" (Heb. 8:1 NIV). There is no greater glory than the glory of the ascended and exalted Lord. Jesus, the priest, possesses the majesty of God.

B. *Jesus is the master in ministry.* No priest can perform the priestly ministry better than Jesus "who serves in the sanctuary, the true tabernacle set up by the Lord, not by man" (Heb. 8:2 NIV). "The ministry Jesus has received is as superior to theirs as the covenant of which he is mediator is superior to the old one" (v. 6 NIV). Many priests of the Old Testament rendered their service with great skill. But when you examine the priestly ministry of Jesus, you discover a superiority. Jesus is better than the Old Testament priesthood.

III. Jesus is better than the old covenant.

After discussing the Old Testament sanctuary and priesthood, the author then turns to the Old Testament concept of covenant. The covenant described the relationship of God with his people. The author affirms that God's relationship with people through Jesus is better than the old covenant.

A. *Jesus brought a covenant that every person on earth could enjoy.* The Jews developed classes of people. Some of these classes, such as the Pharisees, were observers of the law and could keep the details of the law. Most of the ordinary people could not observe all the ceremonial laws. Consequently, the common people were despised. But in Hebrews we read, "They will all know me, from the least of them to the greatest" (Heb. 8:11 NIV).

In the new covenant in Jesus, classes of people do not exist. All people—wise and simple, small and great—can relate to the Lord. The new covenant in Jesus is better because of its universality.

B. *Jesus brought a covenant that is written on the heart.* "I will put my laws in their minds and write them on their hearts. I will be their God, and they will be my people" (Heb. 8:10 NIV). The law written on the heart means that people would relate to God, not just laws. People would obey the Lord not because of the dictates of the law but because of their desire to obey him. Jesus is better, for he indeed brought a better covenant.

IV. Jesus is better than the old sacrifices.

The author continues with his comparisons of Jesus with Judaism. He turns to the Old Testament sacrificial system and proceeds to show that Jesus is better.

A. *The sacrifice of Jesus is an unrepeatable sacrifice.* The priests had to make many sacrifices on many different days. The most significant sacrifice took place the day the high priest had to enter the Holy of Holies and make atonement for the sins of the people. All the sacrifices had to be repeated each year. There was no final sacrifice until Jesus came.

When Jesus sacrificed himself, he made the final sacrifice for sin. No other sacrifice was needed. This element of finality proves further that Jesus is better.

B. *The sacrifice of Jesus is a more effective sacrifice.* The superiority of Jesus' sacrifice may be seen in its effects. "How much more, then, will the blood of Christ, who through the eternal Spirit offered himself unblemished to God, cleanse our consciences from acts that lead to death, so that we may serve the living God!" (Heb. 9:14 NIV). Jesus' sacrifice cleanses the conscience of a person. It releases one from the slavery of sin to become a servant of the living God. The animal sacrifices could not change a person's heart. For this reason, Jesus' sacrifice was better.

Conclusion

Many religions exist in today's world. Take the time to look at Jesus. You will discover that Jesus is better. Give your life to someone superior.

WEDNESDAY EVENING, MAY 24

Title: God's Part in Temptation

Text: "But each one is tempted when he is carried away and enticed by his own lust" *(James 1:14 NASB).*

Scripture Reading: James 1:13–18

Introduction

One of the funniest TV comedians—yet with the saddest message—was Flip Wilson. Flip became known for the quote "The devil made me do it." Regardless of Flip's wrongdoings in any of his skits, it seemed always to have been the Devil's fault.

While that is not totally false, it is not totally true either. The big problem with such a belief is that people can too easily blame someone else and avoid their own responsibility in sin. That's dangerous. Only one attitude could be worse than blaming the Devil—blaming God. James deals with both options in our text.

I. God is not responsible for evil.

A. *People are naturally inclined to shift the blame for their shortcomings to someone, and God always seems to be available.* Actually there is no better option from the perspective that if we can make God do wrong, then surely our wrongdoing will give us less guilt. After God charged Adam with committing the first sin, Adam responded, "The woman *whom thou gavest to be with me*, she gave me of the tree, and I did eat" (Gen. 3:12).

    James, however, says that because of God's very nature, he cannot tempt people to do wrong.

B. *God is completely free of sin.* God is also perfectly holy. That puts God beyond the reach of temptation. In God there is no weakness for temptation to grasp.

II. Sin begins in the human heart.

A. *In figurative language, James declares in verses 14 and 15 that temptation to evil comes from elements that have their roots in the human heart.* The words "drawn away" and "enticed" are taken from the language of fishing. The imagery is that of a fish swimming in a straight course and then drawn off toward something attractive, only to discover that with the bait is a deadly hook. By this expression James rejects all attempts to shift the blame for the wrongdoing from ourselves to outward circumstances or biases or persons.

B. *James makes no reference to Satan in his discussion of temptation.* Two considerations may explain this.

   1. His intention was not to give a technical instruction on the origin of sin but only to show how enticement could *not* come from God.

   2. He also stresses that the inward nature of temptation precludes people from excusing their sins. God is not to be blamed. Even Satan is not wholly to be blamed. Sin is ours.

III. God is the source of all good (vv. 17–18).

A. *James's corollary is that God is the source of all good.* God gives every good thing and every perfect gift. Probably the two phrases are synonymous here and used for emphasis. These good gifts come down to us from the "Father of lights."

B. *God, in contrast to those things that seem to be most stable, is unchanging and unchangeable.* God's will is not shown by enticing people to evil, but by bestowing on them that which is very good—even to the benefit of a new birth.

Conclusion

    There once lived in Dundee, Scotland, a man who had fallen and broken his back as a boy of fifteen. For forty years he lay in bed and moved only with the most terrible pain. One day a visitor asked him, "Doesn't Satan ever tempt you to doubt God?"

    "Oh, yes," he answered, "he does try to tempt me. I lie here and see my old schoolmates driving by in their carriages and Satan whispers, "If God is so good, why does he keep you here all these years?"

When his visitor asked, "What do you do when Satan tempts you?" he replied, "Oh, I take him to Calvary and show him Christ and point to the deep wounds and say, 'Doesn't God love me?' And the fact is that Satan got such a scare there 1,900 years ago that he cannot stand to be reminded of Calvary; he flees from me every time." That bedridden saint had little trouble with temptation, for he was too full of God's good gift—Jesus Christ.

SUNDAY MORNING, MAY 28

Title: The News We Want to Hear

Text: "Is the young man Absalom safe? . . . And the king was much moved, and went up to the chamber over the gate, and wept: and as he went, thus he said, 'O my son Absalom, my son, my son Absalom! Would God I had died for thee, O Absalom, my son, my son!'" *(2 Sam. 18:32–33).*

Scripture Reading: 2 Samuel 18:1–5, 24–33

Hymns: "O Master, Let Me Walk with Thee," Everest

   "O Love That Wilt Not Let Me Go," Matheson

   "Near to the Heart of God," McAfee

Offertory Prayer: Dear Lord, we are overwhelmed by your love. Everywhere we turn we are confronted with reminders of it. Your love truly will not let us go. All of our attempts to express our love to you seem to fall so short. We are imperfect in our lives, imprecise in our commitment, and impervious to your call. But one thing we can do is to express our love by practicing our stewardship. O Lord, this day help us to remember your love for us as we return to you our offerings. All that we have comes from your hand. Freely you have given to us. Freely we give to you. Strengthen us in our love, guide us in our stewardship, and forgive us our sins, we pray. In Jesus' name. Amen.

Introduction

Does your television station carry the public service announcement that asks, "It's ten o'clock. Do you know where your children are?"

That is a good question. Periodically parents should stop and ask themselves that question. The most obvious meaning of that question is, "Do I know where my children are physically, where they are right this moment?" But the application could, and should, be carried further: "Do I know where my children are intellectually, morally, spiritually?" The one overriding question that comes into our minds is, "Is it well with my child?" And the news we want to hear is that all is well.

King David once asked that question. His army was fighting for the life of his nation, but he was concerned about his boy. David was not interested in hearing reports of battles or the disposition of enemies. All he wanted to hear was news of his son Absalom. Absalom was the son who had rebelled against David and led the army in opposition to him. Despite that, the news that David still wanted to hear was that all was well with his son.

As we join with King David in wanting to hear that same news about our children, we become aware that there are some things that can help us hear the news we want to hear.

I. Contact helps us to hear the news we want to hear.

A. *Contact with our children is essential.* David had lost contact with his son Absalom. One of the results was the rebellion of Absalom against his father.

Actually, the seeds of rebellion had been planted years before. Absalom had killed Ammon, his half brother, in revenge and had fled the land. Later he returned and stayed in Jerusalem for two years before he saw his father. During all this time he was laying the groundwork for revolt.

Although this incident is extreme, it still shows us the necessity of maintaining contact with our children. We must maintain regular contact if love and trust are to be built.

B. *Contact with our children is worth the effort.* David obviously knew that Absalom was in Jerusalem; surely his military intelligence system was that efficient. But apparently David did not make the effort to establish contact with his son. He could have and should have.

Sacrificing for your children has great benefits. One man felt so strongly about time with his son that he resigned the vice presidency of a large corporation to be with his son. The father reasoned that the years that the boy would grow and the father could spend with him were limited. He could get other jobs; he only had one son. He felt the contact was worth the sacrifice. This was his priority.

II. Communication helps us to hear the news we want to hear.

There was no communication between David and Absalom. When communication did occur, it was strictly confrontational. Here are some guidelines for effective communication that will help parents.

A. *Tell them that you care.* A sociologist once interviewed some teenagers regarding their impressions of their homes and their parents. He discovered that those who had been brought up permissively were not grateful for it. One girl told the interviewer that she lived in an apartment in a big city. After supper in the summer, the children on the block gathered in the streets to play. But after a while one child would say that she had to go home because her mother had told her to be in before eight o'clock. Or a father would whistle and a boy would have to leave. Another mother would call, and others would have to go. The girl said that they would all go. It would get dark and she would be there all alone waiting for her parents to call her in, but they never did.

B. *Listen to what they have to say.* It is hard for a parent to listen. We always want to be talking. But listen, really listen, to what the children have to say to you.

C. *Give them credibility.* Children may actually know some things that their parents don't know. Particularly this is true of their own feelings. They know how they feel and why they feel that way. The parents should be open to listen to this. Parents also need to listen to their children's perceptions. By listening, a parent can learn the perception a child has of an incident or practice, and it may be totally different from what the parent thinks he or she is expressing.

D. *Communication is a two-way street.* The parent may know something too. Each should listen to the other. Each should express himself or herself to the other.

III. Concern is a way to hear the news we want to hear.

A. *Parents should be concerned about their children.* David was concerned about his son Absalom. Other parents are also concerned about their children. But the concern may be expressed in wrong ways. It may come across as meddling, commanding, or living in anxiety. Concern should be expressed for all points of the child's life, not just the incidental things.

B. *Concern can be expressed too late.* David was concerned about Absalom, but he expressed his concern too late. After the damage had already been done, after the rebellion had already gotten under way, David expressed his concern.

C. *Concern should be focused.* In the end, David focused his concern. He became willing to die for his son. When it mattered, however, he would not share time with his son, even though in the end he was willing to die for him.

Conclusion

What is the news that you want to hear concerning your children? It is the same news that David wanted: to know that it was well with his son. It is possible for us to hear that news as we do some positive things to strengthen our relationships with our children. With God's help we can build better relationships.

SUNDAY EVENING, MAY 28

Title: The Supreme Sacrifice

Text: "And by that will, we have been made holy through the sacrifice of the body of Jesus Christ once for all" *(Heb. 10:10 NIV).*

Scripture Reading: Hebrews 9:23–10:18

Introduction

Hymn writer Robert Lowry asked a probing question and gave an assured answer when he wrote:

> *What can wash away my sin?*
> *Nothing but the blood of Jesus;*
> *What can make me whole again?*
> *Nothing but the blood of Jesus.*

With these words we celebrate the fact that Jesus made the supreme sacrifice for sin.

The author of Hebrews acknowledges that Jesus has made the only true sacrifice for sin. It is the supreme sacrifice. No other offering for sin can begin to compare with Jesus' offering of his life for the sins of the world.

The world searches for cleansing. People observe all kinds of religious rituals to be clean and obey all kinds of religious rules in an effort to be right with God. They give time, money, and other items searching for that which will make them right with God. No sacrifice other than Jesus' atoning work can cleanse from sin and create a right standing with God. Let us examine Jesus' supreme sacrifice for sin.

I. Jesus' sacrifice is unrepeatable.

A. *The Old Testament priests had to repeat sacrifices continually.* Year after year the priests made sacrifices for the people. And once a year on the Day of Atonement the high priest had to offer sacrifice. The very fact that the sacrifices had to be repeated furnished proof that they were not ultimate sacrifices. There was a kind of priestly treadmill of sacrifice: there was no end.

B. *Jesus made a sacrifice that never has to be repeated.* "But when this priest had offered for all time one sacrifice for sins, he sat down at the right hand of God" (Heb. 10:12 NIV). There is no need for any other sacrifice. The life and death of Jesus was one act of perfect obedience, and therefore it was the only perfect sacrifice. Perfection cannot be improved. Therefore the sacrifice of Jesus cannot and need not ever be made again.

II. Jesus' sacrifice is incomparable.

A. *The Old Testament sacrifices reminded the people of their sins.* "Day after day every priest stands and performs his religious duties; again and again he offers the same sacrifices, which can never take away sins" (Heb. 10:11 NIV) shows that the Old Testament could only remind people of their sins. Each sacrifice the priest made was a reminder that both the priests and the people were sinners. "But those sacrifices are an annual reminder of sins" (v. 3 NIV).

No Old Testament writer ever affirmed that the sacrifices were perfect purifications from sin. They realized that the sacrifices looked toward a greater reality, the purification accomplished through Jesus Christ. When Jesus came, he made the better sacrifice. "It is impossible for the blood of bulls and goats to take away sins" (Heb. 10:4 NIV).

B. *Jesus' sacrifice removes sins from people.* "Because by one sacrifice he has made perfect forever those who are being made holy" (Heb. 10:14 NIV). The Old Testament sacrifices cannot begin to compare with the sacrifice of Jesus. He made the supreme sacrifice whereby a person may find removal of sin's guilt, sin's power, and ultimately sin's presence. Nothing compares to Jesus' sacrifice.

III. Jesus' sacrifice is costly.

A. *The Old Testament sacrifices cost the lives of animals.* Countless numbers of lambs were slain in the Old Testament sacrificial system. Every day in the temple a year-old male lamb had to be sacrificed as a burnt offering. Along with the burnt offering there was a meat offering and a drink offering. Sacrifices became a costly operation to the temple.

B. *Jesus' sacrifice was the ultimate cost.* "Then Christ would have had to suffer many times since the creation of the world. But now he has appeared once for all at the end of the ages to do away with sin by the sacrifice of himself" (Heb. 9:26 NIV). Think of all the sacrifices Jesus made to help people. He had to leave heaven where he was worshiped to come to earth where he was despised. He made the supreme sacrifice when he gave his life on the cross. No other sacrifice has been as costly.

IV. Jesus' sacrifice is effectual.

A. *The Old Testament sacrifice intended to make people holy.* God wanted his people to be holy. The temple and its sacrificial system was a means of teaching and exhorting people to greater holiness. But the blood of lambs could not change people. Jesus came to give the sacrifice that could change the lives of people and make them holy.

B. *Jesus' sacrifice has the power to make people holy.* "Because by one sacrifice he has made perfect forever those who are being made holy" (Heb. 10:14 NIV). The phrase "made holy" could refer to the process working in the lives of believers. God is at work in the lives of his people, making them different. That is to say, the one who sacrificed his life also lives within believers, allowing them to live a Christlike life.

Conclusion

Maybe you are asking, "What can wash away my sins? What can make me whole again?" People ask those questions because sin is a great burden. Listen to the testimony of people who have found the answer to those questions: "Nothing but the blood of Jesus." Join the celebration:

> *Oh! precious is the flow*
> *That makes me white as snow;*
> *No other fount I know,*
> *Nothing but the blood of Jesus.*

WEDNESDAY EVENING, MAY 31

Title: I Believe the Bible

Text: "But prove yourselves doers of the word, and not merely hearers who delude themselves" *(James 1:22 NASB).*

Scripture Reading: James 1:19–27

Introduction

At a large dinner party in New York, several well-known celebrities were gathered. At one end of the long table, a wealthy woman sat next to a famous scientist. During their conversation the woman, as was her habit, remarked, "The Bible says so and so."

The scientist drew back in shock and said, "The Bible? You don't believe the Bible, do you?"

"Yes. Indeed I do," said the woman.

The scientist laughed and chided her by saying, "Why I didn't suppose that any intelligent person today believed the Bible."

"Oh, yes," said the lady. "You see I know the Author."

The scientist was silenced with her remark.

We will stand either for or against the Bible. We first must be sure that our approach to the Bible follows God's directives.

I. We must hear God's Word (vv. 19–20).

A. *God's Word demands our attention.* The thought seems to be that those who have received so freely of God's goodness and especially those who have been regenerated by the Word of God ought to conduct themselves in the manner described in James 1:19–27. It is this same Word that provided life and rebirth that now deserves to be heard. It is the Word of God—not merely the word of man.

B. *The Bible is like a telescope.* If we look *through* a telescope, we see worlds beyond; if we look *at* the telescope, we do not see anything but that. The Bible is a thing to be looked through to see that which is beyond. Most people only look at it, and so they see a dead letter.

C. *Many people have not given the Bible a chance because they have not heard its message.* They have no idea of what it contains.

One little girl was asked by a pastor who visited her home, "What's in your Bible?" The little girl answered honestly, "A lot of birthdays and dates of weddings and deaths, a lock of hair, some clippings from old newspapers, some photos, and two valentines."

If we believe God's Word is God's Word, then it's time we hear it as God's Word. That's the first step to receiving it.

II. We must receive God's Word (v. 21).

A. *Receiving God's Word intimately requires a great deal of faith.* Faith is described by Jesus as a mustard seed that grows. Here James alludes to the same comparison.
B. *We have a duty to receive God's Word.* We must peel off the filth that would hinder its growth. God's Word loses its roots when we are more faithful to preconceived notions, traditions, and social ethics.

III. We must practice God's Word (vv. 22–27).

We have had a conversion experience—but that is only the beginning. Too many see it as the ultimate end. Here again in verses 22–27 James presents us with two pictures of people.

A. *First he speaks of the man who goes to church, listens to the reading and expounding of the Word, and thinks that listening has made him a good Christian.*
B. *A second picture is of a man before a mirror.* He looks, he sees smudges on his face, messy hair, and buttons unbuttoned—but chooses to do nothing about it. Listening to and receiving God's Word shows the smudges. If he hears and does not do, his hearing is for nothing.

Conclusion

The Bible is life's greatest resource to us. It holds the best advice for our homes, business dealings, church, worship, parenting, economics, politics—in short, it is advice for all phases of life. It's God's holy Word. Because it is God's Word, it demands practice.

JUNE

■ **Sunday Mornings**

Continue the series "Enriching Marriage and Family Relationships."

■ **Sunday Evenings**

Continue the series "The Superlative Christ" based on the book of Hebrews.

■ **Wednesday Evenings**

Continue the series "The Practice of Genuine Religion" based on the book of James.

SUNDAY MORNING, JUNE 4

Title: Living in a Haunted House

Text: "'Then [the evil spirit] goes and takes with it seven other spirits more wicked than itself, and they go in and live there. And the final condition of that man is worse than the first. That is how it will be with this wicked generation'" *(Matt. 12:45 NIV).*

Scripture Reading: Matthew 12:43–45

Hymns: "Jesus Is Lord of All," McClard

"O God in Heaven, Whose Loving Plan," Martin

"I Need Thee Every Hour," Hawks

Offertory Prayer: Our Father, bless this day and its activities. Bring us close to you in a spirit of love. Help us find security and strength through your Spirit in this service of worship. We give to you an offering. We pray that you would accept it, bless it, and use it for your work throughout the world as well as in this community. We thank you for the strength that allowed us to earn the money and the love that prompts us to give the money. Continue to work within our lives to make your will known and our hearts receptive to it. We pray in Jesus' name and for his sake. Amen.

Introduction

Many of you have probably visited the Haunted Mansion at Disneyland or Disney World. At one place the trolley passes a mirror, and as you and your fellow rider look into the mirror, you are startled to discover that another ghostly occupant is sitting between you.

Or maybe you had a "haunted house" in the neighborhood you lived in as a child. It seems that every community has an old, abandoned house about which scary stories are told.

Jesus told an interesting parable about a haunted house. The application of the parable focused on good and evil. If you want to reform, it is not enough to rid yourself of evil; you must also fill yourself with goodness. Otherwise, the evil will not only come back but will increase. Using the house metaphor, then, we see it is not enough to empty the house of evil, for then it will be haunted. We must pack the house to the rafters with God. That is the way to destroy haunted houses. But how many of us are living in haunted houses even now?

Many of us are. It's a sad truth but a truth nonetheless. Our individual lives and our family lives are empty. So let us take this parable of Jesus and apply it to ourselves and to our families.

What exactly does it mean to live in a haunted house?

I. You live in a haunted house when you try to be neutral about religion.

A. *There is no neutrality in life.* This parable teaches that there is no neutrality in life. The evil spirit was driven out, but nothing else was added. Empty houses never remain empty. Dust and cobwebs gather in the corners and mice and rats move in.

B. *Particularly, there is no neutrality about faith.* We sometimes hear about people who try to be neutral about religion. They do not want to force their children to go to church. They do not want to influence them toward any particular expression of faith. Usually this is accompanied by a story of how they were forced to go to church when they were young and how they reacted against it. Of course, this approach actually turns children against the church and God. It is an undisciplined, godless life. There is no neutrality when it comes to faith: either one accepts and serves God or rejects and opposes God.

Some years ago the New York City Youth Board did a study related to juvenile crime. They sent experts into the homes of five hundred six-year-old boys. These social workers and psychologists tried to make an estimate of the potential of each of these young people. The basis for their estimate was the quality of family life in the home, the style of supervision, attendance at church services and other religious training, and the type of discipline used.

The children from homes deficient in each of these areas were forecast as potential delinquents. The children from homes with good parental attention and basic religious training were forecast as potential good citizens.

The records of these children were then watched for ten years. The experts found that by the time the children without supervisory structure from the parents and church had reached sixteen years of age, 85 percent of them were in serious trouble with the authorities, many of them repeat offenders. On the other hand, 95 percent of the children from the homes that provided training and discipline and religious life could be described as good citizens. The predictive value of this variable is utterly amazing.

II. You live in a haunted house when you are negative in spirit.

A. *Some goodness is only a negative goodness.* The house of which Jesus spoke was only negatively good. The evil spirit had been swept out, but nothing good had replaced it. Many people practice a negative goodness. It consists only of the command "Do not." The Pharisees were "good," but they were not doing anything positive to bring about goodness.

    1. Look for good in attitude. What has been said and done positively in your home this week? The one thing children need from their parents is love. Is love the overriding attitude toward your children? Have you—particularly you fathers—given your children enough time to let them see your attitudes?

    2. Look for good in the home. What has been emphasized in your home? Some homes emphasize only what a person *is not* and what that person *has not* done. How about putting a positive emphasis on what the person *is* and what he or she *has* done?

B. *Much can be accomplished by a positive goodness.* The positive goodness that gives a positive witness can accomplish much. A boy on a cross-country motorcycle trip returned home to tell his parents that his most impressive experience was the night he had spent in a country home in the Midwest. Caught in a rainstorm, he had stopped at the farmhouse to ask if he could spend the night in the barn. Instead, they invited him to spend the night with them. At the breakfast table the next morning, the family read the Bible together and prayed for him by name. That positive witness was the most impressive experience of his trip across the nation.

III. You live in a haunted house when your life is empty.

A. *Houses, while filled, can still be empty.* The life Jesus mentioned in the parable was empty, terribly empty. A lot of houses that are filled with fine furniture—costly antiques, matched sets, color-coordinated rooms—can be terribly empty. They can be empty of love, mutual concern, kindness, Christian teaching, acceptance, trust, and confidence. This is the worst kind of emptiness.

B. *A home, or a life, without Christ is hopelessly empty.* Mrs. Ethel du Pont Warren was once described by artist Dan Flowers as the most beautiful and eligible woman in the United States. As the oldest child of Eugene du Pont, she was the heiress of one of the world's largest fortunes. Her subsequent marriage to Franklin D. Roosevelt Jr. was one of the great society events of the century. However, by the age of forty-nine, she hanged herself from the bathroom shower fixture by the belt of her bathrobe. Beauty, fame, fortune, social prestige, and everything else did not meet the longing of her heart. A life without Christ is empty, hopelessly empty.

Conclusion

We have been talking about empty, haunted houses. Is there any way to change? The answer is to fill life with something positive. The ultimate positive element is Christ. We need to fill our houses with Christ and seek his will as a family.

SUNDAY EVENING, JUNE 4

Title: Challenge to Discipleship

Text: "Let us hold unswervingly to the hope we profess, for he who promised is faithful" *(Heb. 10:23 NIV).*

Scripture Reading: Hebrews 10:19–39

Introduction

Guy H. King, in a provocative book entitled *A Belief That Behaves: An Expositional Study of the Epistle of James,* quoted an old preacher: "My brethren, there are two sides to the Gospel; there's the believing side, and there's the behaving side." These are two important sides of the gospel.

The New Testament epistles commonly consist of two parts—the doctrinal and the practical. The first sets forth Christian truth. The second applies the truth to life. In the opening chapters of Hebrews, there is the believing side of the doctrine of the atoning work of Christ under the types of the Old Testament priesthood (1:1–10:18). The closing chapters of Hebrews contain challenges to discipleship. The challenges were given by the author to those who had accepted the salvation provided by Christ. Let us notice these challenges so that we may see how God's people are to behave in reference to the gospel.

I. The challenge for worship.

Notice the challenge for worship. "Let us draw near to God with a sincere heart in full assurance of faith, having our hearts sprinkled to cleanse us from a guilty conscience and having our bodies washed with pure water" (Heb. 10:22 NIV). The challenge "Let us draw near" refers to the believer's worship.

A.   *The basis of the believer's worship. Christians respond to Jesus because of what he has done for them.* Two primary actions of the Master are described. First, there is the action of sprinkling hearts "from a guilty conscience." This refers to Christ's cleansing the person's attitudes. Second, there is the action of washing bodies "with pure water." This expression refers to Christ's cleansing the person's actions. Christ has done a marvelous work for his people. Because of who Christ is and what he has done, he is worthy of worship.

B.   *The response of the believer's worship.* In view of what Christ has done by his atoning death and by his transforming power, Christians are exhorted to draw near to God. The expression "draw near" means to get close to the Lord in worship and in service. When a Christian thinks of what Christ has done, the response is to adore and thank Jesus Christ for his marvelous work.

II. The challenge to keep the faith.

Another challenge came for the believer's orthodoxy: "Let us hold unswervingly to the hope we profess, for he who promised is faithful" (Heb. 10:23 NIV).

The challenge "Let us hold unswervingly" refers to the spirit of the believers. In the midst of antagonism, they needed to hold fast. They needed to keep the faith.

A. *The threat to a believer's faith.* Judging by the author's words in Hebrews 10, various matters threatened the believer's faith. Evidently myriad teachings and actions bombarded the believers. In the face of all these mysteries, discouragements, doubts, ridicule, and unbelief, times were tough. The mocking and cynical voices were trying to eradicate the believers' faith. Some were wavering.

B. *The disclosure of the believer's hope.* The author speaks of the believer's hope. In light of the hope of better times, Christians were exhorted to endure. The Christian hope is not wishful thinking. Union with God is a fixed reality. Because of this, believers have a real reason to persevere even in difficult times.

III. The challenge of togetherness.

A third challenge the writer gave to the Hebrew Christians was to encourage one another: "Let us consider how we may spur one another on toward love and good deeds" (Heb. 10:24 NIV).

A. *The promotion of fellowship.* One of the great truths of Christianity is that Christians belong to each other. "Let us consider how we may spur one another on." They are brothers and sisters in the same family, partners in the same mission, and members of the same household.

Not only should Christians consider the reality that they belong to one another, but they need "to spur one another on toward love and good deeds." Christians need to watch over each other in the same way committed family members look after each other.

B. *The regularity of worship.* The author of Hebrews acknowledged that regular attendance at worship was an opportunity for togetherness. "Let us not give up meeting together, as some are in the habit of doing, but let us encourage one another—and all the more as you see the Day approaching" (Heb. 10:25 NIV). The meeting of believers affords times of mutual help in "exhorting one another." Being a Christian means living in unity with God's people.

IV. The challenge of hope.

Beginning in Hebrews 10:19, the author gives one challenge after another. We have looked at three challenges. Now we will look at still another—the challenge to hope in the future. "So do not throw away your confidence; it will be richly rewarded" (Heb. 10:35 NIV).

A. *The hope of the Lord's return.* The basis for the Christian's optimism about the future is the Lord's return. The author of Hebrews gives the guarantee of the Lord's return. "For in just a very little while, 'He who is coming will come and will not delay'" (Heb. 10:37 NIV). Other New Testament writers viewed the Lord's coming as an imminent matter. It was to be close at hand. The Lord's return should always be regarded as being near. The Lord's promise to return should challenge God's people to remain faithful to his commands and to his mission.

158

B.   *The Christian's response to the Lord's return.* In light of the promise of the Lord's return, the Christian can make various responses. One response is not to relinquish the idea of reward: "Do not throw away your confidence; it will be richly rewarded" (Heb. 10:35 NIV). Another response is to exercise patience: "You need to persevere" (v. 36 NIV). A third response is to continue to live by faith: "My righteous one will live by faith" (v. 38 NIV). One who gives up does not please the Lord. The challenge to discipleship is one of confident hope.

Conclusion

Whenever we see a "therefore" in the New Testament, we ought to examine what it is "there for." In Hebrews 10:19, the first verse of our Scripture reading for this evening, the writer says, "Therefore, brothers...," referring to the work Christ has done to make a way for believers to draw near to God. He then proceeds to challenge believers to commitment. Why are *you* a Christian? You are a Christian to follow the Christ. Follow him!

WEDNESDAY EVENING, JUNE 7

Title: The Problems with Partiality

Text: "If you show favoritism, you sin and are convicted by the law as lawbreakers" *(James 2:9 NIV).*

Scripture Reading: James 2:1–13

Introduction

James's concept of partiality is a snobbery and favoritism always predicated on exterior conditions. No matter what the expression of favoritism, favoritism is always wrong. Conceivably it could be done by giving preference to the poor over the rich since the predominance of people in the early church were poor. But this is not what James had in mind. His readers were not being tempted to distrust and dislike the rich but were in fact courting their favor by showing partiality to them.

I. Partiality is contrary to faith in Christ (vv. 1–4).

A.   *James's readers were their own examples of this sin.* James shows them a "home movie" of themselves so they can see their own faults.

B.   *Let's examine the situation he outlines.* He says hypothetically, "Suppose a man comes into your meeting wearing a gold ring and fine clothes" (v. 2 NIV), yet he knows that such a man does, in fact, come. The assembly mentioned here is the gathering of the church. The word "your" identifies this meeting as a Christian one. This man's fine jewelry and clothing indicate that he is obviously wealthy in contrast to the majority of churchgoers wearing plain clothing.

C.   *The greatest contrast, however, is not the man's clothing but how he is treated by the believers in the church.* James delineates how the believers' attitudes contrast with the fundamentals of their faith. Their arbitrary show of respect and disdain was reprehensible. It is even more distinct when we realize that the word for "respect" (NIV, "special attention") in verse 3 is the same word for the esteem God had for Mary in Luke 1:48, indicating his profound affection in selecting her to be the mother of Jesus. The contrast of attitudes toward the rich and the poor is further reflected by those assembled offering the rich man a seat yet telling the poor man to stand or sit at their feet.

D. *Their behavior belied their faith in Jesus.* They set themselves up as judges according to the worldly standards by which they would themselves never want to be judged.

II. Partiality is contrary to God's purpose.

A. *Partiality defies God's will.* Look closely at verse 5 for this truth. God's choice is not limited to the poor, nor have all the poor necessarily been chosen. But Jesus elaborates in verse 5 why the poor have dignity. He writes:
   1. They are chosen by God.
   2. They are the rich in faith.
   3. They are heirs of the kingdom.

B. *If anyone deserves our special attention, it is the poor.* If anyone deserves our concern and outreach, it is the poor. If anyone deserves our generosity and ministry, it is the poor—they are the specially chosen people of God.

III. Partiality is not in the best interests of Christians.

A. *Now it would seem that favoring the rich would be an astute maneuver from a practical standpoint, doesn't it?* After all, can't they tithe more? Don't they have a stronger power base in the community? Possibly so. Wealthy people, however, can also be the biggest problem for a church.

B. *A pastor recently related the dynamics of his church.* Their weekly receipts were astonishingly high. Despite the financial security, he said, "I'd trade these finances any day for a church that was struggling financially but trusting in God as they did so." He went on to say that in his church were a few men who are so wealthy that they believed they owned the church—and therefore tried to run it.

IV. Partiality is a violation of the law of love (vv. 8–13).

A. *The main point is that partiality violates the law of love.* The Golden Rule is to love our neighbor as ourselves whether our neighbor is wealthy or poor.

B. *It must be conceded that James is in no way suggesting that the wealthy man be ignored.* But deference to him at the expense of the poor violates the law of love also.

Conclusion

Prejudice is a problem. Although racial prejudice has been a primary focus in the United States throughout our history, other prejudices are thriving and are equally heinous. There may be a bigotry based on economic status, educational status, appearance, vocation, or gender, to name a few. They all are wrong! Yet the heart of the believer is not exempt from any of them.

A blind man, an adulterous woman, and a man with a withered hand were brought before Jesus by, or in the presence of, the Pharisees. The Pharisees looked at these underprivileged people as opportunities to exalt themselves. Jesus saw them as opportunities for ministry. The difference was in the heart of the viewer. This is where the problem of partiality must be solved. Let us ask Christ to change our hearts now.

SUNDAY MORNING, JUNE 11

Title: What Is the Foundation of Your Home?

Text: "Therefore whosoever heareth these sayings of mine, and doeth them, I will liken him unto a wise man, which built his house upon a rock: and the rain descended, and the floods came, and the winds blew, and beat upon that house; and it fell not: for it was founded upon a rock" *(Matt. 7:24–25)*.

Scripture Reading: Matthew 7:24–27

Hymns: "When We Walk with the Lord," Sammis

            "The Solid Rock," Mote

            "O the Deep, Deep Love of Jesus," Francis

Offertory Prayer: Dear Father, for your manifold blessings we are grateful. For the new life that you have given us in Jesus Christ we are thankful. For the opportunities of service afforded each one of us we are appreciative. For the gifts with which you have blessed us we thank you. Now to you we give back some of these material gifts. Use them for your glory. Magnify them with your Spirit. Multiply them with your power. And accept them with your grace. We ask these things in the name of Jesus Christ, your dear Son and our Savior. Amen.

Introduction

In the Pacific Palisades in California at the ocean's edge, it is common to see houses built on the top of high hills. It must be marvelous to live in one of those houses: each night one could watch the sun sizzle into the sea, spreading behind it a glittering path of gold. But some of the families who live in those houses have problems. Land has crumbled away from beneath the foundations and left the houses hanging perilously from hillsides. Because of that, many of the houses have had to be abandoned.

In the final sentences of the Sermon on the Mount, Jesus commented on two foundations for houses. This is simultaneously a conclusion to the Sermon on the Mount and a call to commitment to Christ. Ancient law codes often ended with a blessing or a curse. Jesus completed his sermon and called for a decision in these sentences.

Jesus elucidated that one place a person can build his house is on a rock. Because such a house has a strong base, it can stand up against any sort of violence. The other place a person can build a house is on the sand. Houses built on that foundation cannot hold up when winds and floods press against them. They are torn from their places, wind and water bouncing them about until they look like little mounds of toothpicks.

As we continue to think of the responsibilities before us in our Christian homes, one question comes to mind: On what are we building our homes?

I. We are faced with alternatives.

A. *Unsure, unsafe foundations.* One of the alternatives before us is to build a home on an unsure, unsafe foundation. Remember that Jesus was a carpenter. He knew how important the foundation was to the strength and security of a home. The tragedy of modern life is that so many homes are built on the wrong foundations. Such foundations as popular opinion, instant gratification, and worldly power are hardly foundations for strong homes. Or what is worse, some homes do not appear to be built on any foundation at all; they are just built.

Well over 20 percent of Americans move to a new residence each year. In some areas the telephone company disconnects 50 percent of the residents annually. With this kind of mobility, there must be some kind of stabilizing force for homes to be strong.

B. *Sure, safe foundations.* The stabilizing force necessary for strong homes that can withstand the pressures, is Christian faith. The greatest legacy a father could leave his family is a legacy of faith. That legacy will still continue when money has run out and stocks have lost their value.

II. We must face reality.

A. *The reality is that we will face troubles.* Did you notice that the Scriptures say that the rains descended, the floods came, and the winds blew? It does not say *if* the rains descended, the floods came, and the winds blew. The actuality is that those kinds of events will descend on every home at some time.

These troubles may come from many sources and they may bear many different names and faces. But the reality of life is that each one of us must face these times.

B. *How will you face them?* Since the actuality is that you will face trouble, trial, and difficulty at some time, the question before us is how you will face them. Where will you find the strength? What will your resources be for those times of trouble? I often tell young people when counseling them prior to marriage that they must have a reservoir of faith from which to draw when difficult times come. There is no question but that the times will come. And if we do not have that reservoir of faith beforehand, we will not have it when it is needed.

III. We can achieve.

A. *Achievement is possible.* The positive promise of this parable is that we *can* achieve. We *can* stand to face life. We *can* build our homes properly. When

Jesus offered the alternatives to us and set before us a choice, he was also assuring us that success was possible.

B. *Achievement depends on obedience to Christ.* Whether we build a stable home or an unsafe one depends on obedience to Jesus Christ. We can achieve stability with Christ as the foundation. When a family obeys Christ, when a family turns in faith to Christ, when a family acts on the teachings that Christ enunciated in the Sermon on the Mount, that family builds its home on the solid foundation.

C. *Faith makes the difference.* There is a marked difference in building a home on faith or floundering around in the world. Faith makes the difference between success and failure in the home. In his book *Fresh Every Morning*, Gerald Kennedy contrasts the difference faith made in the lives of two of his friends.

One friend was not a believer. His only son, a brilliant boy headed for a medical career, was killed at a railroad crossing on the way back to the university. With the son's death came the death of meaning in the father's life. He found it difficult to carry on his work. Whenever Kennedy would meet him and talk with him, no word could bring him healing.

Kennedy had another friend who was an active believer who suffered similarly when his daughter was killed in an automobile accident. But here was a difference: while his sorrow was deep, it did not overthrow his life. She was a Christian girl, and he spoke confidently of meeting her again. He published a little booklet giving excerpts from her letters and expressions of her faith. It showed the difference faith makes.

Conclusion

On what are you building your home? Every home is built on some foundation. The foundation that Christ offers through faith in him and obedience to his Word is the foundation that stands.

SUNDAY EVENING, JUNE 11

Title: The Faith of Our Father

Text: "By faith Abraham, when called to go to a place he would later receive as his inheritance, obeyed and went, even though he did not know where he was going" *(Heb. 11:8 NIV).*

Scripture Reading: Hebrews 11:8–19

Introduction

Christians have a great legacy when it comes to faith. In his inspiring chapter on faith, Hebrews 11, the writer begins by giving a succinct definition of faith (vv. 1–3). He says that faith is taking God at his word, and it is understanding many great mysteries. After defining faith, the author highlights Old Testament people who exercised faith (vv. 4–40). The author stresses that Christians are to live by faith. People before the first century lived in faith, and first-century believers should continue that legacy.

Although many examples could be chosen from Hebrews 11 for our consideration, we will examine the faith of Abraham. In the Old Testament, Abraham occupies the important place as the father of the race. Also, in the New Testament, Abraham is regarded as the father of those who have faith. Using Abraham's story, we may learn about what accompanies faith in the believer's life.

I. Obedience accompanies faith.

Abraham's life is summarized in three succinct statements: he obeyed God; he sojourned in the land of promise; and he offered his son as a sacrifice. Let us examine these three actions of faith. The first action is obedience.

A.   *The call of God.* "By faith Abraham, when called to go to a place he would later receive as his inheritance, obeyed and went, even though he did not know where he was going" (Heb. 11:8 NIV). God called Abraham to leave one land to go to another. He was to leave home, family, career, and business.

The Christian also has a call of God. It is the call from the Lord to put loyalty to Jesus Christ first. To follow the Lord, our old way of life must be forsaken. God's call is a demanding one and involves an exclusive relationship.

B.   *The response of faith.* The author of Hebrews summarized Abraham's response to God's call with one word: "obeyed" (Heb. 11:8). Then the author amplified the response of faith: "He . . . went, even though he did not know where he was going" (Heb. 11:8 NIV). Abraham responded to God by leaving Ur of the Chaldeans and plunging into the desert on the way to the place God wanted him to go.

Faith necessitates obedience. In the New Testament, faith is not found by itself. There are always verbs after the response of faith. Look in Hebrews 11: "By faith Abraham . . . obeyed"; "By faith Jacob . . . blessed"; "By faith Moses . . . refused." In every incident a verb follows faith. Faith is not simply a set of creeds. It is a response to the Lord that results in obedience.

II. Righteous submission accompanies faith.

In recounting Abraham's life, the author of Hebrews moves from Abraham's obeying God by leaving the land to his submitting to God on the way to the Promised Land. This stage in Abraham's life is captured with the sentence: "By faith he made his home in the promised land" (Heb. 11:9 NIV). This sentence helps us see that Abraham righteously submitted to God's guidance.

A.   *The necessity of submission.* "By faith he made his home in the promised land like a stranger in a foreign country; he lived in tents, as did Isaac and Jacob, who were heirs with him of the same promise" (Heb. 11:9 NIV). In following God's leadership, Abraham learned to go where God guided him. Previously Abraham had lived in a walled city, but God led him to Canaan and he had to live in tents. Abraham submitted to these circumstances.

Christians are pilgrims. Following the Lord's leadership involves adapting to diverse circumstances. Even if God's people are living in uncomfortable circumstances, God is still leading.

B. *The necessity of patience.* "By faith Abraham, even though he was past age—and Sarah herself was barren—was enabled to become a father because he considered him faithful who had made the promise" (Heb. 11:11 NIV). Abraham's faith was communicated to his wife Sarah. God promised them a son. But no son came, and the time of childbearing was past. Nonetheless, Abraham and Sarah continued to trust God's guidance.

Christians need not grow weary in submitting to God's guidance, for God's guidance is assured. God will always lead his people in a confident manner. Nor should Christians become impatient in following God. God leads his people in his time—not in theirs.

III. Sacrifice accompanies faith.

As we continue to follow the intriguing story of Abraham, we see a crucial venture in his life—the sacrifice of his son Isaac. "By faith Abraham, when God tested him, offered Isaac as a sacrifice" (Heb. 11:17 NIV). In addition to obedience and submission, sacrifice also accompanies faith.

A. *The test of faith.* Abraham's faith was tested when God told him to sacrifice his son Isaac. To have sacrificed Isaac would have meant the destruction of the last hope for descendants. Nonetheless, Abraham was willing to do as the Lord commanded. The severity of the test was that there seemed to be an apparent contradiction between the promise of God and the command of God. Nevertheless, Abraham believed that God's promises would be fulfilled even if Isaac was slain. Thus he was willing to sacrifice his son if that was what God wanted.

Having faith in God means that we are willing to make a sacrifice. Real faith is not cheap. It is a great demand.

B. *The triumph of faith.* Abraham experienced great triumph because of his willingness. "Abraham reasoned that God could raise the dead, and figuratively speaking, he did receive Isaac back from death" (Heb. 11:19 NIV). This verse shows Abraham's willingness to sacrifice because of his belief in the mysterious providence of God.

Christians are willing to sacrifice because of confidence in God's providence. Christians sacrifice because eternity will disclose the worthiness of their sacrifices.

Conclusion

Abraham had great faith in the Lord. His faith was accompanied by obedience, submission, and sacrifice. We cannot appropriate Abraham's faith as our own. Each person stands alone before God. But God does promise that we can have a faith like Abraham's earmarked by obedience, submission, and sacrifice.

WEDNESDAY EVENING, JUNE 14

Title: A Faith That Is Alive

Text: "What good is it, my brothers, if a man claims to have faith but has no deeds? Can such a faith save him?" *(James 2:14 NIV).*

Scripture Reading: James 2:14–26

Introduction

A preacher once said, "Brethren, whatever the good Lord tells me to do in this blessed book, that I'm going to do. If I see in it that I must jump through a stone wall, I'm going to jump at it. Going through it belongs to God—jumping at it belongs to me." Doing something of that nature demands a living faith that responds in obedience to God's will.

James talks about a living faith that changes lives, a faith that causes believers to do things they otherwise would not do.

I. Living faith is not an empty claim.

A. *For many, faith is only a word.* Note in verse 14 that James does not imply that a man can have faith and no works. Instead, James raises a rhetorical question: What is the profit if a person says he has faith but has no works? James will not even admit that it is a possibility. The man pictured is one who talks of faith, talks of things of a spiritual nature, talks of religion, but does not evidence change.

B. Pilgrim's Progress *by John Bunyan is a book about a community and its spiritual pilgrimage.* Bunyan uses various characters who are familiar in any community, and he identifies them by giving them names that suit their personalities. One character is named Talkative. Of him Bunyan says, "Religion hath no place in his heart or house or conduct. All he hath lieth in his tongue and his religion is to make a noise therewith."

C. *James illustrates his own case in pointing to the tradition of almsgiving.* One was expected to give to the poor in those days. Simply giving lip service to the poor left them just as destitute. So it is true today. If one sees a brother starving, do his hunger pains go away on well-wishing? Do nice remarks warm the body and shield from the bitter winds? Likewise, faith must be accompanied by action (1 John 3:18).

II. Faith is not an intellectual creed.

A. *The Bible is clear that if you have not come to God through Christ, you have not come to him at all.* Knowing about God will get you nowhere. James makes that clear. He points out that even the Devil believes in God; surely he is not going to heaven. John Calvin said, "Knowledge about God can no more connect man with God than sight of the sun carry you into the heavens."

B. *People may be the proponents of great doctrine, and they may be sticklers for orthodoxy, but their orthodoxy is meaningless until they come to a living faith in Jesus.* This faith surpasses word with deed, knowledge with relationship, and importance with obedience.

Conclusion

James invites you to learn about living faith in verse 20. Those who put trust in words of faith and knowledge of faith alone are foolish. They are so puffed up with spiritual insight that any higher wisdom is shut off. But they can learn—maybe by looking at two Old Testament examples: Abraham and Rahab.

An authentic faith is one that works. Faith and deeds are not opposites; they are inseparable. What kind of faith is yours—dead or alive? Look at the evidence. Evaluate yourself by James's principles and by answering this question: If you were put on trial for being a Christian, would there be enough evidence to convict you?

There will be enough only if yours is a living faith.

SUNDAY MORNING, JUNE 18

Title: Duties of a Daddy

Text: "But thou, O man of God, flee these things; and follow after righteousness, godliness, faith, love, patience, meekness" *(1 Tim. 6:11)*.

Scripture Reading: 1 Timothy 6:11–16

Hymns: "Faith of Our Fathers," Faber

"God, Our Father, We Adore Thee," Frazer

"Be Thou My Vision," Byrne

Offertory Prayer: Our Father, on this Father's Day we are grateful that we can call you Father. By addressing you as Father, we are aware that this expresses the love, the care, the protection, and the provision that you have given to us. Help us as earthly fathers, our Father, to express some of these same qualities in our relationships. You are infinite and all-knowing; we are finite and limited in our knowledge. Help us to pattern our lives on you and to use what knowledge we have in an effort to find and do your will personally and in our families. Please accept our gifts this morning as expressions of our love and commitment to you. Please bless them and use them in your own ways. And please forgive us our sins and guide us with your Spirit. This we pray in Jesus' name and for his sake. Amen.

Introduction

Kenneth Chafin, in his book *Help! I'm a Layman,* wrote of a time several years ago when he came home from the office just in time for the evening meal. They had hardly begun to eat when his five-year-old daughter asked if he would be home that night. He was embarrassed to answer because he was to speak that night to a group on the topic "What a Good Father Ought to Be." To soften the disappointment of his daughter at his leaving, he decided that he would ask her to give him a little help with the talk. He placed a piece of paper and a pencil on the table and asked her to tell him what it meant to be a good daddy. Throughout the meal she would come to his chair and whisper her ideas in his ear. He wrote each of them down. This was the list: (1) Catch a fish. (2) Build a fire. (3) Fly a kite. (4) Catch a butterfly. (5) Plant a flower. (6) Get a kitty cat out of the mud.

Chafin took the list with him to the meeting. As he waited to be introduced, he was looking over the list. Suddenly it hit him: nothing that his daughter wanted in an ideal father required his buying anything; but everything she mentioned required *him.* From that he wondered if many of us do not spend most of our lives working to purchase things for our children instead of giving them what they need more than anything else—ourselves.

On this Father's Day let's consider some duties of a daddy. For that consideration we will turn to 1 Timothy 6. This is rather a summing up of the things that Paul had written to the young minister. While these suggestions are not primarily intended for fathers, they can surely be applied that way. These are some of the spiritual duties of a daddy.

I. Continuation is one duty of a daddy.

A. *There is a heritage of faith.* Timothy had a good heritage of faith (2 Tim. 1:5). He came from a family where Christian faith was strongly held and vigorously practiced. This was obviously important to Timothy's early spiritual maturity.

B. *A continuation of the heritage of faith.* One duty of a daddy is to continue that heritage of faith. Timothy is urged here to "fight the good fight of faith" (v. 12). The heritage of faith is not just for women and children. It is carried on by people who see its worth and catch a vision of its greatness.

C. *The strength of the continuation of the heritage of faith.* How much stronger our churches would be and how much deeper Christian faith would penetrate the world if this could be the natural, unembarrassed, unashamed approach of fathers. Their faith would be something that they wore with naturalness and expressed without embarrassment. When the heritage of faith is continued by fathers, it is done unashamedly.

II. Character building is one of the duties of a daddy.

A. *The importance of character.* Character is important. We must have men of character who will stand for God in their homes and in the nation.

B. *The indications of character.* Verse 11 gives some of the characteristics of a godly man: righteousness, godliness, faith, love, patience, and meekness. This kind of character will pay dividends for the family.

III. Confession is one of the duties of a daddy.

A. *A confession of faith in Christ.* Another duty of a daddy is to make a clear confession of faith in Christ as Savior. In verse 12 Paul called on Timothy to lay hold of the eternal life to which he had been called and to profess it strongly before others.

B. *This confession is necessary for Christian homes.* We cannot have Christian homes without Christians in the home. The father sets the pace for the family. If he is the head of the household, the leader of the family, he should certainly lead in this area also.

C. *This confession is comparable to Christ's confession.* In verses 14–16 Paul compares the confession that Timothy would make before people to the confession that Christ made before Pilate. It is the kind of confession that is consistent with the commitment that has been made to Christ.

A certain father was the manager of a feed store, where Purina feed was sold. He was offered a position as manager of a competitor's feed store, where he would have made considerably more money. When he refused the offer, his son asked him why. To him the answer was clear. "Why, son," he said, "all these years I have been telling these people that Purina feed was the best feed for their livestock. If I quit them now and started selling some other kind of feed, they would think that I had been lying all that time." This man was equally consistent in his witness for Christ.

Conclusion

These are some of the duties of a daddy. When fathers accept these duties and begin to carry them out, homes will be stronger and the Christian testimony greater.

SUNDAY EVENING, JUNE 18

Title: Living by Faith

Text: "By faith Moses' parents hid him for three months after he was born, because they saw he was no ordinary child, and they were not afraid of the king's edict" *(Heb. 11:23 NIV)*.

Scripture Reading: Hebrews 11:23–29

Introduction

Every Christian would affirm that the Christian life begins with faith. Faith opens the door to an amazing relationship with God. But not many Christians emphasize that the Christian life is to be lived by faith.

The author of Hebrews cited many examples of God's people who lived by faith. To the Hebrews, Moses was one of the most prominent figures. He had rescued them from slavery in Egypt, led them across the Red Sea, and received God's law. To the writer of Hebrews, Moses was a person who lived his life by faith. In the story of Moses there are five stages that illustrate how Moses and those around him applied faith in various situations. Let us notice these stages and the actions that faith needs to take.

I. Faith takes risks.

A. *Moses' parents took a risk to save Moses' life.* "By faith Moses' parents hid him for three months after he was born, because they saw he was no ordinary child, and they were not afraid of the king's edict" (Heb. 11:23 NIV). Pharaoh had ordered the execution of all male infants; Moses' parents sought to save their child's life by hiding him in the bulrushes.

Moses' parents were motivated initially by the physical beauty of their child. But greater than the physical reason was the spiritual reason: they believed that God would do something through their child. They risked their lives to save Moses.

B. *To have faith means to take great risks.* When subjected to undesirable situations, the person who really believes in God's way and in God's sovereignty may have to take risks.

By faith the people of God have overcome their worst fears. Necessary actions have taken precedence over consequences. The example of godly parents taking a risk helps us to see that having genuine faith will often require God's people to step out in obedience to him.

II. Faith chooses the better life.

A. *Moses chose to live with God's people.* "By faith Moses, when he had grown up, refused to be known as the son of Pharaoh's daughter" (Heb. 11:24 NIV). Moses came to a place in his life when he had to choose to live with Pharaoh's people or with God's people. He chose to live with God's people, seeing it as the better life. He gave up all earthly power and riches for spiritual power and riches. This constitutes a better life.

Moses could have had a good life in the courts of Pharaoh. He could have been socially prominent, materially rich, and physically satisfied, yet he "chose to be mistreated along with the people of God rather than to enjoy the pleasures of sin for a short time" (Heb. 11:25 NIV). Moses chose to suffer for the right rather than to enjoy luxury with the wrong.

B. *Having faith means choosing loyalty to God's way.* God's people live constantly with the choices of living for God or living for self. Choosing to live for God means the renouncing of a self-centered, self-gratifying lifestyle. Living God's way means gaining the ultimate reward of God rather than receiving the transient, unsatisfying prizes of earth. Real faith chooses to live the better life with God than to live with the world.

III. Faith follows God's orders.

A. *Moses obeyed God's orders to withdraw from Egypt to Midian.* "By faith he left Egypt, not fearing the king's anger; he persevered because he saw him who is invisible" (Heb. 11:27 NIV). The Lord ordered Moses to flee from Egypt. The reason for that could have been protection from Pharaoh's wrath over Moses' killing of an Egyptian or to temper Moses by teaching him patience. Moses did learn to wait on the Lord. He learned to wait until God said: "Now is the hour."

B. *To have faith means to obey the commands of the Lord.* Often on the surface the Lord's command may not seem logical, but the end result is always logical. God's people are to obey God's commands. At times the way of forgiving, loving, and returning good for evil may seem absurd. But ultimately the results will demonstrate the logic of God's command.

IV. Faith trusts God's promises.

A. *Moses believed that God would deliver his people.* "By faith he kept the Passover and the sprinkling of blood, so that the destroyer of the firstborn would not touch the firstborn of Israel" (Heb. 12:28 NIV). Moses made the arrangements in Egypt for the Passover (Ex. 12:12–48). The lamb had to be slain. The unleavened bread had to be baked. The doorposts had to be smeared with the blood of an unblemished lamb so the death angel would see the blood and pass over the house and not slay the firstborn.

Moses not only made preparations for the first Passover, but he also stipulated that the Passover was to be observed annually. Moses never doubted the success of God's getting his people out of the land of Goshen. Real faith is the kind that trusts the Lord.

B. *To have faith means learning to trust God's promises.* God does not promise his people something and then not fulfill it. God summons his servants to a great task. He will give his people exactly what he has promised and help them accomplish that task.

V. Faith overcomes difficulties.

A. *By faith Moses overcame many difficulties.* One of the greatest barriers in Moses' life was the Red Sea. Yet faith helped him to overcome that obstacle. "By faith the people passed through the Red Sea as on dry land; but when the Egyptians tried to do so, they were drowned" (Heb. 11:29 NIV). Moses would not let any difficulty detour his faith. He was willing to ask God to help him with seeming impossibilities.

B. *By faith we can overcome the difficulties of our lives.* The living of the Christian life will mean the inevitable occurrences of difficulties. Real faith is the faith that believes that God will help us either cope with or be delivered from our troubles.

Conclusion

If you are not now trusting the Lord, let me ask you to consider a new way of living. It is the way of living by faith in the Lord.

WEDNESDAY EVENING, JUNE 21

Title: The Powerful Tongue

Text: "No man can tame the tongue" *(James 3:8).*

Scripture Reading: James 3:1–8

Introduction

There may be considerable disagreement over which is the strongest muscle of the body. The biblical view, however, is that the most powerful muscle of all is the tongue. With the tongue great kingdoms have been created and destroyed. With the tongue life and death orders are pronounced. With the tongue people demonstrate their greatest moments of wisdom and worst moments of stupidity. Homes are either helped or devastated by words formed with the tongue. The tongue has tremendous power.

I. The tongue's power.

A. *Because the tongue is so powerful, the Bible as a whole emphasizes the controlling of it.* James writes more strongly about the tongue than any other New Testament writer. Thus this passage revolves around a discussion of the power of the tongue and the related dangers of indiscreet speech.

B. *James indicates that the tongue is so powerful that it is indeed the hardest muscle for a person to control or coordinate.* James illustrates this power with these vivid figures.

The power of the tongue is analogous to the bit in a horse's mouth. The horse, which is by nature wild and unruly and large (often weighing as much as 2,000 pounds), may have its fiery temper subdued and its movements regulated by a bit of metal weighing only a pound or so. The application is obvious.

It is said that a Greek philosopher once asked a servant to provide the best dish possible. The servant prepared a dish of tongue, saying, "It is the best of all dishes because with it we may bless and communicate happiness, dispel sorrow, remove despair, cheer the fainthearted, inspire the discouraged, and say a hundred other things to uplift mankind."

Later the philosopher asked the servant to prepare the worst dish he could think of. The servant prepared a dish of tongue, saying, "It is the worst because with it we may curse and break human hearts; destroy reputations; promote discord and strife; and set families, communities, and nations at war." He was a wise servant.

Solomon said, "He who guards his mouth and his tongue keeps himself from calamity" (Prov. 21:23 NIV).

II. The vicious nature of the tongue.

A. *James introduces an additional idea—the vicious nature of the tongue.* We see this nature come out in the way gossip comes so easily from all conversations. To make his point, Jesus uses a string of metaphors in verses 6–7.

The tongue is like fire because, while fire can have the good uses of driving out chill and dampness from one's house or cooking one's food, out of control it can consume forests and homes.

172

B. *The tongue is a world of iniquity for at least three reasons mentioned in verse 6.*
1. It defiles the whole body—that is, the tongue pollutes a person's whole personality, soils one's whole nature, and leaves a deadly stain on it.
2. It upsets the course of nature—that is, it works against the wholesome character of a person by destroying any good that may remain.
3. It is set on fire by hell—that is, it is under Satan's influence—and thus is brazen and frightening.

C. *James continues by saying that the tongue is like a wild animal, only worse (v. 7).* While humans have learned to control and tame the wildest animal, they have never quite mastered their own mouths. The poison spewing from an untamed tongue is lethal in any dosage.

III. Many should not become teachers.

In light of these difficulties, we can readily understand James's advice in 3:1. He begins with his conclusion: "Not many of you should presume to be teachers" (NIV).

A. *The words offer a sober reminder that we ought not rush too hastily into the work of teaching.* A ready tongue without an informed mind, a devout character, and a holy life will hinder more than help the cause of Christ. It is extremely easy for vanity, self-conceit, and spiritual pride to creep in. It is, therefore, necessary to be on guard against such influences.

B. *Yet in another sense we all are teachers.* As Christians we teach with everything we do, everywhere we go, everyone we meet. The question is what do we teach others? And how? In light of that question, we must watch our tongues!

Conclusion

The Bible sees the tongue in all its glory and in all its honor. At best it is a means to praise our God; at worst it is a way to vilify our brothers and our Creator. Let us rely on our Creator to control our tongues solely to give honor to him.

SUNDAY MORNING, JUNE 25

Title: The Recovery of Family Life

Text: "The LORD said to me, 'Go, show your love to your wife again, though she is loved by another and is an adulteress. Love her as the LORD loves the Israelites, though they turn to other gods and love the sacred raisin cakes'" *(Hos. 3:1 NIV).*

Scripture Reading: Hosea 1:2–9; 3:1–3

Hymns: "I'll Live for Him," Hudson

"Jesus Is Tenderly Calling," Crosby

"Lord, I'm Coming Home," Kirkpatrick

Offertory Prayer: Dear Father, we are overwhelmed by your love. We come before you today very much aware of our unfaithfulness to you, our failures with one another, and our need for restoration. The assurance that we have from your love is that these may be forgiven, that we will be accepted, and that our relationship with you can be totally restored. For that we thank you. You have given so much to us. We come now to give to you. Help us to be generous. Help us to practice good stewardship. Help us to have the strength and the commitment to return to you your portion of our gain as we have received the full measure of your love. Bless and multiply these gifts, we pray. In Jesus' name and for his sake. Amen.

Introduction

Many of the problems that face our nation can be traced to one root: the destruction of wholesome family life. With this deterioration, we see lack of values, the renunciation of basic virtues, distrust of others, and rebellion against authority and regulation. Many of these things can be traced to the lack of family strength and discipline.

Pauline and D. Elton Trueblood assert in *The Recovery of Family Life* that "the withering away of the family" has occurred because "we have done by neglect much that the Marxists have done by social planning." For this message I will borrow this title and talk about the recovery of family life. I will focus on a Bible family that was destroyed then later recovered through love.

Hosea was a prophet of God. He married a wife named Gomer who was unfaithful to him. After the birth of three children, each of whom had a symbolic name, she left him and actually became a prostitute. Possibly Gomer never believed God. She may have worshiped Baal or one of the Canaanite fertility cults that practiced sacred prostitution as a part of their worship. At any rate, she later sank to such depths of immorality that she was sold as a slave. Prompted by God's Spirit and displaying a love like God's, Hosea bought her. He restored her to a place of love and usefulness. He recovered his family. Hosea used his tragic domestic experience as a vehicle for teaching about God's love. He likened Israel's rebellion against God and their departure from him to his experience of his wife going into adultery and forsaking him. He loved his wife and brought her back. God loves his people and will bring them back to him if they respond.

Look at this story from the vantage point of the recovery of family life. From Hosea's tragic experience we can find some helpful priorities for our lives. Trueblood says that just as a physician can't diagnose an illness until he has a vision of what a well body is, so we can't work toward the recovery of family life until we first have a model of wholesome Christian family life.

I. We must focus on persons.

A. *In the family, each individual is important.* Hosea loved Gomer as a person. He loved her so much that he was willing to relinquish his pride and purchase her as a slave so that she could be a wife again. In some families causes or appearances are so important that persons are obscured.

B. *A family begins with the love of two persons.* The family's life can never be healthy if that original love is not healthy.

C. *Guard the personhood of each family member.* Family life experts tell us never to attack the personhood of a child when correcting that child. You could say, "I don't like children *to* lie," not "I don't like children *who* lie." That safeguards the personhood of the child while expressing displeasure at the child's action.

II. We must find our priorities.

A. *What is our top priority?* The recovery of family life must become a top priority for us just as it did for Hosea. Can you imagine the shame he must have felt at Gomer's behavior? Can you imagine the jests and the jeers he received from his friends at her actions? But he was willing to forgo all that because he had a priority: the recovery of his family life. No other success can compensate for failure in the home.

B. *How do we achieve this priority?* It must be an internal matter rather than an external matter. It will not come by changes in the structures of society as much as by the intent of the individual. When you choose the family as a top priority and begin to work toward the recovery of family life as a goal, it can be achieved.

III. We must consider our pride.

A. *We must forget our personal pride.* Hosea forgot his personal pride to purchase his wife in the slave market. Pride often stands at the base of family problems. We are too proud to reconsider a position, too proud to admit guilt, too proud to allow someone else to have an opinion, too proud to say the important but difficult words "I'm sorry—I was wrong."

B. *We must foster family pride.* Individual family members should be able to take pride in being a part of the family to which they belong. Religious life and witness should be a normal part of family life. Children want to admire their parents, and parents should conscientiously shape their children's lives by living as godly examples.

IV. We must pay the price.

A. *We have paid the price for fractured family life.* The price for fractured family life has been costly. What it has cost in the lives of persons has been very dear when you consider the hurt, the maladjustments, and the pain.

B. *We must be willing to pay the price for recovered family life.* It cost Hosea something to recover his family life. The money that it cost to purchase Gomer was incidental. The real price was the personal cost to Hosea. It will cost us something too. The place to begin is in personal surrender to God and commitment of the family to him.

Conclusion

The key to the book of Hosea is the intensity of his love for Gomer, his wife. God loves us even more intensely. He wants us to be in fellowship with him. When we are right with God, we can be right with our families as well. And that is where we begin the recovery of family life.

SUNDAY EVENING, JUNE 25

Title: Getting Ready to Race

Text: "Let us run with perseverance the race marked out for us" *(Heb. 12:1 NIV).*

Scripture Reading: Hebrews 12:1–2

Introduction

A high school cross-country team established the goal of running three miles in fifteen minutes. This would allow them to finish high in the state finals. The preparation for the achievement was arduous. Besides running each day, the team members were required to eat properly, drink plenty of liquids, and get proper rest. The coach instructed them diligently on running strategies. For weeks the team readied for the race. The preparations were profitable: the team finished high in the state meet.

The author of Hebrews compares the Christian life to a race. Let us examine the process of preparation for running the race of life.

I. Remove the impediments.

Christians cannot afford to be hindered in living the Christian life. The author of Hebrews told believers to "throw off everything that hinders and the sin that so easily entangles" (Heb. 12:1 NIV).

A. *The Christian needs to take action.* The author of Hebrews had probably observed a footrace. Oftentimes runners would train with weights on them. The day of the race, however, the runner would "lay aside every weight" (KJV). In fact, Greek runners ran almost naked. Everything that could hinder the running of the race needed to be removed.

Christians also need to take action on besetting sins. Many hindrances thwart the Christian's progress—for example, fleshly indulgence, faithlessness, lack of dedication, inordinate pride, and laziness. Repentance is the action that needs to be taken.

B. *Without hindrances the Christian can progress.* When the author observed footraces, he probably saw runners with excess fat. They could not run as fast or as far as those who had taken action against that hindrance.

That which seemed to impede the progress of the Hebrew believers was the lack of faith. Those who had achieved did so by opening their lives to the Lord and making progress. The theme of Hebrew is "Let Us Go On." The admonition is "Don't let anything impede your progress in the Lord!" To live a successful Christian life, the impediments to progress must be removed.

II. Examine the race course.

Runners participate in running events on different courses. One of the prerequisites to running a good race is for the runner to walk or run the course prior to the race so that he or she will be familiar with the terrain. The racecourse for the

Christian can only be followed by looking to Jesus: "Let us fix our eyes on Jesus, the author and perfecter of our faith" (Heb. 12:2 NIV).

A. *Jesus is the pattern for the Christian life.* No one needs to wonder how a Christian is to act, think, or speak: the proper behavior is modeled in Jesus Christ. "The race marked out for us" is the life of Jesus Christ. He is our supreme example.

In what way does Jesus set the example for believers? He obeyed the Father's will even when it cost him his life. If Jesus obeyed to the ultimate degree of sacrifice, all of his followers need to be willing to do likewise.

B. *Jesus is the dynamic for the Christian life.* The Lord does not just model the way to live. He helps us achieve the goal. He is "the author and finisher of our faith." He enables those who strive in faith to be victorious.

The word "author" can be translated "pioneer" or "leader." The word "finisher" describes one who is a companion on a journey. Jesus is the one who prepares the way for a person to be right with God, and he is a constant companion to help us on the journey.

III. Look at the legacy of runners.

Runners are inspired by other runners. In many high schools, portraits of past victorious athletes and trophies commemorating past victories are displayed. The author of Hebrews described the legacy of those who had run the Christian race: "we are surrounded by . . . a great cloud of witnesses" (Heb. 12:1 NIV). Why is this so important?

A. *Witnesses testify of the power of faith.* The "therefore" of Hebrews 12:1 is a hinge. It refers to the heroes of faith mentioned in Hebrews 11. The author of Hebrews described the great legacy of those who have faith. These people gave testimony to the worthiness of their faith in the Lord. They finished the race with their faith intact.

B. *Witnesses inspire Christians to be faithful.* Picture racers running around a track in a stadium. The runners are inspired by the spectators in the stands. Modern sports reporters often talk of the crowd "getting into the game." Likewise, those who sit in the stadium of glory cheer on believers on earth.

IV. Work on endurance.

One of the real battles of running is a psychological struggle. The runner has to battle constantly with quitting or continuing. The author of Hebrews encourages believers to work on their stamina: "Let us run with perseverance the race marked out for us" (Heb. 12:1 NIV).

A. *Sometimes we are tempted to quit living the Christian life.* In the mind of every runner the temptation to quit is always present. The runner must fight feelings of fatigue, the possibility of failure, and thoughts about the success of the competition. Nothing should stop the runner from completing the course.

Christians often become easily discouraged. They are tempted to slow down or give up. But believers must not quit. They need to endure. Through Christ they can.

B. *The endurance is worth the effort.* The encouragement to "run with perseverance" is interesting. The Greek word here means having the determination to master something.

Staying with the Christian life has many benefits. First, you experience the joy of running the race. Second, you can relish the accomplishment. Third, you will receive a crown.

Conclusion

The Christian life is a footrace. To run the race effectively, runners must remove impediments, master the course, draw encouragement from the crowd, and run with endurance. How well are you running today?

WEDNESDAY EVENING, JUNE 28

Title: Consistency

Text: "Out of the same mouth come praise and cursing. My brothers, this should not be" *(James 3:10 NIV).*

Scripture Reading: James 3:9–12

Introduction

Many classic pieces of literature demonstrate biblical truths. One from the pen of Robert Louis Stevenson clearly illustrates the truth behind tonight's text. The story is of a doctor named Henry Jekyll. He led a double life. Publicly he was genteel and circumspect, but privately he embraced strange vices without restraint. Becoming obsessed with the idea that people had two personalities, he reasoned that people were capable of having two physical beings as well. He compounded a mixture that transformed his body into a physical representation of his evil self. He became Hyde. In his disguise he was free to haunt the lonely, narrow corners of London and to commit the darkest deeds without fear of recognition.

Stevenson's novelette emphasizes the duality of human nature—the desire to be and to do good and the desire to be and to do evil. In humans there is something of the angel and something of the ape, something of the hero and something of the villain, something of the saint and much of the sinner. Human depravity always causes evil to be the ultimate victor—unless, of course, the heart is changed. Then things will reverse. But that change of heart is the only hope.

People are plagued with inconsistency. Our text tonight illustrates that fact clearly and in doing so also points out that the clearest microcosm of this dual nature is the tongue. It cannot be trusted. One minute it does one thing, the next minute it does another. I think the greatest horror for Dr. Jekyll must have been the insecurity of never knowing what to expect. The horror of the tongue holds the same inconsistency.

So by way of indirect recourse, James describes three areas of our lives that should be consistent because our hearts are changed.

I. Words ought to be consistent with other words.

It is James's conviction that nowhere is man's inconsistency more evident than in the use of the tongue.

A. *We can bless God with the tongue.* This was especially relevant to the Jew. Whenever the name of God was mentioned, a Jew had to respond: "Blessed is he!" This is the highest purpose of the mouth—to bless God.

B. *The tongue is also often used to curse.* Strange as it may seem, the instrument God gave us to bless him is the same instrument that is often used to curse him. How often we see men and women who are consistently inconsistent with their speech—saying good things one minute and negating them the next. In one breath they say one thing and then in the next breath deny it. It is a clear sign of a greater problem.

II. Words ought to be consistent with deeds.

One other problem we often see in people is an inconsistency between their words and their deeds. Here the adage "Your actions speak so loudly I can't hear a word you say" applies. Talk is cheap. Actions are not. By and large a person's true nature is revealed in what he or she does. Actions do speak more loudly than words, and thus our words and deeds need to be consistent.

III. Attitudes toward God should be consistent with attitudes toward people.

A. *Another area in which we need consistency is our attitudes toward God and others.* To curse people is to curse a creation of God and therefore is to curse God. How can we curse God and bless him all at once? The truth is, we cannot.

A mother watched her daughter run and embrace her father and kiss him on the cheek. Then to the mother's surprise, the little girl looked over her father's shoulder and stuck out her tongue at her little brother who was playing on the floor. The mother said to her daughter, "Take your arms from around your father's neck. You cannot pretend to love your father while not also loving his son."

B. *To love God is to love people.* To bless God is to bless others. To honor God is to respect his creations.

Conclusion

We must be consistent in the use of our tongue. This is possible only when God's wisdom controls our words and actions. Then our talk, our deeds, and our attitudes will be consistently pleasing to God and others alike.

JULY

■ Sunday Mornings

On the first Sunday morning of the month, complete the series "Enriching Marriage and Family Relationships."

On the second Sunday begin a series from the book of Isaiah. The courses of our lives depend on our responses to our circumstances. Our lives are better or worse according to our responses—not according to our circumstances. Isaiah spoke a lot about our reactions. These will be brought to light in a series titled "Responding to the Great Irritations of God."

■ Sunday Evenings

On the first Sunday evening of the month, complete the series "The Superlative Christ."

Begin a stewardship series on the second Sunday of the month. Believers today need to grow in their giving of themselves to God and to his work in the world. Many lessons can be learned by looking at the remarkable generosity of the early church. The suggested theme is "The Response of Stewardship to the Living Christ."

■ Wednesday Evenings

Continue the series from James titled "The Practice of Genuine Religion."

SUNDAY MORNING, JULY 2

Title: When Christ Comes to Your House

Text: "When they were come out of the synagogue, they entered into the house of Simon and Andrew, with James and John" *(Mark 1:29).*

Scripture Reading: Mark 1:29–31

Hymns: "Come, All Christians, Be Committed," Lloyd

"Come, Thou Almighty King," Anonymous

"Christ Receiveth Sinful Men," Neumeister

Offertory Prayer: Our Father, we find ourselves at home in your house today. We invite you to come into our hearts and into our homes. As we consider the needs of our homes, we are aware that one of our greatest needs is to invite you in and make you a part of our family. As we are a part of the family of God, help us, O God, to make you a real part of our homes. Be with us now as we make a financial contribution to your work. Help us to determine that our contributions will not only be financial, but that we will give to you our love, our strength, our time, and our devotion. Please accept these gifts we give, use them for the ongoing of your kingdom, and bless both the gift and the giver. We pray in Jesus' name. Amen.

Introduction

When a man came home at the end of the workday, his wife said to him, "The new minister came here today, and he asked a question I couldn't answer."

"What did he ask?"

"He asked me," she said, "Does Jesus Christ live here?"

"And what did you say?" the husband demanded.

"I didn't know what to say," she answered.

"Well, couldn't you tell him that we are respectable people?" he asked.

"But he didn't ask me that."

"Well, why didn't you tell him we go to church when we feel like it?" he queried.

"But he didn't ask me that either," was her reply.

"Then you could have told him that we read the Bible—sometimes," he added.

"But he didn't ask me *that*. What he asked me was, 'Does Jesus Christ live here?'"

That is a good question to put before any home. But an equally important one is, What difference would Christ make in your home?

The New Testament gives us a glimpse into that answer. One time Jesus went to a house—and it made a big difference. This event occurred early in Jesus' public ministry. He had gone from the mountains of Nazareth to the Sea of Galilee. Along the shores of that lake he had taught and healed, and he had begun to call his first disciples.

On a Sabbath day Jesus went to Capernaum. Here Mark shows us one day in the life of the Savior. In the morning he went to the synagogue, where he taught and where he healed a demoniac. In the afternoon he went to Peter's house. There he healed Simon Peter's mother-in-law. Then that evening he went out into the streets where a number of people were brought to him to be healed. Quite a day!

From the experience in the home of Simon Peter, we can see what can happen when Christ comes to one's house.

I. There is healing.

A. *Christ always brings healing to a home.* Apparently this was a morning synagogue service. After the service Jesus went home with Peter. In the ruins of Capernaum today, there is a synagogue. Directly in front of it is a house in which an early church met. It is thought that this house was Simon Peter's house. If this is true, Jesus walked across the street to this house.

Probably he had gone there for rest. After all, he had taught and healed in the synagogue service. He must have been tired. But he was not too tired to heal a sick mother-in-law. In that house there was a need, and he brought the power of God into saving contact with personal need.

B. *Who needs healing in your home?* Does your home need more love or appreciation or understanding or acceptance? Is there competition between family members? Into all this Jesus can bring the healing power of the Holy Spirit.

II. There is help.

A. *One receives help, one can give help.* Did you notice what Simon Peter's mother-in-law did as she was healed? She began to serve others. All the Synoptic Gospel writers—Matthew, Mark, and Luke—noted that. Gratitude to God for the healing he had brought her was expressed in service. This is the way we express gratitude as well—by serving others in Jesus' name.

B. *Help can be given in simple ways.* Helping others can be done in simple as well as complex ways. John Henry Jowett told of a servant girl in his congregation who had a deep concern for her calling as a Christian. When he asked her how she proposed to live the Christian life, she answered that she didn't have much time left from her work and she couldn't attend the church meetings or even many of the services. So he asked her what she did. She replied that she always took the newspaper to bed with her at night. He asked what was the good of that. She said that she read the birth notices and prayed for the babies that had been born. She read of the deaths and prayed for God's comfort to come to the sorrowing families.

C. *Help brings joy and fulfillment.* The help that you give to others, as Christ has given help to you and your family, brings joy and fulfillment. It is joy both to the person helping and those helped. It is fulfillment to the person who helps others.

III. There is hope.

A. *The need for hope.* We do not really know how sick this woman was. Luke, the physician, indicated that she had a high fever. If the fever was high enough, if the illness was severe enough, she may have been in danger of dying. But when Christ came, there was hope. We all need hope.

B. *The assurance of hope.* Jesus *always* brings hope. To the hopelessness of unforgiven sin, Jesus brings forgiveness—and with it, hope. To the hopelessness of habit, like drink or drugs, Christ brings the power to overcome—and with that, hope.

To a home where love seems lost, all is now strife and bitterness rather than rest and tenderness. Christ brings love and reconciliation—and with that, hope.

IV. There is happiness.

A. *Happiness is a result of Christ's presence.* The biblical account does not specifically record it, but can't you sense the happiness in Peter's home after Jesus healed this woman?

B. *Happiness is an evidence of Christ's power.* Perhaps there hasn't been much happiness at your house lately. Perhaps the reason is that Christ has not been there much. An evidence of Christ's power in your life is the resulting happiness and joy.

Conclusion

Invite Jesus Christ into your home. See the difference he can bring. What he does while there can change the home: the persons, the purpose, the pursuits. Let Jesus come to your house, and see the difference he will make.

SUNDAY EVENING, JULY 2

Title: Responding to God's Discipline

Text: "Endure hardship as discipline; God is treating you as sons. For what son is not disciplined by his father?" *(Heb. 12:7 NIV).*

Scripture Reading: Hebrews 12:5–11

Introduction

Perhaps one of the most neglected ideas in the Bible is the discipline of God. Often we hear about the love of God, the wrath of God, and other traits of God. But rarely do we hear about the discipline of God.

The author of Hebrews was not reticent about this topic. He viewed many of the hardships of life as God's discipline. If one takes seriously the biblical idea of the fatherhood of God, one must also look at the concept of God's discipline.

God's people not only need to know about God's discipline, they also need to respond properly to it. The author of Hebrews gives three good responses that a Christian can make to God's discipline.

I. Get a right attitude toward discipline.

A. *Many wrong attitudes exist toward God's discipline.* The author of Hebrews sought to correct some improper attitudes concerning God's discipline: "And you have forgotten that word of encouragement that addresses you as sons: 'My son, do not make light of the Lord's discipline, and do not lose heart when he rebukes you'" (Heb. 12:5 NIV).

Some regard the discipline of the Lord lightly. These Christians may not be aware that God's sovereign hand is at work in the adversities of life. They seem to despise the chastening of the Lord. The discipline of the Lord should not be treated lightly.

Others regard the discipline of the Lord with despondency. Some Christians lose courage when adversity overtakes them. They encounter difficulties and become despondent.

B. *Only one correct attitude exists toward God's discipline.* The correct attitude toward discipline is to treat it as a work of the loving heavenly Father, "because the Lord disciplines those he loves, and he punishes everyone he accepts as a son" (Heb. 12:6 NIV). The right attitude toward discipline is to accept it as coming from a loving, heavenly Father. No good earthly father would send bad discipline. Even more so, the heavenly Father gives to his children those adversities that are necessary to mature their faith.

II. Have a submissive spirit to discipline.

A. *Think good about God.* The Christian attitude toward discipline is often influenced by a person's concept of God. If a person views God as a raging tyrant who seeks to devour his subjects, that person will have a distorted view of discipline. He or she will view discipline as blows sent by God to make people feel uncomfortable for the sake of being uncomfortable.

God as a heavenly Father is a more biblical concept of God. In Hebrews 12:5–11 the writer uses the concept of an earthly father acting with his children. Think of the best father you know, multiply that infinitely, and you will get a glimpse into God's nature. God's discipline is not to make his children uncomfortable but to train them in his ways, which are best for them.

B. *Respond to God's discipline as a child responds to a good father.* "Endure hardship as discipline; God is treating you as sons" (Heb. 12:7 NIV). The comparison is obvious. God treats his people as a good father treats his children. "For what son is not disciplined by his father?" (Heb. 12:7 NIV). The writer of Hebrews describes the universality of discipline. Every earthly child has need of periodic discipline. Likewise, every Christian has need of occasional discipline. Some of God's children may need more discipline than others.

The best way to respond to God's discipline is with a submissive attitude. "How much more should we submit to the Father of our spirits and live!" (Heb. 12:9 NIV). Children should not rebel against an earthly father's discipline. Rather, they should turn to him in obedience. Should not Christians all the more be submissive to God when he does the same?

III. Celebrate the results of discipline.

A. *Discipline has an immediate result.* "Our fathers disciplined us for a little while as they thought best; but God disciplines us for our good, that we may share in his holiness" (Heb. 12:10 NIV). God's discipline is directed to benefit the believer. Good parents discipline children for their immediate good. Because of the goodness of God, he could not induce any form of discipline that would not be of real help to us.

The immediate result of discipline is the making of character: "that we may share in his holiness" (Heb. 12:10 NIV). God disciplines his children so that they will live according to his design and serve the world according to his purpose.

B. *Discipline has an ultimate result.* "No discipline seems pleasant at the time, but painful. Later on, however, it produces a harvest of righteousness and peace for those who have been trained by it" (Heb. 12:11 NIV). The training of a child at the moment is not joyous but grievous. At the moment the child cannot see the profit of the discipline. Yet when the ultimate results are viewed, the picture and concept of discipline changes.

If God's people respond properly to God's present training experiences, they will be victorious. A person who can turn every trying experience into a means of glorifying God in triumphant service for him is a victorious Christian.

Conclusion

Have you felt God's discipline? If you have, you can celebrate the relationship with the heavenly Father. If you have not, you need to so that you can have assurance that you are a child of God. Open your life to Jesus and become one of his children.

WEDNESDAY EVENING, JULY 5

Title: To Be Wise

Text: "Who among you is wise and understanding? Let him show by his good behavior his deeds in the gentleness of wisdom" *(James 3:13 NASB).*

Scripture Reading: James 3:13–18

Introduction

James's comments in this chapter are directed to teachers. James is a teacher himself. He knows full well what he is talking about. His discussion here follows a warning on the tongue—perhaps because a teacher is very vulnerable to such a temptation and can create a mounting effect on students for good or for ill. Here he reminds the teacher of his need for real wisdom and introduces his discussion with a question: Who is wise among you?

I. False wisdom.

Let us look first, then, at false wisdom that we may stay clear of it. Verse 15 describes the basic problem with such wisdom.

A. *It is not from above—that is, not from God.* It is created by the bitterness, jealousy, and selfishness in a person's heart. James says that this wisdom is earthly and is therefore marked by earthly principles.

B. *Now it would only be expected that such an evil-oriented wisdom would have certain bad effects on that person.* So it does. It comes forth with the evidences we see in verse 14: bitter envying and strife.

   1. The literal meaning of the Greek word for envying is "zeal"—an emotion that may be either good or bad. Paul used it in the former sense when he wrote that the Jews had a zeal for God but not according to knowledge (Rom. 10:2). In this passage, however, it clearly has a bad connotation—an unholy zeal. It is a fierce desire to promote one's own opinions to the exclusion of the opinions of others.

   2. There is some uncertainty as to the meaning of the Greek word translated "strife." Perhaps something like selfish ambition best describes it. It is the

notion of rivalry, a party spirit, or factiousness. It is the description of a person who loves to be in the know, that is, to be smart, but only so that he can confound others with his depth.

II. True wisdom.

True wisdom offers us something better. In contrast to the false wisdom, this kind is from above. It is first pure—fundamentally undefiled, free from the self-interest that characterizes false wisdom. James's descriptive words of this wisdom fall basically into three categories.

A. *First, heavenly wisdom is peaceable, gentle, and "easy to be entreated" (v. 17).* These words, expressing qualities that are opposite to the jealousy and selfishness mentioned above, describe true wisdom as it manifests itself in attitudes and actions toward others. Worldly wisdom produces contention and strife.

B. *Second, heavenly wisdom is full of mercy and good fruits (v. 17).* Earlier (2:14) James taught that true faith clothes the naked and feeds the hungry. Here he adds that true wisdom concerns itself with practical things. It is a characteristic of God himself. Good fruits most likely refer to kind actions and helpful deeds promoted by compassion and mercy.

C. *Finally, true wisdom is without partiality and without hypocrisy.* It may in fact also mean "without wavering or doubt," as alternate translations would suggest. Without hypocrisy suggests that true wisdom is sincere, genuine, and unpretentious.

James affirms that this splendid fruit is sown by them that make peace. Righteousness cannot be promoted in ourselves or in others except as we are people of peace. People of peace are those who not only love peace but promote it by every means in their power. Such people truly possess true wisdom. This prayer of Saint Francis of Assisi vividly depicts a man's desire for God's wisdom.

> *Lord, make me an instrument of thy peace.*
> *Where there is hatred, let me sow love;*
> *Where there is injury, pardon;*
> *Where there is doubt, faith;*
> *Where there is despair, hope;*
> *Where there is darkness, light;*
> *Where there is sadness, joy.*
> *O divine Master grant that I may not seek*
>   *to be consoled but to console,*
>   *to be understood but to understand,*
>   *to be loved as to love.*
> *For it is in giving that we receive,*
> *And it is in pardoning that we pardon,*
> *And it is in dying that we are born to eternal life.*

Conclusion

True wisdom is proven by a gentility and openness and respect for others. James says in verse 13 that if people imagine that they are wise and understanding and want to be recognized as such, let them show out of a good conversation their works with meekness of wisdom. The true test of wisdom is not words but works. Mere talk—no matter how fluent, clever, and orthodox—does not of itself prove wisdom.

Spurgeon put it this way: "A man's life is always more forcible than his speech; when men take stock of him they reckon his deeds as pounds and his words as pence. If his life and doctrine disagree, the onlookers accept his practice and reject his preaching."

SUNDAY MORNING, JULY 9

Title: The Great Invitation

Text: "Come now, and let us reason together, saith the LORD: though your sins be as scarlet, they shall be as white as snow; though they be red like crimson, they shall be as wool" *(Isa. 1:18).*

Scripture Reading: Isaiah 1:1–20

Hymns: "Jesus Calls Us O'er the Tumult," Alexander

"Take My Life, and Let It Be," Havergal

"Softly and Tenderly," Thompson

Offertory Prayer: Heavenly Father, we pause to lift our voices in praise and gratitude for the many blessings we have received. We gladly acknowledge you as the source of all that we have and are. Accept these tithes and offerings as an expression of our love and devotion. We dedicate them to you and pray that they will be used to further your kingdom's work. In Jesus' name. Amen.

Introduction

The Bible contains many marvelous invitations (e.g., Isa. 55:1; Matt. 11:28: 22:1–14; Rev. 22:17). None, however, can surpass the invitation of our text. The magnificent aspect of this particular invitation is that it speaks of a holy God condescending to reason with sinful humanity.

I. The invitation God extends.

A. *It is a compassionate invitation: "Come."* One cannot visualize God speaking this word in any tone other than tender compassion. As Ralph Murray writes, this "is the plea of a rejected lover. This is not an affair of the court; it is an affair of the heart. There is not a shred of rationalism in the offer made. . . . This can be nothing but the extravagance of a lover" (Ralph L. Murray, *Plumb Lines and Fruit Baskets* [Nashville: Broadman, 1966], 46).

B. *The word* now *shows that it is an urgent invitation.* Jesus warned that Satan would attempt to steal the seed of the gospel (Matt. 13:4, 9). The writer of the book of Hebrews likewise warns of the danger of "a sinful, unbelieving heart" (Heb. 3:12–13 NIV). The apostle Paul spoke of today as the day of salvation (2 Cor. 6:2). It is imperative that people respond while they can to the gospel and to the convicting influence of the Holy Spirit. A delayed response can be disastrous.

C. *It is a gracious invitation: "let us reason."* This is not a meeting of equals but of a holy God with a sinful people. Such an invitation is totally unreasonable. Yet the wonderful truth of the gospel is that God, who has been offended, and who has every right to destroy humans because of their rebellious spirit, loves them and takes the initiative to reconcile them to himself (1 John 4:10; 2 Cor. 5:19).

II. The people God invites.

The invitation is extended to anyone who will respond. In this chapter Isaiah focuses our attention on four different types of people who are included in the invitation.

A. *The rebellious (v. 2).* The Hebrew word for "rebellion" refers to the breaking of a legal relationship. That legal reference is not absent here, for the break with God has been occasioned by the breaking of God's commandments. This inward breaking of God's laws manifested itself in outward acts of rebellion, apostasy, and idolatry. He who should have been the object of their love and devotion became the one against whom they rebelled (Isa. 30:1–3; 65:2).

B. *The thoughtless (v. 3).* The word "know" is used in the sense of recognizing God, of acknowledging or submitting to him. The words "doth not consider" suggest that the people did not understand completely what they were doing. Their stupidity was greater than that of the animals.

C. *The corrupt (v. 4).* Iniquity is here regarded as a burden that the people must bear. The whole nation is pictured as bowed and weighted down under the crushing weight of accumulated iniquities.

D. *The sick (vv. 5–6).* Notice the words "stricken," "sick," "faint," "no soundness," "wounds, and bruises, and putrefying sores." Sickness has overtaken them. Notice in verse 5 that the sickness is present in the most important parts of the human body: the head and the heart.

We are no different from ancient Israel. We rebel against God (Isa. 53:6), we give very little thought to God (James 4:13–15), or we trivialize the sins in our own life (Rom. 1:32). Modern man is sick with the age-old problem of sin. It has spread throughout his entire being: body, soul, and spirit.

III. The promise God makes.

Our heavenly Father can be trusted to keep a promise (Heb. 6:17–20). He will never go back on his word. The promise included in Isaiah 1:18 involves a thorough cleansing from sin. Sins that are "as scarlet . . . shall be as white as snow," and sins that are "red like crimson," shall be as wool. Notice two things about the sins that are mentioned.

A. *The permanent stain of sin.* The word "scarlet" contains the idea of a fixed or permanent color. Nothing can remove it. Hence, the word is used to represent the fixed or permanent stain of sin that is in the human heart. No human resources can remove it.

B. *The permanent removal of the stain of sin.* Sin will be pardoned, and the soul made pure. The color white has always symbolized purity. "As wool" suggests that the sin will be removed and the heart will be as wool undyed, or from which the color has been removed (cf. 1 Cor. 6:9–11; 1 John 1:9).

IV. The repentance God expects.

Isaiah is quick to point out that there is a blessing and a punishment involved in this invitation.

A. *The blessing for those who repent (1:19).* If the people of Israel would be willing and obedient, they would not only escape punishment but would also be the recipients of God's rich blessings. They would "eat the good of the land." What was the good of the land for Israel is to us the provision made for us in Christ as the nourishing and sustaining power of our life by the Holy Spirit (Rom. 8:17).

B. *The punishment for those who reject (1:20).* Persistence in a wicked way must bring with it the consuming punishment of the Lord. Disobedience to God's commands is the equivalent of rebellion (Matt. 25:41; John 3:18, 36).

Conclusion

In his book of sermons on Isaiah, Dr. W. A. Criswell relates the story of a father and a son who were watching a parade of red-coated British soldiers in London. The father was looking through the window as the soldiers passed by. The little boy, watching the same parade, exclaimed to his father, "Daddy, look at their beautiful white uniforms!"

The father replied, "Son, they're not white. They're red."

"No," said the boy. "Look, they are white, pure white."

The father looked closer and then saw the reason for the discrepancy. Around the window out of which they were viewing the parade was a band of red glass. The little boy, too short to look through the clear pane, was watching the parade through the red glass. When one looks at red through red, it is pure white. Dr. Criswell reminds his readers that this is what God does with our sins. The Lord looks at us through the blood of Jesus, and when he does, he sees us clean and pure and forgiven (W. A. Criswell, *Isaiah: An Exposition* [Grand Rapids: Zondervan, 1977], 44).

SUNDAY EVENING, JULY 9

Title: Compelled to Excel

Text: "But just as you excel in everything . . . see that you also excel in this grace of giving" *(2 Cor. 8:7 NIV).*

Scripture Reading: 2 Corinthians 8:1–15

Introduction

Corinth belonged to a lineage of great communities. From beginnings rooted in the first millennium BC, it had grown to a power status. Before Christ, it survived wars of the fifth and fourth centuries. Even the second-century destruction by the Romans did not prove fatal. By the first century AD, prosperity had restored its status.

Concurrent with this first century of progress was the introduction of Christianity to the city. Pride for the city was carried into the congregation. Jealousy over her preachers created factions. One disciple followed Paul, and another Apollos. Even the quest for deeper spiritual discovery caused problems for the Corinthians. Pride and controversy encircled the exercising of spiritual gifts. But, all in all, the Corinthian Christians had much. Paul affirmed in 1 Corinthians 1:7, "Ye come behind in no gift."

In this single verse, Paul provided a theological paradigm for all Christian churches. We are compelled to excel.

I. We are compelled to excel in faith.

A. *The simple word* faith *in the New Testament means "to trust."* The object of our faith is God. Faith means more than just believing about him. It suggests yielding one's life to him. It is the most comprehensive term for the Christian's response to God. Think how the New Testament writers used faith: "The just shall live by faith" (Heb. 10:38). "Purifying their hearts by faith" (Acts 15:9). We are "sanctified by faith" (Acts 26:18). "I may be comforted together with you by the mutual faith" (Rom. 1:12). "Be justified by faith in Christ" (Gal. 2:16).

B. *Paul used the concept repeatedly.* He wrote, "By faith we stand" (Rom. 11:20); "by faith we live" (Gal. 2:20); "by faith we have access to God" (Eph. 3:12); "by faith we are children of God" (Gal. 3:26); "by faith we have the promise of eternal life" (Gal. 3:22); "by faith we are saved by God's grace" (Eph. 2:8); "by faith, righteousness is attained in Christ" (Phil. 3:9); "by faith we are risen with him" (Col. 2:12).

Charles H. Spurgeon deftly summarized faith's position in the Christian life: "It will not save me to know that Christ is a Saviour; but it will save me to trust Him to be my Saviour." Faith is essential.

II. We are compelled to excel in utterance.

A. *"Speech" corresponds to the public proclamation of the Word.* How important it is for God's ministers and teachers to be faithful to God's precious Word. Pastors are compelled to excel in preaching God's Word. Sunday school teachers expound and explain the Word. God's Word will not return void.

B. *Honor his Word.* If the Word of God is not central in your life, your home, and your worship, you are sinning. Would anyone disagree with the import of God's Word? Certainly not. But we must apply the Word with wisdom.

III. We are compelled to excel in knowledge.

A. *Knowledge means perception.* You have the capacity to listen and learn. A founder of a great seminary once remarked that the Holy Spirit has an affinity for a well-trained mind. The Bible never puts a premium on ignorance.

B. *Do not fear growth.* Peter exhorted his hearers, "Grow in grace, and in the knowledge of our Lord and Saviour Jesus Christ" (2 Peter 3:18). Paul agreed: "I count all things but loss for the excellency of the knowledge of Christ Jesus my Lord" (Phil. 3:8).

C. *Stretch your mind.* Grow. One would be concerned if a child attended school and never gained knowledge. In the same fashion, one should have concern for growing in spiritual perception. The acquisition and application of knowledge is an important dimension to Christian growth.

IV. We are compelled to excel in diligence.

A. *The concept of diligence implies an eagerness and vigor to respond to God.* The author of Hebrews wrote, "We want each of you to show this same diligence to the very end, in order to make your hope sure. We do not want you to become lazy, but to imitate those who through faith and patience inherit what has been promised" (Heb. 6:11–12 NIV). Diligence with proper zeal produces action.

B. *One should sense the same earnestness and diligence in the church.* Diligence may not always be visible but is often in the invisible. The women who prepare a church meal work behind the scenes, but their diligence brings others delight. The preparations of a teacher for a classroom bulletin board may not be seen, but children experience the benefits. What makes the difference? Diligence does.

Few see many of the things done by the members of our church. But where would we be without their diligence? Nevertheless, diligence alone is not the full answer. Our diligence should be seasoned with love.

V. We are compelled to excel in love.

The Corinthian Christians had been upset with Paul. They had divided into factions. Yet love brought them back together.

A. *Love should be expressed in the horizontal and vertical realms.* Love is vertically directed to God. Horizontally it makes us right with others. Where would we be without love? The familiar passage of 1 Corinthians 13 would suffice as an overwhelming response to that question.

B. *We embrace faith, utterance, knowledge, diligence, and love as cardinal virtues of Christianity.* The evidence stands irrefutable. Paul then shocked the Corinthians. If each of the above is important at all, so is giving!

VI. We are compelled to excel in our giving.

A. *The NIV completes the sentence, ". . . see that you also excel in this grace of giving."* The verb "excel" demands a response. It implies action with the potential for obedience or disobedience. Paul suggested that it is possible to have faith, know the Word, gain knowledge, be earnest and loving, yet still lack the concept of giving.

B. *In verse 8 Paul wrote that he was not commanding the people.* He understood that giving could never be forced. He suggested something is wrong in one's spiritual life when giving is absent. Why? Because God owns everything. We are stewards of his possessions.

Conclusion

Dr. Ralph Sockman reportedly told a story about a New York law firm that was attempting to clear the title on some property in New Orleans. Apparently the New York firm engaged a New Orleans attorney to get the dates from the records. The New Orleans lawyer traced the title to 1803 and sent the information back to the East Coast firm. The New York lawyer wrote him back that he had not gone far enough.

In time the lawyer received a letter stating, "Gentlemen, please be advised that in the year 1803 the United States of America acquired the territory of Louisiana from the Republic of France by purchase. The Republic of France in turn acquired title from the Spanish Crown obtained by conquest. The Spanish Crown obtained it by virtue of the discoveries of one Christopher Columbus, a Genoese sailor who had been authorized to embark by Isabella the queen of Spain, who obtained sanction from the pope, the vicar of Christ. Christ is the Son and the Heir of Almighty God. And God made Louisiana."

We are all compelled to excel in each of these areas. Paul said to the Corinthian church, "You excel in so many things, will you not also excel in giving?" What is God saying to you today?

WEDNESDAY EVENING, JULY 12

Title: Self-gratification

Text: "You ask and do not receive because you ask with wrong motives, so that you may spend it on your pleasures" *(James 4:3 NASB).*

Scripture Reading: James 4:1–10

Introduction

One sign we see so often these days is that of the index finger pointing up. People everywhere, especially at football games shout, "We're number one!" It amuses me how many number ones there are and how many different situations call for such a claim. There is always the football team who upon winning the first game of the season claims to be number one. Most amazing is the team that loses all season, then finally in the last game scores the first touchdown and suddenly becomes number one. The one team that can hold up its index finger is the team that has won all year—that team alone is number one in football.

Seeking to be number one puts the Christian in the middle of a great tension—a dual philosophy. One is hedonism, meaning all is geared toward pleasure; the other is Christianity, meaning all is geared toward God. Caught in such a bind, we experience four detrimental results from our pleasure-seeking instincts.

I. The passion for self-gratification causes wars and fightings.

One thing that is sure to happen when we do things our way and seek the glory from it is conflict. James speaks of fights and wars in verse 2. The wars he speaks of refer to chronic hostility with others. The fights are individual conflicts. Thus hostility has two effects:

A. *It damages friendships.* It sets people at one another's throats.
B. *It drives the individual to commit greater and greater sins.* One things leads to another—coveting to envy to jealousy to hate to theft to murder.

II. The passion for self-gratification negates prayer.

A. *James implies it may well be a possibility that we ask for the right things.* Even if we do ask for the right things, we may ask wrongly and fail to get an answer. Then we protest to God. We may be denied because we ask for wrong things or, more likely, for the wrong reasons.
B. *Our basic problem is that we stand in the way of our own prayers.* The great painter Raphael is said to have worn a special hat when he painted. The hat had a candle mounted on top. He said he could often not paint correctly because his shadow spoiled the image he wished to portray.

III. The passion for self-gratification is abhorrent to God.

A. *A third disastrous effect of self-gratification is its offense to God.* This is really the most heinous aspect. God abhors those who are pleasure-seeking and not purity-seeking. James actually says in verse 4 that the passion for self-gratification is spiritual adultery. It is the very strongest form of faithlessness to God.
B. *James paints the picture here in the context of a home.* The person who is unfaithful to God by feeding his own lusts is likened to the married woman who cultivates a friendship with the man who is trying to seduce her. In biblical times the sin was deserving of death. Such a sin today in the spiritual sense is worthy of death as well.

One day a missionary and his son were to show pictures in a Telugu village. Upon their arrival they found the only place available for showing the pictures was in front of the Buddhist temple. The priest gave his consent for the pictures to be shown there. The first picture to be shown was that of Christ from Hoffmann's "Christ and the Rich Young Ruler." But when the picture was projected on the screen, it showed only a dim shadowy face. Upon investigation the missionary discovered that he had placed the screen directly in front of an idol of Buddha where a tiny light was burning. Because the people were anxious to see the picture, they immediately extinguished the flame. Then the strong appealing face of Christ was clearly visible. Likewise, the light of Christ becomes obscured in our lives if we keep a lamp burning to some selfish worldly desire.

IV. The passion for self-gratification demands repentance.

A. *We must repent of this sin.* James's words in verse 7 carry the weight of a military command pointing to the urgency and necessity of returning to God. We must subordinate ourselves and all that we have to the Lord. We must place our will under his control.

B. *James goes on to promise that when God is allowed back on the throne of our lives, Satan will flee from us.* He will see God's power in us. Submission to God will purify our lives after the Devil flees. James likens this process to the cleansing of the priest before he can sacrifice to God. Such a cleansing does not remove joy—it takes away the hilarity and foolishness of sin and restores the humble joy of knowing God—a joy that is accompanied by sorrow for our sins.

Conclusion

Self-righteous people know nothing of true repentance. A woman told her minister she would leave the church if a young woman sharing the pew was not made to occupy another seat. Said the minister, "Madam, that girl was saved from a terrible life of sin. You say she sits and weeps quietly through the church services and it annoys you, but it is because her heart is so full of the love of her Savior. Can't you try to understand her?"

"No, I can't," said the woman. "People who show their emotion over religion annoy me. I have always lived a good life. I don't make any fuss."

"Well, madam," said the minister, "have a talk with the girl; I believe she can help you."

The self-satisfied woman had no room for Christ. She was number one in her own life. Examine your life. Do your actions show that you are number one—or that Christ is?

SUNDAY MORNING, JULY 16

Title: The Great Encounter

Text: "Also I heard the voice of the Lord, saying, Whom shall I send, and who will go for us? Then said I, Here am I; send me" *(Isa. 6:8).*

Scripture Reading: Isaiah 6:1–13

Hymns: "Holy, Holy, Holy," Heber

"Send Me, O Lord, Send Me," Coggins

"I Stand Amazed in the Presence," Gabriel

Offertory Prayer: To know you and to have fellowship with you is the greatest experience in all the world, heavenly Father. Like the angels who cried, "Holy, holy, holy," we acknowledge your holiness; and, like Isaiah, who caught a glimpse of your glory, we cry, "I am a man of unclean lips." We thank you for loving us in spite of our sins and for the privilege of calling you "Father." May we ever be obedient to you and thus bring honor and glory to your holy name. Accept these gifts of tithes and offerings as an expression of our desire to follow you. In Jesus' name. Amen.

Introduction

It has been said that until a person has seen God in some sense, he or she begins at no beginning and works to no end. Isaiah saw the Lord. His encounter with God is recorded for us in Isaiah 6. It is a truly great chapter; it provides a glimpse of the marvels of God. It tells us how Isaiah came to be a prophet of God.

I. A glorious vision of God (vv. 1–4).

"I saw the Lord." Isaiah had a vision of God. What did he see? It is interesting to note that, although he describes the throne, the robe, and the heavenly attendants, he does not attempt to describe God. Nevertheless, certain truths about God were indelibly etched on him.

A. *He saw that God is sovereign.* It was a time of crisis, confusion, and change. Yet above all the tragedy and turmoil, Isaiah saw the Lord as the sovereign ruler of the world. Uzziah, the earthly king, was dead, but the divine King never dies. The throne in Judah was empty, but the throne in heaven was occupied by the eternal King whose glory filled the earth. Isaiah never forgot this vision. No matter how black life about him became, he was held by the conviction that God is the sovereign Lord of the universe.

B. *He saw that God is majestic.* Isaiah saw the Lord "sitting upon a throne, high and lifted up, and his train filled the temple" (v. 2). Seraphim were present, crying, "Holy, holy, holy, is the LORD of hosts: the whole earth is full of his glory" (v. 3). Each of the seraphim had six wings; with two wings each covered his face, a symbol of reverence and awe; with two wings each covered his feet, a symbol of humility; and, with two wings each flew, a symbol of their readiness for service. Isaiah never lost sight of the majesty of God. Throughout his long and eventful ministry, he manifested a consciousness that God is great and glorious.

C. *He saw that God is holy.* The word "holy" (v. 3) means "separate or remote." The word designates God as separate from and other than man. Isaiah was preeminently the prophet of the holiness of God in Old Testament days and may have coined the phrase found so frequently in his prophecy: "the Holy One of Israel."

We need such a vision of God. We need to realize afresh that God is; that he is on his throne; that he is great, majestic, and holy.

II. A vivid awareness of sin (vv. 5–7).

A profound awareness of God always brings a painful awareness of sin. After their sin of disobedience, Adam and Eve were very much aware of their sinfulness

(Gen. 3:8). Moses felt it at the burning bush and hid his face from Lord's presence (Ex. 3:4–6). Peter felt the heavy weight of guilt and cried, "Depart from me; for I am a sinful man, O Lord" (Luke 5:8). The more we see of God the more we are conscious of our sin.

A. *The conviction of sin (v. 5).* Isaiah was convicted of his sin. Listen to him as he cries, "Woe is me! For I am undone; because I am a man of unclean lips." The literal meaning is, "I am cut off; destroyed!" John R. Sampey translated it, "Woe is me, for I am a goner!" (cf. John 16:7–11; Acts 2:37–38).

B. *The confession of sin (v. 5).* Isaiah could not help but admit that he was a man of "unclean lips" and that he dwelt in the midst of an "unclean people." Isaiah confessed that he was unworthy either to join in the praise of God or to deliver a message in his name. The vision of the majesty and glory and holiness of God made him acutely aware of his own unworthiness (Ps. 32:1–5; 1 John 1:8–9).

C. *The cleansing of sin (vv. 6–7).* Fire has always been regarded as an emblem of purifying: one of the seraphim laid the hot coal on Isaiah's mouth and declared that his sin was purged. The word for "purged" means purified or removed. The Hebrew word was used to refer to an atonement for sin. The fact that the coal was taken from the altar of sacrifice was an indication that he was pardoned through the atonement. Fire burns, but it also cleanses. God did not tell Isaiah to take a bath, or to wear better clothes, or to get an education. He touched a hot coal to his lips and said, "Your guilt is taken away, and your sin forgiven."

III. A willing commitment to service (vv. 8–13).

For the first time in the vision, God speaks: "Whom shall I send, and who will go for us?" God's call to service comes in different ways. For Jacob it was angels and a ladder; for Moses it was a burning bush; for Samuel it was a call in the night; for Elijah it was a still, small voice; for David it was the anointing by Samuel; for Peter it was a call to be a fisher of men; for Paul it was a blinding light on the Damascus road. For Isaiah it was a vision from God.

A. *The response Isaiah gave (v. 8).* Isaiah was willing and eager. His urgent response suggests that he was afraid someone else might be chosen. One can almost see him waving his hand and shouting to gain God's attention. He did not know the nature of the mission, but he made himself available. He would go wherever God sent him.

B. *The difficulty Isaiah faced (vv. 9–12).* The people of Israel were a rebellious people. They would resist him as a prophet and harden their hearts against his message, covering their ears, refusing to hear, and covering their eyes, refusing to see their sinful condition. In spite of this difficulty, Isaiah was given no time limit. He was to continue until his job was complete.

C. *The assurance Isaiah received (v. 13).* Even though the people would reject the message and be destroyed, there was still a ray of hope. As a felled tree retains a spark of life in its stump and begins to grow again, so in Judah there would be left a righteous remnant through whom the purposes of God would ultimately be realized.

Conclusion

Isaiah had a life-changing encounter with God. Nothing in the ministry or message of Isaiah can be properly understood apart from this experience.

We are in a different time and country than Isaiah. Many things are different; many are the same. Our world, like that of Isaiah, is in a state of crisis, confusion, and change. Although we live in a highly technological age, the basic needs and issues of life are still moral and spiritual.

Robert Louis Stevenson once said, "No man can truly say that he has made a success of life unless he has written at the top of his life journal, 'Enter God.'" Let us do so with awe.

SUNDAY EVENING, JULY 16

Title: The Impulse to Give

Text: "Prove the sincerity of your love" *(2 Cor. 8:8).*

Scripture Reading: 2 Corinthians 8:8–12

Introduction

Remember the joke about the little boy whose father gave him a dollar and a quarter to take to church? His father instructed him to think about which one he would put into the offering plate. During the service the ushers handed the plate to the lad. He cheerfully dropped in the quarter. As the plate passed by, his father leaned over and said, "Why did you give the quarter instead of the dollar?" The boy looked up at this father and answered, "The preacher just said, 'The Lord loves a cheerful giver,' and it sure made me a lot happier to give the quarter than the dollar."

Why do we give? I want to suggest the levels of motivation in giving.

I. We may be motivated by the negative.

A. *Some people give for negative reasons.* This is really a wrong reason for giving. Some give to get. An immature Christian may take Proverbs 3:9–10, which says, "Honor the LORD with thy substance . . . so shall thy barns be filled," to mean that if one gives, one will automatically receive a monetary blessing. Unfortunately, that is a misinterpretation of that particular verse. The term "substance" is the term "wealth." The writer assumed that one had something to give!

B. *Other negative givers do so out of pride.* Remember the sin of Ananias recorded in Acts 5:1–11? He gave out of pride. He thought he could gain more recognition than he actually deserved.

C. *Some people give to avoid embarrassment.* Jesus scolded the Sadducees and the Pharisees for this sin (Matt. 6:1–4). Too often people tremble as the offering

198

plate passes on Sunday. They reach into their wallets and purses to avoid shame and to gain recognition, not to worship God.

D. *Other people give out of a sense of guilt.* They try to pay penance for guilt from past sin. They do not understand that giving expresses our appreciation to God for all he has done. It does not rectify the past. Only Jesus Christ has the power to do that by forgiving us!

II. We may be prompted by necessity.

In verse 8 Paul wrote, "I speak not by commandment, but by the occasion of the forwardness of others, and to prove the sincerity of your love." Paul suggested we should compare our sincerity, not our giving. Sacrifice built the church. Positive examples should motivate us.

A. *Paul described the greatest sacrifice in verse 9.* "For ye know the grace of our Lord Jesus Christ, that, though he was rich, yet for your sakes he became poor, that ye through his poverty might be rich." Paul reminded church leaders that Christ emptied himself, assuming the role of a servant, to be obedient unto death. His sacrifice should prompt us to give! The example of Jesus Christ alone should cause us to respond.

B. *The church has a responsibility to spread the gospel in our community and to expand the mission ministry of our congregation abroad.* What we have begun we must continue. Stop and ask yourself a question. Through the ministry of my local church, will what I give this year help influence a lost world for Christ? We should be prompted by these necessities.

III. We may be motivated by Christ's example.

A. *Paul said in verse 11: "As there was a readiness to will, so there may be a performance."* In other words, do something about your willingness to give—give!

A man visiting a florist asked for some flowers. The clerk brought the flowers and attractively wrapped them. He asked, "For your wife?" The customer said yes. "Since it is not a holiday, it must be her birthday or your anniversary," remarked the salesman. The customer startled the florist with his reply, "There's no special occasion. I love her, and want to give her something special for no other reason."

B. *The highest motivation a Christian has for giving should be to show appreciation to Jesus Christ.* A natural, spontaneous gratitude should cause a Christian to respond to God's grace. Have you ever given that way before?

Conclusion

A little girl in a church service handed the offering plate to the usher and said, "Sir, would you put it a little lower?" He accommodated her request. She asked again, "Would you put it lower?" The usher stooped down even more. This continued until the usher was agitated and the plate was on the floor. The little girl stood up and stepped into the plate. She looked up at the puzzled gentleman and remarked, "I want to give everything to Jesus." Give because he gave!

WEDNESDAY EVENING, JULY 19

Title: To Criticize Is to Crucify

Text: "Do not speak against one another, brethren" *(James 4:11 NASB).*

Scripture Reading: James 4:11–12

Introduction

We're all familiar with the expression "Sticks and stones may break my bones, but words will never harm me." It is surprising that this slogan has survived through time, especially because it is so ridiculously incorrect. To say that words do not hurt is a blatant lie. Words can crucify a person. Our text shows that James says this also.

Criticism is characteristic of a very negative person. It paints a person as someone who is against other people, against the law, and furthermore against God. In a day when it is popular to be positive, it is peculiar that criticism is so prevalent.

I. To criticize is to be against people.

A. *To criticize is first to be against people.* The word James uses in the Greek means literally "to talk against" or "to talk down." It is to run someone down. It is to defame, to slander, to speak disparagingly, to backbite. Criticism or gossip is among the vilest sins because, rather than ministering to people, it mutilates them.

B. *You never know the damage a comment can make.* You never know whom it will hurt. In many ways we are blind to the harm we cause.

II. To criticize is to be against the law.

A. *To be guilty of this sin is to be guilty of violating the royal law, which James states in 2:8:* "Thou shalt love thy neighbor as thyself." To violate the law is to say that you do not think the law is right. It is to say, "I do not agree with God and what he set out for people to follow—therefore I will do it my way."

B. *That is precisely what we say when we violate any law—religious or civil.* Those who drive 58 mph are saying, "I do not want to get a ticket, so I will not exceed 60. But I think going 55 is silly and does not do any good—so I will drive at *my* speed. Besides, my time is more important than saving lives."

It has been suggested that a way to avoid breaking the royal law is to do the following: "Say nothing, do nothing, be nothing." Jesus has a better suggestion than such apathy and passivity. He (as James repeats) says, "Love thy neighbor as thyself."

III. To criticize is to be against God.

A. *The most serious offense to criticism, however, is that it is a vote against God.* That is to say, the conduct prohibited involves usurping a prerogative that belongs to God alone. He may delegate various functions and responsibilities to human representatives, but he permits no human to share his judgment seat or to cancel or modify his laws. He has the exclusive right to judge because he alone is lawgiver and he alone is able to save and to destroy. In other words, God is Lord of life and death.

B. *To speak evil of our neighbor, to criticize, slander, or insult is to pass judgment on what belongs to God.* Our criticism is unwarranted, unfounded, unneeded, and basically incorrect and unimportant anyway.

There is a story of two taxidermists who stopped before a window in which an owl was displayed. They immediately began to criticize the way it was mounted. Its eyes were not natural, its wings were not in proportion with its head, its feathers were not neatly arranged, and its feet could certainly be improved. When they had finished with their critique and were just about to leave, the owl turned its head and winked. Only God can determine which of his people are truly good and which are truly bad. To God alone belongs the right to judge.

Conclusion

People are slow to realize that there are few sins the Bible so unsparingly condemns as the sin of irresponsible and malicious gossip. Yet there are few activities in which the average person finds more delight than spicy gossip, to tell and to listen to a slanderous story—especially if it is about some distinguished or respected person. It is for all people a fascinating activity—which is against people, against the law, and against God.

Therefore what James is basically asking in verse 12 is "Who are you to judge? Who do you think you are? Who are you to presume to be God?" To criticize is to crucify.

SUNDAY MORNING, JULY 23

Title: The Great Promises of Peace

Text: "Thou wilt keep him in perfect peace, whose mind is stayed on thee" *(Isa. 26:3).*

Scripture Reading: Isaiah 26:1–4

Hymns: "Like a River Glorious," Havergal

"My Faith Has Found a Resting Place," Edmunds

"I've Got Peace Like a River," Traditional Spiritual

Offertory Prayer: Heavenly Father, thank you that in a world of turmoil and uncertainty, when many are frantically searching for peace, we who know you have the peace that passes all understanding. As we present our gifts of tithes and offerings, it is our prayer that you will bless them and use them to further your kingdom of peace. May we strive each day to be peacemakers among people who are strangers to the Prince of Peace. In the name of Jesus we pray. Amen.

Introduction

That the Bible has much to say about peace is evident by the fact that the term occurs some four hundred times. In fact, the Bible can be regarded as God's testament of peace. Much is said about the peace of God (Phil. 4:7), peace with God (Rom. 5:1), and peace from God (2 Cor. 1:3). God the Father is the God of peace who will sanctify the believer (1 Thess. 5:23). God the Son is the Prince of Peace, on whose shoulders the spiritual government will rest (Isa. 9:6). God the Holy Spirit produces the fruit of peace in the life of the believer (Gal. 5:22). The Bible assures us that when our ways please the Lord, God makes our enemies to be at peace with us (Prov. 16:7). At the birth of Jesus, angels praised God, saying, "Glory to God in the highest, and on earth peace, good will toward men" (Luke 2:14). Other verses of Scripture about peace include Matthew 5:9; Romans 12:18; 1 Timothy 2:2; and James 3:17. But of all the verses in the Bible about peace, the favorite of many is Isaiah 26:3. From this verse we can draw personal inspiration and strength.

I. The protection of this peace.

Notice the word "keep." The idea behind this word is a sentinel standing watch or keeping guard. A passage from the New Testament that expresses the same meaning is Philippians 4:6–7. Paul was assured that God's peace would keep (or stand watch) over his readers' hearts and minds. How can we be assured of this for ourselves?

A. *Proven by God's performance.* God reminded Moses and the people of Israel by his faithfulness in protecting them (Ex. 19:3–6). Joshua had a monument erected that would serve as a memorial to remind the people of God's faithfulness (Josh. 4:1–9). Samuel set up stone between Mizpeh and Shen and called it "Ebenezer" to remind the people that they were where they were because of God's faithfulness (1 Sam. 7:12). God's past performance of faithfulness is proof that he will keep his promise of peace.

B. *Maintained by God's power.* In describing the government that the Prince of Peace would establish, the Lord declared, "The zeal of the LORD of hosts will perform this" (Isa. 9:6–7). God's power will bring about this peace, and his power will maintain this peace.

C. *Supervised by God's presence.* In Isaiah 41:10 God encouraged Isaiah, "Fear thou not; for I am with thee: be not dismayed, for I am thy God: I will strengthen thee; yea, I will help thee; yea, I will uphold thee with the right hand of my righteousness." God will not forsake his own. He has promised to be our constant companion throughout life (John 14:18; Heb. 13:5).

II.The description of this peace.

The word "perfect" is not in the original text. The noun "peace" is repeated to denote emphasis and means undisturbed, perfect peace. God's peace is unique in three ways.

A. *It surpasses human understanding.* God's peace is indescribable (Phil. 4:7). It is totally foreign to human experience and reason. Jesus himself said that the peace he would give would be unlike anything the world could offer (John 14:27).

B. *It surpasses human capability.* Three times in Ephesians 2:11–22 the apostle Paul writes of Christ that "he is our peace" (v. 14); he is "making peace" (v. 15); and he "preached peace" (v. 17). No man can remove the enmity between himself and God. It is a miracle of grace through Christ.

C. *It surpasses human expectations.* In writing to the Christians at Ephesus, Paul told them of his prayer request. It was his desire that they might come to a better understanding of God's revelation (Eph. 1:15–19). The richness of God's peace is overwhelming. The gospel of the Lord Jesus Christ involves more than anyone can imagine; it will never disappoint our most grandiose hope.

III. The conditions for this peace.

Although the peace that God offers the believer is a free gift, certain conditions must be met.

A. *A mind "stayed" on God.* The word for "stayed" means "to lean, rest upon, support." Therefore, the mind that is at peace is the mind that is supported by the Lord. We must discipline our minds to dwell on the Lord (Job 37:14; Phil. 2:5; 4:8).

B. *A heart that "trusts" in God.* Isaiah 26:4 reads, "Trust ye in the Lord for ever: for the LORD JEHOVAH is everlasting strength." We must place our confidence in God. No calamity, adversity, persecution, poverty, or trial of any kind should prevent us from trusting him. Hezekiah was a man of faith whose example of trusting encourages us to do the same (2 Kings 18:1–7). And who can forget the inspiring faith of Job who declared, "Though he slay me, yet will I trust in him" (Job 13:15)? One of my favorite Bible passages is Proverbs 3:5–6: "Trust in the LORD with all thine heart; and lean not unto thine own understanding. In all thy ways acknowledge him, and he shall direct thy paths."

Conclusion

Notice that Isaiah 26:3 begins with God ("Thou") and ends with God ("thee") and the trusting soul is in between. Perfect peace is to get between these two words, "Thou" and "thee," and to stay there. Let us recall the poignant words from Frances Havergal's hymn:

> *Like a river glorious is God's perfect peace,*
> *Over all victorious in its bright increase;*
> *Perfect, yet it floweth fuller every day;*
> *Perfect, yet it groweth deeper all the way.*
> *Stayed upon Jehovah, hearts are fully blest;*
> *Finding, as he promised, perfect peace and rest.*

SUNDAY EVENING, JULY 23

Title: The Meaning of Stewardship

Text: "For I testify that they gave as much as they were able, and even beyond their ability" *(2 Cor. 8:3 NIV).*

Scripture Reading: 2 Corinthians 8:1–5

Introduction

Waiting for friends to arrive at a restaurant, a gentleman overheard a lively conversation at a nearby table. A woman questioned her companion, "How much are you going to give me? I am just dying for that new fur coat. Let's go shopping after dinner." The observer of that conversation could not help but chuckle when the couple later left the restaurant and drove off in their Mercedes. The drama exemplified a classic question many people ask, "What am I going to get out of this?"

The Corinthian church had asked Paul what he could do for them. Paul scolds them in 2 Corinthians 11:8, "I robbed other churches, taking wages off them, to do you service." The Corinthians had not supported the ministry of the apostle financially. They concerned themselves with themselves. They majored in what they could get out of Christianity, not what they could put into it.

Paul offers some advice about stewardship. Such knowledge implies more than a casual acquaintance. It connotes intelligent comprehension. Hence, Paul suggests a thorough knowledge of stewardship. What did he want the Corinthians to learn?

I. Christian stewardship grows out of grace.

A. *God has appointed you a steward of certain possessions.* Stewardship means management. A salesman minds the store while the owner leaves for the warehouse. Just because the boss leaves does not suggest a change in ownership. The employer entrusts the employee with possessions. The worker owns nothing.

B. *How much can one bring to life from his own birth?* How much can one take with his dream? Never lose the perspective that life is a gift. We are to be responsible stewards of that gift.

II. Christian stewardship continues in spite of circumstances.

A. *The churches of Macedonia had suffered great hurt.* Rome had impoverished these people. The churches of Philippi, Thessalonica, and Berea had been persecuted. Yet they trusted God's grace and continued to be good stewards of God's gifts.

Examine verse 2: "Out of the most severe trial, their overflowing joy and their extreme poverty welled up in rich generosity" (NIV). In hard times they persevered; they continued to share more than they were humanly able.

A student mission group visited homes in a poverty-stricken area of a city. On a cold windy day, a knock on a door brought an invitation for the students to enter. What they discovered impressed them. A family merely existing offered them food and friendship. The man of the house showed his love for Christ. He exclaimed, "You are welcome to come to our home. Come and visit us again. Have a meal with us. Everything that we have is God's. We would share it with you gladly!" As the students left that physically modest home, they rejoiced over the spiritual wealth they had observed.

B. *God challenges us to give.* Remember the story from Mark 12: A widow gave her last modest coins. Jesus commended her. Contrast that to the sad parable of Luke 12. The rich fool had so much and only wanted more. Jesus taught us to give in spite of circumstances.

III. Christian stewardship goes beyond a tithe.

A. *The Macedonian Christians were not affluent, but they still gave.* The NIV translates verse 3: "For I testify that they gave as much as they were able, and even beyond their ability." New Testament language indicates one must choose to give. One has the privilege of deciding for God's kingdom.

B. *Some Christians are unfamiliar with tithing, the practice of giving the first tenth of one's income back to God.* Tithing is nothing new. Archaeologists have discovered from ancient cuneiform inscriptions that even Babylonian pagans supported their temple with a tithe. The Old Testament supports the tithe. In Genesis 14:20 Abram gave a tithe. In Numbers 18:21 Aaron spoke of giving the Levite priests one-tenth. Deuteronomy 14:22–27 records the festival of the tithe.

C. *One might argue that the tithe applied only during the time the people were under the law.* Yet Jesus gave much deeper insight into the law. The laws of the Old Testament guided. Now the light of Christ reveals new insights. To tithe means to take a first step in giving. Today, under grace, our giving should go beyond a tithe. We must remember that God entrusts us with everything. We own nothing.

A businessman delivered a paper bag to his pastor. It contained $1,000 in $20 bills. The startled minister asked the layman to explain, since the businessman was already a tither. The response touched his minister's heart. "Pastor, we did not have any accidents on the job the last six months. Our insurance company gave back $1,000 as a rebate on our policy for good experience. I know we have been raising money to expand the church. I felt this would help us in achieving our goals. God has been so good to me. This is the least I can do." Stewardship goes beyond a simple tithe.

IV. Christian stewardship deals with your spiritual life.

A. *Verse 7 teaches that stewardship influences one's joy in Christian ministry.* The Macedonian believers had asked for the opportunity to give. Thank God for Christians who understand the spiritual nature of stewardship. Stinginess toward God suggests spiritual trouble. Failure to tithe is not a financial problem. It is a spiritual problem. If one does not share the resources God has given, something is wrong spiritually.

A pastor and a layman in the western United States were driving by a large ranch that covered thousands of acres. The layman related a tragic drama to his minister. He told how the original owner of the land had gambled it away. He had also washed his wealth down his throat with alcohol. He squandered his fortune and finally lost it all. If only he had learned to be a steward of what God had given to him! Where did he go wrong?

B. *The NIV translation of verse 5 provides an answer.* "They did not do as we expected, but they gave themselves first to the Lord and then to us in keeping with God's will." We must commit ourselves first to the Lord. Stewardship begins with commitment to Christ.

Conclusion

Someone once suggested that if Christians totally committed themselves to Jesus Christ, there would be little need for any special appeal for stewardship. Get a man right with God, and his stewardship will be right. A corollary might be suggested. Giving is not just a matter of stewardship. It is a matter of salvation. We give because Jesus gave.

WEDNESDAY EVENING, JULY 26

Title: The Self-made Man

Text: "Now listen, you who say, 'Today or tomorrow we will go to this or that city, spend a year there, carry on business and make money.' . . . Instead, you ought to say, 'If it is the Lord's will, we will live and do this or that'" *(James 4:13, 15 NIV)*.

Scripture Reading: James 4:13–17

Introduction

The issue of tonight's text is how much is too much? Can you ever have too much money? What is wrong with having money? If it is wrong to have much money, why is it? James answers these questions.

In Palestine the Jews generally adhered to agricultural life, but in the dispersion they were frequently merchants and bankers. The dispersion gave them connections all over the world and afforded them new openings for trade. This led to their becoming itinerants. They were full of confidence in facing the future—but they faced it without God. Herein lay the problem. As James explained, the problem had three facets.

I. They were acting without knowledge of the future.

Planning can become a dangerous thing when it disregards the element of the unknown. We do not know the future. Things change. That is all the more reason to depend heavily on God for wisdom. This is exactly James's criticism of these Christians. They counted only on themselves and were fools—self-made, self-led, and self-defeated fools.

II. They were emphasizing the wrong things.

James's readers valued the wrong things: "Your life . . . is even a vapor" (v. 14). Other biblical texts characterize life in this manner as a declining shadow, a breath, and a vanishing cloud. The thought is of something fleeting and transient: here one moment and suddenly gone.

The brevity of life should compel us to emphasize only the truly important. We pour too much of ourselves into the meaningless. Consider this true story of children of a family who were left largely in the care of servants. When the father lost his fortune, the servants were discharged and the parents cared for the little ones. One evening when the father returned home after a day of anxiety and business tension, his little girl climbed up on his knee and wrapped her arms around his neck. She said, "Papa, don't you get rich again. You didn't come into our rooms when you were rich, but now we can come around you and get on your lap and kiss you. Don't get rich again, Papa."

This story illustrates how zealous and ambitious we are to provide the things our family supposedly wants, yet in our efforts we leave out what they really need. We work long and hard to give them many things, but the real effect of our labor is to leave them in abandonment. So it is with our relationships to God.

III. They were committing sin.

James says that such arrogance of presuming to know the future is evil. Hence we see that the problem was one of sin. James's readers knew very well that their future was really in God's hands. They knew that they could not be sure of a single day. They knew that they were absolutely dependent on God for the preservation of their lives. And they knew that any prosperity came from him. But in spite of their knowledge, they continued in their proud ways. They pretended to control the future. They put their priorities on the wrong things. They lived in arrogance rather than by faith in God.

Conclusion

Possessions are not the problem. The problem is with the person whose world revolves around possessions. When material things become our goal, our security, our greatest desire, they are our god. That is when we have problems.

SUNDAY MORNING, JULY 30

Title: A Great Call

Text: "Ho, every one that thirsteth, come ye to the waters, and he that hath no money; come ye, buy, and eat; yea, come, buy wine and milk without money and without price" *(Isa. 55:1).*

Scripture Reading: Isaiah 55:1–7

Hymns: "Come, Thou Fount of Every Blessing," Robinson

         "Satisfied with Jesus," McKinney

         "'Whosover' Meaneth Me," McConnell

Offertory Prayer: We thank you, heavenly Father, for the spiritual life you have given us. Your spiritual blessings satisfy us beyond anything else this world has to offer. We realize that what has been received has been given because of your gracious Spirit. We love you for loving us despite our sins. Among our many blessings are the material possessions you have entrusted to us. We pray that we may be faithful stewards of all you have given. Please accept these tithes and offerings as a demonstration of our faithfulness. In Jesus' name we pray. Amen.

Introduction

Isaiah 55 is one of the truly great chapters in the Bible. In a jubilant and triumphant manner, it presents an unusual call from God. God, the Creator, is portrayed as a merchant pleading with man, the creature: "Ho!" This word calls attention to the subject as an important one. It is as though the merchant is saying, "Stop! Listen! Eyes this way! Ears alert! I have something worthy of your attention!"

I. The people who are invited.

God's call is not based on one's moral goodness but on one's need. Isaiah identifies whose who are issued this call by four types of needs.

A. *Those who are thirsty (55:1).* "Thirst" often indicates intense desire. In the Middle East water is quite scarce. It is easy for a body to dehydrate in the arid atmosphere and merciless sun. But physical thirst is not all that is being discussed here. The text includes other kinds of thirsts: the thirst of the mind for knowledge, the thirst of the heart for affection, and the thirst of the soul for the spiritual things of God (John 4:13–14; 7:37–39).

In Matthew 5:6 Jesus says, "Blessed are they which do hunger and thirst after righteousness: for they shall be filled." Robert Hastings suggests that the word "filled" is a term used for feeding cattle. Just as a well-fed cow stands with sides bulging, so the satisfied Christian can expect ultimate realization of his dreams (Robert Hastings, *Take Heaven Now!* [Nashville: Broadman Press, 1968], 67).

B. *Those who are destitute (55:1).* Those who are unable to purchase salvation are invited to come and spend "money for that which is not bread." In Matthew 5:3 Jesus speaks of those who are spiritually poor. In Revelation 3:17–18 the call is given for those who are naked and sick to come. Jesus welcomes them.

C. *Those who are deceived (55:2).* These destitute people were deceived into believing they could find satisfaction in laboring for and purchasing bread that could never satisfy. There is a void in the heart that things do not and can never fill. A story vividly illustrates this point.

Jay Gould was the richest man in the world many years ago. He had all he wanted. Despite his wealth and power as a railroad tycoon, he spoke of his life like this: "I suppose I am the most miserable man in the world" (W. A. Criswell, *Isaiah: An Exposition* [Grand Rapids: Zondervan, 1977], 256–57).

D. *Those who are wicked (55:7).* "Wicked" refers to those who are guilty of sin against God and following an evil course in life. The "unrighteous man" is the man of iniquity, of evil, of falsehood. All goodness is absent from him (cf. 1 Cor. 6:9–11).

This glorious call is for everybody, regardless of color, class, or condition. It is for saint and for sinner. It is for God's people and for pagans. It is for you and for us. If we are conscious of our need and of our inability to meet that need, God says, "Come!"

II. The conditions that are imposed.

God imposes certain conditions on those who respond. These conditions are designed to help, not hinder. We are talking about coming in contact with a holy God. We could not expect to approach and touch him with sin-stained hands any more than we would expect a surgeon to perform an operation with dirty hands or filthy instruments. So, if we accept his call, we must meet his conditions (Matt. 22:11–14).

A. *An attentive ear (55:2–3).* "Hearken" means to give respectful attention, and "diligently" means to do so with speed. We are to put forth an earnest effort to hear what God has to say. We are to shut out all other voices and listen to God (Matt. 13:10–17; James 1:22–25).

B. *An urgent search (55:6).* "Seek" means "to tread" and refers to the steps taken to come to God. "While he may be found" suggests that there will come a time when he cannot be found; therefore, there is urgency to seek him now (John 12:35; 2 Cor. 6:2).

C. *An earnest call (55:6).* Throughout the Bible one may find one encouragement after another to "call" on God (Matt. 10:46–52; Rom. 10:13).

D. *A genuine repentance (55:7).* The sinner is commanded to "forsake his way." This involves a complete abandonment of all evil—including evil thoughts. The sinner is admonished to return to God, who will pardon and cleanse.

III. The blessings that are included.

The purpose in the call that God extends is that all might be blessed. This blessing is twofold:

A. *The fullness of life.* "Water" suggests the refreshment of life; "wine" suggests joy, exhilaration, comfort. "Milk" speaks of nourishment. "Bread" stands for the staple of life, and "fatness" represents the best of extravagant food, in contrast to the leanness of what the people were striving after. They are invited to eat what will nourish the soul and fill them with joy (John 10:9–10). All of these words represent the rich life one has with God and the abundance of the blessings bestowed on those who come into his kingdom.

B. *The forgiveness of sin.* When we turn to God in true repentance, God turns to us in pardoning grace. Forgiveness of sin is our deepest need, and it is God's greatest gift. When one truly repents, God pardons abundantly.

Conclusion

In his book *Plumb Lines and Fruit Baskets*, Ralph L. Murray tells of a scrubwoman in London who became sick. Her friends made it possible for her to go to the hospital. While she was convalescing there, she became acquainted with other patients. Across the hall from her was a twelve-year-old boy, redheaded and freckle-faced. They talked daily. Then one morning she was awakened early by commotion in the hall, and before long the boy's mother came in to say, "The doctors say Johnny has about ten minutes to live. Won't you say something to him?"

Although this assignment was difficult, the woman, with the courage of a great Christian, walked quietly across the hall and sat down beside the boy. She took his thin hand and looked at him. Quietly, she said, "Listen, Johnny. God made you. God loves you. God sent his Son to save you. God wants you to come home to live with him."

The little fellow turned his eyes weakly toward her and said in a whisper, "Say it again."

Quietly she repeated the same words: "God made you. God loves you. God sent his Son to save you. God wants you to come home to live with him."

Johnny looked into the calm face of his friend and said, "Tell God, 'Thank You'" (Ralph L. Murray, *Plumb Lines and Fruit Baskets* [Nashville: Broadman, 1966], 73–74).

In Psalm 116 David spoke of his love for the Lord and of God's delivering him from sorrow. In verse 12 he asks, "What shall I render unto the LORD for all his benefits toward me?" Then he answers his own question in verse 13: "I will take the cup of salvation, and call upon the name of the LORD." That's what God wants from us. The proper response to God's call is to accept it.

SUNDAY EVENING, JULY 30

Title: A New Day in Giving

Text: "For if any Macedonians come with me and find you unprepared, we—not to say anything about you—would be ashamed of having been so confident" *(2 Cor. 9:4 NIV).*

Scripture Reading: 2 Corinthians 9:1–7

Introduction

From a heart of stewardship flows the lifeblood of giving. God gave. Jesus gave. What would the church be like today if all Christians gave as graciously as they expected God to give to them? Catch a vision of what God wants to do through our church by looking at three simple principles.

I. We must be ready to help.

A. *Give because Christ gave.* In this sense the subject of giving needs no discussion. Paul writes in verse 1 that it is "superfluous" to discuss the topic. Why then does he proceed to do so?

B. *Look at other disciplines.* Christians should pray. But one must be disciplined in learning how to pray. Does one automatically listen to a sermon? Are believers verbal witnesses of their faith in Christ naturally? They may have a desire to witness, but do they act on it? The practices of the faith are cultivated by discipleship. Young Christians grow into mature believers. Likewise, young Christians must be trained to understand the importance of stewardship.

C. *Keep an open door for ministry.* Stand ready to help. Edward Everett Hale stated it this way: "I am only one but still I am one. I cannot do everything but still I can do something. And because I cannot do everything I will not refuse to do the something that I can do."

D. *Look at the ministry of Jesus.* People always asked him for help. In Luke 10:40 Martha asked Jesus to tell her sister to help her. In Mark 9:24 the father of the boy with the evil spirit cried for help. In Matthew 15:25 the Canaanite woman cried, "Lord, help me." Does one hear Jesus requesting help? No. Why? Because he came to give. We must be ready to help.

II. Our help proves our sincerity.

Paul boasted about the accomplishments of the Corinthian Christians. He spoke positive words about their ministries. He added that their performance should match their potential.

A. *Match the ideal with the real.* Growing churches want to expand ministries, reach out to hurting people, and increase mission efforts. If the church dreams of doing, then it must do!

Have you ever casually invited an old friend who lives far away to drop by anytime? One day your friend may call and announce, "Hello, we're getting ready to take a vacation to see you." Suddenly you are put to the test. Was your promise a serious invitation or an empty courtesy? Let's not fill the churches with empty courtesies.

B. *When there is no planning and no preparation, goals are usually not accomplished.* In a typical church fewer than half of the members provide financial support. The problem for many people is that they do not plan to give. What a tragedy!

C. *A person who gives nothing to support the ministry of the local church needs to take a personal spiritual inventory.* Helping proves sincerity, according to Paul. Authentic Christian giving is rooted in the fertile soil of God's love.

III. Sincerity grows out of love.

A. *Paul suggests, "Give a bounty."* The term comes from a concept that means blessing. Literally, will you bless God by your giving? Paul said that one should have a contagious enthusiasm and excitement in sharing and supporting the ministry of the local church. A wise philosopher once said that Christians are obliged to witness because believers see the message as a particle of light, which would be extinguished if too protected. God has placed in your possession the light and the life of Jesus Christ. Give them to the world.

B. *Think about giving love.* Is the real reward in giving love, the love that one receives from others? Could it be the deeper reward of an increased capacity to love? The real joy of sharing Christian love is that one's circle of love increases to more people. Giving increases the capacity to share. Paul exclaimed, "God loves a cheerful giver!" The term "cheerful" here comes from the same Greek word from which we get our word "hilarious." The joy resulting from giving to God should be like that of a parent watching a child at Christmas opening a special gift.

C. *Sincerity grows out of love, and love must come from the heart.* The real source of financial support of the church is not the checkbook, but the heart. Paul says in verse 7 that "each man should give what he has decided in his heart to give" (NIV). A committed heart will love enough to care and to give liberally.

Conclusion

Helping proves sincerity. Sincerity stems from love. John summarized the basis for this love when he wrote, "We love because [God] first loved us" (1 John 4:19 NIV).

AUGUST

■ Sunday Mornings

Christ loved the church and died for it. We need to love the church better—despite its imperfections. We can better love the church by understanding the privileges we have in being part of it. A series titled "The Nature of the Church" will help us do so.

■ Sunday Evenings

God has given Christians access to his wisdom. Many of us, however, are not guided by his wisdom but by our emotions. This often leads to upheaval, chaos, and distress. "Facing Emotional Problems from a Biblical Perspective" is the suggested theme for messages to help us handle our problems using God's wisdom instead of our feelings alone.

■ Wednesday Evenings

Continue the series from James entitled "The Practice of Genuine Religion."

WEDNESDAY EVENING, AUGUST 2

Title: Man, That's Living!

Text: "Your gold and your silver have rusted; and their rust will be a witness against you and will consume your flesh like fire. It is in the last days that you have stored up your treasure!" *(James 5:3 NASB).*

Scripture Reading: James 5:1–6

Introduction

A wealthy man many years ago was somewhat of a free spirit and requested a very special burial congruent to his lifestyle. After his death the burial took place as he had directed: donned in a sports jacket and hat, with his cigar in his mouth, he was placed in a sitting position at the wheel of his brand-new Cadillac convertible, with the speedometer set at 80 mph—then he was lowered into the tomb. A friend nearby said through his tears, "Man, that's living!"

In truth, that is not living at all. Those niceties of life may be put in the grave, but that is exactly where they will stay.

I. They labor for things that do not last (vv. 1–3).

A. *In the East there were three main sources of wealth, and James shows the transience of each.*

213

1. Food: corn and grain, that is, the kind of wealth that can rot.
2. Clothes: a symbol of wealth seen throughout the Bible. All of them, regardless of the splendor, will serve only to feed the moths.
3. Even gold and silver would corrode.

B. *It is James's conviction that to concentrate on material things is not only to concentrate on a decaying delusion, it is to concentrate on a self-produced destruction.*

> *Out of this life, I never shall take,*
> *Things of silver and gold I make.*
> *All that I cherish and hoard away,*
> *After I leave, on the earth must stay.*
> *Though I have toiled for a painting rare.*
> *To hang on my wall I must leave it there.*
> *Though I call it mine and boast its worth,*
> *I must give it up when I quit the earth.*
> *All that I gather and all that I keep,*
> *I must leave behind when I fall asleep.*
> —Author Unknown

II. They labor for things that fail to satisfy.

A. *We work today for the things that will make us happy and comfortable—yet somehow we are never satisfied.* If there is any satisfaction at all, it is temporary. And the lack of satisfaction leads us to greater greed and the greed directly to death.

B. *James gives us an illustration of what he is saying so that all may understand.* He likens us to a cow that does nothing really productive except feed her appetite. She is always hungry, never content, and yet the more she eats to satisfy that hunger, the fatter she gets and the closer to the slaughter she comes.

In 1923 a very important meeting was held at the Edgewater Beach Hotel in Chicago. Attending this meeting were eight of the world's most successful financiers. Their prodigious wealth, however, was meaningless by 1948: Charles Schwab died bankrupt and lived his last five years on borrowed money; Samuel Insull died a fugitive from justice and penniless in a foreign country; Howard Hepoor died at an early age; Richard Whitney was incarcerated in Sing Sing penitentiary; Albert Fall was pardoned from prison so he could die at home; Jesse Livermore, Ivan Kreuger, and Leon Fraser all committed suicide. All of these men had learned well the art of making money; none had learned how to live.

III. They labor for things and neglect people (vv. 4, 6).

A. *There can be little doubt about the harmful effects of materialism on us, but just as important is the effect it has on others.* First, greed obscures our love for others. James addresses particularly those who exploit others for personal financial gain.

B. *The second negative effect on others is injustice.* When wages are withheld, James says they will cry out to God for vengeance. It is incredible how people love to own and control others and oppress the poor.

Conclusion

God cares for his people. He wants them to be happy and comfortable. Christianity should not be equated with an anti-money attitude. Rather, it should be equated with an anti-greed, sacrificial love.

SUNDAY MORNING, AUGUST 6

Title: How Do You Describe an Elephant?

Text: "To the church of God which is at Corinth, to those sanctified in Christ Jesus, called to be saints together with all those who in every place call on the name of our Lord Jesus Christ, both their Lord and ours" *(1 Cor. 1:2 RSV)*.

Scripture Reading: 1 Corinthians 1:1–19

Hymns: "Holy, Holy, Holy," Huber

"I Love Thy Kingdom Lord," Dwight

"In Christ There Is No East or West," Oxenham

Offertory Prayer: Almighty God, you have given us so much. In a world of givers and receivers, you have blessed us with the privilege and opportunity to be among the givers. Accept our tithes and offerings that we give this day, we pray, to further the cause of Christ. In his strong name. Amen.

Introduction

Once upon a time a certain king called on three blind men to describe an elephant. The first, who was touching a leg, said, "An elephant is much like a tree trunk." The second blind man, who was holding on to the tail, said, "An elephant is like a snake. It is much smaller around than a tree and does not come to the ground." The third blind man reached for the elephant and felt its trunk. He said, "You are both wrong. The elephant is like a giant vacuum cleaner."

Descriptions of the church are much like this story of the three blind men and the elephant. Each person who comes into contact with the church has a different impression of what the church is like.

I. The church is a geographical location.

A. *The least appropriate answer to our question is that the church is a geographical location.* Paul wrote his longest and most practical letter to the church in Corinth, one of the four most important cities of that day. A "sunbelt city" of the time, Corinth was on a narrow isthmus linking northern and southern Greece and had the strategic value of Panama.

B. *This was the city of Corinth.* But a church is far more than a geographical location. Its geography is only incidental. We live in a time when many denominations include some geographical reference in their official name, for example, the Church of England. We would do well to see the potential danger of allowing geographical boundaries to circumscribe theological and missionary vision. A church is more than geography.

II. The church is a building.

A. *In common parlance, we refer to the church as a building.* Biblically speaking, a church is far more than an edifice of mortar, stone, carpet, and pews. And so it was for the Corinthians.

B. *The Corinthians had no "official" church building.* Instead, the congregation gathered in private homes, hearing messages from Paul read by the pale light of an oil lamp. A church is more than a building.

III. The church is "of God."

A. *If the church is neither a building nor a geographical location, then just what is the church?* Verse 2 explicitly states that the church is "of God." In addition, Paul mentions some form of the name of Jesus no fewer than ten times in the first nine verses of 1 Corinthians. The church is indeed "of God." It centers around Christ. Paul uses the word *ekklesia* ("church") twenty-two times in 1 Corinthians and nine additional times in 2 Corinthians. Paul speaks of the church more in his Corinthian correspondence than he does in all of his other letters combined. In these writings, Paul stresses that the church is "of God."

B. *A New Testament church is not autonomous; it is theonomous.* The church does not rule itself: God rules it! The New Testament church is not a democracy: it is a theocracy or a Christocracy. The church is "of God."

C. *This truth applies in many directions.* For one thing, it helps us remember that the church belongs to God, not God to the church. Sometimes we forget this and assume that God is the church's talisman God. Second, in the context of 1 Corinthians, Paul surely means us to see something else in this description of the church. Paul wrote this letter largely to address the problem of factions besetting the church. Evidently many were rallying around any one of the several prominent personalities—Apollos, Peter, Paul, and Christ—and fragmenting the unity of the congregation. So, with the very first stroke of his pen, Paul declares that the church is "of God"—and this precludes the possibility that it is "of Apollos," or "of Peter," or "of the denomination," or "of the parachurch." The church is "of God."

IV. The church is both local and universal.

A. *Paul declares that the church is both local and universal.* Devout believers across the years have argued for first one and then the other part of his definition. The truth is that the church is both. Paul addresses his letter "to the church of God which is at Corinth" and then in the same sentence writes, "with all of those who call upon the name of the Lord in every place."

B. *Paul may have chosen his words to correct some proud Corinthians who saw themselves as the center of the Christian universe.* His words remind us as well: the local church is but one fragment of God's entire church. We belong to a local church meeting in a given neighborhood and to a worldwide movement as well. A bank may have several branch offices. Each separate branch is the bank, and then again, it is not. It takes all of the branches together to comprise the bank. So it is with the church. Paul was writing to the Corinthian "branch" or manifestation of the church of God.

V. The church is holy.

A. *Paul says we are "sanctified" in Christ, and we are "called saints" (v. 2).* In the Bible "calling" is not restricted to a few of the spiritually elite or to those who attend seminary. Calling is prerequisite for Christian living. Every Christian has responded to God's call in Christ. When we respond so, God "sanctifies" us— he sets us apart to do his work.

B. *It seems preposterous to us that of all people, Paul called the Corinthians "saints"—"holy ones."* He says this to a congregation riddled with factionalism that had lawsuits among its members, problems with sexual morality and incest, drunken observances of the Lord's Supper, and raucous commotion and uncontrolled speaking in tongues in its worship. Paul calls *this* church "holy" and its members "saints." Given modern definitions of sainthood, this seems impossible! Then we remember: sainthood is not some future distinction but rather a present condition, namely, a response to God's call to be set apart for his service.

VI. The church is an expectant community.

A. *The church is an expectant community in that it awaits what God will do in the future.* The Corinthians' faith evidently centered on the ecstasy of the present moment. "We have it all now," some evidently said. In verse 7 Paul said that the present does not exhaust the riches of our faith, and that we await the revealing of our Lord. Then, in the following two verses, Paul affirms that God is faithful to preserve until the end whom he calls.

B. *We have largely lost this description of the church.* We typically do not conceive of the church as the people of God oriented toward the future. We more usually tie the church to the "old-time religion" and the reputed glories of a distant past. Paul contends that in reality we are awaiting the revelation of Jesus Christ. We are looking expectantly to God's great future. The good news of Christ is more current than high-tech computer software and space shuttles. The church is the people of God living in anticipation of what God is going to do.

VII. The church is the community of grace.

A. *No definition of the church is complete without the affirmation that the church is the community of grace.* In his greeting to the church, Paul wrote, "Grace to you and peace from God our Father and the Lord Jesus Christ." Paul pronounced God's grace on a church that had disgraced itself. We might rather have expected Paul to have "read the riot act" to the problem-ridden Corinthian church.

B. *Instead, Paul declared to them God's undeserved favor—grace.* He continued in the same vein in verse 5, where he affirmed the church in what little progress it had made. He declared God's grace to these struggling Christians, scarcely five years out of raw paganism.

C. *The church is the community of grace.* Because God has given grace freely to us, we ought also to give it freely to others. For all of our talk about "salvation by grace," sometimes Christians show surprisingly little of it toward one another. Grace is the theme of the entire Christian life, but Paul pronounced God's *grace* to them. We need to show grace to *our* fellow Christians like that. A fault-finding, petty attitude is foreign to the Spirit of Christ and should be foreign to his church.

Conclusion

God has given the church many gifts. These are to be used for a purpose. Through this holy, expectant community of grace marching forward under the lordship of Christ, God calls us to mission.

SUNDAY EVENING, AUGUST 6

Title: The Biblical Perspective on Bitterness

Text: "When ye shall have done all those things which are commanded you, say, . . . we have done that which was our duty to do" *(Luke 17:10).*

Scripture Reading: Luke 17:3–10

Introduction

Bitterness is a malignancy of the spirit: it is a cruel disease that does to the soul what cancer does to the body. Intense, internalized anger produces emotional, spiritual, and physical consequences.

Several years ago a man came into my office for counseling. He complained of migraine headaches that could be somewhat controlled only with strong drugs. He was obviously a very unhappy man, even apart from his physical complaint. As we talked I discovered that he harbored an intense hatred for a wife from whom he had been divorced twenty years earlier. She had been dead for nearly ten years. In one of our early sessions, I said, "I regard bitterness toward a living person a very unproductive venture, but what possible good can you attain by hating a dead person?" The man recognized the destructive force that he had allowed to infest his life, and with God's help he freed himself of this bitter spirit. In the same act, he also gave up the chronic headaches.

In Luke 17:3–10 Jesus instructs his disciples with practical suggestions for handling the anger that can sour quickly into bitterness. The Lord speaks of aggressive and courageous forgiveness as a Christian alternative.

I. Confront the offender (v. 3).

The Bible encourages loving, truthful confrontation. This passage gives the offended party the responsibility for open communication. Other New Testament passages require the one who has created an offense to initiate reconciliation. Combining these messages, this means that two mature Christians, upon realizing there is a breach in their relationship, should metaphorically meet one another on the path, each on the way to see the other to resolve the conflict.

II. Forgive without limits (v. 4).

A. *The Lord says that seven times is not too much to forgive the same person for the same offense in one day.* Elsewhere the number used is seventy times seven! Jesus says that we are to forgive others with the same infinite grace with which we are forgiven by God.

B. *Victims often respond to forgiving their offenders with the attitude reflected in this statement: "Forgive? But you don't understand what he [or she] did to me!"* This is a misunderstanding of the issue. The bitterness that grows from the seeds of unforgiveness produces a deadly poison that destroys the vitality of the host. Even more ironically, it does nothing to hurt the offender.

III. Forgive because you want to be obedient to God, not because you feel like forgiving (vv. 5–9).

A. *The disciples responded to this command of Jesus by pleading, "Lord, increase our faith."* They weren't really saying that they couldn't do this; God would have to empower them. Christ indicates that the real issue here is not faith, but obedience and discipline.

B. *Jesus then tells a parable about a servant who returns weary from his day's work yet proceeds to prepare and serve his master's evening meal.* The servant did not "feel like" doing this chore, but he did it because it was his duty as a servant. It is our job to forgive; it is not an option.

IV. Forgive out of obedience to God, not because the offender deserves forgiveness (vv. 5–9).

A. *Nothing in this passage relates forgiveness to a person's worthiness to be forgiven.* God does not gauge his forgiveness of sinful humanity by our worthiness, and for this blessed fact we will be eternally grateful.

B. *The demanding master may not deserve to be served, and the overworked servant may not deserve to be abused.* Nonetheless, the servant quietly lives out his servanthood. So the Christian goes through life forgiving those who offend him as a witness to the grace by which he has been forgiven. After all, grace, by its very definition, is undeserved.

V. Forgive without being proud (v. 10).

There is a subtle kind of pride that we can develop when we forgive. It is an attitude toward the forgiven that implies, "I have forgiven you, you rotten sinner, because I'm so much more righteous and spiritual than you." If bitterness can make a person the town Scrooge, this kind of self-righteousness can make a person the town Pharisee. This proud piety can make a person as obnoxious and unchristian as hateful bitterness can. So we are to forgive in a spirit of humble obedience to the God by whom we have been forgiven.

Conclusion

There are some very good psychological as well as spiritual reasons for not harboring bitterness in your heart. Consider the following priority of reasons for forgiving as an accurate summary:

1. Forgive others for Jesus' sake. It is his will for you to forgive others as an act of devotion to him.
2. Forgive others for your own sake. Even selfish motives ought to move us to want to get rid of self-destructive bitterness.
3. Forgive others for their sake. The Christian duty to allow God's love to flow through us to others is fulfilled in extending forgiveness.

There is a frightening phrase in the model prayer in which we say, "And forgive us our debts as we forgive our debtors." What if God answered that prayer and forgave you in precisely the same measure you extended forgiveness to others?

WEDNESDAY EVENING, AUGUST 9

Title: Precious Patience

Text: "You too be patient; strengthen your hearts, for the coming of the Lord is near" *(James 5:8 NASB).*

Scripture Reading: James 5:7–11

Introduction

In previous chapters James has been quite terse with his audience, but in verse 7 his tone softens even to the point of being warm and sympathetic. The entire section is something of a conclusion made in light of the "coming of the Lord." It is as if James is saying, "A reckoning day is coming for your oppressors, a day of glory is coming for you. Meanwhile here are some things to which you need to give your attention."

I. The appeal.

A. *Patience is the key concept.* The word suggests the self-restraint that enables one to bear an insult or injury without a hasty retaliation. That sort of patience is described as an attribute of God according to Exodus 34:6; Romans 2:4; 1 Peter 3:20. It is also a distinctive Christian character.

It is the characteristic Dr. David Burton writes of: "Keep still. When trouble is brewing, keep still. When slander is getting on its legs, keep still. When your feelings are hurt, keep still till you recover from your excitement at any rate."

B. *In the present passage James teaches that Christians are to be longsuffering in reference to hardships.* He does not say that we are to be patient as in waiting listlessly doing nothing. Patience and procrastination are not the same. Many excuse their laziness with a false definition of patience. James is saying that we must "be patient" in not seeking retaliation or harboring resentment.

I. The illustration.

A. *The illustration James offers is that of a farmer.* He patiently waits for his land to produce precious crops. He does not simply sit; he is not lazy. Instead, he prepares the soil, sows seed, and keeps his fields free of grass and weeds. But for the germination of the seed and the growth of the plants, he must trust the providential care of God. Patience, therefore, suggests the attitude of watchful and constant expectancy.

B. *The conclusion James draws is expressed in verse 8: "Establish [or strengthen] your hearts."* This suggests mustering courage or strengthening your inner being because of the imminent coming of the Lord.

Doubtless, early Christians hoped that Jesus would come back soon to deliver them from the trying conditions of a hostile environment. They were not at all confident that he would return immediately, and they became impatient—even with others who were closely associated with them. James concludes in verse 9: Do not complain against one another; do not blame your troubles on one another; do not envy another whose suffering is less. God is in control.

III. The victory.

A. *Because God is in control, there is victory in patience.* It is always a comfort to feel that others have gone through what we have to go through. In verses 10–11 James reminds his readers that the prophets and the people of God never could have done their work and borne witness had they not patiently endured.

B. *James reminds them that Jesus had said that one who endured to the end was blessed and would be saved.* Then he reminds them of the victory won by Job because of his patience.

Conclusion

We generally speak of the patience of Job. Job was anything but passive. As we read the tremendous drama of his life, we see him passionately resenting what had come on him. He passionately questioned the conventional and orthodox arguments of his so-called friends. He passionately agonized over the terrible thought that God might have forgotten or forsaken him. Few people have spoken such passionate words as Job. But the great fact about Job is that in spite of the barrage of questions that tore at his heart, he never lost faith in God. He said, "Though he slay me, yet will I trust him." The very greatness of Job lies in the fact that in spite of everything that tore at his heart, he never lost his grip on faith and his grip on God.

SUNDAY MORNING, AUGUST 13

Title: The Church in Unity and Diversity

Text: "I appeal to you, brothers, in the name of our Lord Jesus Christ, that all of you agree with one another so that there may be no divisions among you and that you may be perfectly united in mind and thought" *(1 Cor. 1:10 NIV)*.

Scripture Reading: 1 Corinthians 1:10–17

Hymns: "How Firm a Foundation," Rippon

"Let Us Break Bread Together," Spiritual

"The Bond of Love," Skillings

Offertory Prayer: Almighty God, you shower gifts upon us from the coffers of your grace. As your grace multiplied the loaves and fishes so long ago on the lakeshore, we pray that it might multiply these tithes and offerings that we bring to you in this hour that your name might receive the honor due it. Because of Christ and in his name. Amen.

Introduction

Someone has called the book of 1 Corinthians "Paul's special delivery letter to the twenty-first-century church." The factions that riddled that local body have increased exponentially in the fragmentation of contemporary Christendom. Perhaps no passage in the entire book speaks more to our day than these eight verses comprising our Scripture reading. Paul's thesis statement is this: The church finds unity in its Lord.

I. Explanation

A. *Paul wrote to a church familiar with quarrels.* Paul's choice of words suggests the presence of rival factions gathered around favorite leaders. Apparently the factions had not yet resulted in the break-up of the church along party lines, but Paul feared this as a real possibility. In verse 10 Paul calls the Corinthians "brothers," as he does again in verse 11, and encourages them all literally "to say the same thing," so that no *schismata* ("divisions") might develop among them. The picture behind the Greek word is that of a "tear" or "break." Mark 2:21 uses the word to describe the tear resulting from sewing a new patch on an old garment. Paul urges the church to be "united" (v. 10). He uses the same word here that Mark 1:19 uses of Peter and Andrew's "mending" their fishing nets—a word used elsewhere to describe the setting of a broken bone after a fracture. Paul sees the congregation in danger of unraveling if things continue to deteriorate and urges it to "mend" its fellowship, to be "knit together."

B. *Interpreters "spill a lot of ink" trying to identify the thinking of the four factions mentioned in verse 12.* Paul tactfully does not even mention the faction that is the real culprit, and he identifies four groups that are more or less his "friends" to

222

make his point. Our only certainty is that factions existed in the congregation at Corinth. We should note that Paul is not concerned in this passage to take sides with one group or another and to rebut the others. Instead, he attacks the spirit that allows such groups to form in the first place.

Paul responds pastorally to this conflict-charged situation by taking the Corinthians straight to the source of Christian unity: Christ and his cross. The humility and self-sacrifice that led Christ to Golgotha comprise the antithesis of and antidote for self-assertion, self-righteousness, and rivalries that manifest themselves in a factional spirit. Christ and his good news constitute the foundation of Christian unity. Whenever we attempt to substitute any other foundation for that one, trouble comes quickly.

II. Application

A. *Contemporary evangelicals are a diverse lot, even within any particular denomination.* This diversity includes such things as church organization, worship styles, leadership styles, ministry emphases, and theological stances. Can we find an integrating center? Yes! We will find it in exactly the same place that Paul recommended for the Corinthians over nineteen centuries ago: in Christ and his cross. We cohere in Christ. No other foundation for unity except this one will endure. We will not find lasting unity in our views of baptism or the Lord's Supper or in some special theory about the end of the world. Our unity is in Christ and in nothing less.

B. *Today's text reveals a primary cause of factions.* We have conditioned ourselves to think that the reason for most factions is a difference in beliefs. But it isn't that simple! Apparently the disunity in Corinth grew out of the personality cult that was emerging there. Whenever disunity divides Christian ranks today, as often as not personalities are as much at the root of the problem as any other factor. We may unintentionally fall into the trap of following a favorite pastor, Christian celebrity, or revered teacher. Our call is to follow not the proclaimer but the one proclaimed.

Conclusion

Paul's remedy for disunity among brothers and sisters is a summons for all concerned to submit themselves to the church's crucified Lord. God also calls us to live in oneness in him.

SUNDAY EVENING, AUGUST 13

Title: The Biblical Perspective on Anxiety

Text: "For God hath not given us the spirit of fear; but of power, and of love, and of a sound mind" *(2 Tim. 1:7).*

Scripture Reading: 2 Timothy 1:7–13

Introduction

We all have our terrors. Will I be able to pay all these bills? How many cavities will the dentist find this checkup? How much will it hurt when she fills them? What if I flunk next week's test? Am I going to lose my job? Is this investment going to pay off or cost me my savings? Are my children going to turn out right?

Uncertainty. Pressure. They add up to anxiety. Anxiety—the great plague of our generation. Anxiety snatches away happiness like a pickpocket at a county fair. Anxiety in primitive humans was surely a God-given glandular reaction to prepare them for fight or flight. The physiological reactions that once enabled humans to run from danger or fight with fury now create problems for them. Since it is not appropriate in most social situations to fight physically or run away, anxiety becomes a confusing and paralyzing reaction.

The collision of a personal desire with a natural fear expresses the essence of most of our anxiety. My desire to pass a course collides with my fear of failing the final exam. My desire to have my tooth filled confronts my fear of the dentist's drill. Anxiety, then, is the natural result and manifestation of fear. This means that if you can understand and resolve your fears, you can overcome the anguish and trauma of chronic anxiety.

I believe that the simple but profound truths that God has shared with us in 2 Timothy 1:7 can help you deal victoriously with fear. The verse states very concisely, "God hath not given us the spirit of fear; but of power, and of love, and of a sound mind."

I. God does not want you to be afraid.

A. *The fears that plague your life are not coming to you because God wants you to have them.* He does not place a fearful, trembling spirit in man; his will is to fill his children with a victorious spirit. But you are not the only person who has had the tendency to be afraid and intimidated. The Bible is full of examples of people who made mistakes, lost precious opportunities, and displeased God because of their fear.

B. *In Matthew 25 we find the familiar account of the man who gave three servants five talents, two talents, and one talent, respectively, to manage during his absence.* Returning, he found that two servants had invested and doubled their money. But the servant with one talent still had only one. When asked to explain his failure, the servant answered, "Master, I know that you are a hard man, and I was afraid of you." The servant was scolded and punished because he had allowed his anxiety to keep him from being faithful and useful to his lord.

C. *In John 20 we read that the apostles were shocked and frightened because of the crucifixion of Christ, and they huddled together, hidden in a secret room with the doors tightly locked.* Why were they so anxious? Because, John says, they were afraid of the Jews harming or killing them.

D. *In Luke 10:38 we read of Jesus' visit to the home of Mary and Martha.* Before dinner Mary sat at the feet of Jesus to hear what he had to say and enjoy his presence. Martha was rushing around preparing the meal, straightening the house, and being generally burdened with all that needed to be done. Finally, in exasperation she said, "Lord, doesn't it matter to you that I'm working myself to death while Mary sits there loafing?" Jesus said to her, "Martha, you get too upset and anxious over things that aren't that important. You are wrong to be so worked up. Mary has been much wiser in her use of this time we have together." Where did Martha go wrong? What caused her to deserve this rebuke from Jesus?

Her problem was anxiety. She was being driven by fear. Being a conscientious hostess, she was afraid Jesus or his disciples would think the house wasn't tidy enough or that they wouldn't like the food she had prepared. Her ill-founded fear of what people would think or say about her caused her to miss the blessing of Christ's presence in her life.

II. God has given his Spirit to overcome your fears.

Those who know God personally through placing their faith in Jesus Christ have received the Spirit of God to dwell within them (2 Thess. 4:8). The Holy Spirit is described in three ways in 2 Timothy 1:7 to show that his presence is God's answer to the Christian's fears. He is the Spirit of power, the Spirit of love, and the Spirit of self-control.

A. *The Spirit of power.* One of the fears that plagues people is the fear of inadequacy—the fear that they will not meet certain challenges or solve certain problems. We fear the possibility of failure and the humiliation of personal inadequacy. In relation to this type of fear, God has given us his spirit—the spirit of power.

There are two Greek words that are commonly translated by the English word *power.* One means the power of authority, such as kingly or political power; the other means the power of ability, such as the power to lift a weight or run a race. The latter is the word *dunamis* used in 2 Timothy 1:7, and it means that God's Spirit gives us ability, competency, adequacy. As Christians, then, we need not suffer anxiety because of fears of inadequacy; God has given us his Spirit to become our adequacy in every situation. In all honesty I can say, "I am inadequate, but the Spirit of power within me is adequate to equip me for doing every good thing God wants me to do."

B. *The Spirit of love.* Many of our anxieties relate to our relationships with people. We fear being abandoned or being betrayed by friends. We fear conflict and tension in our social situations. Responding to these fears, God has given us his Spirit of love, because love is the key to maintaining and nurturing these relationships. If I truly love a person, I do not feel insecure in our relationship, and I am prepared to accept that person regardless of how he or she treats me. This agape love is not an easy way of life for us, but as Christians we have God's Spirit available to love others through us.

This "fear-exorcising" power of love is clearly set forth in 1 John 4:18, where we read, "There is no fear in love; but perfect love casteth out fear." This is the truth that helps free us from anxiety about our relationships with people. We must learn to let God's Spirit enable us to love actively and positively those whom we would otherwise fear or distrust.

C. *The Spirit of self-control.* Sometimes you may be anxious because you fear yourself. You think you are going to make a fool of yourself in public; you fear that your judgment will be faulty—that you will make a foolish decision; you fear that you will lack the necessary discipline in a given situation to do the right thing.

Totally relevant to this kind of anxiety is Paul's reminder that God has given his children the spirit of "a sound mind" or, as the NIV puts it, a spirit of "self-control." If you have the Holy Spirit of God living in you, you can trust yourself. You can feel confident about yourself and comfortable with yourself. God offers you help for keeping your life from swerving out of control. His Spirit serves as a guardrail if you accept his guidance for your life.

Conclusion

When you experience anxiety, ask yourself, "What is it that I am afraid of right now?" If you can identify the specific fear that lies behind your uneasiness, you can begin to deal with it. Anxiety is usually a sort of general, nebulous feeling, but with some thought we can often come to a conscious understanding of the fear that lies below the surface.

You need not fear inadequacy—just let God make you adequate for relationships with people—let God love them through you. You need not fear yourself—let his Spirit of self-control make your judgment sound and your life disciplined.

The apostle deals with anxiety also in Philippians 4:6–7 where he exhorts us, "Have no anxiety about anything, but in everything by prayer and supplication with thanksgiving let your requests be made known to God. And the peace of God, which passes all understanding, will keep your hearts and your minds in Christ Jesus" (RSV).

WEDNESDAY EVENING, AUGUST 16

Title: Taking Oaths

Text: "But above all, my brethren, do not swear, either by heaven or by earth or with any other oath; but your yes is to be yes, and your no, no; so that you may not fall under judgment" *(James 5:12 NASB)*.

Scripture Reading: James 5:12

Introduction

Repeated utterances of an expression often dull its meaning. For instance, we profess to be greatly opposed to "taking the Lord's name in vain." We think that command merely refers to cursing. Actually that is not what the Old Testament quote means at all. A correct understanding of this prohibition will reveal that we may be guiltier of violating the commandment than we realize.

For something to be "in vain" simply means that it is without profit or advantage. Thus, any time we use God's name without a particular purpose, it is used in vain. That is precisely what James is addressing here. Let's examine the context of his statement.

The problem with taking oaths was not so much that it was evil; it was just unnecessary. Jews believed that an oath was binding only when God's name was used. The result of this was that the people in James's day swore oaths frequently. Likewise, they became experts at evasive speech. Finding a promise that was not binding became a matter of skill and practice. The practice of oath-taking became nothing more than an illustration of the prevalence of lying, cheating, and falsehood.

In an honest society, no oaths are needed. It is only when people cannot be trusted that they feel the need to punctuate their promise with oaths. James warns that the practice is not only unnecessary but harmful.

I. Say what you mean.

A. *James's words simply tell us to say what we mean.* We have assailed the English language with our flippant use of it. We throw about empty phrases, we exaggerate so frequently that no one knows when to believe us. How frequently do you hear someone saying, "Everybody's doing it" and you know that only a few really are. How often do you preface your remarks with introductions like "Now, to tell you the truth" or "To be honest with you," both of which only imply that you do not always tell the truth or speak honestly.

B. *The point is that we have diluted our language to the point that it no longer reflects the personal integrity to which we aspire in all areas of life.* We ought to tell the truth without exaggeration and say what we mean.

II. Mean what you say.

A. *The corollary to saying what you mean is to mean what you say.* If we promise something, we ought to follow through with it. Otherwise we will lose our credibility.

B. *This is especially difficult for parents.* We are experts at threats and novices when it comes to follow-through. Many parents dole out punishments for their children in a fit of anger, only to find they later regret the severity of their demands. How many of you have grounded your child for a week only to find that, after two days, you couldn't bear to be true to your word? We must be consistent with our children. We parents must be cautious to mean what we say and say what we mean. We are judged by what we say and by what we do.

Conclusion

The most frequent criticism leveled against modern Christians by outsiders is that "the church is full of hypocrites." What a shame that Christians are seen this way!

It is true perhaps that people would criticize the church even if it was full of committed people. But it is true also that we Christians give outsiders much to criticize. We grumble and mumble. We are unkind and unfair. We criticize and complain. We debate and argue. And we are judged.

Imagine how different our mission would be, how much better our task would be, if when we approached lost persons with the gospel, they knew that our church had a track record of love, compassion, and honesty. Imagine how different their responses might be if we were to say what we mean and mean what we say.

SUNDAY MORNING, AUGUST 20

Title: The Ties That Bind

Text: "According to the grace of God given to me, like a skilled master builder I laid a foundation, and another man is building upon it. Let each man take care how he builds upon it" *(1 Cor. 3:10 RSV).*

Scripture Reading: 1 Corinthians 3:1–23

Hymns: "The Church's One Foundation," Stone

          "Now Thank We All Our God," Rinkart

          "Word of God, Across the Ages," Blanchard

Offertory Prayer: Almighty God, you have called us to missions. Accept these tithes and offerings as symbols of our offering our whole selves to fulfill this missionary call. We pray this in the name of the Lord of the harvest. Amen.

Introduction

The bulletin misprint that read, "The church was untied," instead of "The church was united," perhaps reveals as much as it amuses. The church at Corinth was an "untied" rather than a "united" church. Much of Paul's purpose in writing to them in 1 Corinthians was to get them "tied up" to one another again. First Corinthians 3:1–23 records several "ties that bind" diverse individuals and factions in the church into a cohesive, ministering body.

I. Spiritual maturity.

A. *The first "tie that binds" a congregation is progressing in spiritual maturity.* For jealousy, strife, and group loyalties to infect a church, as happened in Corinth, is to give clear evidence of spiritual immaturity.

B. *Paul addresses the Corinthians as "babes in Christ," not as spiritual Christians.* They are attempting to live in the world as practical atheists. They are living a self-centered instead of Christ-centered existence, with the first proof of the fact being their partisan spirit. The opposite of living according to the flesh is living a life dominated and determined by the Spirit. The Corinthians had received the Spirit, but they were not living like it. As a result, they remained in spiritual preschool.

C. *Christians are "born again" to grow.* The ancient church supplied a drink of milk to newly baptized converts on the basis of this text, in order to say to them by way of a powerful and dramatic symbol, "You are born into Christ to grow in Christ."

228

Babies are cute in the "cooing" stage, but something has gone dreadfully wrong if they are still "cooing" when they are five years old. We are born to grow.

II. A ministry of servanthood and sharing.

A. *A second "tie that binds" (vv. 5–10) is the realization that we are all servants sharing different roles in our Christian calling.* Paul uses Apollos and himself as examples to remind the Corinthians that they are all teammates playing on the same team. Paul calls Apollos and himself "deacons." A *diakonos* in the first century was a household table waiter. Paul is saying, "Look! We are not chairmen of the church board. We are household servants!"

A few verses later, in the first verse of chapter 4, Paul uses another lowly word devoid of all status, the word "ministers," to describe Apollos and himself. The word comes from the galley ships of the time and denotes the "under-rowers"—the slaves manning the oars on the lowest deck of the ship. In essence Paul is saying, "This is who we are: not the pastor, not the chair of the deacons, and not a mover and shaker in the denomination. We are only table waiters and under-rowers sharing in the ministry of Christ."

B. *In these verses Paul uses both agricultural and architectural metaphors to say that good harvests and successful building projects are team efforts.* Christians are only colleagues together in God's construction crew. In verse 10 Paul calls himself the "skilled master of works," literally the *architekton*—the "architect"—who laid the foundation as the original evangelist in Corinth. But he does not seem concerned in the least that another has built on his foundation.

III. The foundation of Christ.

A. *The third "tie that binds" is the foundation of Christ himself on which the church rests.* Verse 11 has served as the inspiration for the great hymn of faith "The Church's One Foundation." Remembering "the Rock from which we are hewn" can serve as a powerful impulse for Christian unity, because factions usually grow up around some leader or theological program, which in subtle ways attempts to usurp the place rightfully occupied by Christ.

B. *Evidently something like this was in danger of happening at Corinth.* Paul recognized that we can build poorly by attempting to alter the foundation (as perhaps some Judaizers were trying to do in Corinth). Christ is our only choice for the foundation of the church; without him it will not be the church. We can also build poorly by using inferior construction materials on the foundation. God will test the durability of our work. Someone has remarked that the test of a pastor's ministry in a church is not so much what the church does while he or she is there as much as what it does five years after he or she has gone. Paul reminds us that on Judgment Day some "divine pyrotechnics" will test all combustible material that we may have contributed to the life of the church!

IV. The temple-hood of the church.

A. *Paul's thought in verse 16 requires that we coin a word to describe what he says.* The fourth "tie that binds" the church together is the recognition by its membership of the church's "temple-hood." Ordinarily we think of our individual bodies as "temples of the Holy Spirit," and so 1 Corinthians 6:19 teaches. But in our text, as we find again at the conclusion of Ephesians 2, the Bible speaks of the entire church as the temple of God, as "God's house." The church as a corporate body enshrines God's Spirit. Literally, Paul says, "You *all* [second person plural] are the temple of God [God's house], and the Spirit of God dwells in you."

B. *Living along a fault line in the earth's crust reminds us that no building can stand if the cracks in its walls and foundation become too large.* Take a few pillars out of the ancient temples, and the structures will fall. Similarly, Paul reasons, division is a tool used by the Devil's demolition squad against God's temple, the church. To destroy the unity of the church is to raze the temple of God in that locality. Strife and gossip and their fiendish friends unforgiveness and impatience still can drive the Spirit out of the church and shatter its unity today, destroying strategic building stones in the temple of God. We as a corporate body are God's temple.

V. The true wisdom: that we belong to Christ, not to our leaders.

In the concluding verses of our text, Paul speaks of true wisdom. The Corinthians debated one another concerning true wisdom. Rival factions each claimed to have "cornered" it. The pith of what Paul says about true wisdom we find in verse 23: "You are Christ's." Paul reminds them and us that we belong to Christ and not to anyone else. True wisdom unites us in Christ.

Conclusion

In these early years of the twenty-first century, it may seem that the people of God are hopelessly fragmented. Both local congregations and larger Christian bodies know of disunity and strife that bring reproach to the name of Christ. But if we will look again to the spiritual resources that God has placed at our disposal so that we may meet the challenges of this hour, we will be assured again that some eternal "ties that bind" unite us.

SUNDAY EVENING, AUGUST 20

Title: The Biblical Perspective on Worrying

Text: "Sufficient unto the day is the evil thereof" *(Matt. 6:34).*

Scripture Reading: Matthew 6:25–34; Philippians 3:13–14

Introduction

Wilbur was a world-class, veteran worrier. He was once asked, "What if you woke up in the morning with nothing to worry about—totally carefree, content, secure, and happy? Wouldn't that be great?" Wilbur replied, "Oh, if that happened, I'd be worried that I had lost my mind."

For a confirmed worrier like Wilbur, there is probably no cure. But for those of us who are still amateurs, dabbling in the fine art of fretting, the Bible offers some hope for improvement, if not cure.

Worry relates primarily to two of the three tenses. We worry about things that happened in the past tense, and we worry about what may happen in the future tense. (This makes for a lot of "tenseness.") But the general emphasis of the Bible is on the present—the "now."

I. Don't carry the burdens of the past.

A. *The apostle Paul says in Philippians 3:13–14 that a runner has to erase from his mind the track he has covered and keep his attention on the finish line.* Paul speaks in these verses of a deliberate effort to forget about past problems and failures, and perhaps even past glory. The finish line and the prize motivate the runner to press ahead.

B. *You cannot effectively live today if you are still carrying yesterday's burdens.* Worries related to wrongs suffered in the past need to be resolved with forgiveness. Worries related to guilt over sins committed in the past need repentance and acceptance of cleansing. Worries involving unsettled obligations from the past need to be handled with complete restitution. Allow the past to recede into the past; wash your hands of its lingering foul residue.

II. Don't presume the problems of tomorrow.

A. *Matthew, in his gospel record, urges us not to worry about the future.* The NASB renders the text for this message, "Each day has enough trouble of its own." God promises sufficient grace for us to meet and victoriously deal with each day's problems. But if we use up vast amounts of today's grace supply to deal with next week's problems, we soon find ourselves unable to cope with today's demands. Grace, like manna in the wilderness, is a daily provision. We cannot successfully store it up for future use, and we cannot get "credit" to extract an advance on next week's allotment.

B. *James 4:13–15 reminds us not to presume that tomorrow will even come.* Worrying about the future, for the Christian, reflects this kind of arrogant presumption. James and Matthew both seem to be advising us, "Allow God to enable you to

231

cope with this present moment, and trust him to be able to do the same when the future moment of need arrives." Don't worry about the future. Someone has said, "Life by the mile is hardly worthwhile, but by the inch it's a cinch."

III. Act now!

A. *The person who is doing wrong in the present has some justification for worrying about the future.* Today's misdeeds will taint tomorrow. And upon arriving at tomorrow, there will be a past to regret. Today is vitally important. Yesterday is a cashed and canceled check. Tomorrow is a promissory note with no collateral or signature. But this present moment is precious. It provides the possibility of taking action, making a change, doing right.

If you have something important to do, do it now. Much worry can be avoided by taking constructive action. Worry is often the poor substitute a lazy or cowardly person uses for not doing what needs to be done.

Second Corinthians 6:2 says, "Now is the accepted time; behold now is the day of salvation." If you need to make an important decision about your relationship with God, do it now! If you need to express love to a family member or friend, do it now! If you need to make a wrong right, do it now!

B. *The Christian faith is a present tense way of life.* Had Jesus been a procrastinator, we would still be wretched lost beings without a Savior. God described himself to Moses as the eternally present one. He said simply, "I am." The present tense of "to be" is the best understanding we can grasp concerning his nature. He "is," and he wants us as his heirs to "be"—now.

Conclusion

This present moment is the most valuable possession you own. Material things can disappear in an instant. Yesterday is spent and tomorrow isn't yours to spend. Use this gift of the present wisely.

Apply forgiveness to the past, apply faith to the future, and apply yourself to the present.

WEDNESDAY EVENING, AUGUST 23

Title: Proper Prayer

Text: "The prayer of a righteous man is powerful and effective" *(James 5:16 NIV).*

Scripture Reading: James 5:13–18

Introduction

James's sequence of thoughts here is easy to follow. He describes when to pray, why to pray, and then how to pray.

I. Pray always.

A. *Verse 13 is a picture of the early church at its best.* In times of suffering they prayed. In times of joy they sang. In times of sickness they healed. Against a pagan world that offered only a bleak hopelessness, these Christians operated with expectation and power. They loved to sing: a clear sign of joy is evident in someone's singing or whistling or humming. When the occasion was less joyous, they prayed for help and acted on their requests as far as they could.

B. *The point is that they drew together to pray and do what they could to help remedy the situation.* They asked God to take their efforts and perform healing. But they were not prone, as we often are, to ask God to do the miraculous while we passively do nothing.

II. What prayer accomplishes.

James's enthusiasm regarding prayer comes from high expectations of what prayer can accomplish.

A. *First, the prayer of faith will save.* The fact that the promise is stated in unqualified terms raises a problem. Not even the apostles believed that prayer *always* resulted in healing. Paul remained sick and so did Trophimus.

This statement, then, must not be taken as a guarantee that every prayer offered in sufficient faith will be answered positively. It is mainly intended to show that every possible need of the Christian can be brought to God in prayer.

B. *Second, the Lord will raise him up (v. 15).* Note James's emphasis that it is the Lord who raises him up. The elders, the oil, the prayer—these are simply instruments that the Lord uses to restore one's health.

C. *Third, if he has committed sins, they will be forgiven (v. 15).* No one can know real health of soul, mind, or body until he or she is first right with God. A right relationship with God is a prerequisite for *total* good health.

III. How to pray.

How can we pray best? James gives two answers.

A. *First, there is a need for the confession of sins—not just to God but to each other.* It is sometimes easier to confess sins to God than it is to confess to other people. Yet in sin two barriers are often created. One is between us and God; the other is between us and our fellow humans. To remove both barriers, both types of confession must be made. This principle is clearly one that must be used with caution. It is quite true that there may well be cases where confession of sin to each other may do infinitely more harm than good. Only where a two-way barrier has been erected because of a wrong ought one to feel the necessity to confess to the other. Otherwise, just work to remedy the problem and do not cause more trouble than necessary.

B. *Second, James says to pray for one another.* Here we see the mark of pure unselfish intercession. Saturating oneself in prayer for others is a wonderful spiritual experience. A prayer may be quiet and private, but it avails much.

Conclusion

Prayer is both necessary and helpful. We should develop the habit of being prayerful. Talking to God in praises and petitions should be second nature to us. We can know God intimately through prayer. Let us not only develop the habit, but persevere in it.

SUNDAY MORNING, AUGUST 27

Title: What about Church Discipline?

Text: "Cleanse out the old leaven that you may be a new lump, as you really are unleavened. For Christ, our paschal lamb, has been sacrificed" *(1 Cor. 5:7 RSV)*.

Scripture Reading: 1 Corinthians 5:1–13

Hymns: "O God, Our Help in Ages Past," Watts

"Crown Him with Many Crowns," Bridges

"Lord, I Want to Be a Christian," Spiritual

Offertory Prayer: Almighty God, you have called us to live lives under the lordship of Christ. Accept these tithes and offerings as our pledges to acknowledge his lordship and authority over every part of our lives. In the name of Jesus Christ the Lord, we pray. Amen.

Introduction

For most Christians the term "church discipline" is as palatable as a brier under the tongue! For us, the term connotes "discipline meetings" of a bygone era called by a church to denounce various members and sins, both real and imagined. Church discipline is also known as "shunning," "churching people," "withdrawing fellowship," and "backdoor revivals." What exactly is church discipline?

I. A historical view.

Historically, the church has not had a good experience with discipline. The term itself calls to mind memories of the Spanish Inquisition, the martyrdoms of Hus and Tyndale, Calvin's Geneva, and New England Puritanism. We have equated the practice as seen in the more recent past with a petty, legalistic spirit intent on banishing such ruinous "sins" as dancing and card-playing from the face of the earth!

While American Christianity has heard increasingly less about church discipline over the last century, it made national headlines in the 1980s when a midwestern church and one of its members became embroiled in a dispute concerning church discipline that led to a lawsuit in which a jury awarded the member almost half a million dollars in damages. In a time when many believers apparently regard their church and their Lord with increasing nonchalance, a growing number of persons are expressing the need for constructive church discipline.

II. A biblical view.

Jewish and early Christian groups practiced the discipline of their membership widely. In Acts 5 Ananias and Sapphira were struck dead for attempting to deceive the church. In particular, the writings of Paul show a concern for a disciplined church membership. In 2 Corinthians 2:5–11, for example, Paul urges the Corinthians to forgive a disciplined brother and to restore him to their fellowship. Similarly, he advises the Galatians, "Brethren, if a man be overtaken in a fault, ye which are spiritual restore such a one in the spirit of meekness" (Gal. 6:1).

234

The New Testament church arose out of a Judaism that took the discipline of its adherents seriously. The scrolls of the Dead Sea community existing at the time Paul wrote 1 Corinthians contain a passage specifying penalties that the community should impose on its membership for specific offenses. The scroll reveals that annually each community member was assigned a rank accordingly to the progress he had made in his faith. The writings of Paul imply the influence of the synagogue, with its four distinct levels of discipline, on the early church.

III. A textual view.

In 1 Corinthians 5:1–13 Paul writes opposing a case of incest in the Corinthian church. Apparently the Corinthians were bragging about this man's freedom from the law. For them this sin seemed to represent a "new" and more enlightened morality. Paul found the church's attitude as horrible as the sin itself. He commands the church to break table fellowship with the offender. Social acceptance implies ethical acceptance, so Paul charges the entire church, not a special delegation of church officials or the pastor and deacons, with making this decision. He hoped that lack of fellowship would prove redemptive by providing relational "shock therapy" to bring this man to his senses. His further concern in verse 6, as we would say, was that "one bad apple will ruin the whole barrel."

In the Jewish mind, leaven stood for an evil, corrupting influence. Immediately *before* the Passover Feast, Jewish households discarded the old year's leaven (dough retained from previous baking that had fermented) and made a fresh start with the grain from the new harvest. This illuminates Paul's point in our text: "Christ our Passover Lamb has *already* been sacrificed; but you Corinthians still have not removed the evil (leaven) from your lives, which you should have done *before* the Lamb was slain. Now remove it at once!" Christians celebrate a perpetual Passover, and in so doing observe a suitable purity of life.

In the concluding verses of our text, Paul taught that Christians are not to withdraw from the immoral of the world, since that will be impossible so long as we live! Paul did command the Corinthians, however, to withdraw from a brother guilty of any one of several sins. The Corinthians evidently had things backwards. They withdrew from immoral non-Christians but maintained fellowship with immoral believers.

IV. A practical view.

Our dilemma is that we find it difficult to decide when to forgive and when to discipline for sin. We live in the tension between the danger of "judging" and the necessity of "inspecting fruit."

A. *Church discipline is to be redemptive, not penal.* Paul's first concern is for the good of the erring member. He hopes that *outside* the fellowship of the church the man will reflect on his wrongdoing and repent of it. We do well to remember that the root meaning of "discipline" is "learning," not "punishment."

B. *Church discipline is covenantal and corporate, not isolated and individual.* Paul appeals to the covenantal community of the church as a whole, not to the church's leadership. We have largely lost the New Testament view that the

235

church is a body, a corporate unity. Sin is a contagion that can infect it as a whole if action is not taken. Devoid of this understanding of the church as a covenantal community, permissive nonchalance that allows the other guy to "do his own thing" has become the order of the day!

C. *Church discipline is comprehensive, not selective.* The bane of church discipline in American Christianity is that we have selected only a narrow band of sins for which we will discipline. Traditionally, church discipline has pertained to strong drink, sexual immorality, or cultural mores. Paul is not selective in our text. In verse 11 he expands the list to include greed, idolatry, reviling, drinking, immorality, and theft. At least one sin on that list may apply to everyone! But when was the last time we saw or heard of a church member being disciplined for greed, and what American has escaped the taint of materialism? Are we ready to exercise the church discipline of comparing income tax forms with tithing records? Church discipline covers a multitude of sins, not a select few.

D. *Church discipline is preventive, not prognostic.* While this point is not explicit in the text, nothing in the Bible contradicts it, and many portions of Scripture support it. The church can do much to prevent disciplinary problems from arising in the first place. New member training, marriage enrichment retreats, prayer seminars, special Bible study emphases, and a Sunday school class contacting weekly absentees all represent much needed forms of preventive church discipline. Preventive and positive concern may preclude the need for any negative rebuke.

Conclusion

Jesus invites us to follow him as his disciples. The call to discipleship is both a call to become a "learner" and to bring ourselves under the lordship of Christ as we live in loving fellowship with his people.

SUNDAY EVENING, AUGUST 27

Title: The Biblical Perspective on Depression

Text: "He requested for himself that he might die; and said, It is enough; now O LORD, take away my life" *(1 Kings 19:4).*

Scripture Reading: 1 Kings 19:1–13

Introduction

Depression has become epidemic in America. Millions of Americans suffer from the misery and sadness of emotional depression. Some years ago an article in a leading national news magazine said, "There is no doubt that depression, long the leading mental illness in the U.S., is now virtually epidemic—and suicide is its all too frequent outcome."

The Bible is not silent about this. Christianity is not a pie-in-the-sky philosophy; it is a relationship with a Savior who "became flesh and dwelt among us." Even in the Old Testament there are illuminating case studies of God's pastoral care for specific people with acute needs.

Elijah is such an example. He was one of God's great prophets. The moment of truth came in his ministry when he met 450 prophets of Baal for a duel of prayer on Mount Carmel. The pagan prophets failed, and Elijah succeeded, vindicating the name of Jehovah God and Elijah's prophetic ministry. Elijah experienced his greatest spiritual victory that day. But the account doesn't end there. After this resounding success, Elijah, exhausted and drained, fell into a deep depression.

I. Elijah's symptoms (1 Kings 19:3–4, 9–10).

Elijah presents us with some classic symptoms of the devastation precipitated by emotional depression.

A. *Elijah is fearful and anxious.* Depressed persons frequently experience a nebulous, generalized sense of malaise. There is a pessimism about the future that causes fear, sometimes without the victim being able to identify the cause or object of the fear. Elijah feared for his life, even though it would appear that the greatest threat to him had already been overcome at Carmel.

B. *Elijah is physically and emotionally spent.* There are many human experiences that extract a heavy toll on our emotional strength and ability to cope. Physical illness, deep grief, stress from radical changes in our lives, and a multitude of other factors can create the weariness of spirit in which depression thrives.

C. *Elijah is feeling low self-esteem.* He states that he wishes he were dead. This feeling of worthlessness that causes people to consider their lives an unnecessary burden to the earth is common in depression. Elijah seems to feel guilty and ashamed about being tired and afraid, and he cannot forgive himself for this human frailty.

D. *He indulges in self-pity.* Depressed people generally do not need the pity of their friends because they are so enthusiastic in their own production of pity for themselves. This private "pity party" is common to depression.

E. *Elijah is feeling lonely and rejected.* There is a sense that no one really cares or understands. He feels rejected by his countrymen. Rejection, genuine or perceived, delivers a destructive blow to the human personality, and depression is often the response.

F. *Elijah becomes critical of other people and hostile toward them.* Depression involves guilt that causes self-depreciation and anger that lead to criticism of others. Elijah is convinced that all others have forsaken God, and they want to destroy him.

So God's great prophet huddles alone in a cave, praying to die and trying to sleep away what remains of his miserable existence. But Elijah isn't alone. The holy God of the universe peers through the darkness of the cave, and his gaze even penetrates the shadowy gloom of the depressed soul. He cares and he acts. With love and firmness God ministers to Elijah.

II. God's therapy (1 Kings 19:5–8, 11–13).

God sends an angel to minister to Elijah. The creator of human beings seems to have a remarkable understanding of how they work and what they need. The angel confronts Elijah with specific therapeutic instructions. Elijah is instructed to perform a number of significant actions.

A. *Get up and take care of yourself.* Depression creates a kind of paralysis that causes people to become neglectful of the most basic daily tasks. Elijah has stopped eating, and he must be told to feed himself. Some depressed people will try to medicate themselves by stuffing their bodies with food; others will attempt to starve themselves. Elijah is the latter. Proper nutrition is an important part of overcoming depression.

Depressed people often must be encouraged to engage in a productive daily routine. They may stop taking care of their daily hygiene, become lazy, and/or retreat into a hypnotic obsession with watching television. The person who speaks for God may need to say, "Get up and stop neglecting the basic chores you should be doing." The person who says this takes a big risk, to be sure. But we are called to be courageous in our care.

And of course a key component of getting help is to get medical attention. Sometimes all the prayer and prodding in the world won't help a depressed person until he or she gets the proper medication to correct the chemical imbalance that has caused the depression.

B. *Busy yourself with productive activity.* God gave Elijah specific instructions about his future ministry and the selection of his successor. Depressed people need assignments to complete. A sense of accomplishment can reverse the downward spiral of worthless feelings. When a person lacks inner motivation, the necessary motivation to keep on living may need to come from external sources. God cared enough about Elijah to provide discipline for him during the time when he lacked the inner strength to discipline himself.

C. *Renew your relationship with God.* We see Elijah meeting God in a new way and hearing the still, small voice that speaks forgiveness and love. Depressed persons need to be reminded that God is still present with them and that he has a word for them. His coming to them may be a whisper rather than an earthquake, but that is just as real for those who are willing to listen carefully.

D. *Admit your limitations and get help.* Elijah becomes a healthier human being because he begins to understand and accept his own humanity. He sees that he needs help, and God has help available for him. There were still seven thousand who had not forsaken God, and they represented potential support for Elijah. But that support was not operative for Elijah's benefit until he admitted that he needed it. The depressed person who refuses to accept help in the midst of his misery is not strong or admirable; he is unrealistic and self-destructive.

Conclusion

Because we are children of an omnipotent Father, we can have hope. Because unique resources are available to the Christian, we can have hope. Even as we confront the hellish demon of depression, we can have hope.

WEDNESDAY EVENING, AUGUST 30

Title: Bringing Back Backsliders

Text: "Remember this: Whoever turns a sinner from the error of his way will save him from death and cover a multitude of sins" *(James 5:20 NIV)*.

Scripture Reading: James 5:19–20

Introduction

One of the great enigmas of most churches is an accounting problem. Specifically, we have trouble accounting for a group referred to as backsliders.

We might be inclined to scold them for their failures, but James would have us seek them to restore them. They have strayed from their Christian convictions; they no longer care about the things of Christ; they are on a dangerous course. It is these for whom we need to account. They need to be brought back.

I. Some do stray from the truth.

A. *The grammar of the text suggests a condition that is not necessarily true but at least probable.* The text does not imply that backsliders are spiritually dead or going to die—only that they are in a dangerous condition. Therefore, the issue here is not that of falling from grace, but rather of drifting from a meaningful relationship and fellowship with God.

B. *This may be true of many modern Christians in light of the fact that what is being wandered from is "truth."* Christian truth is more than a matter of knowledge or an intellectual exercise. Christian truth is always moral truth; it always manifests in action. It is a way of life. It is something to which we must submit our minds, bodies, and hearts. It is from this that Christians often drift.

II. It takes people to restore backsliders.

A. *It is really not unusual for adults to miss the security of truth that they knew as children and seek to come back to that from which they drifted.* Most often someone is needed to help that person return.

B. *James encourages us to be instruments in restoring backsliders.* It is interesting to note, however, that as much as he wants that done, he never tells us how to do it. From the context we may infer that this mission has to do with intercessory prayer. We can also assume that the restoring process must include good teaching, confronting, and befriending people, and ultimately accepting them. Basically, the process does not include anything new and different. People have always and will always be brought back to truth by Christian love and concern.

In the last century international attention was drawn to the famous Egyptian sphinx. The 4,500-year-old structure had gradually eroded to the point of possible collapse. Various methods of restoration were considered and rejected. The final conclusion was that it be restored over a five-year period by using ancient Egyptian methods. Modern equipment and chemical treatments were turned down for fear of causing greater damage in the future. Likewise, in restoring backslidden Christians, it is hard to beat the proven methods of ancient days—prayer, ministry, sound teaching, and love.

III. The rewards are great.

A. *First, there is a great benefit to the backslider who is restored.* James's first comment apparently applies to him. His soul is saved from death. Perhaps James uses the word "death" here as he did in 2:17. There it would certainly have a dead faith by James's definition. Thus, being brought back to close fellowship with God and the church would make his life productive and meaningful and alive again.

B. *But a second reward is for the one who helps bring that person back.* A faithful missionary was asked, "What pay do you receive for the hardships you undergo and the sacrifices you make, living and working among these people?" The missionary took a note from his pocket, worn by much handling, and read two sentences from it written by a Chinese student: "But for you, I would not have known Jesus Christ our Savior. Every morning I kneel before God and think of you, thank God for you, and pray for you." "That," said the missionary, "is my pay."

Conclusion

The road of restoration is long, hard, and rocky. We are naive if we think that is a simple process. We are called to have compassion on these backsliders, and we are called to suffer with and for them. Why? To enhance the honor of Jesus Christ.

SEPTEMBER

■ Sunday Mornings

Evangelism is the primary emphasis for the month of September. We will examine how to share the good news of God's love revealed in Jesus in a series called "The Conversations of Jesus That Led to Discipleship." Jesus himself is our model.

■ Sunday Evenings

The four final, short epistles of the New Testament are often overlooked. They have much to contribute to our sanctification and are filled with practical, relevant encouragements to our faith. Therefore we will engage in a series entitled "Edifying Elements in the Epistles."

■ Wednesday Evenings

We will begin a series of devotional studies of 1 Thessalonians using the theme "Measuring Ourselves by a New Testament Pattern."

SUNDAY MORNING, SEPTEMBER 3

Title: Conversations of Jesus: Nicodemus

Text: "Jesus answered and said unto him, Verily, verily I say unto thee, except a man be born again, he cannot see the kingdom of God" *(John 3:3)*.

Scripture Reading: John 3:1–12

Hymns: "Holy, Holy, Holy," Heber

"He Lifted Me," Homer

"Jesus Saves," Owens

Offertory Prayer: Heavenly Father, we rejoice today over your sending your Son to be our Savior. Thank you for rescuing us from the waste, the ruin, and the disappointment of sin. Today we come to give ourselves to you for the sake of others that they might come to know Jesus Christ as their own personal Savior. Accept and bless these tithes and offerings to the preaching of the gospel. For your sake. Amen.

Introduction

Dr. Norman Vincent Peale once had an interview with a very prominent businessman in New York City. The businessman came into his office and laid out before Dr. Peale a very tragic tale of years of confusion, frustration, tragedy, and misplaced values. Over a series of years his life had painted a very dark picture. He said to Dr. Peale, "What do you think I should do?"

The minister said, "I have a solution for you. It's simple, and you're a very sophisticated and intelligent man. I doubt you would want to hear it."

The man said, "I think I would like to hear it."

The minister said, "No, I don't believe you would. It's too simple."

Again the man responded by saying, "I want you to tell me."

Dr. Peale repeated, "I really don't think you want to hear it."

After a while the fellow became incensed and he pressed him and said, "Look, tell me what your answer is."

Dr. Peale said, "What I think you really need to do is get down on your knees and tell God that you are a sinner and ask God to forgive you and change you."

The gospel of Jesus Christ is profoundly simple and simply profound. The Bible speaks of another conversation between a minister and businessman. In this conversation with Nicodemus, Jesus articulates the simple and profound truth of his gospel.

To discover and experience a personal and life-changing relationship to a living God is so profound that it is like a birth. It's like being born all over again. To be born again will not turn you into some kind of a weird personality, but it will actually complete your personality so that you will become the person God intended for you to become. When Jesus said, "You must be born again," what was he saying?

I. This new birth is a beginning.

A. *Just as you have to have a physical birth to begin a physical life, you must have a spiritual birth to begin a spiritual life.* There must be a beginning. You don't become a Christian by accident. You don't drift into it or wander into it. It doesn't happen to you without your knowing about it. It doesn't come about by a process of absorption or association; you cannot be reborn just by being around Christian people or attending church.

B. *Neither do you become a Christian by inheritance.* Just because you were born into a Christian family, just because your wife or husband or your brothers or sisters are believers, does not mean that you are a Christian. No, you must have a beginning.

C. *You don't become a Christian just by having some kind of a good warm feeling about God, or about the world, or about religion, or about life.* It's good to have those feelings, but you do not become a Christian just by experiencing some kind of nebulous, vague emotion. You become a Christian when you come to that time and place in your life when you are willing to personally and intelligently accept Jesus Christ into your life. That's the beginning.

D. *Spiritual birth is experienced in different ways.* Some people's spiritual birth is very dramatic and emotional. They weep many tears. They tremble and experience an inward ecstasy. I think that's the way Saul of Tarsus had his beginning. But other people's beginning is very matter-of-fact, very simple. They don't hear an audible voice. They just make a simple decision. Some people have their spiritual beginning when they are very young. Others begin as adults. Usually when a person begins with Christ as an adult, the change is more dramatic and more difficult.

For some it is difficult to say the exact moment they began with Christ. Ruth Graham has said repeatedly that she does not know for sure the first time that she trusted Christ. G. Campbell Morgan, one of the greatest biblical expositors who ever lived said, "We cannot tell the first time the sun came up, but we knew that it had come up. To be born again means that I am able to say, 'I have had a beginning. My relationship to God is personal.'"

II. To be born again is to experience an inward change.

A. *The Bible says that you and I have a basic problem and that problem is sin.* We are sinners, not just because we do bad things or because we commit individual acts of sin, but because the Bible says it is our nature. It is our nature to be selfish and sinful. We are born with that nature, and therefore we commit individual acts of sin.

When Jesus told Nicodemus that he had to be born again, he was telling him that what he needed was an inward, radical revolutionary change that had to do with that sinful nature. A little reformation is good, but it is not enough. A little religion is good, but it is not enough. Change must occur on the inside.

Let's suppose I bought a pig and decided to keep it for a pet. I kept the pig in the house and cleaned it, bathed it, and dressed it. Do you know what would happen the first time that pig got out of the house? It would find the closest mud puddle and get as dirty as it could. Do you know why? Because that is its nature. Our nature will experience a radical change when we accept Christ as our Lord and Savior.

B. *When a person by faith accepts Jesus Christ, a beautiful thing happens: a change takes place on the inside.* Things you once loved, you begin to despise. Things you once despised, you begin to love. Scripture says, "If anyone is in Christ, he is a new creation; the old has gone, the new has come!" (2 Cor. 5:17 NIV). God gives you new values, new priorities, new goals.

III. This new birth is a miracle.

A. *It's not something you do for yourself; it's something God does for you.* Nicodemus said, "I don't understand how this happens." Jesus said, "Nicodemus, do you feel the wind blowing on your face? You don't know where the wind is coming from or where the wind is going. So is everyone that is born of the Spirit." It's a miracle.

B. *Being born again doesn't mean our struggles are over.* In fact, the opposite is true: we will have even greater struggles because the Holy Spirit comes in to do battle with our old sinful nature. But because of the miracle of the new birth, we are promised a new life.

243

Conclusion

The good news is that you can be born again. You don't have to live the same old frustrating sinful life. You can have a new life, a new beginning. You can experience change. You can have a miracle in your life if you will come to Jesus Christ just as you are and trust him. Will you do it?

SUNDAY EVENING, SEPTEMBER 3

Title: Saved and Sure of It!

Text: "I write these things to you who believe in the name of the Son of God so that you may know that you have eternal life" *(1 John 5:13 NIV)*.

Scripture Reading: 1 John 5:13–15

Introduction

Every one of us shares the need for security. The fact was captured in comic form by the late Charles Schultz in his comic strip *Peanuts*. Schultz pictured one of the characters, Linus, tenaciously clinging to his security blanket. Wherever he goes or whatever he does, Linus must have his blanket. He feels insecure without it. This may be humorous, but actually all of us have to have our security blankets of one kind or another. No one knows this any better than God. So he inspired the apostle John to write this letter to meet this very need. Thirty-four times the word *know* is used in these five chapters. This is an average of almost seven times per chapter.

John's purpose for writing this letter is clearly stated in 5:13. The good news to all is that one can be saved and sure of it. In anticipation of the question, "How can I be saved and sure of it?" John offers four answers.

I. The fellowship you have (1 John 1:3–7).

Our world is too often cold, aloof, and openly hostile. There is within every one of us, however, an intensive hunger for warm personal fellowship. This is found only among those who are bound together by a common love for Jesus Christ.

This is why ours is a "blessed fellowship." The warmth and love, the gracious spirit and generous attitudes, the delight of each other's company—all of these and more characterize the blessed fellowship we have.

II. The source of that fellowship (1 John 1:3).

A. *Our fellowship with the Father.* Someone perhaps asked John, "How can such a diverse group of men as you apostles possibly have the fellowship you have? You have Simon the Zealot, and in contrast to him, Matthew the tax collector; there are also the ambitious James and John and the retiring Andrew." John may have answered, "Truly our fellowship is with the Father and with his Son, Jesus Christ."

Our fellowship with the Father necessitates our fellowship with each other. You cannot love the Father without loving the children too.

Our fellowship with the Father removes any cause of offense. In verse 5 John states, "In him is no darkness at all." Actually John is saying there is no cause of stumbling, no occasion for offense, in the person of Jesus Christ. Therefore, as we walk in the light with Christ, fellowship with others becomes a reality. It is only in "darkness" that people stumble.

1. Our experience with his Son (1 John 1:3). As we have a saving experience with his Son, we become changed people, and in the words of Paul (2 Cor. 5:17), we become a new creature with old things having passed away and all things becoming new.

2. Our infilling with the Holy Spirit (John 2:27). At the point of salvation, the Holy Spirit takes up residence in us and, if given freedom, he will produce the "fruit of the Spirit" (Gal. 5:22–23). All of these products of the Holy Spirit inevitably lead to fellowship both with one another and with our heavenly Father.

B. *The necessity of that fellowship (John 1:7).* This fellowship makes operative the blood of Jesus Christ. The one factor that a church cannot afford to lose is its fellowship! It can lose its income, buildings, social acceptability, and dearest and most dedicated members, but it cannot lose its fellowship and remain a New Testament church.

1. Fellowship is essential to the life of the church. In Acts 2:42 we are told, "And they continued steadfastly in the apostles' doctrine and *fellowship,* and in breaking of bread, and in prayers" (emphasis added). The New Testament chooses to define the church in terms of "fellowship." In fact, practically all definitions of the church use the word *fellowship.*

2. Fellowship is essential to the development of the Christian (1 John 1:7). The problem between the two sons in Christ's parable of the prodigal son is a lack of fellowship. Both were separated from their father. One was separated by selfish willfulness that took him into a far country. The other was separated from his father by a wall of self-pity and legalistic piety. The fact remains that both had arrested their development until they entered into fellowship with each other and with their loving father.

3. Fellowship is essential to converting the world. Paul spoke of our fellowship in the gospel in Philippians 1:3, 5. By this he is referring to our cooperative work together in spreading the gospel of Jesus Christ. People are attracted to a church by its Christian fellowship. To prove this, try opening up your home. Invite the unchurched and the unsaved into your house. Then surround them with warm Christian fellowship, and you will see at least some of them attracted to Christ and his church.

C. *The sharing of that fellowship (1 John 1:3).* John wants those who have not "seen and heard" to have fellowship with him and enjoy all that he enjoys. Fellowship with one another is more than union, it is a sharing together of the blessings of God. This fellowship must be shared corporately as a church, such as time together in Sunday school classes and worship services. It must also be shared individually by caring people.

III. The live you live (1 John 2:3–6).

A. *Verse 3 is paraphrased in the Living Bible in this manner: "And how can we be sure that we belong to him?* By looking within ourselves: are we really trying to do what he wants us to do?" Christians must strive for obedience.

B. *On one occasion Dr. R. A. Torrey asked the wayward son of a Baptist minister, "Are you a friend of God?"* The young man said, "I think I am." Dr. Torrey replied, "Our Lord said, 'You are my friends if you do whatsoever I command you.'" The young man replied, "In that case, I suppose I have not been a very good friend of God." You can be saved and sure of it because of the life you live.

IV. The purpose of Christ's coming (1 John 3:5).

"And you know, moreover, that Christ became man for the purpose of removing sin, and that he himself is quite free from sin" (1 John 3:5).

The first recorded words of Jesus were, "Didn't you know I had to be in my Father's house?" (Luke 2:49 NIV), and his last words on the cross were "It is finished" (John 19:30). From the first to the last words, the purpose of his coming was that we might be saved and sure of it.

V. The love you share (1 John 3:14–18).

Our loving each other reveals a spiritual kinship. If a child of God means more to us than the rank and file of humanity, if the society of the church is more precious to us than the society of the world, if God's love is working consciously in us, then we can be *sure* we are saved! We can know "that we have passed from death into life."

A. *A prohibition (1 John 3:15).* Here John prohibits ill will and hatred in any form. He states that a persistent pattern of hatred reveals that we have no saving relation with Christ. Hatred not only leads to murder; it is murder. That is a very strong statement, but it is supported by the words of Jesus in the Sermon on the Mount.

B. *A perception (1 John 3:16).* We are not left without an example to follow. In Christ's dying on the cross, we perceive how we should be willing to live with each other. We do well to remember that Christ did not die for his friends, but for his enemies: "While we were still sinners, Christ died for us" (Rom. 5:8 NIV).

C. *A practice (1 John 3:17–18).* Sooner or later in life we will all stand face-to-face with the clear-cut opportunity to "practice what we preach" about love. This opportunity may come in the form of a person in need or one who has wronged us. But the command still stands, "Let us not love in word . . . but in deed and in truth."

Conclusion

The Greeks said, "I know God," but it made very little difference in the way they lived. They reasoned through an intellectual acceptance of deity, or they moved through various rituals and rites in an effort to experience deity. But all of this had no effect on their lifestyle.

In stark contrast, fellowship with Christ involves imitation of Christ. As we imitate Christ and become more than simply hearers of the Word, there is a growing level of assurance of our salvation. When we reach that point of competent assurance, then the purpose of this letter has fulfilled itself in our lives. For the purpose of 1 John is stated clearly in 5:13: "I write these things to you who believe in the name of the Son of God so that you may know that you have eternal life" (NIV).

WEDNESDAY EVENING, SEPTEMBER 6

Title: What Kind of Christian?

Text: "We give thanks to God always for all of you" *(1 Thess. 1:2 NASB).*

Scripture Reading: 1 Thessalonians 1:1–4

Introduction

A pastor awakened in the middle of the night with a question running through his mind. He awakened so suddenly and completely that it was as if the question had been shouted audibly. The question that had so abruptly captured his attention was, "What kind of Christian am I?" As he struggled with the issue that night, he was forced to acknowledge some painful realities about his own spiritual life. Out of that soul-searching experience, he was led to a recommitment of his life to Christ that has changed his manner of living to this day.

The question is very basic, but one we all need to deal with from time to time. "What kind of Christian am I?"

The apostle Paul gives us a description of an admirable Christian as he opens his first epistle to the Thessalonians. He begins his letter by expressing thanks for them because of the qualities of Christian life he has observed in them. His expression of thanksgiving and commendation toward the Thessalonian believers provides us with a useful description of the kind of Christians we should strive to be.

I. A lifestyle of faith.

A. *Paul talks of the work of faith that he observed in these Christians.* The word "work" here should not be understood to refer to one's vocation. Rather, it refers to the working out of a person's entire life, a total lifestyle. Paul implies that Christians should conduct their lives with continual evidence of faith at work.

247

B. *In Romans Paul says that the Christian life is to progress "from faith to faith."* In other words, we are to move through life step-by-step from one faith experience to the next. The faith that enabled us first to trust Christ to be our Savior is the same faith by which we are to live a trusting lifestyle. Living in a deceitful and untrustworthy world as we do, it is most difficult for us to exercise the simple Christian quality of childlike trust. How long has it been since you made a major decision or took an important step in your life solely on the basis of faith? This is the kind of Christian lifestyle we are called to live.

II. A labor of love.

A. *The "labor" referred to in this context is "arduous toil."* Paul gave thanks for those in the church who work hard.

B. *He also notes this work is motivated by love.* It is possible for church workers to give themselves on the altar of service to the church but to do so with a sense of resentment and self-pity. The model presented is one of hard work motivated and characterized by genuine, self-giving love. Our church work should come from a genuine love for the Christ who first loved us and died for us. Our work should be inspired by a love for the church, which is his body. Our work should be motivated by a love for individuals for whom Christ died. First Corinthians 13 reminds us that without this kind of love, all of our eloquence, all of our self-denial, all of our mountain-moving faith amounts to nothing.

III. A steadfastness of hope.

A. *The steadfastness that is to be a part of the Christian life is firmness in the faith.* It is a kind of stability that allows the Christian to be consistent in lifestyle.

B. *The kind of stability that Paul commends is based on an unwaning hope.* This hope is more than wishing: it is confident expectation. Our hope is in the Lord; our confidence is in him. We may not always understand the mysteries of life or the paradoxes of the faith, but we remain firm and patient in our relationship with Christ because of the hope we find in him.

Conclusion

The same three concepts that Paul mentioned here in describing an ideal Christian are also mentioned in 1 Corinthians 13, the love chapter. These three important qualities—faith, hope, and love—appear to be a key to the apostle's theology and practical Christianity. Faith is that Christian quality that helps us survive day-to-day life. Love is the Christian quality that helps us work hard and yet do so with joy and thanksgiving. Hope is that which enables a Christian to remain firm and steadfast in the Christian life. Paul expressed thanksgiving to God for people who live this way. Can't we all join him in thanksgiving for this kind of Christian? Don't you want to be this kind of Christian?

SUNDAY MORNING, SEPTEMBER 10

Title: Conversations of Jesus: The Woman at the Well

Text: "Jesus answered and said unto her. Whosoever drinketh of this water shall thirst again; but whosoever drinketh of the water that I shall give him shall never thirst; but the water that I shall give him shall be in him a well of water springing up into everlasting life" *(John 4:13–14).*

Scripture Reading: John 4:7–14

Hymns: "Joyful, Joyful, We Adore Thee," Van Dyke

"Blessed Redeemer," Christiansen

"The Old Rugged Cross," Bennard

Offertory Prayer: Father in heaven, we thank you for giving heaven's best for us in the person of Jesus Christ. We thank you for giving us the gift of eternal life and membership in your family. Today we come giving tithes and offerings that your kingdom may advance and that others may come to know you in the forgiveness of sin and in receiving the gift of eternal life. Bless these gifts to that end, we pray, in Jesus' name. Amen.

Introduction

The woman at the well of Samaria was a loser—a five-time loser, in fact. She was born a woman—a Samaritan woman. She had failed miserably in marriage. In all likelihood she had come to the well at noon instead of late evening to avoid associating with the respectable women of Sychar. She was a loser. Jesus' conversation with her is a dramatization of his concern for losers.

In his love and compassion for this woman, Jesus used the occasion of their meeting to speak to her about her soul. She had come to a well to draw water, and he was thirsty and asked her for a drink. When she responded to his request in a rather negative way, he offered her living water. He used the occasion of his thirst and her task of drawing water to teach an eternal truth. This conversation of Jesus covered a wide range of subjects, but the idea of water is central. He used the human experience of thirst and the need for water as an analogy, and he applied that analogy to the human spirit.

At the center of all this is a fundamental truth: the human heart thirsts for something that only Jesus Christ can satisfy. Sinclair Lewis in one of his novels draws a picture of a respectable businessman who has run away with a girl he thinks he loves. She says to him, "On the surface we seem quite different, but deep down we are fundamentally the same. We are both desperately unhappy about something— and we don't know what it is." In every person there is this nameless, unsatisfied longing, this vague discontent and frustration. In every soul there is a thirst that only the waters of eternity can quench.

249

I. Jesus said he was the source of living water (vv. 13–14).

Jesus was claiming in these words to be the one who alone can satisfy human longing. He was offering himself as the one to quench the thirst of the soul. He said to this woman what he later said to a great throng of people at a Jewish feast: "If any man thirst, let him come to me, and drink" (John 7:37).

A. *Jesus Christ satisfies the deepest longings of the mind.* His gospel offers a worldview and a philosophy of life that is logical, sensible, and consistent with experience. And though it doesn't answer every question, it satisfies the deepest probings of the mind. The gospel of Jesus Christ is intellectually solid, credible, and profound. Don't let anybody ever tell you that only those who don't think are Christians. For one who says that has obviously not read history and does not know that Jesus Christ satisfied the minds of Augustine, Blaise Pascal, William Blake, Søren Kierkegaard, Leo Tolstoy, Dietrich Bonhoeffer, and countless others.

B. *Jesus Christ also satisfies the deepest longings of the emotions.* Though his gospel is surely a worldview, it is more than that. It's more than a system of thought or a coherent set of ideas. It is a relationship—a personal relationship—with God. In that relationship Christ provides comfort in sorrow, peace in turbulence, strength in difficulty. Jesus Christ can meet every emotional need we may have.

C. *Jesus Christ also satisfies the deepest longings of the will.* What we are powerless to do in our own strength, he will enable us to do by his saving and redeeming grace. He will not only show us how to live, but he will also empower us to do it. Jesus Christ satisfies the thirst of the mind because he is the embodiment of truth. Jesus Christ satisfies the thirst of the emotions because he is the embodiment of love. Jesus Christ satisfies the thirst of the will because he is the embodiment of God.

II. Jesus claims to be the continual supply of this water (v. 14).

A. *The last phrase of verse 14 paints a beautiful image: it is the picture of a spring or a fountain bubbling forth with a continual supply.* The picture is not that Christ gives you a drink of water and then in a matter of hours you are thirsty again. But the picture is of an endless, inexhaustible spring within your heart that never ceases to satisfy your thirst. This spring or fountain is free, joyous, and self-sufficient. It isn't dependent on the outward circumstances of life. It is one that flows in all seasons of the year—in prosperity or adversity, in health or in sickness, in life or in death—this water continually refreshes and cleanses the soul. Some of you have been Christians for many years and can testify that the Christian life gets sweeter every day. It may get harder in that you are called on to face new challenges and more difficult tests—but it gets better. The satisfaction, the joy of Christ, becomes more intense as you walk with him. His supply of living water is endless.

B. *Jesus said that this spring of water springs up into everlasting life.* One of the elements of human thirst for God is the longing for eternity, for existence that is not subject to decay, vanity, or death. Although you and I live in time, we have an eternal soul. We thirst for life that can express the eternality of the soul. We yearn for endless existence, for everlasting life. Literature expresses that inward wish in a number of ways. Poets and philosophers have written of utopias, a golden age, a heavenly existence. The longing for heaven is inherent in the human soul. It is thrust so deep that it expresses itself in every single one of us. Jesus Christ promises that in him there is eternal life. He offers living water that springs up forever. He says to us that death is not the end of existence. In him there is everlasting joy and fulfillment. Heaven will not only be endless existence. It will be an endless and unbounded and unlimited experience of God. Our thirst will be quenched forever.

Conclusion

Once a person tastes of the living water that Jesus gives, nothing else will satisfy. Once a person drinks of the fountain and experiences Jesus' quenching of one's deepest thirst, nothing else will satisfy. Have you tasted this living water? Why not say to Christ:

Fill my cup, Lord.
I lift it up, Lord.
Come and quench this thirsting of my soul.
Bread of heaven, feed me till I want no more.
Fill my cup. Fill it up and make me whole.

—Richard Blanchard

SUNDAY EVENING, SEPTEMBER 10

Title: An Old Man's Love Letter

Text: "Now I beseech thee, lady, not as though I wrote a new commandment unto thee, but that which we had from the beginning, that we love one another. And this is love, that we walk after his commandment" *(2 John 5–6).*

Scripture Reading: 2 John 1–6

Introduction

Have you ever been guilty of reading someone else's mail? It can be exceedingly interesting, can't it?

I have been reading someone else's mail of late. Perhaps my most intriguing bit of snooping was the reading of a love letter. It was just a brief letter that required no more than a single piece of paper. But the truth is that love letters are never judged according to their length, but according to their content.

What makes this letter so special is that it is an old man's love letter. If some of you young Romeos think you know how to write a love letter, you need to take a few lessons from some older men who have had far more experience from which to draw, and consequently, a far more expressive vocabulary.

Just such an experienced older man was the apostle John. He is not ashamed of his age. In fact, he calls himself "the elder," that is, "the old man." He is not referring to an office he holds, but to an age he has attained.

It is his age that qualifies him to write his love letter. A person without his experience or with fewer years could never have written such a letter. Four facts about Christian love surface in this letter.

I. There is a personal delight in love (v. 4).

Phillips translates this verse in these words: "I was overjoyed to find some of your children living the life of truth."

A. *Randel Harris says that 2 John is a Christian love letter.* And it is, but not from John to a particular person but from John to a particular church, which he calls "the elect lady," and to the members of that church, whom he addresses as "your children."

B. *Because of the fidelity of the members of that church, John found a special delight in expressing his love for them.* It is always so: the fires of love are fanned by the fidelity of those with whom we have labored.

II. There is practical definition of love (vv. 5–6).

A. *In verse 6 of this letter John offers a practical definition of love.* "And this is love. . . ." Here John dares to define love in terms of conduct, not conversation; in terms of practice, not pronouncements; and in terms of behavior, not belief. Within the church to which John is writing there are things that make him glad and things that make him sad. He is joyful that some of the church's members are walking in the truth. But he is sorrowful that others have departed from the truth. Thus there was a division within the church. John offers one remedy: the remedy of love.

B. *John's practical definition of love is couched in terms of doing.* There is a personal delight in love and a practical definition of love, but John warns:

III. There is a possible destruction of love (vv. 7–9).

The Living Bible paraphrases the first part of verse 7 in this manner: "Watch out for the false leaders—and there are many of them around." More highly than any other Christian virtue, John cherished the virtue of Christian love. He knew all too well that if love is lost, all is lost.

Because of the devastation the loss of love brings to a church, John warns us that there always is a possible destruction of love. He mentions two ways that love may be destroyed.

A. *By the wrong kind of belief (vv. 7, 9).* The wandering prophets had a propensity to abuse their position. An enormous amount of prestige went with their calling. It was possible for the most undesirable characters to enter into this particular religious profession since they moved from place to place. In light of the economy of their day, such wandering prophets could live in considerable comfort at the expense of local congregations. During the early days of the church, some of these wandering prophets became nothing more than con artists who found an easy way to make a comfortable living. William Barclay points out that this is the picture behind 2 John. The wrong kind of beliefs proclaimed by these false teachers were destroying love in the church and thus disrupting fellowship. Any time wrong beliefs are allowed to be perpetuated within a church, you can be certain that it is disruptive to the fellowship of the church and ultimately to its total ministry.

B. *The wrong kind of behavior (v. 8).* This portion of verse 8 is paraphrased in *The Living Bible* in these words: "Beware of being like them." Always there is the temptation to be like our teachers, especially if we hold them in high esteem. John is saying here that we must resist the temptation to match wits with the "advanced thinkers" of our day. If we are not careful, we will behave as they behave and become arrogant advocates of our own ideas. To do this is to be guilty of the wrong kind of behavior.

IV. There is to be a continual defense of love (vv. 10–13).

Since love is indispensable to the fellowship of the church, and since there are those who would destroy it, it must be defended continually.

Someone said, "Love may not make the world go around, but it surely makes the trip worthwhile!" John mentions two fronts on which we must maintain a constant defense system if the trip is to be worthwhile.

A. *There must be a personal defense in dealing with those who would disrupt the fellowship (vv. 10–11).* Dr. Henry Halley, in his famous Bible handbook, claims that John is clearly stating "that the practice of Christian love does not mean that we should give encouragement to the enemies of the truth." John clearly states that those who would disrupt the fellowship of the church are to be offered no hospitality whatsoever. They are not even to be given a greeting on the street, since doing so would be interpreted as extending sympathy and support for their false cause. It must be made clear to the world that the church has no tolerance of those whose teaching would destroy its faith.

How, then, are we to treat the people of more than 350 religious cults in the United States? Many of them are very evangelistic. When they come to your door and offer you free literature or express a desire to explain some new, allegedly divinely inspired book, how should you respond? Second John 10–11 answers the question very explicitly. You must maintain a constant defense against those who would disrupt the fellowship and destroy the truth, whether it be in your home or in your church.

B. *There is to be a continual defense of love in dealing with those who are a part of the fellowship (vv. 12–13).* John says that he will write no more because he intends to come and meet with these people face-to-face. John realized that letters often can only confuse the situation, whereas a face-to-face encounter can often clear up a seemingly insoluble problem. Often a letter or document carefully written is misinterpreted and only adds fuel to the fire. There are times when we must sit down in Christian love and in face-to-face encounter correct problems that are potentially explosive.

Conclusion

Jerome, in his *Commentary on Galatians,* told of John when he was an old man and had to be carried to the church. Unable to speak many words, John would say at the conclusion of each service, "Little children, love one another." Members grew weary of always hearing the same words Sunday after Sunday. On one occasion a member asked John, "Why do you always say, 'Little children, love one another'?" John's answer was profound. He replied, "It is the Lord's command, and if it is done, it is enough. Little children love one another."

An old man's love letter when taken to heart can help us make our circle of love wide enough to take in all others. If this is done, I suppose it isn't so bad to read someone else's mail after all.

WEDNESDAY EVENING, SEPTEMBER 13

Title: What Kind of Gospel?

Text: "Our gospel did not come to you in word only, but also in power and in the Holy Spirit and with full conviction" *(1 Thess. 1:5 NASB).*

Scripture Reading: 1 Thessalonians 1:5

Introduction

After describing the kind of Christian he admired in the Thessalonian church, Paul addressed the kind of gospel he valued (v. 5). The question for us in this study is, What kind of gospel do I believe? What kind of gospel does my church teach and preach? Paul implies that there are various forms of the gospel floating about. We know he believes in one true gospel, but he is aware, as we should be, that there are numerous false ones too.

Paul described in this single verse the kind of gospel that he believed and preached. It is the kind of gospel that we also want to affirm and proclaim.

I. Not just words.

Paul indicates that the gospel is more than words spoken into the air or written on paper. The gospel is not simply a litany that we recite in public worship. It is not just a creed that we memorize and by which we judge the faith of others. Verbal witness is important, but the gospel is more than just words spoken or written. Paul commends the Thessalonians for their multifaceted devotion to the gospel. Their actions fleshed out their words.

II. The gospel of power.

A. *The apostle believed in a gospel that was alive and dynamic.* The gospel Paul proclaimed had a power to affect lives beyond ways that people could explain or understand.

B. *We are inclined to want to explain church growth in terms of a formula guaranteeing success.* We look for a pastor who is a charismatic leader. We want to explain church growth in terms of effective public relations or well-organized machinery. However, any church growth that can be explained in human terms is not genuine church growth. Only the gospel has power to affect lives supernaturally. This is the gospel of power that we believe.

III. Holy Spirit involvement.

A. *The gospel that we believe is that which proclaims Jesus Christ to be Son of God and Savior.* The Bible assures us that in the living and proclaiming of the gospel the Holy Spirit is present in a mysterious but real way.

B. *If we forget the Holy Spirit and his involvement in the gospel, several unfortunate things can happen.*
    1. We are subject to err without the guidance of the Holy Spirit.
    2. We lack confidence that anything significant will happen by our own efforts. The Holy Spirit helps us to know that the sowing of seed will eventually produce a harvest.
    3. We feel alone and rejected without the Holy Spirit at work in our gospel proclamation. When people say no or slam doors, we may feel personally rejected unless we realize the Spirit stands with us.
    4. We try too hard without a conviction about the involvement of the Holy Spirit in evangelism. Lacking faith in God's power to make a difference, we attempt to force decisions on people. As one preacher has remarked, "We go out to harvest, and we pick green fruit" if we go without the guidance of the Spirit of the Lord of the harvest.

IV. A gospel in which we have full conviction.

The literal Greek phrase may be translated "much full assurance." The gospel that we believe is one that we should believe absolutely. Do you really believe that Jesus is the way? Do you truly consider him humankind's *only* hope for salvation? Do you believe this with sufficient conviction that you would stake your life on it? You are staking your life on it whether you realize it or not.

V. A gospel demonstrated in life.

Paul spoke of a gospel that was confirmed by what he proved to be while among the people. The Christian gospel causes people to enter an exciting pilgrimage of becoming—of becoming more than they are, becoming Christlike in character. We should be able to look at our churches and from every angle observe people who are in the process of becoming.

Conclusion

An inadequate gospel produces inadequate Christians. To our shame, there have been Christian churches through the centuries that have diluted and adulterated the clear, powerful gospel in ways that robbed it of its vitality and power. We need to understand the kind of gospel that Paul describes in this verse, and this should be the gospel that we live, believe, and proclaim.

SUNDAY MORNING, SEPTEMBER 17

Title: Conversations of Jesus: Paul

Text: "He fell to the ground and heard a voice say to him, 'Saul, Saul, why do you persecute me?'

"'Who are you, Lord?' Saul asked.

"'I am Jesus, whom you are persecuting,' he replied. 'Now get up and go into the city, and you will be told what you must do'" *(Acts 9:4–6 NIV).*

Scripture Reading: Acts 9:1–9

Hymns: "Praise to God, Immortal Praise," Barbauld

         "Christ Receiveth Sinful Men," Neumeister

         "Have Thine Own Way," Pollard

Offertory Prayer: Heavenly Father, today we come to bring our tithes and offerings to you. Help us to do so with joy in the privilege of giving, even as you gave your Son for us on the cross. Help us to make known the good news of your love to the ends of the earth through our tithes and offerings. In Jesus' name we pray. Amen.

Introduction

The drama of conversion to Christ is portrayed in the conversation between Saul and Jesus in a very vivid manner. The dynamics of conversion, the nature of conversion, and the ingredients of conversion are all here. In fact, the experience of Saul on the road to Damascus is considered by most to be the best example of a radical conversion. Often someone will remark, "I've never had a Damascus road experience with Christ." By that they mean they've never seen a blinding light or heard a voice from heaven. They've never been struck down in quite as dramatic a way as was Saul.

Yet in a very real sense every person who becomes a Christian experiences what Saul experienced on the road to Damascus. Saul's conversion was really no different from other conversions except that it was more concentrated, more focused. The attendant physical manifestations—such as the voice and the light—are really insignificant in comparison to the deeper dynamics of what occurred on that road. In fact, I am convinced that many other people have been made aware of the reality of Jesus Christ in just as dramatic a way as Saul and yet have refused to be converted.

But it is because Saul's conversion was so dramatic that it offers a good example of conversion. It teaches us the nature of conversion and the absolute necessity of it and helps us understand what it is.

I. Conversion always occurs because of Christ's compelling.

He takes the initiative in it.

A. *He always inaugurates it or begins the process by which we are able to come to faith in him.* The farthest thing from Saul's mind was that he might become a Christian. He was going in the opposite direction with great zeal when the Lord took the initiative in regard to him. Verse 1 says, He was "breathing out threatenings and slaughter against the disciples of the Lord," when suddenly Jesus Christ dramatically reached out to him.

The first ingredient in all conversions is Christ's taking the initiative. He seeks us before we ever seek him. In fact, our seeking of him is a result of his seeking us. If God didn't take the initiative and reach out to us and make us aware of our need of his love, none of us would ever believe in him. If we were left to ourselves, we would continue to be like sheep—going astray, going our own way.

B. *The conversation that marked Saul's conversion began with Jesus calling, "Saul, Saul."* In the Scripture when there is a repeated name or phrase, it is usually the evidence of great compassion and sorrow. In the Old Testament David cried after the tragic death of his son, "O Absalom, O Absalom, my son." When Jesus stood over Jerusalem and wept over its sin, he cried out, "Jerusalem, O Jerusalem." So with Saul, Jesus calls out in love and sadness.

II. In that compelling there is a conviction of sin and need.

A. *The question that Jesus asked of Saul was, "Why do you persecute me?"* The acts of cruelty that Saul was performing against the Lord's disciples were acts of cruelty against him. And those acts were expressions of his own sin and need. In conversion the Lord makes us aware of our need—whatever that need may be. He makes us aware of our need and our inadequacy. He causes us to see ourselves as we are and the need to be changed. That awareness is what the Bible calls conviction. It is an inward consciousness of sinfulness and worthiness, a stark realization of failure. It is an acknowledgment of guilt, an admission of sin.

B. *Conversion is also an awareness of the absurdity and foolishness of sin.* Conviction is the realization of how futile and foolish it is to set one's will against God. Conviction is admitting that living life apart from God is hurting ourselves and others, and it is unnecessary.

III. In conversion there is a confrontation.

A. *After Jesus' question, "Why do you persecute me?"* Saul himself asked a question, "Who are you, Lord?" Realizing that it was God himself who was speaking, Saul now inquired of God. It was, I believe, an honest inquiry. Saul really wanted to know the Lord in a personal way. So the Lord identified himself and revealed himself to Saul. The Lord said, "I am Jesus, whom you are persecuting." Verse 6 says Saul began to tremble and was astonished.

B. *This is the crucible of conversion.* A confrontation, a face-to-face meeting, took place between Jesus Christ the Son of God and Saul of Tarsus. Surely every person's conversion will not be like this one in that everything occurs so dramatically and quickly. Yet for a person to say, "I have been converted," he or she must be able to say, "I have had a confrontation with Christ."

Confrontation is not just acceptance of ideas or intellectual assent to a plan of salvation. It is not just agreeing to some facts. It involves acceptance of a person and acknowledgment of that acceptance to him. Confrontation is saying to Jesus Christ, "I accept you as my Lord. I trust you for my salvation."

IV. In that confrontation there is commitment.

A. *The most significant words Saul spoke in this personal conversation with Jesus were, "What shall I do, Lord?" (Acts 22:10).* Those words reflect a change of heart and mind in Saul.

B. *There can be no conversion apart from personal commitment to Jesus Christ.* Jesus said, "If anyone would come after me, he must deny himself and take up his cross and follow me" (Matt. 16:24 NIV). It's not enough just to be sorry for your sins. It's not enough just to want to go to heaven when you die. It's not enough just to desire to live a better life. Conversion requires commitment. You must be willing to say what Saul said: "What shall I do, Lord?"

Conclusion

Many of us were converted to Jesus Christ in ways that were just as decisive and dramatic as Saul's conversion. They just weren't as quick. God's work in lives is very deliberate, but it is usually done over a period of time. Conversions can be as much a process as an event. Many cannot tell of the exact moment they first trusted Jesus Christ as Savior and Lord. But one thing is sure. If they have felt the compelling of God's Spirit, if they have been convicted of sin, if they have confronted Jesus Christ and have personally committed their lives to him, they are his. Are you?

SUNDAY EVENING, SEPTEMBER 17

Title: The Many Faces of Love

Text: "Beloved, I wish above all things that thou mayest prosper and be in health, even as thy soul prospereth" *(3 John 2).*

Scripture Reading: 3 John 1–7

Introduction

A hundred years ago, the majority of babies under age one who were placed in children's institutions did not live. Later research proved that the absence of a mother's love was a major factor in so many deaths.

One study conducted by René Spitz of New York City surveyed children in two similar institutions. The only difference in the children was the amount of love they received: in the first home the babies were cared for by their mothers; in the second home the infants were raised by a few nursing personnel so overworked that one nurse cared for up to twelve children. In two years 37 percent of the babies not receiving a mother's love died, but after five years none of the babies cared for by their mothers had died. This shows the power of a mother's love.

But love has many faces. It may take on the face of a child, a parent, or a friend. Christian love has just as many faces. Christian love is dynamic. It is not static, nor can it be stereotyped.

The many faces of love are seen in John's letter addressed to Gaius. This is a letter that the apostle intended for Gaius to share with his church.

I. The greeting love sends (vv. 1–2).

A. *Twice in this greeting John uses the word "beloved."* In these three letters John uses the word "beloved" ten times. This is a very important fact, because even though these letters are full of warning and rebuke, their accent is on love.

B. *In verse 2 John expressed an interest in both the spiritual and physical welfare of Gaius.* Like his Savior, John never lost sight of the fact that people have bodies as well as souls. God is equally concerned with both parts of us.

C. *We must never fail to show the face of love when we are called to warn or rebuke.* John *has some stern things to say.* But he did not come out shooting from the hip like a religious cowboy drunk on the wine of his own spirituality. He remembered the greeting love sends.

II. The joy love brings (vv. 3–4).

A. *In verse 4 John tells of the teacher's greatest joy—the joy of seeing his pupils walking in the truth.* The truth of which he speaks in the latter part of verse 4 is that which causes a person to live like God and think like God.

B. *When we, like John, can see in those with whom we have labored a lifestyle that "walks in the truth," there comes to us the joy that only Christian love can bring.* This love in turn shines forth and brings joy to others.

III. The hospitality that love extends (vv. 5–8).

A. *John speaks of his listeners doing a good work for God by taking care of the itinerant teachers and missionaries.* Because they were traveling for the Lord, they took with them neither food nor clothing. But the love of God's people prompted them to extend hospitality.

B. *Second John warns against extending hospitality to missionaries who were bearers of Gnostic heresy.* On the other hand, 3 John concerns itself with encouraging hospitality to missionaries who were orthodox in their views.

As pastors we should encourage our people to use the hospitality of their own homes to cultivate evangelism. Christ's love can be shown in their warmth and joy as they extend hospitality. But surprisingly, their Christian love may incur opposition!

IV. The opposition love incurs (vv. 9–10).

Once upon a time there was a member of a church who loved to think of himself as a "great leader." For some reason, perhaps because he had been a member of the church a long time, or because of his family name, or because he had given money in the past, he felt that he should be consulted about everything that occurred in the church.

This man did not need to be chairman of anything. Simply because of who he was he felt he should approve everything, including those who would speak in the church. He did not like the idea of having so many guest speakers. If any member extended hospitality to one of these traveling preachers, this self-appointed church spokesman would actually try to get that member kicked out of the church.

"This can't really be true," you say. "A church member would never act like that!" Wouldn't he? I'll tell you this man's name. I think you ought to know when someone acts that way. His name is Diotrephes. You can read an actual account of his misbehavior in 3 John 9–10.

Not only did this man not love, he could not stand the fact that others loved each other. There will always be those who oppose any expression of hospitality or generosity toward others. How do you handle people like this? John's advice is, "Don't become like them, but rather follow the example love sets" (v. 11).

V. The example love sets (vv. 11–12).

A. *John says, "Do not follow the example of Diotrephes, but follow the example of Demetrius, for this is the example love sets."* Dr. C. H. Dodd said, "There is no real religious experience which does not express itself in love." This is why in spite of all of his innate ability as a leader, Diotrephes was not a real Christian, at least as John saw it.

B. *We must never forget that behavior is as important as belief, and conduct is as critical as one's creed.* It is possible for a person's theology to be as sound as a rock and his or her heart as correspondingly hard.

John says that in choosing an example to follow we should choose a person who has the habit of doing good (v. 11) and we should follow the example of a person who has a good report among all people (v. 12).

VI. The peace love produces (vv. 13–14).

The words "peace be to thee" are far more than a formal farewell. They are a reminder of the peace that love produces. Soon John will come and talk face-to-face with the church. His presence will do what no letter can ever do. John is saying that the peace love produces will never come through "pen and ink" but through one life touching another life.

Conclusion

Do you have this peace? Have you allowed the love of God to produce this peace in you? Are you willing from this day on to allow your face to be one of the expressions of love?

WEDNESDAY EVENING, SEPTEMBER 20

Title: What Kind of Church?

Text: "You became an example to all the believers" *(1 Thess. 1:7 NASB).*

Scripture Reading: 1 Thessalonians 1:6–10

Introduction

A man once remarked to a friend that he was looking for the ideal New Testament church. The friend replied, "If you do find the perfect New Testament church, I hope you won't join it and destroy its perfection." We understand that any church made up of imperfect human Christians cannot be a perfect church. But we need ideals to strive for, and the apostle Paul provides us with a description of the kind of church that he would consider ideal.

I. Imitators of Christ.

A. *Verse 6 speaks of the ideal of Christians modeling their lives after Christ.* Surely it would be an ideal church if all of us were thoroughly committed to being like Jesus in every situation.

  1. In tribulation Christ provided us with a model of Christian attitude and behavior. He suffered but submitted to God. When bad times come, let us respond in like manner.

  2. Christ lived a life of tranquility and joy. The ideal Christian, then, lives with a profound joy that comes from the Holy Spirit.

B. *We are also to be examples for others.* The apostle Paul indicated that Christians should make themselves copies of Christ so that others could imitate them and thus be Christlike.

II. Heralds of the gospel.

A. *In verse 8 Paul speaks of the kind of church that is actively involved in spreading the gospel everywhere.* It is easy for us to develop a spiritual myopia that allows us to see only the physical needs around us. We cannot get sidetracked.

B. *The ideal church has a world vision and is responsive to the needs of the entire world.* The world doesn't end in our backyards. We must extend ourselves to include supporting missions.

III. Welcomers.

A. *Verse 9 refers to the qualities of hospitality that Paul would encourage in the church.* We are to be constantly opening our arms to receive people with love. The church of Jesus Christ is to be inclusive, but all too often we are exclusive. We are to welcome all into our homes and into our church.

B. *We are able to be open to receive the living and true God as an integral part of our lives.* We are to be open to his presence, open to his Word, and open to obeying his commandments.

C. *Christians need to be ready to receive and welcome a returning Savior.* With regard to the second coming of our Lord, some have been so confused by the multitudinous interpretations of the prophecies that they avoid thinking about his coming altogether. Other Christians don't care that Jesus is coming again. Informed and sensitive Christians, however, eagerly await his coming. Will it not be a welcome day when Christ is openly acknowledged as King and Lord of all that belongs to him?

Conclusion

What kind of church will we be? Let us be imitators of Christ, our supreme example. Let us be busy broadcasting the gospel near and far. Let us be open and receptive to one another, to those outside the family of faith, and to the Lord himself.

SUNDAY MORNING, SEPTEMBER 24

Title: Conversations of Jesus: Mary Magdalene

Text: "'Woman,' he said, 'why are you crying? Who is it you are looking for?'

"Thinking he was the gardener, she said, 'Sir, if you have carried him away, tell me where you have put him, and I will get him'" *(John 20:15 NIV)*.

Scripture Reading: John 20:11–18

Hymns: "A Mighty Fortress Is Our God," Luther

        "He Included Me," Oatman

        "Faith Is the Victory," Yates

Offertory Prayer: Holy Father, thank you for meeting with us today in the house of prayer and worship in the person of your Son, Jesus Christ. Thank you for the gift of your Spirit as an indwelling presence. Thank you, Father God, for giving us the privilege of partnering with you in winning a world to faith in your Son. Bless these gifts to that end. Amen.

Introduction

When was the last time you cried? Psychologists tell us that tears can be a sign of emotional health. Expressing emotion instead of keeping it all bottled up inside can be one of the most health-giving things you do. But psychologists also tell us that tears can be a sign of emotional sickness. Uncontrollable weeping or even sentimental weeping may be a sign of guilt or an evidence of unresolved grief. I've known some for whom tears were a defense mechanism or an escape from reality or a substitute for positive action.

The Bible is surely no stranger to crying. It gives innumerable accounts of people who shed tears for all kinds of reasons. Jesus wept over Jerusalem, and Hebrews 5:7 says that in the days of his flesh he offered up prayers and supplications with strong crying and tears. Paul said to the Ephesian elders that for three years in Paul's ministry with them he ceased not to warn them with tears. There's one entire book in the Bible that sounds like one great sob—the book of Lamentations.

The conversation of Jesus with Mary Magdalene had to do with tears. The first recorded words of Jesus after his resurrection were, "Woman, why are you crying?" Her tears were a strange mixture of unbelief and love, affection and fear. And in response to her weeping, Jesus appeared and spoke words that are a strange combination of comfort and rebuke. We are so much like Mary Magdalene, and our tears—whether they are shed with the eyes or only in the heart—are so much like her tears.

I. Hers were tears of sorrow, and Jesus spoke to her words of comfort.

A. *It is not difficult for those who have suffered the death of a close loved one or friend to understand Mary's grief.* She was brokenhearted, crushed, overcome with sorrow. Not only was Jesus dead, but now his body was missing. No piece in the puzzle fit. There was no rhyme or reason in her pain. So she wept.

B. *If you have known the chilling hand of death to touch someone you love, you too have wept tears of sorrow.* If you have known the loneliness of separation, you too have wept the tears of sorrow; but if you listen, Jesus will say to you what he said to this grieving woman. After he asked her, "Why are you crying?" she supposed he was the gardener and answered, "Sir, if you have carried him away, tell me where you have put him, and I will get him." To those pleading, pitiful expressions, Jesus spoke only one word, her name, "Mary."

C. *In the time of sorrow what a person needs more than anything else is the comfort of God's presence and love.* When I weep tears of sorrow, I need to hear the voice of Jesus speak my name. If I am still and listen, I will hear it. Oh, not in an audible voice, but in the quiet of the soul the risen Christ will come to comfort and console me. For the Christian the time of sorrow is a bittersweet time in life. It is bitter because of the pain of loss and the suffering of separation. But it is also sweet in the experience of the nearness of God and the reality and the power of God.

II. Mary wept tears of love, and Jesus spoke to her words of assurance.

A. *Mary Magdalene loved Jesus.* Her tears were a sign of that love and evidence of her devotion. In response to that love and devotion, Jesus appeared to reassure her that her love was received. By speaking to her personally, he was saying, "I know of your devotion. I receive your love." By speaking to her personally, Jesus was assuring her of his love for her.

B. *All of the postresurrection appearances of Jesus were only to people who loved him—except one.* After his resurrection Jesus did not appear to Pilate, Herod, Caiaphas, or the Roman soldiers. Why is that? Why did he not dazzle them or overwhelm them by showing that he was alive and that he was real? He knew that such appearances would not accomplish any real purpose. He knew that such appearances would at best frighten them and at worst solidify their resistance even more. The postresurrection appearances of Jesus were to those who loved him, whose hearts were already turned to him. The same is true today. Jesus is real only to those who love him and will commit their lives to him. In John 14:21 we read, "He that hath my commandments, and keepeth them, he it is that loveth me; and he that loveth me shall be loved of my Father, and I will love him and will manifest myself to him." Jesus Christ will manifest himself only to those who love him.

C. *Do you know how one comes to know God?* It's not by analytical thought or logical reasoning. You may come to know a lot about God that way, but you do not come to know *him* that way. God becomes real in a person's life through the instrumentality of the heart: as one is willing to trust God, make a commitment to him, and obey him, God will manifest himself and make himself real. Jesus Christ gives assurance of his presence and love only to the devoted heart. Mary's tears were expressions of love and devotion. So Jesus made himself real to her and appeared to her.

III. Mary wept tears of unbelief, and Jesus appeared to her to challenge her.

A. *Mary's tears showed great love but little faith.* Her grief blinded her to the facts—the empty tomb, the way in which the linens lay, the presence of the angels. All of these should have reminded her of Jesus' own words that he would rise again on the third day. Even Jesus' voice did not penetrate her grief. She was oblivious to everything except her own feelings. So Jesus' question "Why are you crying?" was asked to open Mary's eyes and quicken her faith. There is even a hint of rebuke in the question. It's as if Jesus was saying, "Mary, your weeping is unnecessary. Remember what I promised you. Believe in me. I am alive just as I said I would be."

B. *We are so like Mary.* How many times do we weep for something that is already within our grasp? How many times do we weep for fear of what will never actually happen? How many times do we weep for some unnecessary thing? Jesus challenges us just as he challenged Mary. "Put away your tears of anxiety, fear, and unbelief. Trust in my power, love, and providence."

Conclusion

If you are weeping in this place of worship today, Jesus asks you, "Why are you crying?" Your tears may be shed or unshed; he knows your sorrow. If you are weeping in defeat and discouragement over the apparent weakness of the kingdom of God, Jesus says, "Weep not for me, but weep for yourselves." If you are weeping in concern for lost souls, Jesus says, "They that sow in tears shall reap in joy. He that goeth forth and weepeth, bearing precious seed, shall doubtless come again with rejoicing bringing his sheaves with him." If you are weeping in sorrow or sadness, Jesus says to you, "Come unto me all you that labour and are heavy-laden and I will give you rest. Take my yoke upon you and learn of me and you shall find rest unto your souls, for my yoke is easy and my burden is light." If you are weeping over the spiritual need in your life and the leanness of your own soul, Jesus says to you, "Blessed are they that mourn, for they shall be comforted."

SUNDAY EVENING, SEPTEMBER 24

Title: The Faith Once Delivered

Text: "Beloved . . . earnestly contend for the faith which was once delivered unto the saints" *(Jude 3)*.

Scripture Reading: Jude

Introduction

The faith once delivered to the saints is a simple faith. People—not God—have complicated that faith. The gospel in itself is the power of God unto salvation to all who believe. But proud and arrogant people come along and either explain it away or pollute it with their own theories and interpretations. This is nothing new. As long as there has been a gospel, there have been those who would pervert it. They even lived in Jude's day. His brief but powerful letter hit those who read it like a hammer blow. Its call to defend the faith is as clear and rousing as the blast of a trumpet.

Its message is also meant for our day. William Barclay says that Jude is not far from being "the most relevant book in the New Testament." In our day when personal interpretations can so easily destroy our fellowship, we are wise to hear and to heed what Jude says about "the faith once delivered."

I. The call to defend the faith (vv. 3–7).

Even as Jude had intended to do, so we should major on proclaiming the gospel rather than protecting the gospel. But there come those rare occasions when the faith is so attacked from without and so perverted from within that we can do nothing else than hear and respond to the call to defend the faith!

A. *The call to defend the faith is a call to alter our plans for the future (v. 3).* Often we
   need to alter our plans for the future. Jude is simply saying that he had planned
   on writing these people some other thoughts about the salvation that God had

given them, but because of the pressing urgency of the hour, it was necessary for him to write something different. The different message he wrote was a defense of the faith.

B. *The call to defend the faith is a call to protect the faith in the present (v. 3).* Phillips translates this verse in this manner: "I felt compelled to make my letter to you an earnest appeal to put up a real fight for the faith, which has been once for all committed to those who belong to Christ." From this we learn several things.

1. The faith is something that is delivered to us. Our Christian theology is not something that we have concocted ourselves. It is a divine trust of a divine message given to us.

2. Our Christian faith is something that is once and for all delivered to us. There is an unchangeable quality and permanency about our faith.

3. Christian faith is something that is entrusted to the family of God. By this Jude is saying that the Christian faith is not the possession of any one individual. Rather, it is the possession of the total family of God.

4. The Christian faith is something that must be defended. Every one of us is called upon to be both a proclaimer and a defender of the faith.

C. *The call to defend the faith is a call to remember the experiences of the past (vv. 4–7).* The problem that had created the need to contend for the faith was a problem from within the church, not from outside the church. Jude says that these troublemakers had "crept in unawares."

These false teachers had sought to turn the grace of God into an excuse for open immorality. These heretics believed, or at least claimed they believed, that since the grace of God covers any sin, a person may sin as much as he or she likes. These false teachers also denied Jesus Christ (vv. 5–7).

II. The conduct of those who would destroy the faith (vv. 8–15).

Because their conduct was such a contradiction of every Christian principle, Jude did not see that it was necessary to refute their doctrine. So that we might be spared the condemnation that comes to such people, Jude describes their conduct (vv. 8–13).

Jude says that these people defiled their flesh and spoke evil of angels, even when Michael the archangel would not speak evil of the Devil. Furthermore, these wicked individuals condemned everything that they did not understand. They were like hidden rocks on which a ship may crash and be destroyed. In verse 12 Jude compares them to clouds without rain and trees without fruit. He continues in verse 13 to say that they were like lost stars, roving recklessly throughout the heavens.

III. The course for securing the faith (vv. 17–23).

The call to defend the faith cannot be denied, and the conduct of those who would destroy the faith is a sober warning to each of us. But how shall we go about "defending the faith once delivered"? What is the course for securing the faith? Jude outlines the course with four Rs.

A. *Remember what God has said in the past (vv. 17–18).* In these verses Jude shows that nothing had happened that they should not have expected; God had spoken of these things in the past. In light of the past, nothing should take us by surprise in the future.

B. *Rebuild your Christian faith (v. 20).* The NIV translates this verse: "You, dear friends, build yourselves up in your most holy faith and pray in the Holy Spirit." Our entire Christian life is founded on faith. In other words, the life of a Christian is built not on something that he or she has invented, but rather on something he or she has received by faith.

C. *Remain in the boundaries of God's love (v. 21).* "Stay always within the boundaries where God's love can reach and bless you" (TLB).

D. *Reclaim those who have drifted from the faith (vv. 22–23). The Living Bible* brings out this truth most clearly. In our effort to reclaim those who have drifted from the faith, we are admonished to be merciful and to be kind and careful. We are told to hate even the trace of their sin, but at the same time to be merciful to them as sinners.

IV. The consolation for following the faith (vv. 24–25).

What consolation is ours for defending and following the faith? It is the consolation of knowing that:

A. *Christ is capable of keeping us from failing on earth (v. 24).*

B. *Christ is capable of presenting us faultless to heaven (v. 24).*

C. *Christ alone has all glory and majesty and dominion and power in heaven and on earth (v. 25).*

Conclusion

In whatever pulpit we may stand, and whatever problems may be represented in the pews before us, we have but one message, and that is "the faith once delivered unto the saints."

WEDNESDAY EVENING, SEPTEMBER 27

Title: What Kind of Preaching?

Text: "So we speak, not as pleasing men, but God who examines our hearts" *(1 Thess. 2:4 NASB).*

Scripture Reading: 1 Thessalonians 2:1–6

Introduction

Preaching has been central to the life of the church and the proclamation of the gospel since New Testament times. Despite this long background of preaching in the church, many of our people are still uninformed about what constitutes good preaching. Some of them are inclined to evaluate preaching in terms of the decibels of the delivery. Others expect preaching to be entertaining or glib. Some listen to preaching hoping that they will hear simple dogmatic answers to complex problems. Some people want preaching to heap guilt and punishment on them because they somehow feel that they become more spiritual as they are spanked from the pulpit.

In writing to the Thessalonian church about some very basic issues, the apostle Paul provides a valuable description of what good preaching really is.

I. Good preaching is not cowardly.

A. *In verse 2 Paul refers to preaching as a bold and courageous delivery of a word from God.* Good preaching does not take place if the overriding concern of the preacher is what the people's response may be.

B. *Preaching is to be a prophetic word from God, not weakened by a fear of those who listen.*

II. Good preaching is not dishonest.

A. *Verse 3 implies that preaching can be manipulative in its efforts to guide persons toward certain responses.* It can be an erroneous proclamation if in its zeal to produce results it is not true to the biblical record, interpreted in context.

B. *Good preaching scrupulously avoids inaccuracy and dishonesty.* It is characterized by integrity in the handling and application of Scripture.

III. Good preaching is not grandstanding.

A. *Preaching can be designed to please the crowd.* Perhaps you can remember those occasions when you heard a preacher address a crowd whose mood he understood, and you heard him evoke great responses of agreement and encouragement by saying the things they wanted to hear. In verse 4 Paul indicates that good preaching is not designed to stir the emotions of people momentarily or satisfy their itching ears.

B. *Those who listen to preaching are too frequently impressed by clever clichés that actually mean very little.* Emotions may be aroused that lead to immediate feelings of great impact from a sermon, but the real proof of good preaching is whether genuine, lasting change is effected.

IV. Good preaching is not self-serving.

A. *The Christian pulpit should be used to honor Christ, not to bring glory to a preacher.* The genuine pastor-shepherd understands that his feeding responsibility is to the flock—not to his own ego. Sometimes when people walk out the exits exclaiming how eloquent and entertaining the preacher was, good biblical preaching has not taken place.

B. *Genuine Christian proclamation causes people to experience and maintain a sense of awe about the holiness of God and the magnificent greatness of Jesus Christ.*

Conclusion

There is a challenging educational process ahead for many of us. We need to be taught to value preaching that boldly proclaims the truth of God, is faithful to the Word, clearly reveals the living Word, and honors the one proclaimed rather than the proclaimer.

OCTOBER

■ **Sunday Mornings**

Understanding our salvation is contingent on understanding God's grace: salvation is by grace in its commencement, in its continuance, and in its consummation. This month's series is "The Grace of God."

■ **Sunday Evenings**

"Facets of the Stewardship Gem" is the title of the first message and also the suggested theme for the month.

■ **Wednesday Evenings**

Continue the devotional studies of 1 Thessalonians using the theme "Measuring Ourselves by a New Testament Pattern."

SUNDAY MORNING, OCTOBER 1

Title: The Grace of Salvation

Text: "For by grace you have been saved through faith; and that not of yourselves, it is the gift of God" *(Eph. 2:8 NASB).*

Scripture Reading: Ephesians 2:8–10

Hymns: "All Hail the Power of Jesus' Name," Perronett

"Redeemed," Crosby

"Amazing Grace," Newton

Offertory Prayer: O gracious heavenly Father, how you have supplied our needs by your grace! You have given us your Son to save us; now you have given us the privilege to give to you. Grant that our hearts may be clean so we may give in a spirit of generosity and praise, for your glory. Amen.

Introduction

Someone once said, "If there were only a half-dozen words in our vocabulary, 'grace' should be one of them." Grace is the difference between the sinner's plight and the believer's position. If we are to grow in God's grace, we must understand what has happened to us by his grace. It is by grace that we are saved (Eph. 2:8). There is no greater need in a person's life and no greater provision from God. There are five truths that will help us to understand the grace of salvation.

I. The source of salvation.

"For by grace are ye saved" (Eph. 2:8). This means that God both initiated salvation and completed it. What is grace?

A. *Grace has been called the unmerited favor of God.* It is that but is also more than that. Grace is the desire and power to do God's will (Phil. 2:13). The grace of God is one of his attributes, all of which are active. God expresses his love by giving. He expresses his grace to us by giving us the desire and power to do his will. In 1 Corinthians 15:10 Paul says, "By the grace of God I am what I am." God's grace works in us to do his will; it is not accomplished by our own volition. It cannot be accomplished by our will—only God's.

B. *The verse further says that salvation is "not of ourselves," not anything of our doing; and it is "not of works," so that it is not self-achieved.* However, humans have historically tried to save themselves by self-affliction, by human sacrifice, by good works, or by religious ritual. But God's Word is very clear on this point: It is "not of works"! It is by grace.

II. The provision of salvation.

Our focus on grace needs to be centered on the one through whom God's grace of salvation comes.

A. *Ephesians 2:6–10 clearly affirms that this is possible through Jesus Christ.* We are quickened together with Christ (v. 5). We are allowed to sit in heavenly places together with Christ Jesus (v. 6). God's purpose is to show the exceeding riches of his grace in his kindness toward us through Christ Jesus (v. 7). Finally, we are his workmanship, created in Christ Jesus (v. 10).

B. *Acts 4:12 says, "Salvation is found in no one else, for there is no other name under heaven given to men by which we must be saved"* (NIV). Acts 16:31 says, "Believe in the Lord Jesus, and you will be saved" (NIV). Romans 3:24 says we "are justified freely by his grace through the redemption that came by Christ Jesus" (NIV). This is how God saves us. Jesus Christ is the Savior by God's grace!

III. The nature of salvation.

Two important words in verse 10 describe the nature of salvation.

A. *The first is "workmanship."* The verse says, "We are God's workmanship" (NIV), establishing the fact that salvation exists because of his work.

"Workmanship" is from the Greek word *poiema*, which may be translated "poem." It also may be translated "art" or "masterpiece." The believer, then, is God's masterpiece! Everywhere we look we see the works of God's hands (Ps. 19), but God's greatest masterpiece is a new creation in Christ!

B. *The second word is "created," as in "created in Christ Jesus."* It is the word for creation that is used only of God and refers to the creative energy that only he can exert.

Salvation is a divine creation, not an evolution. It is experienced in a moment of time, as Zacchaeus (Luke 19:9) and Saul of Tarsus experienced it (Acts 9:3–6).

"Create" means to bring something out of nothing. Only God can create! Humans cannot create anything—not even an insect or a sunbeam. Our new nature is of God. It is not reformed or remade: it is *new*, the old is gone. We are new persons in Christ (2 Cor. 5:17). This provides for new relationships in life as the new people of God. This can only be God's gracious doing!

IV. The condition of salvation.

Verse 8 says, "For by grace are ye saved through faith." It is important to see the network: salvation is *by* grace *through* faith.

A. *Faith is the means by which we appropriate salvation.* It is the hand that receives the gift. It means "to trust" or "to rely on." John Calvin said, "Faith brings a man empty to God, that he may be filled with the blessings of Christ."

B. *Saving faith has three parts.* Faith is hearing (Rom. 10:17); it is accepting the truth you hear; and it is committing yourself to it. It is a sailor trusting the compass and the stars. It is a patient trusting his or her doctor. It is a traveler trusting the pilot of a plane. To be saved, we must trust Jesus Christ to save us! Faith is the acrostic: Forsaking All I Take Him.

V. The purpose of salvation.

"We are ... created ... unto good works ... that we should walk in them" (v. 10). This is why we are created in Christ Jesus. The purpose of salvation is twofold.

A. *God purposes good works in our lives.* Good works affirm the reality of salvation, because we prove our faith by our works (James 2:14–16). These good works are not human works; they are works God prepared beforehand for us to do. They are eternal works that relate to his eternal plan. They are works like those Jesus did (John 14:12–13). They are prepared works, as the word *ordained* means. We do not manufacture these works; God works in us and through us.

B. *God purposes a new walk for believers "that we should walk in them."* These good works should be our way of life. This new walk in doing God's good works brings glory to God. Consider this example:

A Christian woman often visited a retirement home near her house. One day she noticed a lonely man sitting, staring at his dinner tray. In a kindly manner she asked, "Is something wrong?"

"Is something wrong?" replied the man. "Yes, something is wrong! I am a Jew, and I can't eat this food!"

"What would you like to have?" she asked.

"I would like a bowl of hot soup!"

She went home and prepared the soup and after getting permission from the office, took it to the man. In succeeding weeks she often visited him and brought him the kind of food he enjoyed. Eventually she led him to faith in Christ. Even preparing soup can be a spiritual sacrifice, a good work to the glory of God. It is the grace of salvation continuing to give.

Conclusion

The strength of our salvation and of our continuing in good works lies in the grace of our God. By his grace our lives have new dimensions. Grace enables us to sit in heavenly places in Christ's authority. Grace enables us to walk on earth in Christlike service. This is what salvation by grace is all about. Are you still in the plight of an unbeliever, or are you enjoying the position of a Christian? You can trust Christ and be saved!

SUNDAY EVENING, OCTOBER 1

Title: Facets of the Stewardship Gem

Text: "As each has received a gift, employ it for one another, as good stewards of God's varied grace" *(1 Peter 4:10).*

Scripture Reading: 1 Peter 4:7–11

Introduction

The Christian gospel is a treasure chest of valuable gems, and one of them is stewardship. When most Christians hear the word *stewardship,* their initial thought is probably not diamonds but money, budgets, or offerings. Like a gem whose facets reflect different colors, biblical stewardship involves much more than our offerings. The apostle Peter enables us to see some of these facets of the spiritual gem of stewardship.

I. Stewardship involves the person we are.

The Christian steward has undergone a spiritual transformation more radical than the cutting, grinding, and polishing required for a finished gem. The love of God manifested in Jesus Christ has transformed us and brought us into his family. Once we are in God's family, we are stewards of his grace. The word *steward* means "house manager" and describes an individual entrusted with something for supervision and management. We are to be God's steward—administering God's world according to his will, for the benefit of others, and accountable to the Lord who owns it all.

A. *The scope of our stewardship.* A Christian is a steward of "God's varied grace." The word "varied" means "many-colored" and refers to the multiple ways we experience God's grace. Stewardship involves the gifts of the Spirit for ministry; the blessings of the creation, our environment, and our physical bodies; the gifts of time, intellect, abilities, influence, and possessions. All we are and all we have are the scope of Christian stewardship.

B. *The potential for stewardship.* Every Christian possesses potential for effective stewardship. Equal response from all is not possible, but equal commitment and sacrifice will erupt from a life truly changed by God's grace. Kenneth

Wuest translates this verse: "In whatever quality or quantity each one has received a gift, be ministering it among yourselves as good stewards of the variegated grace of God" (Kenneth S. Wuest, *Studies in the Greek New Testament,* vol. 2 [Grand Rapids: Eerdmans, 1966], 117).

II. The standard for God's steward.

A standard of quality is applied to a finished gem: it is valued according to size, color, and purity. Likewise, the Scriptures have a standard for an effective steward.

A. *Good, faithful, wise.* A "good" steward seeks excellence and desires to please the Master. Paul adds a second requirement: "It is required of stewards that they be found *trustworthy*" (1 Cor. 4:2 NASB, emphasis added). Jesus gives a third requirement: "Who then is that faithful and *wise* steward, whom his lord shall make ruler over his household?" (Luke 12:42, emphasis added). Good, faithful, wise—all of these traits will be expressed in the way we use what God entrusts to our care.

B. *Apply the standard.* Jesus pronounced a blessing on the steward "whom his lord when he cometh shall find so doing" (Luke 12:43). Doing what? Doing a good job, doing it faithfully, doing it wisely. The stewardship standard must be applied. In the parable of the talents (Matthew 25), two servants were commended: "Well done, good and faithful servant!" The third servant received a word of judgment: "You wicked and lazy servant." He didn't do anything! The test of authentic stewardship is in the doing. We need to apply the standard to *all* God entrusts to us.

III. The power for effective stewardship.

A. *How can one achieve the standard and live as a good, faithful, and wise steward?* Peter cites the key—"by the strength which God supplies" (v. 11 NASB). God enables us to use the time wisely. He can enable us to maintain balance between labor and rest.

B. *Christ can supply the power to cope with greed and materialism.* "By the power at work within us [he] is able to do far more abundantly than all that we ask or think" (Eph. 3:20 RSV).

Conclusion

Will you be available for the Lord to work in you? This is the day for good, faithful, wise stewards. "The end of all things is at hand" (v. 7). The world, "lost in the darkness of sin," hastens toward ruin, desperately in need of Christ. Will you give yourself to reach the world before it is too late? Don't wait until some mythical "better day" to become the steward God desires. He wants you now. The end is near. You are needed today.

WEDNESDAY EVENING, OCTOBER 4

Title: What Kind of Ministry?

Text: "We were well-pleased to impart to you not only the gospel of God but also our own lives" *(1 Thess. 2:8 NASB).*

Scripture Reading: 1 Thessalonians 2:7–12

Introduction

Within the fellowship of the church, our attitude and behavior toward one another and toward those to whom we minister is vitally important. Paul suggests the desirable ways of relating to people.

I. The gentleness of a mother (v. 7).

Imagine the tender scene of a young mother cradling her infant. This is the tender care that we are to extend toward those around us. We need to minister with methods that reflect sensitivity.

We are often afraid that if we are gentle, we will be used. God calls us to love with a gentleness and tenderness that compel people to see Christ—regardless of others' responses.

II. The generosity of a brother (vv. 8–9).

We are to give the gospel to people, but also we are to give *ourselves* to people. Our ministry should be characterized by generosity in sharing all of our resources with those to whom we minister.

III. The firmness of a father (vv. 10–12).

We are to relate with a "tough love" that does not compromise the principles of Christian faith. We are to encourage by affirming one another. We are to warn one another about the dangers of wrong behavior.

Conclusion

Churches may be tempted at times in their pursuit of the appearance of success to use methods that violate the dignity of persons. The methods by which we work should be guided by gentleness, generosity, and firmness.

SUNDAY MORNING, OCTOBER 8

Title: The Grace of Serving

Text: "I have written you quite boldly on some points, as if to remind you of them again, because of the grace God gave me to be a minister of Christ Jesus to the Gentiles with the priestly duty of proclaiming the gospel of God, so that the Gentiles might become an offering acceptable to God, sanctified by the Holy Spirit" *(Rom. 15:15–16 NIV).*

Scripture Reading: Romans 15:14–19

Hymns: "Serve the Lord with Gladness," McKinney

   "My Faith Has Found a Resting Place," Edmunds

   "Great Is Thy Faithfulness," Chisholm

Offertory Prayer: Heavenly Father, our hearts are filled with your innumerable blessings. We praise you in your awesome attributes. We present ourselves to you as a living sacrifice. Thank you for the joy of giving. Here are our gifts of tithes and offerings to be used in your storehouse for your glory. Amen.

Introduction

God gives us grace to be saved, grace to live, and grace to serve. To see this truth, we need to remember that grace is an active attribute of God. It expresses his power in us, giving us both the desire and the dynamic to do things his way (Phil. 2:13). This is how we have grace for serving. His power is at work in us, giving us the desire and power to serve his way.

Look at Jesus Christ. He was full of grace and truth, and he went about doing good, condescending to serve (Phil. 2:5–8). His whole life was given to ministry (Matt. 20:28), and he exemplified the spirit of humble service (John 13). He had the grace of serving. Do we have this kind of grace?

I. The grace of serving is the grace of serving practically.

A. *Romans 15:15–16 tells us that God gives grace to serve, and Paul is a living testimony to that.* The word for "minister" means "public servant" and "to fulfill a function."

B. *This kind of serving is to the Lord.* This concept is not an abstraction, however. We serve our Lord by serving others, and by serving them in very practical ways.

Dr. Chester Swor tells about a bedridden woman who formerly taught the largest Sunday school class in her church, sang in the choir, and was active in many ways. She had contracted an incurable illness. She could have complained and said that her days were over; however, in a new spirit of courage, she said, "I will look for new ways to serve."

She became a most powerful witness. During one week alone, she telephoned 150 church members from her bedside, urging them to go to an important meeting. She also invited young people to sit by her bedside. She led seven to Christ, and five made commitments of life to Christian service. This woman served mightily, and she never left her bed. This is grace for serving!

II. The grace of serving is the grace of serving spiritually.

This is seen in Romans 12:3: "For I say, through the grace given unto me, to every man that is among you . . . to think soberly, according as God hath dealt to every man the measure of faith." This kind of serving is expressed in three ways.
A. *Serving according to spiritual guidelines (vv. 1–2)*. Serving is not a matter of just doing an activity; it is an expression of a life presented to God. Notice the flow of the first three verses: service is a response to worship! Service expresses sacrifice. Service is devotion, not duty.
B. *Serving according to a sober spirit (v. 3)*. Sound judgment means that we are not thinking of ourselves more highly than we ought to think, but according to God's measure of faith. It means that we know that we have been given grace to serve and faith to exercise, and that not all have the same function. If we do not "function," we fail to fulfill God's grace in our lives, so that the church suffers from the lack of Christians who serve.
C. *Serving according to spiritual gifts (vv. 6–7)*. We have gifts according to the grace given to us. Each of us has a spiritual gift, a grace gift. Seven are listed: prophecy, serving, teaching, exhorting, giving, administering, and showing mercy. Our best service will be rendered in the knowledge of the spiritual gift God has given to us.

III. The grace of serving is the grace of serving cooperatively.

This is best seen in Galatians 2:9–21. Three concepts are given.
A. *The grace of serving together (v. 9)*. Peter, James, and John gave the right hand of fellowship to Paul and Barnabas in serving Christ and the gospel. This was a means of endorsing one another in the ministry of grace. Notice in 3 John 9–10 the condemnation of Diotrephes, who thwarted collective serving.
B. *The grace of serving sincerely (vv. 11)*. Peter, serving in fear of others, separated himself from other servants. Paul was given grace to oppose Peter to his face and warn him of hypocrisy. Service is to be done in openness, not secrecy.
C. *The grace of serving effectively (v. 20)*. The secret of serving is found in verse 20, which speaks of being "crucified with Christ." This is the perfect tense that emphasizes a past event with continuing effects. Not only are we crucified with Christ, but he also lives in us. The reality of this truth lifts the pressure of serving. It means that Christ is living in us and serving through us! This is the secret to victorious service.

IV. The grace of serving is the grace of serving trustingly.

A. *Ephesians 3:2 speaks of serving as a stewardship*. Grace is a sacred trust given; true serving in doing so trustingly and faithfully. Verse 7 says that Paul testifies that in that spirit he became a minister, a *diakonos*, a servant willing even to serve tables.

277

B.   Diakonos *is also a word that describes urgent, diligent service in God's grace.* Verse 8 says that this grace was given to preach, to evangelize the riches of Christ. Every believer has been given this grace to evangelize.

V. The grace of serving is the grace of serving seriously.

First Corinthians 15:9–10 is a testimony from the apostle Paul explaining why he served. He said, "By the grace of God I am what I am" (v. 10). It was God's grace flowing through him not with him in service. He says further, "But I labored more abundantly than they all" (v. 10); yet it was not he, "but the grace of God which was with [him]."

The following Scriptures emphasize the seriousness of serving labor and toil: Matthew 11:28; Acts 20:35; Romans 16:12; Ephesians 4:28; Colossians 1:29; and 2 Timothy 2:6. The last reference describes the hardworking farmer who toils from dawn till dark.

Conclusion

God gives us grace to serve him so that we meet the needs of others now and eternally! My challenge to you is to respond positively to this aspect of his grace.

SUNDAY EVENING, OCTOBER 8

Title: From Heart to Hand

Text: "They came, every one whose heart stirred him up, and every one whom his spirit made willing, and they brought the LORD's offering to the work of the tabernacle of the congregation, and for all his service, and for the holy garments" *(Ex. 35:21).*

Scripture Reading: Exodus 35:20–29

Introduction

What determines a good steward? Can stewardship be measured with tangible things—the amount of an offering, the time invested in church work, the pledge made to a special campaign? God focuses first on the heart rather than on what is in our hand. Biblical stewardship moves from heart to hand.

This movement is illustrated in the Hebrews' response to the building of the tabernacle. At a worship assembly, Moses challenged the people to obey the Lord and bring materials to erect the tabernacle. They listened, went home, and later "they came, every one whose heart stirred him, and everyone whose spirit moved him and brought the Lord's offering." This is a paradigm for our behavior. When the direction of our stewardship moves from heart to hand, it includes these important areas.

I. Inadequate motives are refused.

What motivates you to give? The heart can be very deceitful and lead one to give for the wrong reason. Some are motivated to give to the Lord's work out of fear. One person expressed fear when he said, "If you don't give the tithe, the Lord will take it another way." Others give from a sense of duty, but duty can become cold, mechanical, and legalistic. Self-respect moves some; they are most concerned about what others might say or think of them. The prospect of material reward motivates the hand sometimes. The Lord does promise to bless those who give, but the nature of that blessing is not necessarily material. Atonement for sin lies behind some giving, but God can't be bought. When the heart is right, these inadequate motives will be refused. Giving needs to be motivated by something else.

II. The highest motive.

A. *A heart stirred by thankful love is the highest motivation: ". . . whose heart stirred him."* The Hebrews had been together and heard Moses tell of his encounter with God. They saw his shining face reflecting the Lord's glory: what a powerful stimulation! Only those who experience the glory of the Lord will have a heart rightly motivated for giving. Paul wrote, "The love of Christ constrains us" (2 Cor. 5:14).

B. *Love brought Christ to die.* "God so loved the world that he gave."

> *Love ever gives—*
> *Forgives—outlives—*
> *And ever stands*
> *With open hands.*
> *And, while it lives—*
> *It gives.*
> *For this is Love's prerogative—*
> *To give—and give—and give.*

The gift in the hand is not enough. What is in the heart? "If I give all my possessions to feed the poor, and if I surrender my body to be burned, but do not have love, I gain nothing" (1 Cor. 13:3 NASB).

III. A willing spirit (vv. 21–22, 29).

A. *Moses did no begging, no extreme urging, no pleading.* He presented the cause and left it to God to deal with the hearts of the people. There was no assessment. The people gave spontaneously, freely, joyfully. They heard; they came; they gave "a freewill offering to the Lord.

B. *Paul described the spirit of authentic Christian giving.* "Each man should give what he has decided in his heart to give, not reluctantly or under compulsion, for God loves a cheerful giver" (2 Cor. 9:7 NIV).

Conclusion

Exodus 36:5 reveals the marvelous results of hearts stirred by love and possessed with a willing spirit. "The people bring much more than enough for the service of the work, which the LORD commanded to make." Adequate resources are available to fulfill the mission of our Lord. The issue is personal. Jesus asks, Do you love me? Are you willing? The Christian steward has the joyful experience of moving from heart to hand in sharing Christ with the world.

WEDNESDAY EVENING, OCTOBER 11

Title: A Spiritual Checkup

Text: "We sent Timothy . . . to strengthen and encourage you as to your faith" *(1 Thess. 3:2 NASB).*

Scripture Reading: 1 Thessalonians 3:1–5

Introduction

Paul sent his trusted colleague Timothy to check on the Thessalonian church. The concerns he expressed for their spiritual status give us a "spiritual evaluation" of sorts that we should consider for ourselves.

I. The temperature of our zeal (v. 3).

Paul was hoping to prevent discouragement from dampening the enthusiasm of the Thessalonians as they heard about his afflictions. He understood that the element of morale is vitally important in the spiritual life. We may become discouraged by a lack of results, a lack of appreciation or support from others, or a lack of opportunity to succeed. We have a spiritual problem if our zeal has been quenched.

II. The pulse of our faith (v. 5).

The pulse is the indicator of the strength and regularity of the pumping of the heart. The pulse of our spiritual lives that keeps us functioning with constancy and vitality is faith. A strong, consistent faith enables us to survive crises and live stable lives.

If we yield to temptation, it is as if we are saying our faith is futile. Conversely, our faith needs to remain strong, like the pulse of a healthy person, to withstand Satan's attacks.

III. The vigor of our moral purity (v. 5).

Sin is the infection that sickens and kills the soul. Paul was concerned about the work of the tempter that could destroy his investment in God's people.

God's power flowing through us is the only antibiotic that can thwart the spreading of sin's infection. We need to appropriate his power more so we can faithfully fight off Satan's attacks.

Conclusion

Paul has identified for us three of the spiritual problems that create sickness in our Christian lives and in our churches: discouragement, the nagging chronic affliction; unfaithfulness, the lack of efficient and healthy functioning; moral breakdown, the cancer that destroys vitality.

SUNDAY MORNING, OCTOBER 15

Title: The Grace of Growing

Text: "Grow in the grace and in the knowledge of our Lord and Savior Jesus Christ. To him be glory both now and forever! Amen" *(2 Peter 3:18 NIV)*.

Scripture Reading: 2 Peter 3:17–18

Hymns: "To God Be the Glory," Crosby

        "Draw Me Nearer," Crosby

        "Open My Eyes That I May See," Scott

Offertory Prayer: Dear heavenly Father, Father of all mercies and God of all grace, who is at work in us and through us to do your good will, thank you for your daily provision for our needs. Our gifts this morning are in honor of your name and for the fulfillment of your work. To you be the glory, in Jesus' name. Amen.

Introduction

The Bible speaks of grace in many beautiful ways: the exceeding riches of God's grace, his abundant grace, and his manifold grace. We sing of his grace, we confess it, and we glory in it.

Our Scripture reading today emphasizes a new relationship to grace. It is not enough to be saved by grace, or to live or to die by it, or even to know grace; we must grow in it! As 2 Peter 3:18 says, "Grow in . . . grace."

This is the final verse of Peter's two letters. In 1 Peter the theme is "the grace of God," and the letter describes the sufficiency of God's grace in salvation, submission, and suffering. Second Peter has assurance and growth in spiritual knowledge as its theme. So verse 18 summarizes these letters by the thought of growing in grace and knowledge.

First Peter 5:12 says, "Stand firm" in God's grace; 2 Peter 3:18 says, "Grow" in God's grace. When we do both, we know the wonderful work of the Lord. Let's examine three ideas about "the grace of growing."

I. The imperative of growing in grace.

A. *"Grow" is a word of command.* God commands us to grow in grace, just as he commands us to do many other things, such as repent, believe, and love. Growth should not be something difficult to do. Where there is life, there is growth. A little baby grows without exertion. So where there is spiritual life, there is spiritual growth.

B. *"Grow" is a word of continuity.* It is in the present tense, so it has the idea of continuing to grow in grace. To do so is to bring glory to Christ, now and forever. Not to grow spiritually is to grow cold in our hearts (Matt. 24:12).

There are three ways to tell when Christians are not growing, according to 2 Peter 1:5–11:

1. They are idle, not working for Christ.
2. Their lives are unfruitful.
3. They are blind, lacking spiritual insight. They are spiritually nearsighted, with poor memory, forgetting what God has done for them.
God expects us to grow in his grace continually. It is his will.

II. The alternative to growing in grace.

We can do something other than grow in God's grace. Verse 17 says that we are either growing or falling. It is important to examine some key words.

A. *"Carried away" (NIV) means "led away" and is always used in the passive voice.* Therefore, it describes being strongly influenced by someone. If you are not growing, you need to be aware of who is influencing you. According to Galatians 2:13, Peter, the Jews, and Barnabas were carried away from the truth by hypocrisy. We need to be cautious about whom we allow to influence us.

B. *"Error of lawless men" (NIV) refers to the sin of those who wander or who have forsaken the right path.* It may be in the area of doctrine or morals—two realms inextricably linked.

C. *"Lawless men" are wicked people who are not living according to the law.* They are living without principles. In 2 Peter 2:7 this word is used to describe the population of Sodom and Gomorrah. Lot was oppressed by the sensual, immoral conduct of unprincipled people.

D. *The word "fall" used here is from a Greek word used to describe flowers that wither and die with the seasons.* It is also used to describe a ship out of control, running aground. This is what will happen to us when we respond to wrong influences. We will fall away from the course set for us in God's Word. This is a serious alternative. It is time to stand guard. It is time to grow!

III. The superlative of growing in grace.

God's goal for our lives is for us to grow in grace and knowledge. To grow in grace is to increase in it, expand our lives by it. It carries with it several superlative meanings.

A. *Growing in grace is growing in Christlike character.* Verse 18 truly means "Christlikeness." We need to grow to be like him in spiritual qualities (Rom. 8:29).

B. *Growing in grace is growing in Christlike responses.* Matthew 5:41 teaches the "second mile" principle. The first mile is the law mile; the second mile is the grace mile. Treating one another in this spirit is indeed a Christlike response.

C. *Growing in grace is growing in Christlike knowledge.* Verse 18 speaks of the "knowl- edge of our Lord and Savior Jesus Christ." We do this by growing in the Word of God, as seen in Acts 20:32; 1 Peter 1:5; and 2:22.

D. *Growing in grace is growing in Christlike speech.* Colossians 4:6 says, "Let your speech be always with grace." See also Ephesians 4:29 and Luke 4:22 as refer- ences to Jesus' gracious words. We are to speak to one another in such a way that we enable God's grace to penetrate one another.

E. *Growing in grace is growing in Christlike trust.* John 1:16–17 says, "And of his full- ness have all we received, and grace for grace. For the law was given by Moses; but grace and truth came by Jesus Christ." As he constantly trusted his Father, so must we trust him for every need.

F. *Growing in grace is growing in Christlike service.* The grace of Jesus' life was that he did not come to be ministered to, but to minister, and to give his life for many. Gracious serving is not always easy, but it is always valuable.

G. *Growing in grace is growing in Christlike witnessing.* Wherever Jesus went, he spoke the words of God's grace. Recall how he tenderly witnessed to the woman at the well, five times married and living with her current lover. He graced her with life eternal through his witness. Also recall Zacchaeus, a hated tax collector, to whom Jesus spoke words of salvation, so blessing him and his house.

Conclusion

Now you can see why growing in grace is an imperative for our lives. We are to be like Christ in all ways. Now that we have heard this word, we need to obey it.

SUNDAY EVENING, OCTOBER 15

Title: God's Plan of Giving

Text: "On the first day of every week, each one of you should set aside a sum of money in keeping with his income, saving it up, so that when I come no collections will have to be made" *(1 Cor. 16:2 NIV).*

Scripture Reading: Matthew 23:23–24; 1 Corinthians 16:1–2

Introduction

An art contest featured a prize for the best depiction of a dead church. The winning entry pictured a beautiful and fully-equipped church auditorium. A closer look at the canvas revealed mission offering plates with cobwebs over them. One criterion of a successful church is participation in God's plan of giving so the gospel can go into all the world.

Paul's instruction to the Corinthian congregation outlines God's plan of giv- ing. These principles lift the offering far above a traditional line in an order of wor- ship. Giving becomes a crucial part of Christ's mission to the world.

I. God's plan of giving involves every Christian.

Paul exhorted each one in the Corinthian church to participate in giving to meet the needs of the world beyond their city. Giving is not an elective in the Christian curriculum. Christians who fail to give bear part of the responsibility for the gospel remaining unknown in vast regions of the world. Studies of church giving indicate that 20 percent of the members carry the financial load; 60 percent give occasionally, and 20 percent give nothing. The church's world task will remain incomplete until "each of you" gives to support it.

II. Giving is an act of worship.

The Corinthians were instructed to give "on the first day of every week"—Sunday, the day of worship. Our offerings declare that God is worthy. The gift is an act of praise and thanksgiving; it is an admission of trust. Giving affirms God's lordship and our stewardship.

God's people giving together is like a mighty anthem of praise affirming, "Worthy is the Lamb!" Don't miss the opportunity to worship. We haven't totally worshiped until we have given. God's plan includes each Christian giving as an act of worship.

III. The Christian gives first to the church.

Since our gifts are an act of worship, they are to be presented to God through the local congregation where we bear testimony of Jesus. When Paul encourages each Christian to "set aside," he echoes the words of Malachi: "Bring the whole tithe into the storehouse" (3:10 NIV). The church is God's storehouse. The Corinthian church agreed to gather their resources to help meet the needs of the poor in Jerusalem. Compassion and commitment, planning and preparation lay behind their gift. Several churches united their efforts in this love gift administered by Paul. Here is a pattern for today. The world needs to hear the good news and receive the rich gift of salvation. Millions are poor spiritually—that is, impoverished in spirit. Their hearing and believing depends on believers who are faithful in giving and churches that are faithful in sharing a portion of those gifts with those outside their congregations.

IV. God's plan calls for proportionate giving.

Paul anticipates the question, "How much should I give?" and says, "In keeping with [your] income." Give in proportion to what God has entrusted to your stewardship. The tithe as a measure of devotion to Jesus Christ is only the beginning of a sharing life; it is not the place to stop. But for many Christians the tithe is the initial step in moving away from a life dominated by materialism, and it can become a doorway to a life of blessing.

It is difficult to conceive of a Christian wanting to give less than a tenth when the Hebrews gave far more under the law. Jesus said of the tithe, "These ought ye to have done" (Matt. 23:23), but he lifted giving above legalism to the level of love and liberality by saying, "Freely ye have received, freely give" (Matt. 10:8).

This same principle applies to a congregation as well as to individuals. A church with abundant resources is able to give more. Examine what proportion of the gifts coming into your church goes beyond the church for world outreach.

Conclusion

God's will is for all to hear the gospel. "How can they hear without someone preaching to them? And how can they preach unless they are sent?" (Rom. 10:14–15 NIV). How can evangelists and missionaries be sent without resources? Each time the offering plate is passed, an opportunity for God's plan is implemented. Every Christian can participate. With each gift each member worships with other church members and enables the church to do its part in fulfilling God's plan to reach the world.

WEDNESDAY EVENING, OCTOBER 18

Title: A Good Report

Text: "Timothy has just now come to us from you, and has brought good news about your faith and love" *(1 Thess. 3:6 NASB).*

Scripture Reading: 1 Thessalonians 3:6

Introduction

Timothy was sent to observe the Thessalonian church and report on their spiritual health to the apostle. He returned with a good report about several areas of healthy functioning. We need to examine these attributes to evaluate the extent they are present in our own lives and in our church.

I. Strong faith (v. 6).

Timothy found a growing confidence in God and optimism and expectancy about the future. This is what faith does in a church.

All too often we Christians place our faith in ourselves, in our families, or in our jobs. These become idols all too easily. Our optimism about our present or future cannot be based on anything but a firm faith in our Lord Jesus Christ.

II. Genuine love (v. 6).

The healthy church will possess a love that will be reflected in works of local evangelism, missions to the world, and benevolence to the physical needs of humankind.

"Love" has become a cliché in our society and as a result has lost a lot of its original power of meaning. The love a Christian is called to show is a love that takes pleasure in sacrifice, continues despite rejection, and thereby reflects the love of Christ. This is the kind of love that breaks the cliché and speaks to the core of others.

III. Warm affection (v. 6).

Paul expressed his longing to share in fellowship with his dear friends. The healthy church is characterized by a warm relationship of people who love to be together. This gives further witness to the love of Christ for us.

IV. Encouraging stability (v. 8).

Timothy reported a strong firmness in the faith of the church, and Paul found that this report enriched his life. Any church leader would share this feeling.

V. Paul's reaction to this good report.

How will a church leader respond to finding faith, love, affection, and stability in his or her people? Paul said that it gave him great comfort (v. 7), inspired thanksgiving (v. 9) within him, caused him tremendous joy (v. 9), and gave him a strong desire to serve even more and work even harder (v. 10).

Conclusion

How does your church measure up in these areas? Can your leaders respond with the positive feelings and desires expressed by Paul?

SUNDAY MORNING, OCTOBER 22

Title: The Grace of Giving

Text: "Therefore, as ye abound in everything, in faith, and utterance, and knowledge, and in all diligence, and in your love to us, see that ye abound in this grace also" *(2 Cor. 8:7).*

"Every man according as he purposeth in his heart, so let him give; not grudgingly, or of necessity, for God loveth a cheerful giver" *(2 Cor. 9:7).*

Scripture Reading: 2 Corinthians 8:1–7; 9:6–8

Hymns: "I Saw the Cross of Jesus," Whitefield

          "Glorious Is Thy Name," McKinney

          "Take My Life and Let It Be," Havergal

Offertory Prayer: Bless the Lord, O my soul, and all that is within me, bless his holy name. Bless the Lord, O my soul, and forget not all his benefits. In that spirit of blessing and honor, we give ourselves and our gifts to you, dear Father. In your Son's glorious name. Amen.

Introduction

To keep growing in his grace, we need to know the grace of God in giving. God's grace gives salvation, peace, eternal life, access to God, and many other spiritual blessings.

Giving is an outward expression of an inward work of God's grace. When we give according to God's way, it is the grace of God at work in us.

There are countless forms of giving. We give encouragement. We give thanks to God and to others. We give praise, a smile, and a kind word. We give time, money, and offerings.

One of the most beautiful demonstrations of the grace of giving in the New Testament is the generosity of the Macedonian churches. What caused these Christians to give to other Christians many miles away? What caused them to give to people they did not know? Only the grace of God!

Giving of ourselves and our money cannot be dismissed lightly. It is not always easy. God calls us to sacrifice—to give until it hurts. Let's delve into two aspects of giving: What are the causes of an inability to give, and what can we do to enhance our ability to give?

I. What is wrong when we fail to give?

The Macedonian churches had the gift of giving, but the Corinthian church didn't. The Corinthians abounded in many things (2 Cor. 8:7), but the grace of giving was missing. How did this happen? How can it happen today?

A. *Unconfessed sin in the church.* There was immorality in the church in that a man had his father's wife. Sin deadens the spirit of a church.

B. *Bitter strife in the church.* Some of the members were having differences with one another. They were going to court, divided in loyalties, criticizing and complaining. Their selfish preoccupations squelched their desire to give.

C. *Doctrinal instability in the church.* The Corinthians were theologically unstable due to the heresy of Gnosticism and emphasized knowledge over spiritual reality. This was reflected in their family lives through wrong marriages and divided homes, thus making the grace of giving difficult to experience.

D. *A lack of training to give.* Paul received no financial aid from the church at Corinth. He earned his own way by tentmaking. The church received his services for free! This is not healthy for a church. We need training about the grace of giving so we may see God at work at close range.

E. *A lack of personal consecration.* Macedonian Christians gave themselves to the Lord (2 Cor. 8:5). This is Paul's challenge to all of us. It is not enough to be born again; we need to grow in the Christian life. Christians really begin to grow when they commit themselves to giving.

II. How do we give sacrificially?

God wants all of us to abound in the grace of giving, as 2 Corinthians 8:7 and 9:8 indicate. Here are some characteristics of true giving that may help us to experience fully the abounding grace of giving.

A. *We give sacrificially.* "For to their power, I bear record, yea, and beyond their power they were willing of themselves" (2 Cor. 8:3). Sacrificial giving, then, is beyond our ability and alters our lifestyle in giving. The highest example of sacrificial giving is none other than that of Jesus Christ (2 Cor. 8:9). Secondarily, Jesus identified total giving in the widow giving her two mites (Mark 12:41–44).

B. *We give willingly.* A willing mind is first (see 2 Cor. 8:3, 5, 19; and 9:7). Acceptable giving is an act of our will. This is grace in giving–God giving us both the will and the power to give his way!

C. *We give victoriously.* Victorious giving is getting beyond the spirit of covetousness to a spirit of unselfishness, described in Luke 12:15 and Hebrews 13:5. Let us not be like the young man who found a five-dollar bill on the street. It gave him so much "pleasure" that from that time on he never looked up while walking. During his lifetime he accumulated 10,000 buttons, 22 cents, 14,000 pins, a bent back, and a miserly disposition.

D. *We give generously.* Second Corinthians 9:6 says, "He which soweth sparingly shall reap also sparingly." The measure of blessing equals the measure of giving (see Prov. 11:24 and Luke 6:38). Giving is God's way for us to keep his wealth in circulation.

E. *We give purposefully.* Verse 7 says every person should give "as he purposeth in his heart." This means we give decisively and prayerfully. We give not by reason alone, but as the Holy Spirit directs. This delivers us from mechanical, "cut and dried" giving.

F. *We give enthusiastically.* Verse 7 says that we should not give "grudgingly or of necessity: for God loveth a cheerful giver." This means that we are not to give resentfully, but cheerfully—even hilariously. When we surrender to God's will, he gives us grace to give and joy to go with it.

G. *We give testimonially.* This is found in verse 12–14. We give so that we become a testimony. This brings thanksgiving to God and encouragement to others.

H. *We give unconditionally.* God has given to us freely, and we are to give to him freely. We are to give without demands, without telling him how to use his gift. Rather, we are to release it unconditionally and thereby release ourselves to the Lord.

Conclusion

There was once a slave who was a great Christian and often told his master about the Lord. His master came to him one day and said, "You know, whatever you have, I want it. You have peace and joy and contentment. How can I get these things?" The slave said, "Go to the house, put on your white suit, and come down here and work in the mud with us slaves, then you'll have it."

The master answered, "I could never do that. That's beneath my dignity."

The master came back two months later and said, "I must ask you again, 'What is it you have, and how can I have it?'"

The slave repeated, "Go put on your white suit on, come down and work in the mud with us, and you will have it."

The master was furious and walked off.

Finally, in desperation he came to the slave again and said, "I don't care what it takes, I'll do anything."

The slave said, "Go put on your white suit and work in the mud. Will you do that?"

"Yes," the master agreed.

The slave said, "Then you don't have to."

The point is that pride and selfishness were standing between the master and Christ. When he was willing to give, a whole new life was open to him. This is the principle in the grace of giving.

SUNDAY EVENING, OCTOBER 22

Title: Dead but Still Speaking

Text: "By faith Abel offered to God a more acceptable sacrifice than Cain, through which he received approval as righteous, God bearing witness by accepting his gifts; he died, but through his faith he is still speaking" *(Heb. 11:4 RSV)*.

Scripture Reading: Psalm 49:10–11, 16–17; Hebrews 11:4

Introduction

Do people communicate with us from beyond the grave? The writer of Hebrews thought so. But the communication of which the writer of Hebrews spoke was not like that of modern spiritual mediums. He wrote, "Abel died, but *through his faith* he is still speaking." Each person has a stewardship responsibility for the influence left after death.

Part of death's grief is the inability to complete the agenda we have set for life—to say, see, and do all we desire. It was said of Robert Louis Stevenson, "He died with a thousand stories in his heart."

Our stewardship involves what we do with life while we are here. It also involves what we leave behind. The final test of a good, faithful, and wise steward is the disposal of what remains. This is the last opportunity to show sincerity of Christian commitment. Desiring to be faithful to the end, the Christian steward recognizes certain truths about the conclusion of life and his possessions.

I. Death removes us from our possessions.

Few regularly review the psalmist's clear statement: "For all can see that wise men die; the foolish and the senseless alike perish and leave their wealth to others" (Ps. 49:10 NIV).

Alexander the Great inherited an empire and conquered another. The wealth of both West and East was his. Yet he asked that at his death his hands be left unwrapped and open for all to see that they were empty. "For we brought nothing into this world, and it is certain we can carry nothing out" (1 Tim. 6:7). Because we will eventually leave everything behind, we should be convinced that "a man's life does not consist in the abundance of his possessions" (Luke 12:15 NIV). Jesus recounted the sad story of a man with only an earthly vision. He worked, built, invested, and lived as if he would always be chairman of the board. At last death separated him from his possessions. Jesus pronounced the verdict on his stewardship: "Thou fool" (Luke 12:20).

II. Death bequeaths our possessions to someone or something.

The Scripture declares that all "leave their wealth to others" (Ps. 49:10). The foolish man faced the question, "Whose shall those things be?" (Luke 12:20). A Christian has the opportunity and responsibility to decide the proper dispersion of his possessions. While one lives, the question, "Whose shall those things be?" can be answered. The answer can be given through a will, which legally commits the individual's intentions. Without such a document, the decision is left to the state. The state lays aside personal sentiment, emotions, and intentions, and adheres only to the law.

Americans are fortunate to live where individual rights are recognized. Everyone has something that will go to someone or something. Irresponsible stewardship leaves the decision to others. A will relieves the family of much anxiety. A will can stipulate arrangements for the care of dependent children. A will can be written for a minimal cost and when legally prepared is rarely broken. Death bequeaths our possessions to someone or something. A will enables one to decide where those possessions will go.

III. A Christian can speak after death through a will.

Margaret Applegarth said of a Christian will: "It takes a lawyer, in the end, to phrase it legally; but it takes a Redeemer to plan it regally—immortal things in your mortal hands." The bequests made and the causes benefited can reflect Christian faith and values. A vital Christian testimony can continue vividly even after death.

Through endowment gifts, trusts, and grants, there are many opportunities to support Christ's work. The local church, children's home, mission agency, Christian education, student scholarships, and much more await Christians who will speak after death. Through a Christian will, "The righteous will be remembered forever" (Ps. 112:6).

Conclusion

"Whether we live or whether we die, we are the Lord's" (Rom. 14:8–9). Personal stewardship does not stop at death. The Lord will hold each Christian accountable for the manner in which his or her possessions are disposed of. It is a blessing to give now. Now is also the time to prepare to "speak though dead."

WEDNESDAY EVENING, OCTOBER 25

Title: An Earnest Prayer

Text: "Now may our God and Father Himself and Jesus our Lord direct our way to you" *(1 Thess. 3:11 NASB).*

Scripture Reading: 1 Thessalonians 3:11–13

Introduction

This passage gives us an opportunity to listen in on the prayer life of the apostle Paul. He prays for the believers in Thessalonica, suggesting some elements for our intercession and for one another.

I. A straighter path (v. 11).

God has a perfect plan for our lives, and we should ask him to direct our path toward fulfilling his purpose. Satan places obstacles in our way and attempts to force detours. It is sad when people waste time and wander for miles pursuing a crooked path.

How are we to know God's path for us personally? God promises to bless us and direct us as we walk obediently in his Word. So his will becomes evident as we persevere in following his precepts.

Knowing God's best for us is not then a merely mystical experience. It is sheer obedience.

II. A greater love (v. 12).

An overflowing love makes life abundant, and it spills over to flow into and bless the lives of others. Genuine love is more clearly understood as action rather than empty sentiment.

III. A deeper dedication (v. 13).

"Holiness" means separation for service to God. "Established" means firmly set. Paul suggests we pray for one another to be firmly set in our dedication to living out God's purpose for us.

Dedicating our lives to holiness does not mean having a spirit of deprivations. Holiness is actively taking on the fruit of the Spirit (Gal. 5:22) and conscientiously embracing righteousness, not evil. Holiness then does not simply mean saying no to sin; it means saying yes to God.

IV. A fuller preparation (v. 13).

Jesus is coming again, and we need to be constantly prepared to welcome him. Our lives need to be in order, and we need to be expanding his kingdom on this earth to celebrate his victorious return.

Conclusion

May God remind us to pray more frequently and fervently for one another, asking for a straighter path, a greater love, a deeper dedication, and a fuller preparation.

SUNDAY MORNING, OCTOBER 29

Title: The Grace of Sufficiency

Text: "He said unto me, 'My grace is sufficient for thee: for my strength is made perfect in weakness'" *(2 Cor. 12:9).*

Scripture Reading: 2 Corinthians 12:7–10

Hymns: "At Calvary," Newell

        "Come, Thou Fount of Every Blessing," Robinson

        "Grace Greater Than Our Sin," Johnston

Offertory Prayer: Thank you once again, Father, for the privilege of worshiping you through giving our tithes and offerings. Thank you for your generosity to us. Blessed be your name in this special moment of dedication. In the name of Jesus Christ. Amen.

Introduction

Grace is the key to life and is sufficient for every need. Grace emphasizes not what we do for God but what God does for us. But it is not only his activity *for* us; it is his activity *in* us! "For it is God which worketh in you both to will and to do of his good pleasure" (Phil. 2:13).

There are three things that God's grace does for us. First, God's grace will do something for us in the future, in such actions as the delivering of creation (Rom. 8:21), the raising of the dead (1 Cor. 15:51–52), and the gathering up of the living (1 Thess. 4:16–17). All of these actions are passive, not active. It is God's work, not ours!

Second, God's grace has done something for us in the past. Ephesians 2:1 says that the believer has been made alive spiritually, and verses 6–10 state that it was by grace. So, it is not by anything we do, but by the work God does. It is his grace at work!

Third, God's grace is doing something for us in the present in our daily lives. Romans 5:10 tells us that we shall be kept saved by Jesus' resurrection life, so that we now have the privilege of reigning in life through Christ. This is by grace!

Second Corinthians 12 testifies about just how sufficient the grace of Christ is. It is like a many-faceted diamond, and as we look down on it, we can see the sufficiency of God's grace. Let's look at some of these facets.

I. Predicament.

A.   *Verse 7 speaks of revelations a man received.* Most interpreters conclude that the man was Paul himself and that fourteen years earlier he had a divine revelation no other person ever saw or heard. He was caught up to the third heaven into the very presence of God. He said nothing about this experience lest he be honored more than he ought.

B. *So God gave him a "thorn in the flesh" to keep him from exalting himself, to keep him from pride.* We don't know what it was, but his language indicates that it was physical, painful, and humiliating. It was a divinely permitted satanic antagonism. It constantly troubled him, and consequently he suffered acutely.

II. Prayer.

A. *Verse 8 records that Paul prayed about his predicament.* The manner in which he prayed indicates the depth of his spirit.
   1. He prayed specifically: "For this thing."
   2. He prayed earnestly: "I besought the Lord."
   3. He prayed repeatedly: "thrice."
   4. He prayed purposefully: "that it might depart from me."
   The Lord answered Paul's prayer, and that answer is found in verse 9: "He said unto me, 'My grace is sufficient for thee: for my strength is made perfect in weakness.'"

B. *"He said" is in the perfect tense, a tense that describes the action as started in the past but continuing in the present.* So it means that what Christ said still stands. He gave to Paul's definite prayer a definite answer. Paul responds positively to Christ's answer.

C. *"My grace" is the grace of Christ himself.* This is the only time in the New Testament that this expression is found. Christ's grace is found in such Scriptures as John 1:16, "grace upon grace"; Romans 5:20, abounding grace; and Romans 5:21, reigning grace. His grace not only saves us, it also suffices in every situation.

D. *"Is sufficient" means to be possessed of adequate strength, to be strong, to be enough for a thing.* Christ's strength is unfailing—whatever your situation!

III. Perfection.

A. *"For my strength is made perfect [perfected] in weakness" (v. 9).* "Perfected" is a present passive verb. It means that through this "thorn" God was perfecting Paul. He was maturing him, completing him in spirit through this means.

B. *God is perfecting us through the "thorns" in our lives.* He perfects us through our learning to live with something rather than allowing it to be an irritation. It is our transforming an irritation into a spiritual motivation. How is this possible? It is possible only through the sufficiency of the grace of Christ!

C. *To see the difference between the perfect tense and the present tense, compare John 19:30 with this verse.* In John 19:30 the statement "It is finished!" is in the perfect tense. Redemption has been completed and continues to be. Second Corinthians 12:9 says, "is made perfect," a present tense, passive voice verb. The present tense is continual action, meaning that one's strength is continually being perfected. God is not finished with us yet. The passive voice means that the subject is being acted on. So Christ is the one perfecting us.

D. *God uses many things to perfect us.* So this may be the reason for your unchangeable situation, your suffering, your adversity. As your master designer, the Lord has your life on a special easel, putting on his divine finishing touches. As the master teacher, he has you in a special classroom to teach you truths you could learn in no other way.

So what happens? Christ's power is perfected in us. Paul says, "That the power of Christ may rest upon me." The verb here describes Christ's power like a tent covering us. This is the only place this word is used in the New Testament. The simple form is found in John 1:14, "the Word . . . dwelt among us." This is grace in all its sufficiency.

IV. Praise.

A. *Verse 9 expresses the burst of Paul's praise.* "Most gladly, therefore, will I rather glory in my infirmities" (v. 9). Verse 10 describes his deep spirit of contentment and pleasure in his adversities, weaknesses, insults, distresses, persecutions, and difficulties. How is this possible? Only through the sufficiency of God's grace. God's grace is so miraculous that we can even revel in our trials because they are his best.

B. *The great lesson of this Scripture is that grace is sufficient for the unchangeable situations in our lives, the circumstances beyond our control, the handicaps we suffer, our sickness, and all other types of adversities.* Whatever you are passing through, the Lord says, "My grace is sufficient for you."

Conclusion

Horatio Bonar wrote about Richard Cameron's father. The aged saint was in prison for preaching God's Word. The bloodied, mutilated head of his martyred son was brought to him by his abusive persecutors, and he was asked derisively if he could recognize who it was.

"I know it, I know it," said the father, as he kissed the mangled forehead of his son. "It is my son's, my own dear son's! It is the Lord! Good is the will of the Lord, who cannot wrong me or mine, but hath made goodness and mercy to follow us all our days."

This is the sufficiency of God's grace. Do you know it?

SUNDAY EVENING, OCTOBER 29

Title: Sacrificial Giving

Text: "Out of the most severe trial, their overflowing joy and their extreme poverty welled up in rich generosity. For I testify that they gave as much as they were able, and even beyond their ability" *(2 Cor. 8:2–3 NIV).*

Scripture Reading: Mark 12:41–44; 2 Corinthians 8:1–9

Introduction

The highest expression in Christian financial stewardship is sacrificial giving. To sacrifice is defined as "to surrender something prized or desirable for the sake of something having a higher or more pressing claim." The Christian steward gladly sacrifices for the higher claim of Christ. Sacrificial giving is the logical result of Christian discipleship as Paul described it in Romans 12:1. Sacrificial giving may appear to be a logical result of commitment to Christ, but it is a lost grace for most Christians. A recovery of sacrificial giving would supply abundant resources for Christ's work.

I. Sacrificial giving alters our lifestyle.

Two New Testament experiences provide examples of sacrifice that are worthy to imitate. One day Jesus watched the people place their offering in the temple treasury. The wealthy gave large sums, probably in a very pretentious way. Finally, a poor widow silently placed her two small coins in the treasury. No one noticed her but Jesus, and he gave her the eternal honor of being the centerpiece of a lesson on sacrificial giving.

A. *The wealthy gave out of their abundance; she gave out of her poverty.* The wealthy never missed making their gift. It really didn't cost them anything. "She, out of her poverty, put in everything—all she had to live on" (Mark 12:44 NIV). Sacrificial giving affects our way of living.

B. *Paul cited the Macedonian churches as an example of sacrifice.* The Macedonian resources had been drained by the Romans. The province was in the midst of "the most severe trial ... and ... extreme poverty" (2 Cor. 8:2 NIV). If anyone seemed to possess the right to say, "I can't afford to give," it was the Macedonians. However, the love of Christ and the needs of others were greater than their personal needs. They continued to do without; they waited for some things. The Christian ministry had greater priority than convenience, pleasure, or prosperity. Believing God would provide, they sacrificed and gave.

C. *We underestimate our ability and overstate our needs.* "It is in trying to do what we cannot do that we do best what we can do." Sacrifice! It isn't sacrifice when we give out of abundance, passing on to the Lord unexpected bonuses. Sacrifice alters our lifestyle. Sacrifice costs.

II. Sacrificial giving is the result of personal sacrifice.

A. *Sacrificial giving began with the personal sacrifice of Jesus.* "For you know the grace of our Lord Jesus Christ, that though he was rich, yet for your sakes he became poor, so that you through his poverty might become rich" (v. 9 NIV). Our sacrifice flows from his sacrifice. Jesus provides the ultimate pattern. Complete selflessness motivated his gift. He surrendered all for our sakes. Realizing the depths of his love, can any Christian be satisfied selfishly holding on to anything?

B. *The Macedonians understood: "They gave themselves first to the Lord" (v. 5 NIV).* Giving resources of money, time, and ability are of secondary consequence if one has first surrendered self to Christ. When Christ is truly Lord, things fall into the proper perspective and sacrificial giving results. No wonder the Macedonians gave with "overflowing joy ... and even beyond their ability" (vv. 2–3 NIV). They belonged to Christ. It is a privilege to offer possessions when Christ possesses the person.

Conclusion

A group of Christians in a small riverside city of equatorial Brazil had prayed and worked for several months trying to reach more people. A spiritual awakening in the town resulted in numerous conversions. A young missionary provided twenty-five dollars to buy a mud hut for the growing congregation to worship. Soon people began to say, "Our building is overflowing with people. When can we have a real church building?"

One afternoon Dona Silvia, a seventy-year-old woman, asked the missionary to visit her home. She offered the first five dollars toward the building. For three months she and her husband had done without one meal a day. They planned to continue to do so until the new church building could be paid for.

NOVEMBER

■ Sunday Mornings

"Living for the Values of Eternity" is the theme for Sunday morning messages dealing with our stewardship of material things. This is suggested because many churches use the period immediately before Thanksgiving to plan the budget for the coming year. If a different month is used, these sermons could be interchanged with the sermons of that month.

■ Sunday Evenings

"The Realities of Heaven" is the suggested theme for a series of messages. People raise many questions about heaven, and the Scriptures provide answers about life and death.

■ Wednesday Evenings

Continue the devotional studies of 1 Thessalonians using the theme "Measuring Ourselves by a New Testament Pattern."

WEDNESDAY EVENING, NOVEMBER 1

Title: A Wholesome Life

Text: "God has not called us for the purpose of impurity, but in sanctification" *(1 Thess. 4:7 NASB).*

Scripture Reading: 1 Thessalonians 4:1–8

Introduction

In recent years we have heard many news reports about the tragedy of toxic substances permeating the soil, water, or air and destroying an area. The apostle Paul was conscious of the toxic nature of influences that can pollute and destroy us spiritually. He gave guidance to help us fight these spiritually lethal toxins.

I. Abstain from sexual immorality (v. 3).

We all possess, as a part of our human nature, urges and drives that we cannot eliminate and should not deny. There is no cause for us to feel guilty about having interests and urges. We can, however, control our behavior. We are responsible before God to live wholesome lives.

Ultimately the Holy Spirit can free us from bondage to these desires if they have a sinful base. But we also need to see that we make choices daily that lead us either to righteousness or to evil. We must choose, then, to abstain from sexual immorality.

297

II. Appreciate God's plan of marriage (v. 4).

God understands human sexual needs, and he has provided us with ways to discipline and manage these urges. An important part of this provision for our fulfillment is Christian marriage. The meaning of verse 4 is that we can learn how to acquire a Christian mate and share a relationship that is mutually satisfying.

III. Avoid lustful situations (vv. 5–6).

The amazing proliferation of pornography in our day reminds us that sexuality can be exploited, twisted, and tainted. People can be used and defrauded for the selfish purposes of others, and our society is clear testimony of this reality.

The Christian is to avoid habits and actions that unnecessarily fan the flames of sexual lust. We must be careful not to behave in ways that would encourage lustful or inappropriate thoughts to trouble those we associate with in life.

IV. Affirm wholesome values (v. 7).

The Lord's will for his people is that they live happy, winsome lives. He wants us to have loving, faithful families.

Sin hurts people. It hurts the sinner and those near to the sinner. It hurts the church and society. Most of all, sin hurts a loving God who gave his Son to provide atonement for man. As Christians, then, we should affirm, teach, and live godly values.

Conclusion

Christians should not be naive or prudish, but we must not let our desire to be sophisticated make us insensitive to the twisted sexual values of our society. There is much around us that is wrong, and we should be honest with ourselves and others about the evil of sexual sin.

SUNDAY MORNING, NOVEMBER 5

Title: Guidelines for Investing in Eternity

Text: "And I say unto you, make to yourselves friends of the mammon of unrighteousness; that when ye fail, they may receive you into everlasting habitations" *(Luke 16:9).*

Scripture Reading: Luke 16:1–9

Hymns: "Guide Me, O Thou Great Jehovah," Williams

   "I Love Thy Kingdom, Lord," Dwight

   "Take My Life, and Let It Be," Havergal

Offertory Prayer: Holy heavenly Father, thank you for giving us the gift of eternal life. Thank you for inviting us to live for eternal values in the here and now. Help us to invest our time, talents, and treasures in the things of eternal significance. In Jesus' name we pray. Amen.

Introduction

"For the sons of this world are shrewder in their generation than the sons of light." With this statement, our Lord sets forth the primary point of his parables. We are not to copy the method of the unjust steward, but we are to copy his shrewdness. He acted in a way that enabled him to accomplish the goals that he had set. The "sons of this world" are those who handle the wealth of this world without any reference to God. They are the big-time investors who use their wealth to make more wealth. The "sons of light" are the people who have the light of God—the Christians. Christians do not act as shrewdly in handling the goods of this world as do the people of the world.

Wise investors are able to handle their money in such a way that they build up rather sizeable fortunes. Their wealth does not come to them by accident; rather, it is the result of their carefulness and shrewdness. Jesus is saying that we should learn from people like this. The shrewdness they exhibit should become a part of our lives. There are at least three basic guidelines that they follow that are applicable to us.

I. We should set forth our investment goal clearly.

In our text Jesus is using the figure of the steward to set forth our acts of giving. That which the unjust steward gave away in order to make friends for himself was actually the property of his lord. The same is true with us. Everything that we have belongs to God, so whatever we give is actually the Lord's property.

A. *The goal of the world.* It is clear that the unjust steward had a clear goal in mind when he began to give away the goods of his lord. He was using these goods in such a way that he would have friends to help him when he was out of a job. Our Lord commended his shrewdness. He had a clear-cut goal.

If you were to secure the assistance of a good financial advisor, his or her first task would be to help you clarify your financial goals. The goals you set for yourself will determine the kind of investments you make.

B. *The goal for the Christian.* Jesus speaks to this point in his application of the parable: "I say to you, make friends for yourselves by unrighteous mammon, that when you fail, they may receive you into everlasting habitations." Jesus encourages us to set our goal in light of eternity. Our goal must be to have "friends" to welcome us into "everlasting habitations." Just what the Lord means by this has been debated, but some things are clear. Our goal should be to invest our money in such a way that we realize the benefit from it in eternity. Investments that pay off in time are not a part of this goal. We operate on the premise that everything that is of earth will be destroyed in the fire, so we want something that the fire cannot destroy. "Friends" here may be people who have benefited eternally from our giving. These could be people who have received the gospel because of our support of missionaries; or they could be the poor who have had their burdens made lighter because we have given.

The type of investment we make is valuable if we have the right purpose. We need to remember that the goal of the investment is to bring honor and glory to God on earth and to participate in his rule on the earth.

Some people give simply to pay the bills of the church. Some people give simply because they want to be known as generous givers. Their goal is to acquire the praise of people. Some people give because they have heard such giving will lead to earthly prosperity. Jesus calls on us to set a goal for our giving that involves eternity. We should be investing for "treasures in heaven."

II. We should choose our place of investment carefully.

A. *Place determined by goal.* The shrewd steward chose his place of investment carefully. He did not have many options open to him, but he made his decision carefully. This is a principle followed by all of the shrewd investors of the world.

People spend thousands of dollars every year getting counsel about the best place to invest. They subscribe to newsletters and attend seminars to expose themselves to the best financial council. Their goals for investment are clear: they want to preserve their wealth and they want to enlarge it. Why? Many want to give their children a sizeable inheritance to make their lives easier. Their goals have determined the place of investment.

B. *The church—our place.* If your goal is to accumulate a treasure for eternity, where could you give your money? The best place to do this is through a New Testament church of Jesus Christ. On what basis would I make such a bold claim?

1. The church is the institution that Jesus Christ established for the evangelization of the world. It is his creation. He continues to work with and in and through his church: the church is uniquely his.

2. The work of the church is designed to make friends for eternity. The work of the church is always with a view to eternity. The church preaches the gospel, administers the ordinances, sends missionaries, helps the poor, builds hospitals, cares for orphans, and worships Jesus Christ. All that the church is doing should bear fruit for eternity.

3. When we give through the church, the Lord receives the glory. This is important. Our sinful hearts are so tempted to do things for our own glory. When we give through the church, whatever our money accomplishes brings glory to the Lord of the church, not to us. For instance, whenever you help a poor family directly, they may tell others how good you are. But when you give your tithes through the church, and your church is able to help a family in need, they go away giving glory to the Lord. Your gift has lost your imprint and has taken on the imprint of the Lord. He is glorified!

III. We should determine our investment amount deliberately.

A. *The importance of commitment.* A good investment counselor will insist on this. You do not depend on whims and impressions if you are serious about investments. You set forth your goals, determine where you will make your investments, and then make a commitment.

B. *The nature of the commitment.* A shrewd steward of the Lord would at least commit himself to follow the basic guideline that the Lord has given to him. The Lord has called us to commit at least 10 percent of our income to such an investment program. That would surely be the minimum.

I have discovered that if I write down my commitment and sign my name to it, I am much more likely to do it. This is why I am ready to sign my commitment card for this year. I want to be as wise about this as the investors of the world are about their commitments that involve this world only.

Conclusion

These are basic guidelines that every child of God should follow. First, set your goal. Do this in the light of the word of Jesus. Second, decide on the place of your investment. Third, make a definite commitment. Now is the time to do it!

SUNDAY EVENING, NOVEMBER 5

Title: Life after Death

Text: "To an inheritance incorruptible, and undefiled, and that fadeth not away, reserved in heaven for you" *(1 Peter 1:4).*

Scripture Reading: 1 Peter 1:3–4

Introduction

All of us have an *instinct* about heaven. Our instinct tells us that heaven must exist because of the nature of human personality. It seems absurd to our instinct to think that human personality with all of its complexity ceases to exist at the moment of death just as a snail or a tadpole ceases to exist. Our instinct tells us that heaven must exist because justice demands it. So much good here goes unrewarded. So much truth here goes unheralded. So much that is noble and beautiful here is never recognized. Instinctively we believe that somewhere, somehow, right will be requited.

All of us have an *intuition* about heaven. We long for it, and we have an occasional inkling of its delight in our consciousness. Something happens, and suddenly we feel a joy that we wish could last forever. A premonition of paradise surges in every one of us.

All of us have an incurable *imagination* about heaven. The imagery of music in heaven comes primarily from biblical images. Both classical anthems and gospel songs stretch our imagination to picture heaven as a celestial city, the sweet by and by, or the promised land. John Milton's imagination portrayed a heaven of majesty, opulence, and power. One cannot read *Paradise Lost* or *Paradise Regained* and not be moved. C. S. Lewis's imagination portrays a heaven of opportunity and endless possibility. One cannot read *The Great Divorce* and not have the imagination stirred.

Yet with all our instinct, intuition, and imagination, we have little real information. Science cannot tell us what is after death. Philosophy cannot tell us what is after death. Human genius in artistic expression can only describe a little of it. Shakespeare said in one of Hamlet's soliloquies:

> *But that dread of something after death,*
> *The undiscovered country, from whose bourn*
> *No traveler returns, puzzles the will,*
> *And makes us rather bear those ills we have,*
> *Than fly to others that we know not of.*

Left to ourselves we know so little about that undiscovered country. But the Good News is that a traveler has returned. Jesus Christ, the Son of God, took on human nature, lived as a man, and died as a man. His body was put in a grave; his disembodied spirit went to God; then his spirit returned to inhabit a raised and glorified body. By the resurrection of Jesus Christ, God has given us hope. We have something to anticipate after death. And that which we can joyfully anticipate is continued existence, continued identity, individuality, personality—life everlasting.

I. Is there really life after death?

Job's question, "Will a man live again after death?" is asked by every serious-minded person. Jesus gives the answer in John 11:25: "I am the resurrection, and the life: he that believeth in me, though he were dead, yet shall he live: and whosoever liveth and believeth in me shall never die." No wonder Peter exclaimed, "Hallelujah!" Whatever your trials, blessed be God who has given us birth to a life with hope.

II. What kind of life is it?

A. *This life after death is so wonderful and so glorious that it is also called an inheritance (vv. 3–4).* "Blessed be the God and Father of our Lord Jesus Christ, which according to his abundant mercy hath begotten in us a lively hope by the resurrection of Jesus Christ from the dead, to an inheritance." Verse 4 describes the afterlife of a believer as an inheritance, a possession prepared for an heir. God has prepared a life after death that is of such bounty and blessedness that it is here called an inheritance.

B. *All through Scripture we are reminded of how God prepares the very best for those who are his.* David said in Psalm 23: "Thou preparest a table before me in the presence of mine enemies," and in Psalm 31: "Oh, how great is thy goodness, which thou hast laid up for them that fear thee." Jesus often spoke of the kingdom of God as being like a banquet table. In fact, he said on one occasion, "Blessed is the man who will eat at the feast in the kingdom of God" (Luke 14:15 NIV). We find all throughout the Scriptures promises that God has prepared many blessings for those who love him.

In Jesus' parable of the sheep and the goats in Matthew 25, he says that when the Son of Man comes in his glory, "The King will say to those on his right, 'Come, you who are blessed by my Father; take your inheritance, the kingdom prepared for you since the creation of the world'" (v. 34 NIV). He also says, "Let not your heart be troubled: ye believe in God, believe also in me. In my Father's house are many mansions: if it were not so, I would have told you. I go to prepare a place for you" (John 14:1–2). Paul wrote, "No eye has seen, no ear has heard, no mind has conceived what God has prepared for those who love him" (1 Cor. 2:9 NIV). That which we anticipate is a life after death that is prepared for us by a loving heavenly Father, an eternal Savior, and a divine Comforter. It is a place prepared as an inheritance.

III. What are the attributes of this inheritance?

In verse 4 Peter describes some of the characteristics of this life—this inheritance.

A. *Life after death is incorruptible.* Most of us have stood by the bedside of the sick and dying, watching human suffering and pain. We have all probably stood beside a grave of a young child who has tragically been killed, or of a young man in the prime of his life, or of a mother who has left precious children, and we have felt the pain and hurt of the family. But the life God has prepared for us as our inheritance is deathless. Revelation 21:4 says, "And God shall wipe away all tears from their eyes; and there shall be no more death, neither sorrow, nor crying, neither shall there be any more pain: for the former things are passed away."

B. *Life after death is undefiled.* Life in the presence of Christ will be holy, pure, and sinless. Do you get tired of the sinful world? Some of you work every day in a world where you see backstabbing, greed, lust, hate, rivalry, and jealousy. Do you ever get tired of the sin that is inside you? Do you get sick of your impure motives, your impure thoughts and attitudes? Our inheritance is a life free of sin—no Satan, no temptation, no wrong desires to tarnish or taint that life.

C. *Life after death doesn't fade.* This means that it is unimpaired by time. Its beauty never fades or tarnishes.

> *When we've been there ten thousand years,*
> *Bright shining as the sun,*
> *We've no less days*
> *To sing God's praise*
> *Than when we've first begun.*
>
> —John Newton

D. *Life after death is reserved in heaven for you.* The phrase "in heaven" suggests that there is a definite location where Jesus in his glorified humanity is even now—though in his deity and by his Spirit, he is everywhere. The verb "reserved" means that our inheritance is kept safe. We who believe in Jesus Christ are not only protected and preserved by God's power in this world, but our inheritance is secured for the next world. Our inheritance is awaiting us when we are ready for it. It wouldn't do much good to try to teach a five-year-old child algebra. She's not ready for that. But when her mind is ready and the time is right, then that which is prepared for her will be taught her. Likewise, in this world we are not ready for heaven. Therefore our inheritance is being reserved for us.

Conclusion

Oh, what a hope we have! What an inheritance—a life after death that is incorruptible, undefiled, unfading, and reserved in heaven. Is this inheritance for you? The only way you can receive it is by personal faith in Jesus Christ.

WEDNESDAY EVENING, NOVEMBER 8

Title: Death and Grief

Text: ". . . that you will not grieve, as do the rest who have no hope" *(1 Thess. 4:13 NASB).*

Scripture Reading: 1 Thessalonians 4:13–18

Introduction

Paul wrote to the church in Thessalonica in part to deal with potential problems. He saw the possibility of discouragement as Christians experienced the death of their fellow church members. Thus he addressed a brief message to the church about a Christian understanding of death.

I. Christians should be informed about death and grief.

There is no premium on ignorance. Death is a reality of human experience, and Christians should have a theological understanding of it. Because we believe in a God who has power over the ravages of death, we need not deny or fear it.

Much study has been done in recent years on the grief process. Christians should be informed in this area for their own understanding and to be more effective in ministering to others.

II. Christians understand death as sleep.

Paul is not teaching "soul sleep" here, the idea that the human spirit sleeps unconsciously until the resurrection. He is comparing the state of the *body* to sleep. The spirit of the deceased goes immediately to heaven or hell, but the spiritless body silently and motionlessly awaits eventual resurrection. There is nothing in Scripture to imply reincarnation or disembodied human spirits lingering around earth.

III. Christians grieve in a different way than others do.

The distinctive difference in the Christian's response to death is *hope*. We feel the same sorrow and weep the same tears as others do. But underlying all of the pain and sadness is a deep, abiding hope. We have the hope of a victorious Savior, the hope of resurrection and eternal life, the hope of an indwelling Comforter to stand alongside us to help heal the wounds of the spirit.

IV. Christians believe in resurrection and a returning Lord.

We do not understand all we would like to understand about the resurrection and the return of the Lord, but we believe that the same power that raised Jesus from the grave will also resurrect those who belong to him. The Bible describes a joyous reunion of all believers of all times at Christ's return.

Conclusion

Death brings the pain of separation and the grief of readjustment to living without a person who was important to us. In Christ, however, we have the future hope of resurrection and eternal life to temper the pain of the present.

SUNDAY MORNING, NOVEMBER 12

Title: The Great Impossibility

Text: "No servant can serve two masters: for either he will hate the one, and love the other: or he will hold to the one, and despise the other. Ye cannot serve God and mammon" *(Luke 16:13)*.

Scripture Reading: Luke 16:9–13

Hymns: "O Worship the King," Grant

          "Glory to His Name," Hoffman

          "Our Best," Kirk

Offertory Prayer: Holy heavenly Father, today we come to worship you in spirit and in truth. Thank you for giving us the inward disposition that causes us to love you and to desire your commendation and leadership. Bless us as we bring our gifts so that your kingdom will come to the hearts of people everywhere. In Jesus' name we pray. Amen.

Introduction

Jesus never uttered anything more absolutely: "Ye cannot serve God and mammon." He spoke of this as the one who knows the secrets of life itself.

The language of the verse calls for some explanation. "No man can serve two masters." Is that true? Can a person not work at two jobs and thus serve two masters? In our modern world many people do this. However, the word "serve" here means to serve as a bond slave. The master in this case is more than a boss: he is a lord, an owner.

What are we to understand by mammon? Our English word has been brought into our language from the Greek text. The Greek word was probably derived from the Hebrew word for that which is trusted—riches, wealth, material things. But our Lord says that we cannot be a servant of God and a servant of riches at the same time.

I. Our nature precludes serving God and gold.

As the creator of humans, Jesus knows us better than we know ourselves.

A. *In human nature one's heart follows one's treasure.* In a very practical passage, Jesus instructs his disciples to make sure that they place their treasure in heaven, and he warns about earthly treasures. He warns that at their very best they are perishable. Then he gives the reason it is so important to have one's treasures in heaven, "For where your treasure is, there will your heart be also." It's just human nature that one's interest and devotion follow one's treasure.

When Jesus talks about treasures in heaven, he is not speaking of material wealth. We do not accumulate material wealth to be received later in heaven. Our Lord himself is the great treasure of heaven. His instruction is that we so use the material things we receive on earth in the service of Christ that when we get to heaven we will receive his approval and blessing. It is a matter of having Christ, not the riches of the world, as the first love of life. Your heart is going to follow your money. If you put your money in the stock market, you develop an interest in the stock market. If you put it in the service of Christ, you will be interested in the welfare of the kingdom of God. You are so created that your heart will follow your treasure.

B. *Divided devotion leads to darkness.* The other fact about human nature that our Lord puts before us is that attempts at divided devotion produce confusion and darkness. "The light of the body is the eye: if therefore thine eye be single, thy whole body shall be full of light" (Matt. 6:22). Our Lord is using a parable that relates the relationship of the eye to the body. If you have good eyes, your body will be full of light. If you have blurred eyesight, your body will be full of darkness. In the spiritual life singular devotion is to the spiritual life what good eyes are to the body. But an attempt at divided devotion is what bad eyesight is to the body. "If thine eye be evil, thy whole body shall be full of darkness. If therefore the light that is in thee be darkness, how great is that darkness!" (v. 23).

It may be that our Lord is using the illustration of a cockeyed person. He would be saying that if you are a person who is trying to keep one eye on the Lord and another eye on the things of the world, you end up not seeing anything correctly, you get everything in life out of perspective. It is simply human nature that we cannot live successfully with a divided devotion.

II. Conflicting demands preclude serving God and gold.

The word Jesus used for "master" emphasizes that he is Lord. He views mammon as a competitor with God for the place of lordship in our lives. We might have expected that he would present Satan as the alternative, but he knew that Satan gains control through fronts. Satan rarely ever bargains for control personally; instead, he uses good things. We must not understand Jesus to be saying that wealth and riches are evil in themselves. God is the creator of all the gold, silver, oil, and land in the world. He declared that everything he made was very good. Mammon is evil only when we allow it to be the lord of our lives.

A. *Both God and gold demand first place.* Jesus says, "Seek ye first the kingdom of God, and his righteousness" (Matt. 6:33). God will not accept a second place in your life. Mammon says, "If you want what I have to offer, you must be willing to set your goals high and pay the price." Both God and gold demand total allegiance from you. You can give total devotion and first place but to one lord at a time. If God has first place, then gold does not. If gold has first place, then God does not. You can determine which is first with a little reflection. Which determines your decisions, your relationship to God, or your desire to make money and get things?

B. *Both God and gold demand complete trust.* They also are in conflict because they both demand complete trust. God says, "Trust in me and I will see you through all of your difficulties." We may be placing our trust in mammon without realizing it. In which do you have your trust today?

    A little reflection will help you determine the answer to this question. If your family gets into a financial pinch, which is cut first, your contributions to the work of the Lord or your insurance premiums? Which would be the more important matter to you, keeping your insurance current or your tithes? I do not discount the importance of a good insurance program, but surely God is more to be trusted than our insurance program. It is so easy for us to unconsciously begin to trust in mammon rather than God.

C. *God and gold conflict in the values they thrust upon us.* When you look at another person, what do you see? How do you evaluate that person's worth? Do you value her on the basis of her relationship to God or on the basis of how much of this world's goods she may have? Are you more interested in him if you find out that he is an oil mogul or that he is the president of a successful corporation? It is so easy for us to accept the values of mammon and to evaluate others by the standards of mammon rather than God's.

    What would it take to make you absolutely happy? How much would that happiness, as you see it now, depend on mammon? How much of it would be related to God? Do you not see that God and mammon make conflicting demands on our lives? You cannot have both of them as master of your life. If you make gold the center of your life, you have thereby excluded God.

Conclusion

Almost all of us have made a decision about this matter at some point in our lives. In our profession of faith and baptism, we declared that we wanted God to be first in our lives and that we wanted only one Lord. The question we must face this morning is, Have we changed this decision?

How we are treating the wealth we have is a good sign of who is lord. When Jesus is Lord, our wealth is used in his service.

SUNDAY EVENING, NOVEMBER 12

Title: Heaven: What Will It Be Like?

Text: "Let not your heart be troubled: ye believe in God, believe also in me. In my Father's house are many mansions: if it were not so, I would have told you. I go to prepare a place for you" *(John 14:1–2)*.

Scripture Reading: John 14:1–14

Introduction

What is heaven like? And what shall we do there? Let's be honest in admitting that heaven has little appeal for many of us. Even though we do believe in and love Jesus Christ, if the truth were known and we were honest, we would rather be living here in a full way than be living in heaven. Particularly is this true if we are somewhat healthy and active and are enjoying a degree of personal fulfillment and social benefit. It is not that we resist or disbelieve the idea of heaven, but it is simply the fact that heaven has little or no appeal to us.

Our feelings are colored in part by our common conceptions of heaven—conceptions that are often caricatures. Biblical imagery is pressed too far. Personal preferences are made uNIVersal. Ideas are forced that include sheer speculation and outright absurdity.

Some of us think of heaven as an interminable religious meeting. We picture it as an eternal church service where we will all be given wings and a place in the heavenly choir or orchestra. Sir Walter Scott confessed that he dreaded heaven as "an eternity of music." And Lloyd George wrote, "When I was a boy the thought of heaven used to frighten me more than the thought of hell. I pictured heaven as a place where time would be perpetual Sundays, with perpetual services from which there would be no break. It was a horrible nightmare and made me an atheist for ten years."

Others think of heaven as the perfect monastery where we will contemplate God in cloistered piety. The traditions of asceticism have had a great influence on the historical church and have also influenced our collective consciousness concerning eternity. Now some, who by temperament or discipline have perfected meditation and solitude, would anticipate such a heaven. Some who have tasted the ecstasy of enlightenment or the soul rapture of revelation would surely look forward to such a heaven. But to the vast majority of people who have practiced prayer but have lived in the pressures of an everyday world, such a concept of heaven is not too inviting. For those whose lives have been more public than private, more social than solitary, more communal than celibate, such a concept of heaven is not very appealing.

What sort of place, then, is the Father's house? What can be said about heaven and what we will do there? Much is said negatively about heaven, that is, what it is not like and what will not be there. First Peter 1 describes our inheritance as incorruptible (no death), undefiled (no sin), and unfading (no time limit). But what can be said positively about the place where Jesus has gone to make preparation?

I. Heaven is a place of untiring service and work without weariness.

A. *Heaven will be anything but boring and dull.* We won't be lollygagging on a cloud or serenely listless for eternity. We won't be a winged creature playing a harp or a disembodied spirit floating idly around the stratosphere. Isaac Taylor wrote, "It is surely a frivolous notion that the vast and intricate machinery of the universe, and the profound scheme of God's government, are now to reach a resting place, where nothing shall remain to active spirits through an eternity, but recollections of labor, anthems of praise and inert repose."

B. *The specifics of how we will serve in heaven are not clear, but the principle is implied all through Scripture.* In his parable of the talents, Jesus showed that initiative and industry, diligence and labor are rewarded with more of the same. He spoke a parable in which the master said to the servants who had worked and doubled what they were given, "Well done, thou good and faithful servant: thou hast been faithful over a few things, I will make thee ruler over many things" (Matt. 25:21, 23). Jesus said on another occasion, "My Father is always at his work to this very day, and I, too, am working" (John 5:17 NIV). In his description of the celestial city in Revelation 22, John said, "His servants will serve him" (v. 3 NIV). I do not know what our work will be, but we will work.

The biblical picture of eternity is not one of inactivity and inertia. We will not be destined to idleness. We will work. We will exercise responsibility and will. We will continue to cooperate with God in serving him. We will carry with us the capacity and character that was given to us here, and in some way we will use it there.

C. *Our work in heaven will be without weariness.* We will work without growing tired. No matter how much you enjoy work here, there are times when you get tired. Sometimes you get tired *in* your work, and sometimes you get tired *of* it. But heaven will be a place of untiring service and work without heaviness. Since we will have resurrection bodies, we will not experience physical weariness. Since time will be no more, we will not be emotionally weary at the end of the day or at the end of the week. Since sin and Satan will not be present, there will be no rivalry or greed in work. Rudyard Kipling described activity in heaven in his poem "When Earth's Last Picture Is Painted" in these words:

> *And only the Master shall praise us, and only the Master shall blame;*
> *And no one shall work for money, and no one shall work for fame;*
> *But each for the joy of the working, and each in his separate star,*
> *Shall draw the thing as he sees it for the God of things as they are.*

Work in heaven will not be in forms that are unimagined to us, but it will be in energy that is inconceivable to us now. We will worship and work in a perfect environment. We will worship and work in perfect bodies. We will worship and work in the glory of God.

II. Heaven is a place of unlimited growth and unhindered developments.

There are three reasons why we are going to grow in heaven:

A. *The very nature of mind and spirit implies ever-enlarging capacity; that is, mental and spiritual activity is impossible apart from a degree of enlargement.* E. Y. Mullins, a great Baptist theologian, said, "The true ideal of personal spiritual beings is that of life in which we are ever satisfied and blessed, yet ever aspiring; and which is ever attaining, yet ever hoping for greater attainments."

B. *The idea of development is shown in 1 Corinthians 13: "And now abideth faith, hope and love, these three."* All three of those qualities are not only going to characterize the life of the believer in this world, but they will continue into eternity. If hope is an abiding element, it implies endless growth and attainments.

C. *In John 14:2 the Greek word translated "mansion" actually means "resting place."* It is sometimes translated "room" and connotes the importance of an ornate building. But actually it referred to a resting station on a journey, a comfortable accommodation for the night. The idea implicit in the word is that in the Father's house we will continue to be on a journey where there is unending progress and development.

Nothing disturbs us more about growing old than the thought of atrophy. I have often heard, "I don't want to reach a place where I just stop, where my mind and spirit stop." One of the signs of life is growth. Heaven will be a place of endless growth. And for that reason I look forward to it with great anticipation. I want to grow here. One reason I know I'm spiritually alive is that I have a hunger to grow. I want to grow in knowledge, love, faith, and understanding. I want to grow in holiness. I look forward to heaven as a place of unlimited growth and unhindered development.

Conclusion

How do we know there is a heaven? Jesus said so. After death there is the Father's house—not extinction, not obliteration of personality, not the end of life—but the Father's house. And what is infinitely wonderful is that Jesus said, "I will receive you."

WEDNESDAY EVENING, NOVEMBER 15

Title: The Season of His Coming

Text: "You yourselves know full well that the day of the Lord will come just like a thief in the night" *(1 Thess. 5:2 NASB).*

Scripture Reading: 1 Thessalonians 5:1–3

Introduction

Paul speaks to the early church about a "day of the Lord" when comfort would come to a persecuted community, justice would be established, and peace would reign. Three analogies are used to describe the season of this important event: a thief breaking in, a sudden disaster, and the labor of giving birth to a newborn baby.

I. An unannounced event.

No self-respecting thief calls for an appointment to rob your house. With stealth and cunning he comes under cover of darkness to unexpectedly ransack the place. Jesus' second coming will likewise be unannounced in terms of specific indications of its occurrence.

II. An unexpected event.

While society is lulled to sleep with a false sense of security and an insensitivity to the real undercurrents of the time, the Lord will make his dramatic intervention. An expectant mother knows that the arrival of a baby is in the future, but the beginning of labor pains still comes as a sudden development. The body has its own timetable for such events.

Christians understand that Christ is coming again, yet we do not claim to know exactly when, and we will be surprised, along with everyone else, when he appears.

III. An inescapable event.

Christ's original advent as a babe in Bethlehem came "in the fullness of time," or when the time was right. So it will be with his second coming. The issue is "when," not "if," he will come.

Conclusion

Paul considered this message of future hope and justice an essential piece of information for the early church. Our faith is viable for the present and gives abundantly in the present, but there are times when we also need to take the eternal look and be reaffirmed in our confidence in an eternal God with an ageless plan.

SUNDAY MORNING, NOVEMBER 19

Title: Thankful for God's Best

Text: "His mouth was opened immediately, and his tongue loosed, and he spake and praised God" *(Luke 1:64)*.

Scripture Reading: Luke 1:57–64

Hymns: "We Gather Together," Parker

           "Count Your Blessings," Oatman

           "Make Me a Channel of Blessing," Smyth

Offertory Prayer: Heavenly Father, out of the bounty of your grace, you have bestowed on us the richness of your blessings. Today we come to offer the gratitude of our hearts and the praise of our lips. From our pocketbooks we bring tithes and offerings to dedicate them for use in advancing your kingdom's work here on earth. Bless these gifts to that end, we pray. In Jesus' name. Amen.

Introduction

It was thanksgiving day for Zechariah. The answer to his prayers had arrived after many, many years: his wife, Elizabeth, had given birth to a son. It was the eighth day since his birth, and the friends and family had assembled to celebrate the birth and the circumcision of the child. It was customary to name the son on the day of circumcision. The friends had attempted to name the little son after his father Zechariah, but Elizabeth insisted that his name be John. When they gave a writing tablet to the apparently deaf and mute Zechariah, he wrote on the tablet that the baby's name was to be John. This was the name the angel had given in the temple when his birth was announced. When Zechariah obediently wrote down the name John, his tongue was loosed and his ears were unstopped. He broke out into a hymn of praise to the God of Israel as the Holy Spirit filled his being.

We have come to consider this hymn of thanksgiving during this special season of thanksgiving. It is not surprising that Zechariah was thankful and sang to the Lord; yet, in light of his recent ordeal, we may be surprised to learn what he was most thankful for. Zechariah had at the top of his list the greatest blessing God ever gave to man. Zechariah thanked God for the great salvation he was giving to the world through the coming of the one to be born to Mary. Salvation is God's greatest gift to humankind!

This famous hymn of Zechariah, which has been sung in the church since the early days, can be very instructive to us. It can help us refresh our memory about God's greatest blessing, about the best that God gives.

I. Salvation is God's best because of what it reveals in God.

The hymn has been divided into various divisions, but we will not concern ourselves with them. Rather, we look at the hymn in its wholeness and look for those things that excited Zechariah to thanksgiving concerning the salvation of the Lord being given through the coming Messiah. For this aged priest, the knowledge of

God was rightly held to be the supreme joy of life. The coming of Christ to bring salvation would be above everything else a revelation of God.

A. *His love is revealed in this salvation.* "Blessed be the Lord God of Israel; for he hath visited and redeemed his people." The first line sets forth the nature of this whole passage. It is an ascription of praise to the Lord God of Israel. It is blessing him for his blessing. Everything that follows is to be viewed as a basis for the ascribing of praise to God; note that the very next line begins with "for." God has acted to "visit" and "redeem" his people. "Visit" means that he has come to become involved in humankind's situation. He has moved into action. "Redeem" means that he has come to pay the price required to set people free from their bondage. It is in his saving work that we see the love and mercy of the Lord God, our God.

B. *His power is revealed.* "And hath raised up an horn of salvation for us in the house of his servant David." The "horn" of the bull became the symbol of strength and power in the Old Testament. The "horn" of salvation is then the "power" of salvation. God's saving power is revealed in the coming of Jesus into the world and in our receiving his salvation. We look at the one born to Mary—his life, death, and resurrection—to see the saving power of God. God's power to save is seen in Jesus Christ and in his mighty name.

C. *His faithfulness is revealed.* No truth about God is more important than his faithfulness. It was important to Zechariah that the coming of the Messiah was "as he spake by the mouth of his holy prophets, which have been since the world began." He saw Christ's coming as the fulfillment of all of the prophecies beginning with the first one given in Genesis 3:15.

II. Salvation is God's best because of what it does for humans.

Have you noticed how the aged priest speaks in the plural throughout the hymn? While the salvation of the Lord is personal, Zechariah is fully aware that it includes others. He is celebrating God's saving activity toward all of his people. We need to keep this note in our praise to God. Let us look for the different aspects of this salvation that are suggested in the hymn.

A. *The salvation of the Lord frees from bondage.* It gives freedom. "For he has visited and redeemed his people." The outcome of redemption is freedom. Redemption is what God does, but liberty is what believers receive. This freedom is spiritual freedom from the bondage of sin and Satan. Zechariah may have had in mind some political enemies as he sang this hymn to the Lord, but surely at the deeper level he had in mind the destructive bondage that sin has brought to humankind.

B. *The salvation of the Lord forgives me for my transgressions.* Zechariah says that John's ministry is to be that of giving "knowledge of salvation unto this people by the remission of their sins." John is to declare the message of salvation. As people came to know Jesus and to believe on him, they would know the remission of their sins. John first identified him as the "Lamb that takes away the sins of the world." If you are saved, you are forgiven.

C. *The salvation of the Lord gives hope to humankind.* "Whereby the dayspring from on high hath visited us, to give light to them that sit in darkness and in the shadow of death." This Dayspring is the coming of the Lord Jesus into the world as the Light of the World. As the Light of the World, he brings hope to those who sit in the darkness of despair. The only people who really have hope are those who have been saved by the mighty Savior.

D. *The salvation of the Lord also brings peace.* Zechariah explains the Dayspring's purpose: "To guide our feet into the way of peace." As the Light of the World, Jesus so guides his people. This is most interesting. He does not give an experience of peace but rather leads us into the way of peace. The lifestyle that he leads us to is literally the highway of peace. Walking under his lordship leads to blessed personal peace.

Can you not see why Zechariah considered this to be God's greatest blessing to humankind? Sure, God had given him a son, a good wife, and long life—but salvation is so much more than these. God had met all of his physical needs, but salvation is so much more. God may have withheld some of his blessings from you, but if he has saved you, he has given you the best.

Conclusion

To know that Jesus is your creator is a great insight and an important thing to know. To know that Jesus is your sustainer is equally important. To know that Jesus is your sovereign is also significant. But the greatest truth about Jesus that you can ever know is that Jesus is Savior! Unless you know this, you will never be free from the bondage and the burden of sin, you will never know the heart of God. To know his creation is to know his hand. To know his sovereignty is to know his throne. To know his salvation is to know his heart!

Do you know Jesus as Savior? Then you should praise him all of your days. Do you want to know him as Savior? Then call on him. He has promised to save all who call on him. Call out to him in prayer right now.

SUNDAY EVENING, NOVEMBER 19

Title: Heaven: Will You Be There?

Text: "I say unto you, that many shall come from the east and west, and shall sit down with Abraham, and Isaac, and Jacob, in the kingdom of heaven. But the children of the kingdom shall be cast out into outer darkness: there shall be weeping and gnashing of teeth" *(Matt. 8:11–12).*

Scripture Reading: Matthew 8:11–12

Introduction

Christians have been accused of being so heavenly minded that they are of no earthly good. The accusation may have had some justification in times past. But I doubt that our problem today is that we are too heavenly minded. Indeed, I believe part of our problem as twenty-first-century Christians is that we are too absorbed in the agenda and problems of this world. Not only are we secular and materialistic, but we also have tunnel vision in thinking that the most important issues of life are those of today. We have a "me" mentality—a "now" mentality.

This "now" mentality evidences itself in many ways in today's church. Christians are more concerned about physical healing than eternal salvation of souls. Christians are absolutely absorbed in psychological advice or how to be successful and happy rather than how to be holy and righteous. This is the "me" generation and the "now" generation. We justify this obsession with the now by saying that this generation, this day, is unlike any other. We have an illusion of uniqueness regarding the complexity, stress, and pressure of our day. We think we're different from all who came before us. In reality, I doubt that the average chamber maid of eighteenth-century London or the peasant of an aboriginal tribe has any fewer problems than the average American office worker. I doubt that our day is any more complex, pressurized, and problem-plagued than anyone else's.

In contrast to a "me focus" and a "now focus," Colossians 3:1–3 urges us, "If ye then be risen with Christ, seek those things which are above, where Christ sitteth on the right hand of God. Set your affection on things above, not on things on the earth. For ye are dead, and your life is hid with Christ in God." We need to direct our attention to eternity. We will live better in time if our vision is set on things above.

The story of a Roman centurion is the setting of our text. In response to the centurion's faith, Jesus spoke words that must have startled the Jews who heard: Gentiles would be admitted to the kingdom of God while many Jews in the kingdom of Israel would be excluded. But verses 11–12 are also prophetic in that they give descriptive insight about heaven and hell.

I. Heaven will be a populous place.

A. *Some have taken Matthew 7:13 as evidence that not many people will be saved.* "Enter ye in at the strait gate: for wide is the gate, and broad is the way, that leadeth to destruction, and many there be which go in thereat." Charles Spurgeon has said, "Some narrow-minded people think that heaven will be a very small place, where there will be very few people who went to their chapel or church. I confess I have no wish for a small heaven. Do you think Christ will let the devil beat Him? That He will let the devil have more in hell than there will be in heaven?"

B. *There will be great numbers of children in heaven.* There will be youth and adults prior to the time of Christ who looked forward to the Messiah. There will be the church of all ages. Revelation 7:9 says that John saw a multitude, which no man could number, before the throne with white robes and palms.

II. Heaven will be a diverse place.

A. *Redeemed souls from every culture, every nationality, and every language will gather.* Heaven will be no provincial heaven only for those like our kind. The song "In Christ there is no east nor west; In Him, no north nor south" will be fully realized in heaven. The Jews thought of heaven in very nationalistic and narrow terms, but Jesus exploded that idea.

B. *The diversity of heaven will not only be geographical, but spiritual as well.* Some people such as Abraham, Isaac, and Jacob will be spiritual giants; others will be spiritual babies that have been converted only at the last moment. Some will have been ladies and gentlemen on earth. Others will have been drunkards and dangerous sinners that will have been recipients of grace in the last hours: the thief on the cross and the apostle Peter; the Philippian jailer and the apostle Paul; blind Bartimaeus and the blind John Milton; the woman at the well and Fanny Crosby. "[O Lord], thou art worthy . . . for thou wast slain, and hast redeemed us to God by thy blood out of every kindred, and tongue, and people, and nation" (Rev. 5:9).

III. Heaven will be a social place.

A. *Heaven will not be a solitary contemplation of God or a private experience or a personal cloister.* We will sit down with other saints, friends, and family of God, in fellowship. "Sitting down" sounds like a banquet or feast. What will we do? I don't know.

B. *Our fellowship there will be one of knowing.* We will know one another. I do not by what means of identification we will know one another. I don't know how we will know Abraham, but we will. It would surely be a dreary and dull place should we all be alike unknowing and unknown—but we will have company and social interaction. One of the great fears we have about death is whether it will end friendship and fellowship. It will not. Relationships begun here will continue there. Friendships nurtured here will continue there. Have you experienced the joyous renewal of friendship or recovery of family that was severed by distance or time? That's the kind of renewal and joy there will be in heaven.

C. *Heaven will be a society, a city, a household.* It will be a place where we will commune with each other, talk, rejoice, worship, and work together. What we have known here will be even better there because of the absence of sin.

Conclusion

Now I do not wish to describe the condition of hell from verse 12, but I do want you to notice that phrase at the beginning of that verse. Many of the kingdom shall be cast into outer darkness. The kingdom here is a referral to Israel, that is, many who would think that they automatically would be in the kingdom of God because of position or past will be excluded. Your heritage doesn't qualify you for heaven.

Heaven is a prepared place for a prepared people. One who is not ready for it would feel and be out of place in heaven. It wouldn't be heaven at all. The person whose heart is not tender and receptive to God's love here would not really want to be there. But for the person whose spirit is in tune with the Holy Spirit, whose will is yielded to Christ, and whose heart is trusting in God, heaven will be a joy. Are you ready?

WEDNESDAY EVENING, NOVEMBER 22

Title: Contrasting Children

Text: "You are all sons of light and sons of day. We are not of night nor of darkness" *(1 Thess. 5:5 NASB).*

Scripture Reading: 1 Thessalonians 4:4–10

Introduction

Many of us know siblings who are very different from each other in appearance, temperament, and talent. The contrasts in these brothers or sisters are blatantly obvious. Paul says that the human race is also composed of contrasting children. He calls these the children of light and the children of darkness.

I. The children of light.

The children of light, God's children, are distinctive in terms of attitude, condition, lifestyle, and destiny. Their attitude is one of alert concern: Christians care about themselves and others. Their condition is one of sound thinking and appropriate seriousness about the issues of life. The lifestyle of these children is disciplined. Verse 8 of our passage speaks about faith, hope, and love as qualities to be exhibited in daily life. Finally, the children of light are bound for a destiny of salvation through Jesus Christ.

II. The children of darkness.

Paul describes the children of the darkness as being asleep. Their attitude is one of indifference and unawareness of spiritual things. The condition of these children is comparable to drunkenness. They are desensitized: their senses are dulled; they are unable to enjoy the full richness of life.

The lifestyle of these lost souls, in contrast to that of the children of light, is uncentered. It is uncontrolled and chaotic as it gropes blindly in the darkness. The destiny for those who reject the light is the wrath of God. By their choice they refuse to accept the Master's plan for their salvation.

Conclusion

There is a clear-cut choice to be made by all persons. We choose for light or darkness, good or evil, salvation or eternal lostness.

SUNDAY MORNING, NOVEMBER 26

Title: God Holds the Deed

Text: "The earth is the LORD's, and the fullness thereof; the world, and they that dwell therein. For he hath founded it upon the seas, and established it upon the floods" *(Ps. 24:1–2).*

Scripture Reading: Psalm 24:1–5

Hymns: "Love Divine, All Loves Excelling," Wesley

        "A Child of the King," Buell

        "Jesus Loves Even Me," Bliss

Offertory Prayer: Holy heavenly Father, open our eyes and help us to see the greatness of your grace toward us. Help us to recognize you as creator, sustainer, and owner of all the earth. Help us to see ourselves as your stewards and mangers during our lifetime. Help us to live in time with eternity's values in mind. Bless these gifts to that end, we pray. In Jesus' name. Amen.

Introduction

No one has a clear title to any portion of this world. Your deed may withstand all of the tests that a court might apply to it, but it is still not clear. The primary problem with your deed is that it does not go back far enough. If you live in Texas, your deed only goes back a little over a hundred years in tracing ownership. You will not find an attached release from the original owner of the property—the Creator God.

The first stanza of this beautiful hymn of David states the situation clearly. "The earth is the LORD's, and the fullness thereof." This hymn was originally written to be used in the victorious procession in which the ark of the covenant was brought into the newly created capital, the city of David. The king himself led the triumphant procession. The sons of Levi sang these words of praise as the ark entered the city. The God whose presence was symbolized by the ark is the owner of all that is.

Secular people ignore the truth of this psalm. They foolishly act as though they have the sole rights of ownership. They treat their property and their own lives as though they have no ultimate accountability. They live as though they are accountable only to themselves.

I. The specifications of the divine ownership.

Just what does God own? Where would you find the property that he owns in our community? Would it be limited only to the pieces of property that have been dedicated as places of worship?

A. *He owns the earth.* God holds the deed to the earth. As indicated here by Hebrew parallelism, the earth and the world are one and the same. Writing as a man standing on the earth, and very much earthbound, the psalmist sees the earth as the whole universe. However, the concern of the psalmist is not with the ownership of the planets or the sun and moon, but with the city of Jerusalem—and my city. Who owns the farmland of my state? His emphatic statement is that God holds the deed to every inch of it. "Lord" is emphatic in the Hebrew text. He is the absolute owner.

B. *He owns the fullness.* This includes everything that is in the earth or on the earth. Regardless of how small or how large, it belongs to the Lord. All of the vegetation is his, including the grain and cotton in our fields. All of the trees are his, including those used to construct the house in which you live. All the minerals are his, including the gas and oil that we are pumping out of the earth. All of the gold, silver, and precious stones are his. The oxygen that we breathe is his, as well as the sunshine and rain that we need for the sustenance of life.

C. *He owns us.* The divine ownership extends to those "that dwell therein." This includes every living thing that moves on the earth, including you and me. Of every cow and calf, every horse and chicken, every sheep and dog, God is the ultimate owner. Every man, woman, boy, and girl, regardless of race or nationality, belongs to God. In our day we tend to limit his ownership to the church and to the people who acknowledge him as Lord and serve in some full-time ministry. Not so! God's ownership includes you and everything you claim in the earth.

II. The basis for the divine ownership.

We base our claims to ownership on the payment of a price or on an inheritance. Deeds reflect the basis for ownership. God bases his claim on ownership on more important things, things that take precedence over a purchase price paid by me. "For he hath founded it upon the seas and established it upon the floods." This is a poetic way of setting forth a profound truth about the ownership of the earth and everything in it.

A. *He is Creator.* These words refer to the creative act of the Creator God whereby the earth and all the living creatures came into existence. God wants them because he made them. David is referring to the inspired statement of this activity that opens the Bible. Genesis 1 records how God made out of nothing everything that exists. He made it as an expression of his love and creative power.

The speculation of modern humans about the origin of the earth has created uncertainty in their minds. They have heard just enough about the theory of evolution to make them wonder about the Creator. But to those who have faith, there is no question about the origin of the earth and who is responsible for it. They may not have all of the answers about "how" it happened, but they are sure about who did it. They look at the world about them and, with wonder in their heart, exclaim, "God did it!"

B. *He is God of providence.* These words also refer to the divine providential care of the earth and its fullness. The verbs used by David picture the continued order that is in the earth as the result of God's activity. The world continues to exist in an orderly way because of God's control and care. He causes it to be held

319

together by his power. If it could not exist apart from him, surely it is folly to attribute the ownership of it to anyone else.

III. The acknowledgment of the divine ownership.

If we accept the truth of this inspired statement, then surely there must be some way for us to acknowledge God's ownership.

A. *We acknowledge through worship.* We acknowledge God's ownership of our lives through worship. This hymn is just one expression of worship. From the very beginning humans were instructed to set apart one day out of a week of seven to worship God. The consecration of this day for worship was based on God's being the Creator. Though in the Christian era we have set aside the first day of the week for worship because it is the day Christ was raised from the dead, we are also acknowledging his claims on our lives.

B. *We acknowledge through tithes and offerings that God owns everything material around us.* This is the basic context in which the Bible places tithing. Tithing is not so much a law as it is a way of acknowledging to God his ownership of everything. Your offering above your tithe acknowledges your gratitude for the faithful manner in which God has provided for all your needs. People who do not bring to God a tithe or offering are living as though they are the sole owners of the money and goods they have at their disposal. Do you not see the folly of this? You and I are stewards—not owners. But it is a wonderful privilege to share with God in his creation in this way.

Conclusion

Every Lord's Day is a special acknowledgment day. But then we move from the Lord's Day with a renewed awareness that God owns everything. Are we living in the light of this truth in a fresh way?

SUNDAY EVENING, NOVEMBER 26

Title: Heaven: Be Prepared

Text: "There shall in no wise enter into it any thing that defileth, neither whatsoever worketh abomination, or maketh a lie: but they which are written in the Lamb's book of life" *(Rev. 21:27).*

Scripture Reading: Revelation 21:19–27

Introduction

There is the story of an old-time preacher who after reading a rather cryptic text, took off his spectacles, closed his Bible with a bang, and said, "Brothers and sisters, this morning I intend to explain the unexplainable, define the undefinable, ponder over the imponderable, and unscrew the inscrutable." I confess to you today that my ambitions are not quite that lofty in this final sermon on the subject of heaven. The doctrine of heaven must be discussed with a great deal of humility and a recognition that we see through a glass darkly. Even in its revelation of heaven, Scripture leaves unanswered a great many questions. The revelation itself is often given to us in highly symbolic and picturesque language. This is especially true of today's text.

But I want to focus our attention on verse 27, which speaks about those who will inhabit heaven: "And there shall in no wise enter into it anything that defileth, neither whatsoever worketh abomination, or maketh a lie; but they which are written in the Lamb's book of life."

This verse makes it clear that not everyone will be in heaven. The idea that everyone, regardless of their belief or behavior, will eventually be in heaven is foreign to the Scripture. Many have the sentimental thought that God is like a benevolent and doting grandfather who says to all people at the end of life, "Ah, shucks, it's okay. Sure you did some wrong. But we'll overlook that. Come on in." But that's not what the Bible teaches.

Neither does the Bible teach that after death there is a stage of purging or refining that prepares us for heaven. There is not one word in Scripture about lighting candles or praying for the dead with the hope they will be purged more quickly. There is not one word in Scripture about after-death preparation for heaven. The clear and unmistakable teaching of the Bible is that we make preparation for heaven while on this earth. The tragic but true fact is that not everyone makes that preparation. Therefore not everyone will be in heaven.

Who then will be in heaven? What is the preparation necessary? Two things are said in verse 27 about making preparation for heaven. One has to do with sin, and the other has to do with Jesus Christ. One has to do with repentance, and the other has to do with faith.

I. The text says that nothing impure will enter heaven nor will anyone who is shameful or deceitful (21:6–8; 22:14–15).

Now what are these verses saying? Are they saying that if anyone has ever committed sexual sin, or murdered, or practiced idolatry, or told a lie, that person will be unfit for heaven? If that is what they're saying, there is no hope for any of us, because all of us have sinned and come short of the glory of God. All of us in different degrees have been impure, shameful, and deceitful. What then is this verse saying?

A. *It is saying that to enter and enjoy heaven, we must have had a change of heart about our sin.* We must have experienced godly sorrow for it, holy revulsion to it, and genuine rejection of it. We surely are not sinless or pure, but we have deliberately turned from sin as a practice and sought forgiveness for it.

B. *It is only when we repent of our sin that God changes our hearts so that we no longer love our sin.* Jesus said to Nicodemus in John 3: "Except a man be born again, he cannot see the kingdom of God." Our hearts are so deceitful and so sinful that we must experience the grace of God changing us and transforming us. But God's grace changes us only when we are willing to turn from our sin.

321

I read a story of a very wealthy man who had no close relatives to whom he could leave his wealth, and instead of leaving his wealth to some good institution, he left his wealth to a distant relative. It was a great tragedy, because that relative was totally unprepared for the wealth. He was not qualified by nature or fitted by education to handle the money. He was separated from his old friends because they felt superior. He was wealthy, but he was miserable, for he was incapable of handling what was given to him. Such would be the condition of a person in heaven without a changed heart toward sin. Heaven will be a holy place. It will be a place of fellowship with God and of fulfilling service to him. A person who has never repented of selfishness would be incapable of enjoying selflessness. A person who has never repented of a life of sensuality would be incapable of enjoying a life of spirituality.

II. The second thing this text says about being prepared for heaven is that your name must be written in the Lamb's book of life.

A. *If you are to enter and enjoy heaven, you must not only turn from your sin, but you must in faith trust Jesus Christ as the Lamb of God.* To be prepared for heaven you must not only deal with your sin, you must deal with the Savior from sin— Jesus. Jesus Christ is described in this verse as the Lamb. The Lamb is the one who takes away the sin of the world. Throughout the Bible it is clear that if a sinful person is to be restored to a relationship with a holy God, sin must be paid for by the shedding of blood. Sacrifice must be made. Life is in the blood, and without the shedding of blood there is no remission of sin. If God in his holiness and justice is to forgive sinful humans and restore a broken relationship with them as they come to him in repentance, then atonement must be made for sin.

B. *When John the Baptist saw Jesus standing on the banks of the Jordan River, he pointed to Jesus and said to those around him, "Look, the Lamb of God, who takes away the sin of the world!"*(John 1:29 NIV). In 1 Peter 1:18–20, Peter says, "For you know that it was not with perishable things such as silver or gold that you were redeemed from the empty way of life handed down to you from your forefathers, but with the precious blood of Christ, a lamb without blemish or defect. He was chosen before the creation of the world" (NIV). In Revelation 5 there is a picture of the angelic host of heaven gathering around God's throne. They cry out to God, "Worthy is the Lamb, who was slain, to receive power and wealth and wisdom and strength and honor and glory and praise!" (v. 12 NIV).

Conclusion

The Bible says the only people who are going to go to heaven are those who have trusted in the Lamb. To have your name written in the Lamb's book means you have accepted Jesus Christ as the sacrifice for your sin. Have you trusted Jesus Christ and his shed blood and sacrifice on the cross for your salvation? Or are you trusting something else? Are you trusting your reputation or your status? Are you trusting good works you have done or your heritage? Are you trusting in your church membership?

You must repent of your sin and trust Jesus as the one who died for you. Have you done that? You ask, "How much do I have to turn from my sin and trust Jesus as the Lamb who died for me?" The answer of the Bible is that you have to do it only enough to call upon him and ask for his forgiveness. Come to him sincerely and honestly, saying to him, "I know I have sinned. I don't want to live the way I've been living. I repent. I turn from my sin and come to you with nothing in my hand. I come to trust Jesus Christ, the one who died on the cross for my forgiveness." If you do this, he will forgive you and will fit you for heaven.

WEDNESDAY EVENING, NOVEMBER 29

Title: Final Instructions to the Church

Text: "Encourage one another, and build up one another, just as you also are doing" *(1 Thess. 5:11 NASB).*

Scripture Reading: 1 Thessalonians 5:11–22

Introduction

This epistle is concluded with some very specific and emphatic suggestions for the church. With paternal affection Paul gives guidelines for managing relationships.

I. How to relate to one another (vv. 11–15).

Christians should edify and encourage one another for mutual growth and betterment.

Church members are urged to respect and appreciate their leaders. The leaders carry heavy responsibilities and work diligently and therefore merit the esteem of those they serve.

Christians should live in peace with one another, Paul says. By exercising patience, forgiveness, compassion, and care, the church operates as a peaceful fellowship.

II. How to relate to God (vv. 16–18).

God is honored by the rejoicing of his people. He gave his Son to make their lives abundantly full, and their abundance of joy gives witness to his good gift.

A constant spirit of prayer and an openness to communion with God also strengthens our relationship with him.

Thanksgiving is an important habit for Christians to develop in our relationship with God.

III. How to relate to the Holy Spirit (vv. 19–22).

Avoid grieving the Spirit. Paul suggests several ways in which we may offend and hinder the moving of the Holy Spirit. If we fail to value prophetic speaking, the Spirit is grieved. If we fail to discern spiritual things and attribute to the Holy Spirit of God things for which he is not responsible, we offend him. If we fail to hold firmly to the good, we grieve the Spirit.

Conclusion

Paul pronounces on his readers a final blessing that contains a reminder of the faithfulness of God toward us. Let this challenge us to be faithful to one another and to him.

DECEMBER

■ Sunday Mornings

On the first Sunday of the month complete the series "Living for the Values of Eternity."

The significance of the incarnation of Christ cannot be overstated: it is in him that we have the clearest picture of God. Because of this, "The God Who Revealed Himself in Jesus Christ" is the theme for the Sunday morning messages for the rest of December.

■ Sunday Evenings

"The Human Responses to the Christ of Christmas" is the theme for the Sunday evening messages.

■ Wednesday Evenings

"Hearing and Responding to the Calls of Christ" is the theme for a series of biographical studies based in the gospel of John. John was a careful listener and a diligent learner. He heard and learned much that can be of great profit to us as we consider different lives described in the gospel of John.

SUNDAY MORNING, DECEMBER 3

Title: Jesus' View of Money

Text: "Jesus told his disciples: 'There was a rich man whose manager was accused of wasting his possessions. So he called him in and asked him, 'What is this I hear about you? Give an account of your management, because you cannot be manager any longer'" *(Luke 16:1–2 NIV).*

Scripture Reading: Luke 16:1–9

Hymns: "Rejoice, Ye Pure in Heart," Messiter

             "My Jesus, I Love Thee," Anonymous

             "When I Survey the Wondrous Cross," Watts

Offertory Prayer: Holy Father, your Word teaches us that you are the one who gives us the power to get wealth. We pray that you will deliver us from the peril of living only for materialistic values. Help us to recognize our possessions as being entrusted to us, not just for our use but for the advancement of your kingdom. Bless us as we share and as we care. In Jesus' name. Amen.

Introduction

Jesus did not leave us in the dark about money. He revealed the true nature of money so that we could handle it correctly according to his teaching in the parable of the steward. The details of the parable are familiar. The wealthy businessman had committed the management of his business to a man he believed was a trusted employee. Reports came to him that this employee was not trustworthy, that he had actually been mismanaging the firm. The owner called for an accounting from the employee. Before the accounting could take place, the employee manipulated events for himself. Anticipating that he would lose his position and not wanting to go on welfare or unemployment, he made a deal with the people who owed his boss some money. One who owed a hundred measures of oil, or about nine hundred gallons, had his bill cut in half. Another who owed about twelve hundred bushels of wheat had it reduced by 20 percent. The man acted that way so he would have friends when he was out of a job. Obviously his actions were unjust and wrong, but they were in his apparent interest. He acted shrewdly, in light of his values, to provide for his own future. I do not want to deal with the primary lesson of this parable at this time, but rather to take a close look at what Jesus said about money. To understand money the way Jesus understood it is essential if we are to use it shrewdly as children of light.

I. Wealth is tempting.

Jesus uses an intriguing name for wealth in the passage. He refers to it as "worldly wealth" (vv. 9, 11 NIV). Why does Jesus describe this wealth as worldly?

A. *Jesus is not saying that all wealth is evil.* Like the rest of the material world, it is amoral. It takes on moral qualities according to its use.

B. *I hold in my hand a bill of currency.* Where do you suppose this bill has been? What would be the chances that it has ever been to church before? It may have brought some selfish pleasure in a house of prostitution. It may have been used in a casino. It may have been a part of a bribe to pay off a corruption of justice. It may have been used in a drug buy. There are so many selfish and unjust things that it could have been used for that surely there is validity in our Lord's descriptive term. With this bill I can be tempted to do some things that I would never consider without it.

C. *Worldly wealth is important to the unrighteous world.* It is the thing on which the world is so prone to set its heart. In this matter people are the same regardless of the economic system under which they live. I am grateful that I have been privileged to live under a limited free-enterprise system, but this system does not cure people of their passion for wealth. At times it may actually encourage them in that direction since it makes it possible for them to reach out for more of it.

I. Money is temporary.

Jesus points us to this basic fact about money. "I tell you, use worldly wealth to gain friends for yourselves, so that when it is gone, you will be welcomed into eternal dwellings" (v. 9 NIV).

A. *It is temporary because we hold wealth only until death.* This seems to be the primary application that our Lord is making. He is suggesting that there will be a day, even the day of death, in which regardless of how much wealth you have, it will be of no use.

The apostle Paul states the same truth in a different way. "Godliness with contentment is great gain. For we brought nothing into the world, and we can take nothing out of it. But if we have food and clothing, we will be content with that" (1 Tim. 6:6–8 NIV). Your relationship with your wealth, whether it be little or much, is temporary because of your approaching death.

B. *It is temporary because it will be under the judgment of God.* It will be burned up in the fire at the end of the age. John warns us. "The world and its desires pass away, but the man who does the will of God lives forever" (1 John 2:17 NIV). The verbs used by John indicate that the world is already passing away. The process of judgment has already begun.

III. Wealth is a trust.

This is a truth that our Lord consistently emphasized; this parable asserts it obviously. God is the wealthy landowner, and we are his stewards. We hold everything that we possess in trust for God.

A. *Everything we have belongs to God.* Jesus reinforces this with a question in verse 12: "If you have not been trustworthy with someone else's property, who will give you property of your own?" (NIV). This is where we are now. We are managing a part of the property of the eternal God. We do not own anything. Nothing!

B. *Wealth is the least of the trusts we receive.* This is the startling truth that Jesus puts before us. We make over it so much, but on God's scale of values, it is the least significant thing that he has entrusted to our care. Jesus said, "Whoever can be trusted with very little can also be trusted with much, and whoever is dishonest with very little will also be dishonest with much" (v. 10 NIV). The context makes it clear that our Lord means for us to understand that the worldly wealth is the least of what he has entrusted to us.

Does this tell you anything about us? Do we wonder why God has not trusted us with more blessings? Many of you have not even met the Old Testament level of tithing in your stewardship. You put your tipping on a percentage basis, but not your giving to the God who owns all things. God looks at this.

Conclusion

Since money is tempting, we need to handle it prayerfully. Since money is temporary, we need to handle it deliberately. Since money is a trust, we need to handle it faithfully. Someday the owner will require an audit of our stewardship.

SUNDAY EVENING, DECEMBER 3

Title: Jesus, the Light of the World

Text: "Again Jesus spoke to them, saying, 'I am the light of the world; he who follows me will not walk in darkness, but will have the light of life'" *(John 8:12 RSV)*.

Scripture Reading: Isaiah 9:2–7; John 8:12–30

Introduction

On the evening of the first night of the Feast of Tabernacles, there was a ceremony called the Illumination of the Temple, which involved the ritual lighting of four golden candelabras in the Court of Women. For additional reflection, each person lit four candlesticks and set them in a floating bowl, producing such a spectacle of illumination that it is said that all Jerusalem reflected the light. All night long the light glowed. In celebration and anticipation, the greatest, wisest, and holiest of Israel's men danced before the Lord and sang psalms of joy and praise while the people watched and waited.

They watched and waited, hope and prayed, because this festival reminded the citizens of Israel that God had promised long ago that a child would be born who would be the Anointed One who would redeem his people. The great prophet of the golden age of prophecy, Isaiah, had proclaimed that the coming of God's new age would be as the coming of a great light (9:2–7).

For Israel it was a time of darkness and despair. The nation was occupied by a foreign power, and thus the Jews' aspirations, dreams, and hopes were blunted by reality and blighted by circumstance. So they longed for the birth of the one who would restore their rejoicing and revive their joy, the Prophet who would renew their glory, release them from bondage, and reestablish their independence.

Against this backdrop Jesus defined who he is: "I am the light of the world!" What a magnificent setting—the darkness of the countryside surrounding the brilliance of the light coming from the temple area—for a declaration that God's new age had dawned in the birth, person, and work of the humble Nazarene!

Light enables one to see. It illuminates. "To shed light on the matter" means to reveal, to disclose truth. Jesus is the Light of the World in that he enables us to see the truth about ourselves and the truth about God. He illuminates our understanding both of ourselves and of God. In Jesus, the Light of the World, we see ourselves as God sees us, and we see God as he desires that we see him.

I. The child born in Bethlehem illuminates the way we feel about ourselves.

A. *We live in an age of despair and gloom.* It is an age that tells us that we are not worth much unless we brush with the right toothpaste, wash our hair with the right shampoo, wear the appropriate designer labels, and use the latest jargon. A great sense of worthlessness, of "nobodiness," permeates our day.

B. *But Jesus as the Light of the World can illuminate our feelings at precisely this point.* We have worth because of who our Creator is. "The Word was made flesh" (John 1:14); this reminds us that we are the good product of the creative, loving activity of God as he moved to bring order out of chaos, light out of darkness, and humans out of the dust of the ground. The biblical picture was one of excitement, ecstasy, anticipation, and fondness, as God formed us into his own image and breathed the breath of life into our nostrils. He looked upon creation with delight and declared that it was good.

C. *Not only were we been created by the Word because he loved us, but also the Word became flesh because he loved us.* Sure, we ate the forbidden fruit, but the message of Christmas is that we are still loved and deemed more valuable than precious jewels. That toddler in Nazareth assures us that we are still the apple of the Father's eye—even in our sin. Jesus is the incarnating—the in-the-fleshing—of God's love for us. We are of ultimate worth because we have a Redeemer.

II. The child born in Bethlehem illuminates the way we feel about God.

A. *Where do you think John, the great apostle of love, got the idea to write such a stunning verse as "For God so loved the world that he gave his one and only Son, that whoever believes in him shall not perish but have eternal life" (John 3:16 NIV)?* The Holy Spirit inspired him. During his three years with Jesus, John learned that, indeed, the boy born of Mary was the Light of the World who could illuminate our understanding of how God feels about us.

B. *Where do you think Paul, the great apostle of grace, got such a preposterous idea as to reduce the gospel to "God demonstrates his own love for us in this: While we were still sinners, Christ died for us" (Rom. 5:8 NIV)?* He got it from interpreting the life and ministry of Jesus through the Holy Spirit. To Paul, Jesus was the Light of the World. In Jesus, Paul learned ultimately how God felt about him and that faith in the child born of the Virgin was the way to be right with God.

Conclusion

When a tour group gets to the bottom of the magnificent Carlsbad Caverns in New Mexico, the lights are turned off to show utter darkness. After the lights are turned off, it does not take long before you can even feel the darkness; you start getting anxious for the lights to come back on. The tension is relieved only when the lights return.

In our world of darkness—a world of sin and guilt, desperation and despair, estrangement and alienation—Jesus is the Light!

WEDNESDAY EVENING, DECEMBER 6

Title: The Calling of Andrew

Text: "One of the two which heard John speak, and followed him, was Andrew, Simon Peter's brother" *(John 1:40).*

Scripture Reading: John 1:35–42

Introduction

Apart from the gospel of John, we would know very little about Andrew. He appears three times in John's Gospel—in chapters 1, 6, and 11. In all of these experiences, he is doing the same thing: bringing someone to Christ. But in this study we see how he himself came to know Christ as his own Savior.

I. Situation.

A. *Place.* The experience of the calling of Andrew took place in Bethany beyond Jordan according to A. T. Robertson in his *Harmony of the Gospels.* James Hastings, in his *Dictionary of the Bible,* suggests that it took place in Bethany in Galilee, which was the place of John's baptism.

B. *Time.* Albert Barnes, in his *Notes on the New Testament,* contends that Andrew's calling occurred the day after John's testimony that Jesus was the Son of God. John's testimony is found in verse 29 of this same chapter. Verse 39 tells us that it occurred the tenth hour, which could well have been 4:00 p.m. if we count time from sunrise to sunset as the Jews did.

C. *Circumstance.* Following his baptism Jesus went into the wilderness and encountered what we commonly call the temptation experience. Here he had just come out of this experience, and John the Baptist had just testified that Jesus is the Messiah. The day before, John had addressed a multitude, and on this day he was standing with two of his disciples (v. 35). Verses 36–37 tell us that John the Baptist's statement concerning Christ was not addressed particularly to these two men. In fact, his statement was intended for the prepared hearts of several people. The question we must ask ourselves based on this example is, "Do our words encourage others to follow Christ?"

II. Method.

A. *Description of the person.* Andrew was one who apparently had been looking for Christ (v. 30). He was an honest seeker and an ordinary individual. Andrew obviously had been a disciple of John the Baptist, yet he was not desirous of forming a party or building up a sect. In fact, he was willing that all whom he had led to John become followers of Christ.

B. *Method.* Christ opened the way for John and Andrew to express what he knew was in their hearts. Therefore Christ said, "What are you seeking?" In verse 39 Christ's answer to their suggestion was prompt and cordial: He invited them to his home. In verses 38–39 it is clear that Christ was seeking to relieve their embarrassment and at the same time call for definite action. Christ took people one step at a time; we should do likewise. These verses also indicate that Christ was both kind and respectful.

He used three main steps in his method: (1) the Master's question, "What seek ye?" (v. 38); (2) the Master's invitation, "Come and see" (v. 39); and (3) personal communion, "They came and saw where he dwelt and abode with him that day" (v. 39).

III. Result.

A. *Andrew went after Christ to learn more about him (v. 40).* Verse 41 tells us that Andrew found his brother, Simon Peter, and brought him to Christ. The word "first" tells us it was the first thing he wanted to do and the first thing he actually did.

B. *From this experience Andrew went on to be a great personal evangelist.* He first brought his brother, Simon Peter, to Christ (John 1). Later, he brought the little boy with five loaves and two fishes to Christ (John 6). And then he brought some Greeks to Christ (John 12).

Conclusion

This passage reminds us that God through Jesus Christ is eternally reaching out to lost humankind. At the same time it reminds us that those who have been reached by his grace have the privilege and responsibility to reach out to others.

SUNDAY MORNING, DECEMBER 10

Title: Where Is Christmas?

Text: "When the fullness of the time was come, God sent forth his Son, made of a woman, made under the law, to redeem them that were under the law, that we might receive the adoption of sons" *(Gal. 4:4–5).*

Scripture Reading: Galatians 4:4–5; Luke 2:8–14

Hymns: "Jesus Shall Reign Where'er the Sun," Watts

"Angels, from the Realms of Glory," Montgomery

"Glory to His Name," Hoffman

Offertory Prayer: Holy Father, you are the giver of every good and perfect gift. As we approach the Christmas season, we are reminded of the greatness and the graciousness of your generosity to us. Help us to respond with an attitude of generosity that will express itself in loving service. In Jesus' name we pray. Amen.

Introduction

What is Christmas? Dr. Robert G. Lee said, "Christmas is the joyous celebration of eternity's intersection with time." The apostle Paul said, in Galatians 4:4, "When the time had fully come, God sent his Son, born of a woman" (NIV).

Why do people refuse what Christmas offers?

A sorrowful wife stood just outside a psychopathic ward in a great hospital. Her husband, a patient in the hospital, was with her. He looked vacantly into space as she pleaded, "John, here's a Christmas present for you. Take it, John, and look at it."

John made no move.

Again the plea was made. "John, dear, all of us at home thought you would like your present so much. Look at it, John. Isn't it nice?"

The loving, urging voice failed to reach John's mind. He was powerless to grasp the meaning of a Christmas gift.

Millions in the world today are like John. They refuse God's great gift of love—the Savior. There is this difference, however, between that mentally sick man and those who refuse God's gift: he didn't knowingly refuse the gift offered to him, but many people deliberately and knowingly refuse the gift of God—the Savior and eternal life.

Where is Christmas? Christmas is everywhere Christ and the believer are found. Let's look at what the Bible has to say about this.

I. Christmas in heaven.

A. *What had happened before the fullness of time had come?* The world was being prepared for the advent of Christ. A number of things had taken place:
   1. The announcement of an angel to Zechariah (Luke 1:8–23).
   2. The conception of John the Baptist (Luke 1:24–25).
   3. The announcement of the angel Gabriel to the Virgin Mary (Luke 1:26–38).
   4. The announcement of the angel to Joseph (Matt. 1:18–25).
   5. Mary's visit to Elizabeth (Luke 1:39–56).
   6. The journey of the holy family to Bethlehem (Luke 2:1–5).

   The fullness of Mary's time had come. She had pondered these things in her heart during these months, and now the time had come.

B. *The next event was the incarnation through the virgin birth.* This momentous event on which all history turns was unheralded, unattended, and unknown, except for the animals and the angels.

II. Christmas on earth.

A. *Things had been happening on earth.* Prophecies had been fulfilled. The world had been prepared politically for the birth of Christ. The world conquest by Alexander the Great and the development of a common language—Greek—had helped to show the fullness of time. The world had been prepared morally. Heathenism, paganism, and false religions had buried God in the visible world; a literal God, an almighty God, the God of love was unknown in the midst of superstition and unbelief. All of the religious experience of the

332

day had produced an epoch of despair. Philosophy and moral values had produced widespread corruption and a longing for better things.

B. *The fullness of time had come.* Other events that show this fullness of time are as follows:
   1. Jesus' birth in Bethlehem (Luke 2:1–5).
   2. The announcement that the angels made to the shepherd (Luke 2:8–14).
   3. The visit of the shepherds to the manger (Luke 2:15–20). God's Son had come to earth!

III. Christmas in you.

A. *It is a fundamental truth of God's Word that Christ is reborn in the regeneration of every child of God.* Paul wrote, "I am again in the pains of childbirth until Christ is formed in you" (Gal. 4:19 NIV). When a person is born again, it is literally true that there is another incarnation of God. We can say, "Christ lives in me."

B. *When you are born again, Christmas comes into your heart.* Have you crowned Christ King of Kings in your heart? Are you ready to acknowledge him as Master, Lord, and King?

Conclusion

The wise men brought their gifts because they believed Jesus was the King of the Jews, the King of Kings. Have you worshiped him as King? Do you adore him as the angels did?

Christ is the Savior of the world, and he wants to be your Savior too. He died to make satisfaction for your sins. Will you accept this only authentic Christmas gift?

SUNDAY EVENING, DECEMBER 10

Title: Crowded Rooms and Empty Lives

Text: "She brought forth her firstborn son, and wrapped him in swaddling clothes, and laid him in a manger; because there was no room for them in the inn" *(Luke 2:7).*

Scripture Reading: Luke 2:1–7

Introduction

The first Scripture we learn as children at Christmas is: "She . . . wrapped him in swaddling clothes, and laid him in a manger, because there was no room for them in the inn" (Luke 2:7).

Fourteen years was the usual cycle of enrollment for taxes. But Augustus and Herod quarreled, so a new tax was placed on the Jews, even though only ten years had elapsed.

Each one had to return to his tribal family home. The inns were crowded, so Mary and Joseph, who had traveled eighty miles, were sent to a stable, which may have been a cave behind the inn.

God had been working out his purpose and plans. Caesar Augustus and the divine emperor carried out God's plans without any idea they were fulfilling Old Testament prophecy. God had worked out the time, place, and circumstances of the birth of Christ. "There was no room for them in the inn" (Luke 2:7); the people were living in these crowded rooms, but without Christ they had empty lives.

"Crowded rooms but empty lives" is my message to you today. Let's look at how we can suffer from this syndrome.

I. This occurs if we fail to recognize the Christ of Christmas.

The angel had announced, "Fear not: for behold, I bring you good tidings of great joy, which shall be to all people. For unto you is born this day in the city of David a Savior, which is Christ the Lord" (Luke 2:10–11).

Jesus is the universal Savior and Lord, but many people do not recognize and acknowledge him. They want him out of the public schools, out of government, out of politics, out of social functions, and out of lives.

We need to follow Christ in all we do. The faithful lives of his children will point others to Christ.

II. This occurs if there is no worship of Christ.

The story of the wise man encapsulates the meaning of worship. Jerusalem was the capital of the Jewish people and the center of the religious hope of the world. A short time before Jesus was born, some magi, whose names and number we do not know, started from their homes somewhere in the East and journeyed toward Jerusalem, being guided by a peculiar star. They interpreted the sign and looked for the King of the Jews.

Upon reaching Jerusalem, they asked, "Where is he that is born King of the Jews?" Their question dropped like a lighted match on a dry prairie; soon all Jerusalem was aflame with excitement. Troubled Herod demanded that the chief priest and scribes answer the magi's question. They said, "In Bethlehem of Judea" (Matt. 2:5). The magi, upon arrival in Bethlehem, found the Christ child and worshiped him. They did so in three special ways.

A. *They worshiped a person.*
B. *They worshiped with a purse.*
C. *They worshiped with a purpose.*

We have crowded rooms and empty lives when we fail to worship Jesus.

III. This occurs if we have no time for Christ.

We all claim to be busy. There is no time for him in our world. There is no time for him in our lives! There is no time for him in our homes!

Will you make time for Christ this Christmas and in the new year?

Life is a story in volumes three,
The past and present and yet to be.
The first is written and laid away,

The second we are writing every day,
The third and last of the volumes three
Is locked from sight—God keeps the key.

—Author unknown

The Bible says we need to make time for Jesus today: "Behold, now is the accepted time; behold, now is the day of salvation" (2 Cor. 6:2). Said Emerson: "This time, like all times, is a very good one if we know what to do with it." Follow Christ now!

IV. This occurs if we have no gifts for Jesus.

"And when they were come into the house, they saw the young child with Mary, his mother, and fell down, and worshiped him: and when they had opened their treasures, they presented unto him gifts; gold, and frankincense, and myrrh" (Matt. 2:11). God wants to be worshiped with our gifts. Consider the following story.

A large sum of money was urgently needed by Dr. J. H. Jowett's famous church in Carr's Lane. A special money-raising meeting of the church was called. At the close of the service, the names of all the donors and the amounts they gave were read. The crowd applauded when the names of those who gave sizeable donations were read. The last name read was that of a poor woman who sacrificially gave six-pence. No one applauded. Dr. Jowett stood quietly and said impressively, "I hear the applause of the crucified hands." Jesus takes pleasure in our gifts.

Conclusion

We can easily live empty lives by crowding our rooms with anything other than Christ. We can keep the debris out if we recognize the Christ of Christmas, worship him, and give time and gifts to him.

WEDNESDAY EVENING, DECEMBER 13

Title: The Winning of Nathanael

Text: "Jesus saw Nathanael coming to him, and saith of him, behold an Israelite indeed, in whom is no guile!" *(John 1:47)*.

Scripture Reading: John 1:43–51

Introduction

Jesus came to seek and to save humankind. He won followers one at a time. Nathanael is a particularly interesting case.

I. Situation.

A. *Place.* Verse 43 indicates that Jesus had recently left Bethany beyond the Jordan. Christ was near Cana in Galilee and probably was on his way to Cana when Philip found him. Perhaps Philip had run ahead and told Nathanael the news of Christ's coming.

B. *Time.* This occurred perhaps five or six days after the deputation from the Sanhedrin had visited Christ. It immediately followed the call of Andrew, Peter, and Philip.

C. *Circumstances.* Jesus had just called Andrew, who in turn won Peter, his brother. Philip, only recently having been won, prepared the heart of Nathanael. Verse 43 tells us that he found Nathanael. That simply means that he made a willful, deliberate effort to share his faith. Apparently Nathanael was by himself, and he had never met Christ before. Also, Philip had no opportunity to inform Nathanael concerning Christ prior to this time.

II. Method.

A. *Description of the person.* In verse 46 we read that Nathanael was apparently quite cynical in regard to Nazareth. Perhaps this was a result of small-town rivalry between Cana and Nazareth. It is obvious that Nathanael was hard to persuade yet was an earnest individual. As far as his name is concerned, Matthew 10:3 would indicate that he and Bartholomew are one and the same person, since the name Bartholomew is a last name. He was apparently an upright and honest man and could well have been one of John the Baptist's disciples.

B. *Method.* Christ used Philip to prepare the way, even as he uses individuals today. When Nathanael raised the question concerning Christ, he was invited to view the evidence (v. 46). It is significant that Philip did not choose to argue the issue but rather to confront him with tangible proof. Jesus in verse 48 used his divine knowledge to impress Nathanael. In the statement Christ makes in this verse, he is not so much stressing that he saw Nathanael under the tree as he is stressing that he read his thoughts as Nathanael was undoubtedly praying that the Messiah would come. In verse 47 when Jesus calls him "an Israelite indeed," Christ makes known the unseen potential in Nathanael. Also, it is significant that Jesus took the first step in beginning the conversation. Even today our Lord takes the initiative in touching human hearts. The word "to behold" in verse 47 expresses Christ's joy in Nathanael's coming, and the words "no guile" are Christ's acknowledgment of Nathanael's sincerity.

III. Result.

Nathanael acknowledged the dignity of Christ's person in verse 49 as he called him "Rabbi." He further acknowledged the greatness of Christ's office when he called him "King of Israel." In that same verse when he referred to Christ as "the Son of God," he was accepting Christ openly as God's Son, the Messiah. Christ's response to Nathanael's embrace was to promise him greater things (v. 50). Verse 51 concludes this experience of our Lord with Nathanael by Christ's praising and rewarding Nathanael's faith.

Conclusion

Christ knows the hearts of men and women long before they come to him. He welcomes them and sees within them the potential that can be realized by their allowing him entrance into their lives.

SUNDAY MORNING, DECEMBER 17

Title: Your King Comes to You

Text: "Rejoice greatly, O Daughter of Zion! Shout, Daughter of Jerusalem! See, your king comes to you, righteous and having salvation, gentle and riding on a donkey, on a colt, the foal of a donkey" *(Zech. 9:9 NIV).*

Scripture Reading: Zechariah 9:9–16

Hymns: "There's a Song in the Air," Holland

"Angels from the Realms of Glory," Montgomery

"Come, Thou Almighty King," Anonymous

Offertory Prayer: Eternal King, we worship you for your powerful love. We praise you for your tender mercy. We adore you for your patient help. We offer ourselves to you with our gifts. In the name of Jesus. Amen.

Introduction

"See, your king comes to you!" The prophet came. The priest came. The third "anointed one" in ancient Israel was the king. All three persons—prophet, priest, and king—are fulfilled in the person of Jesus. And so, as we celebrate Christmas, the infinite variety and all-inclusiveness of our Lord shines clear.

The hope for the continuation of the Davidic line was natural. David had been a popular ruler. Even before his accession to the throne, many of the people preferred him to Saul. He was a man of the people, and they treasured his memory. God had guaranteed the succession. He had promised that David's house would last forever.

At times hope was stronger than at other times. If the ruler chanced to be a descendant of David and was a bad ruler, hope was deemphasized. The hope for a Davidic ruler was especially popular during the period between the testaments. The nationalism of the people was tested, and they equated a Davidic descendant with nationalistic hopes.

In Jesus' time the hope for such a Davidic king was closely correlated with the hope for a Messiah. Zechariah himself bore a highly symbolic name. His name means "he whom the Lord remembers." It is at this point that the promise of a king to come became highly personal. The prophet seized upon this hope: "See, your king comes to you!"

I. He is King under God.

What kind of king is this? All too often the people longed for a popular figure to be a king and in their choice doomed the monarchy to be a clear rejection of God's will. The king of God's people is God's choice, not the people's whim. Other prophets spoke as clearly as did Zechariah. Jeremiah, for example, spoke for God on the issue: "Behold, the days come, saith the LORD, that I will raise unto David a righteous Branch, and a King shall reign and prosper, and shall execute judgment and justice in the earth" (Jer. 23:5).

A. *The King is just.* Not only is he King under God, he is just. Again another prophet emphasized the same theme. Isaiah spoke for God: "And there shall come forth a rod out of the stem of Jesse, and a Branch shall grow out of his roots . . . and righteousness shall be the girdle of his loins, and faithfulness the girdle of his reins" (Isa. 11:1–5). He is not concerned with appearances or hearsay. He is clothed with righteousness. There is no injustice in the King who comes.

B. *The King will be victorious.* It is a hope to which we as well as the ancient believers may cling. A prophet of the ancient world, Micah, found in tiny Bethlehem a pocket of hope. Out of insignificance, out of weakness, out of little things, was to come one who would rule in Israel.

C. *The King is lowly.* What sort of king will he be, this one destined to come and rule over God's people? He is just, he is victorious, and he is under God. He is also lowly. God has always been interested in the lowly: "I dwell in the high and holy place, with him also that is of a contrite and humble spirit, to revive the spirit of the humble, and to revive the heart of the contrite" (Isa. 57:15). If there were those who expected the coming King to be mounted on a royal charger, their expectations had to be altered. How clearly the prophet described it: "See, your king comes to you . . . on a colt, the foal of a donkey" (v. 9 NIV). True meekness is not insecurity, but confidence, and confidence does not have to make a show of strength.

II. The King and his kingdom.

Regardless of what royalty may suggest in our day, the king of God's choice was also a spiritual figure. It is in this light that Jesus taught us to pray, "Thy kingdom come!" When we pray in this manner, we remember that his coming fulfilled the ancient hope. This prayer, Jesus' word to his disciples, is full of stern reality. We remember, for example, that the relationship with God is a totalitarian relationship. Although we may legitimately speak of our church relationships as being democratic, the relationship we sustain with God is one of absolute lordship. Further, the prayer reminds us that this relationship with the King is personal. It is after all a personal prayer of commitment, a disciple's prayer.

A. *The kingdom and peace.* The prophets hoped for a kingdom of peace. It is this same kingdom for which the disciple prays. Yet in something of a paradox, this peace is gained by conquest. We have a great deal to learn about peace, and most of it may be learned from God. The King was able to ride on a donkey, the symbol of peace, because of God's power and his victory. Peace is never cheap. Patrick Henry quoted Jeremiah, "Men may cry, 'Peace, peace,' when there is no peace" (Jer. 6:14), so effectively that many suppose the quotation was original with the patriot. His plea was designed to remind the colonists that peace is achieved only through suffering. It is gained through conquest.

We are called to be active in the offense against evil. Only in this manner can peace be achieved. How closely the petitions parallel one another: "Thy kingdom come. . . . Deliver us from evil." The stern reality of the prayer relates us to the prophetic hope: "See, your king comes to you!" Even Jesus, Prince of Peace, said, "I came not to bring peace, but the sword." It is not easy to think of conquest at the Christmas season. All of our thoughts are sweet and compassionate and peaceable and meek. But there is a King to be obeyed, a kingdom to come.

B.   *The kingdom is universal.* It is universal, not in the sense of geography, but in the sense of absolute sovereignty. It thrives on the confidence that there is one God who created the heavens and the earth. It is based on the belief in his supreme power. How clearly Zechariah spoke, "And the LORD shall be King over all the earth" (Zech. 14:9). In this universal kingdom the chosen people then are a means to an end. An earlier prophet had spoken of God's Servant: "I will also give thee for a light to the Gentiles, that thou mayest be my salvation unto the end of the earth" (Isa. 49:6). Being subjects of the kingdom of God involves us in conquest.

To pray earnestly, "Thy will be done," is to be encouraged to have faith in the Lord. It is to realize that the subjects are to act like the King.

Conclusion

A modern poet-storyteller has described the relationship between King Arthur and his knights. Inspired by Arthur's character, those who followed him were to stamp out evil in the name of the king. This was their covenant, their objective. Now we hear the prophetic voice and it rings clear in our ears. "See, your king comes to you!" He comes driving out evil, granting peace, and offering victory. Where is he? Hear the word of the apostle: "The word is nigh thee, even in thy mouth, and in thy heart" (Rom. 10:8).

May it be true in your experience: See, your King comes to you!

SUNDAY EVENING, DECEMBER 17

Title: Missing the Main Event

Text: "Jesus entered into Jerusalem, and into the temple: and when he had looked round about upon all things, and now the eventide was come, he went out unto Bethany with the twelve" *(Mark 11:11)*.

Scripture Reading: Mark 11:1–11

Introduction

When Jesus made his triumphal entry into Jerusalem, he did so in a way calculated to get attention. He used a symbolic animal for his entrance. The donkey was seen as an honorable animal. Kings rode on donkeys in peace and on horses in war. The symbolism, then, is that of a King of Peace, the Prince of Peace. He wanted to be enthroned in his people's hearts.

The crowds wanted a king for a day, a messiah who would overthrow the government of Rome. Instead, Jesus came to be the Lord of their lives. Jesus did not come to be a military ruler. He came to seek and to save the lost. Jesus was determined to sacrifice himself for sinners.

The crowd on that eventful day missed the point. They missed the main event. We can be like those people in the crowd. Let's examine how.

I. We miss the main event when we see the show but miss the message.

People are prone to miss the main event. Some people who go to a circus never get past the side show. They are so caught up with peripheral attractions they never see what's in the center ring.

We cry out, "Entertain me, cater to me, serve me, appeal to my motives, dazzle me." But Jesus didn't enter Jerusalem to dazzle us; he entered Jerusalem to die.

How many this Christmas will see the show but miss the message of Christmas? Programs, gifts, decorations, food—these are all peripheral attractions that certainly can be enjoyed, but we must be care not to miss the message of Christ's birth.

II. We miss the main event when our God is too small.

Jesus was offering himself as the Messiah, the Savior of the world, the Wonderful Counselor, the Mighty God, the Everlasting Father, the Prince of Peace, Immanuel, but they wanted only a political ruler who would serve their selfish purposes. Jesus wanted them to think big, but they were thinking small. Their God was too little. They wanted to think about their culture, their group, their race. Jesus wanted them to see their salvation and the salvation of the world. But their God was too small.

We miss the main event when our God is too small.

III. We miss the main event when we make Jesus king for a day and not Lord for life.

"If thou shalt confess with thy mouth the Lord Jesus, and shalt believe in thine heart that God hath raised him from the dead, thou shalt be saved" (Rom. 10:9).

"Therefore let all the house of Israel know assuredly, that God hath made that same Jesus, whom ye have crucified, both Lord and Christ" (Acts 2:36).

A. *Jesus is Lord because he is God.* "For it pleased the Father that in him should all fulness dwell. . . . For in him dwelleth all the fulness of the Godhead bodily" (Col. 1:19; 2:9). Jesus is man, but he is more than man. He is the God-Man. He is God in human flesh.

B. *Jesus is Lord because he is Creator (Col. 1:16–17).* "All things were made by him; and without him was not anything made that was made" (John 1:3). We know that God made the world and that he made us and gave us the breath of life.

C. *Jesus is Lord because he is Redeemer.* "For it pleased the Father that in him should all fulness dwell; and having made peace through the blood of his cross, by him to reconcile all things unto himself; by him, I say, whether they be things in earth, or things in heaven" (Col. 1:19–20). He died for humanity's sins. He saves us!

IV. We miss the main event when we do not follow him.

Jesus said, "Follow me" (Matt. 4:19).

A. *We belong to him and all that we have belongs to him.* We must recognize that we are not the ultimate owners of anything. We are simply stewards of all we have and all we are.

B. *We must obey him.* Our character, our conduct, our conversation must be regulated by the Word of God. It is not enough to give lip service to Jesus. We must render to him full and unqualified obedience.

C. *We ought to glorify him (1 Cor. 6:19–20).* To glorify Christ is to honor him. We must live in such a way that we will cause others to want to honor him.

D. *We ought to tell others about him (Matt. 28:18–19).*

E. *We should submit to his lordship.*

Conclusion

Will you miss the main event this Christmas? Will you obey Jesus? He said, "Follow me!"

> *To every man there openeth a way, and ways, and a way.*
> *The high soul climbs the high way,*
> *And the low soul gropes the low:*
> *And in between on the misty flats,*
> *The rest drift to and fro.*
> *But to every man there openeth a high way and a low,*
> *And every man decideth. The way his soul shall go.*
>
> —John Oxenham

WEDNESDAY EVENING, DECEMBER 20

Title: Nicodemus

Text: "There was a man of the Pharisees, named Nicodemus, a ruler of the Jews: the same came to Jesus by night" *(John 3:1–2).*

Scripture Reading: John 3:1–22; 7:45–53; 19:38–42

Introduction

Although Christ had a very special place in his heart for the poor and down-trodden, he also had a place in his heart for the financially privileged. His concern was for the souls of people regardless of how affluent or poor they might be. Jesus' conversation with Nicodemus was a classic example of Christ's compassion for and ability to relate to the affluent and educated people of his day.

I. Situation.

A. *Place.* The meeting was in or near Jerusalem—perhaps on the temple porch or at the place where Jesus was living.

B. *Time.* In light of John 2:23, it appears that the conversation took place on the evening of the Passover feast.

That Nicodemus came at night seems to be an important fact in John's mind, for he mentions in each of his references to Nicodemus (chaps. 3, 7, 19) that Nicodemus came to Jesus "by night." The question naturally follows, Why did Nicodemus come to Jesus "by night"? Several interesting suggestions are offered. Some think Nicodemus came to Jesus at night not out of cowardice but rather out of caution. Others say he came at night to avoid the hostility of his colleagues. Still others suggest that he came by night because, as a member of the Sanhedrin, he was a very busy man and had no other time when he could come for a prolonged conversation. Perhaps he realized that as busy as Christ was, Christ would not have time to sit down for an involved dialogue other than at night. One of the suggestions I like best is that Nicodemus came to Jesus at night because it was at that particular time he was most deeply convicted of his need and thus the moment when the Holy Spirit compelled him to go to Christ.

C. *Circumstance.* Nicodemus probably was one of the "many" mentioned in John 2:23 as believing in Jesus because of signs he performed. Nicodemus was well-versed in the history of the Jewish faith. He may have expected that this young rabbi from Galilee might turn out to be a disappointment just like many other false messiahs who had come before. Nevertheless, he continued to investigate. He had to know the meaning of Jesus' healings and miracles.

II. Method.

A. *Description of the person.* Nicodemus was a man of spiritual dissatisfaction: timid, moral, respected, religious. He was also a man of professional success and attainment. He was a member of the Sanhedrin, a professional student of Scripture, and a teacher of the law.

Nicodemus must have been convinced that Christ stood in a very close relation to God in order to be able to do the various miracles he performed (John 3:2). He was open-minded and wanted to know whether God was actually working through this Jesus.

B. *Method.* Christ began at the point of Nicodemus's need. Our Lord explained the essential doctrinal truths involved in being born again. He did so in three steps:

1. The necessity of the new birth (vv. 3, 7).
2. The nature of the new birth (v. 6).
3. The means of receiving the new birth (v. 16).

Christ patiently led Nicodemus to an understanding. He used simple illustrations including the wind, the concept of birth, and a reference to the serpent being lifted up in the wilderness during the time of Moses.

Throughout the conversation Christ spoke with a note of authority, never allowing himself to be sidetracked. He was not impressed or intimidated by the reputation or status of Nicodemus.

In verse 5 Christ calmly and politely informed Nicodemus that he was not in the kingdom of God. But he did not make him look foolish or absurd. He regarded all Nicodemus's questions as sincere. As he answered them he proceeded from the known to the unknown.

III. Result.

John does not record that the results of Jesus' encounter with Nicodemus were immediate. We would be delighted to read of a dramatic and obvious change on the part of Nicodemus, but there is no such report. In John 7:45–53 it is obvious that some kind of change did occur, because Nicodemus reprimanded the Sanhedrin.

The final result can be seen in John 19:38–42. At the point that all seemed lost, Peter had denied Jesus and the disciples were scattered, and it was at that point that Nicodemus stood openly as Christ's friend. It was Nicodemus who assisted Joseph of Arimathea in preparing the body of Christ for burial.

Conclusion

The conversion of some people is seen in immediate and dramatic change. For others like Nicodemus we must be patient to find equally impressive evidences of a change brought about by a new birth. We must not neglect those who, because of the higher degree of their education or status or wealth, seem to overshadow us. They need Christ as much as others.

SUNDAY MORNING, DECEMBER 24

Title: Immanuel—God with Us

Text: "They shall call his name Immanuel; which is, being interpreted, God with us" *(Matt. 1:23).*

Scripture Reading: Matthew 1:21–25

Hymns: "Hail, Thou Long-Expected Jesus," Wesley

"Joy to the World, the Lord Is Come," Watts

"O Little Town of Bethlehem," Brooks

Offertory Prayer: Father, we thank you for Jesus. You gave your Son to the world because you loved the world. We know you still love the world. We love it too. We bring our gifts so that the world may know of your love in Jesus Christ, in whose name we pray. Amen.

Introduction

"What's in a name? That which we call a rose by any other name would smell as sweet." Shakespeare was right insofar as he went, but he was not writing of rational and responsible human beings. Many a young man has experienced the challenge of a great name given him by ambitious parents. There is an interesting story concerning Napoleon's name. On one occasion a coward who was about to desert from Napoleon's army was brought before the general. "What's your name, son?" asked Napoleon. Fearfully the lad replied, "My name is Napoleon, sir." Sternly the general spoke, "Change your ways or change your name."

I had a Nigerian friend whose name was Immanuel. It was his Christian name, for he was born into a pagan environment. If someone in his native country asked Immanuel the meaning of his strange name, he replied, "It means 'God with us.'" To his countrymen his name was quite important. And to those who believe, the name at the center of the Christmas story is life-changing. The stars in the heavens, the lights on the trees, the sparkling icicles—all are intended to illuminate this truth: "Immanuel—God with us."

I. Immanuel: God with us in prosperity.

A. *In every experience "God with us" may be a reality.* We do not always consider God in times of prosperity, but he is with us in prosperity. God knows what happiness is. Look deeply into the eyes of parents or even grandparents when the news of a healthy new baby is announced. God knows about that happiness—he had a son born too.

The Babe of Bethlehem grew up, as Luke describes it, "in wisdom and in stature and in favor with God and man." He was attractive and drew many friends to himself. God knows what personal popularity is. On one occasion 5,000 men along with women and children gathered around him. He fed them with spiritual food and then with physical food, and they thought so highly of him that they wanted to make him king. He, knowing full well what personal popularity is, withdrew into the mountain to pray.

344

B. *One of the joys of the Christmas season is the renewal of friendship.* The cards you receive remind you that others are thinking of you. Likewise, the cards you send let others know that you are thinking of them. God knows about this close fellowship with friends. His son entered into the merriment at the marriage feast in Cana of Galilee. A wedding was the most joyous occasion in the ancient Near East. Jesus seems to have taken great delight in the supper at Bethany with his friends Mary, Martha, and Lazarus. These were good friends. One of his last acts was to cement the fellowship with his disciples in the Last Supper at Jerusalem. He treasured these friends. God knows what happiness is. "Immanuel—God with us."

C. *His presence will always make a difference.* Perhaps this is the reason he is not always welcome. If God is with you, he will have an interest in the way you use your influence. He is very demanding and has little patience with the individual who capitalizes on his church relationships or his divine faculties for personal aggrandizement. Do not take "Immanuel" lightly.

II. Immanuel: God with us in adversity.

A. *Immanuel may be realized in adversity also.* Indeed, the first use of the term as a proper name in the Old Testament was in such a circumstance. In the eighth century BC, Rezin, the king of Syria, and Pekah, the king of Israel, went up to Jerusalem while Ahaz was king of Judah to make war against it but could not prevail. As soon as Ahaz heard the news, he was petrified—or, as the prophet writes, "So the hearts of Ahaz and his people were shaken, as the trees of the forest are shaken by the wind" (Isa. 7:2 NIV). The Lord God sent Isaiah to the king to quiet his fears and told him to take his son Shear-Jashub along. The son's name means "a remnant will return." He challenged the king's faith: "If you do not stand firm in your faith, you will not stand at all" (v. 9 NIV).

The Lord spoke through the prophet to Ahaz, "Ask the LORD your God for a sign" (v. 11 NIV). The king, a pious fraud, refused to "tempt" the Lord by asking for a sign. The prophet replied sharp: "The LORD himself will give you a sign: The virgin will be with child and will give birth to a son, and will call him Immanuel. . . .Before the boy knows enough to reject the wrong and choose the right, the land of the two kings you dread will be laid waste" (vv. 14–16 NIV). Of course it turned out that way: Isaiah's own wife bore a son and the prophet named him Maher-Shalal-Hash-Baz, which means "quick to the plunder, swift to the spoil." The message to Ahaz in trembling fear was simple and straightforward, "Immanuel—God with us."

B. *God knows what sorrow is.* He saw the crowds reject his Son. In the last hours, when his need was greatest, his loneliness was greatest. Few fathers have witnessed the crucifixion of a son as a criminal whose only fault was obedience to the heavenly Father.

It is because God has known such deep sorrow that we count his presence in sorrow a blessing. God is still around when friends forsake us. He is with us in all kinds of adversity. Even those who have completely ignored the Lord God and his church most of their lives will find the ministry of that church welcome in their last hours. He is there if you'll let him be: "Immanuel—God with us."

III. Immanuel: God with us in opportunity.

A. *God will be with us in opportunity—if we will permit it.* God knows what opportunity is. See his Son again at a well in Samaria. It wasn't a very large opportunity—just a woman, a Samaritan woman at that, who came to the well for water. But Jesus gave her water that was not from the well; like a fountain of eternal life, it sprang up within her. He knows what opportunity is.

B. *His presence with us reveals opportunities.* Often in prayer these doors of opportunity open. Our vision is much keener at prayer time. You may need to pray for such a door to open. If you do, pray that it will be an opportunity to serve others and not yourself. If you do, pray that the opportunity will clarify your witness and not glorify yourself. No opportunity that glorifies self or dims our witness is a God-given opportunity.

Conclusion

Keep your eyes open to see the door of opportunity when it opens. God's presence with us changes opportunity to responsibility. When we realize "Immanuel—God with us," we recognize his presence in the "least of these," his brethren. What a halo of responsibility shines about these opportunities—what an aura of heavenly light illumines these who are like sheep without a shepherd. Listen to—no, look at that boy or girl, at that young person, at that senior adult, at that parent. When you see responsibility in these opportunities, then you are near the reality, "Immanuel—God with us." In the power and wisdom of the Holy Spirit who is, in our own experience, "God with us," you can see and understand and serve.

God has tasted the dregs of human misfortune and enjoyed the wine of human happiness. He is "Immanuel—God with us" from our youth to our old age, in good times and bad. We can count on God to be with us if we walk by faith with him.

SUNDAY EVENING, DECEMBER 24

Title: Home for Christmas

Text: "Everyone went to his own town to register" *(Luke 2:3 NIV)*.

Scripture Reading: Luke 2:1–7

Introduction

Since both Joseph and Mary were descendants of David, it was necessary for them to go to Bethlehem of Judea, the city of David, for the taxation enrollment. Little did Caesar Augustus know that by his decree he was an instrument in the divine plan to bring about the fulfillment of prophecy concerning the birth of the Messiah.

Nat King Cole made the Christmas song "I'll Be Home for Christmas" popular. All of us know about crowded bus stations, train stations, airports, and highways during the Christmas season. It seems that everyone is trying to get home for Christmas. On that first Christmas Mary and Joseph were in Bethlehem by the decree of Caesar Augustus for registration and in divine fulfillment of prophecy. They were home for Christmas. Jesus was to be born in Bethlehem.

Why do people go home for Christmas? Let me suggest some answers.

I. Home for Christmas because home is God's primary institution.

A. *God himself established the home.* God said, "The LORD God said, It is not good that the man should be alone; I will make him an help meet for him" (Gen. 2:18).

He also said, "Therefore shall a man leave his father and his mother, and shall cleave unto his wife: and they shall be one flesh" (Gen. 2:24).

B. *The home is God's primary institution, God's first institution.* Helen Hunt Jackson said, "The woman who creates and sustains a home, and under whose hands children grow up to be strong and pure men and women is a creator second only to God."

We ought to major in the making of a home. A reporter asked Henry Ford when he celebrated his golden wedding anniversary, "To what do you attribute your fifty years of successful married life?" Ford replied, "The formula is the same I've used in the making of cars—stick to one model!"

II. Home for Christmas because your loved ones are there.

Strange concepts are associated today concerning the home: we routinely hear of wife abuse, husband abuse, and child abuse. If all of these things are taking place and are as widespread as indicated, then many, many homes are without love and without instruction from the Lord.

Christian love makes a difference (Eph. 5:25–33). A true home abounds with love. This means the type of love that is most difficult to give: unconditional love.

The home is the most difficult place to show this type of love because the home is where people know you best. It is easier to get angry at home than it is at your business. It is easier to be selfish at home than it is at a friend's house. But Christ calls us to love regardless of our feelings—he calls us to a commitment to love despite others' wrongs. Only this supernatural love could bring to fruition Sir John Bowring's thought: "The happy family is but an earlier heaven."

Charles Dickens wrote in *The Pickwick Papers*: "Happy, happy Christmas that can win us back to the delusions of our childhood days; that can recall to the old man the pleasures of his youth; that can transport the sailor and traveler, thousands of miles away, back to his own fireside and his quiet home."

III. Home for Christmas because at home you are somebody.

You cannot be replaced at home. No one can take your place. Regardless of how many times you marry, a child will only have one father, one mother, and a set number of sisters and brothers. No one else can take their places.

Someone said: "Home is where the great are small and the small are great."

IV. Home for Christmas because at home you are loved.

In a true home there is love: love for each other, love for all. An appropriate adage is: "A smart woman can keep springtime in her husband's eyes by keeping a fresh flower in her hair. The husband can keep springtime in his heart by supplying the flower."

Conclusion

We all long to be home for Christmas, but how much better to be in our heavenly home for eternity. Are you on your way to the heavenly home? Let's get a glimpse of that place by reading Hebrews 11:13–16.

> These all died in faith, not having received the promises, but having seen them afar off, and were persuaded of them, and embraced them, and confessed that they were strangers and pilgrims on the earth. For they that say such things declare plainly that they seek a country. And truly, if they had been mindful of that country from whence they came out, they might have had opportunity to have returned. But now they desire a better country, that is, an heavenly: wherefore God is not ashamed to be called their God: for he hath prepared for them a city.

We have two challenges before us then. First, we have to ask Christ to help us make our earthly homes like our heavenly home. Second, we need to see how compelling and sweet our heavenly home is. We should work hard at the first without losing sight of the second. Let's pray that we may be wise and faithful.

WEDNESDAY EVENING, DECEMBER 27

Title: The Samaritan Woman

Text: "There cometh a woman of Samaria to draw water; Jesus saith unto her, 'Give me to drink'" *(John 4:7).*

Scripture Reading: John 4:3–42

Introduction

The vast spectrum of our Lord's love is illustrated as we move from chapter 3 of John, where he deals with a very religious, upright man to chapter 4, where he deals with a self-confessed adulteress. If we would be like our Lord, we must have an equally unlimited and uninhibited compassion for others, regardless of their sins.

I. The situation.

A. *Place.* Very clearly it is stated in verse 4 that this incident took place at Jacob's well. This was not far from Sychar, which is generally identified with the modern city of Askar. Joseph's tomb was nearby.

B. *Time.* This experience of our Lord occurred during his Judean ministry. The exact hour is given by John as being the sixth hour, which would probably be noon. The reason the time is noted by John was probably his recalling the physical exhaustion of Christ occasioned by a long journey.

Perhaps another reason John noted that it was at noon was that a woman of this person's reputation would not come in the evening when most women came, but rather at noon to avoid the crowd.

II. Method.

A. *Description of the woman.* These verses give a detailed description of this woman. She is said to have been a Samaritan (v. 7) and was probably of the city of Sychar. It is obvious that she was well versed in the history and tradition of her people. Just as many people may be well versed in the history and tradition of religion today and yet not be saved.

Christ reminded her that she had lived with five men, and the man with whom she was now living was not her husband. As most individuals would do, she immediately tried to change the subject (v. 19). The Samaritan woman believed that there would be a messiah and that he would come in due time (v. 25).

At first she was astonished at being spoken to in such a friendly manner by a national enemy. She reminded Christ that traditionally the Jews and Samaritans were at odds. She was also spiritually poverty-stricken and bankrupt, and in her heart she knew this to be fact.

B. *Method.* In verse 7 Christ opened the way for friendly conversation. He adapted his speech to hers and gradually unveiled the truth for her. He finally unveiled himself as the Giver of the gift (v. 14). Christ brought her face-to-face with her helplessness and recognized her potential value to the kingdom of God.

Verse 15 indicates that Jesus aroused within the woman an interest in spiritual things. He expressed confidence in her and took occasion from common topics of conversation to introduce spiritual truths. In so doing he used the analogy of water to communicate a profound truth. It is to our own advantage to learn that in witnessing, Christ avoided unnecessary conflict (vv. 12–13). In asking a small favor from her, he expressed confidence in her kindness (v. 7), and this served further to open the door of opportunity.

III. Result.

Unlike the experience of Nicodemus, we see immediate and positive results of this encounter. Verse 28 tells us there was a positive separation—she "left her waterpot." There seems to have been a dawning understanding as she asked if this could be the Christ (v. 29).

In addition to herself, a large number of other people were saved. Some were saved through the testimony of the Samaritan woman herself (v. 39). Others were saved through the direct witness of Jesus Christ (v. 42).

Conclusion

That we should accept people where they are, addressing them in language they can understand, is clearly illustrated by this encounter of Christ. Our Lord teaches us by his own example that in seeking to win others to him we should avoid unnecessary conflict and avoid the temptation of being led astray into peripheral issues. Through it all we must state the main issue: a person's need for Christ and Christ's ability to meet that need.

SUNDAY MORNING, DECEMBER 31

Title: God Is Able

Text: "Whatsoever is born of God overcometh the world: and this is the victory that overcometh the world, even our faith" *(1 John 5:4).*

Scripture Reading: 1 John 5:1–21

Hymns: "Have Faith in God," McKinney

        "O for a Thousand Tongues," Wesley

        "Make Me a Blessing," Wilson

Offertory Prayer: Holy heavenly Father, we thank you for all of the blessings that you have so abundantly bestowed on us during this year. We thank you for truly being "Immanuel: God with us" every day. As we face the new year, we thank you that you are the God who is available and is able to help us become all that you would have us to be. We give ourselves afresh to you that the coming year might be better than the past. In Jesus' name. Amen.

Introduction

Most of us have listened in on the conversation of little children who boast of their father's prowess: "My father is smarter than your father" or "My father is stronger than your father." It is enough for us to say about our Father that he is able to do anything!

God is a worker. Jesus said of him, "My Father worketh, and I work." We gather in the name then of one who is a worker.

I. God is able in us to overcome the world.

A. *He has chosen to overcome the world through us, much as he chose to do it in his Son.* We are born to overcome the world. We sing, "Faith is the victory" and thereby do not make confident assertion of our own abilities, but declare our dependence on God. Jesus challenged us, "Be not overcome with evil, but overcome evil with good." What an exciting prospect!

B. *The incarnation is a pledge of victory over the world.* The Scripture passage offers a series of spiral translations by way of transition. Note them:

    1. "Whosoever believeth that Jesus is Christ is begotten of God!"

    2. "Whatsover is begotten of God overcometh the world."

    3. "Who is he that overcometh the world but he that believeth that Jesus is the Son of God?"

    4. "We know that whosoever is begotten of God does not dwell in sin."

5. "We know that he that was begotten of God keepeth him."
6. "We know that we are of God."

To confess that God was in Christ reconciling the world to himself is to believe that God is able to overcome the world.

II. God is able to give assurance.

A. *This challenges our faith.* Here are three witnesses, and we remember that in Jewish law "at the mouth of three witnesses every word shall stand." Nor were these things done in a corner. God's ability has been manifested. Look at the empty tomb!

B. *We have the witness of the incarnation, the Spirit, and the Word.* Perhaps you will choose to add the witness of John's baptism, Jesus' death and resurrection, and the Spirit's presence. Those who reject these witnesses declare God to be a liar!

III. God is able to give life.

A. *Now life is more powerful than death.* This too was demonstrated in the resurrection. God gave his Son life. Now he gives his children life in his Son. This is about all the truth most of us can absorb. An eight-year-old boy accepting Christ does not understand the meaning of the incarnation, but he can have life.

B. *All of this is a word of assurance.* Let me read some of the verses in a somewhat freer form. [Read 1 John 5:13–20 from a modern paraphrase of the Bible.]

God is able to give life!

IV. God is able to answer prayer.

A. *There is a postscript to the letter in the words "if we ask anything" (v. 15).* God hears us when we pray. This ought not be as incredible as before the days of radio and television. Ethel Romig Fuller has written:

> *If radio's slim fingers*
> *Can pluck a melody*
> *From night, and toss it over*
> *A continent or sea;*
> *If the petaled white notes*
> *Of a violin*
> *Are blown across an ocean,*
> *Or a city's din;*
> *If songs, like crimson roses,*
> *Are plucked from thin blue air,*
> *Why should mortals wonder*
> *If God hears prayer?*

God hears us and he grants our petitions. This is our faith. The strong statement in Mark 11:24 is a challenge: Believe that you have it, and it will be yours! If we ask in terms of God's will, the answer is yes; if not, then the answer is no, to make it accord with his will.

B. *God helps our friends.* Of course the prayer of brother for brother, addressed to the common Father, is out of the question where brotherhood has been renounced. For in prayer we are "bound together with gold chains about the feet of God."

But there is an aura of mystery here. Somewhere beyond the ability of God, inherent in creation and in the eternal purpose of God and basic to the nature of God, is a self-imposed inability. The author himself seems unsure about a "sin unto death." This is a sin that leads to death, but then sin always approaches death.

In the midst of the mystery, there are some things we know: God is able to make us know, for this is a book of assurance as well as affirmations. It is clear in verses 13–15.

Conclusion

God is able to save you. God is able to make your life worthwhile. God is able to answer your prayer. God is love, and so he is willing to do these things. He is both willing and able!

SUNDAY EVENING, DECEMBER 31

Title: He Cared Enough to Send the Very Best

Text: "For God so loved the world, that he gave his only begotten Son, that whosoever believeth in him should not perish, but have everlasting life" *(John 3:16).*

Scripture Reading: Luke 2:1–20; John 3:16

Introduction

The Hallmark greeting card slogan, "When you care enough to send the very best," can be applied to God's gift of love: God thought enough of us to send his very best.

Benjamin J. Hanby wrote:

> *Who is He in yonder stall,*
> *At whose feet the shepherds fall? . . .*
> *'Tis the Lord! O wondrous story!*
> *'Tis the Lord, the King of glory!*
> *At His feet we humbly fall—*
> *Crown Him! Crown Him, Lord of all!*

God sent his best for us—his Son, the Lord Jesus Christ!

I. God thought enough to send his best when he sent his only begotten Son and not another (John 3:16).

A. *John 3:16 has been called the little gospel, the comfortable Word, an epitome of the whole gospel, and a marvelous interpretation of the mission and message of our Lord.*

B. *"God so loved the world. . . . "* The word "loved" refers to love in its highest form. The word here has reference to God's love for humans (Rom. 5:8; Eph. 2:4; 2 Thess. 2:16). The word can also refer to one person's love for another (John 13:34).

C. *". . . that he gave his only begotten Son. . . . "* These words refer to Jesus' eternal relationship with the Father. God sent the best he had—his only begotten Son.

D. *". . . that whosoever believeth in him should not perish, but have everlasting life."* Jesus accomplished what he was sent to do.

II. God thought enough to send his best when he sent light, not darkness, to the whole world.

A. *Christ as the light of the world is a theme throughout Scripture.* Here are just a few pertinent passages:

"The people walking in darkness have seen a great light; on those living in the land of the shadow of death a light has dawned" (Isa. 9:2 NIV).

"In him was life, and that life was the light of men" (John 1:4 NIV).

"This is the verdict: men loved darkness instead of light because their deeds were evil" (John 3:19 NIV).

"When Jesus spoke again to the people, he said, 'I am the light of the world. Whoever follows me will never walk in darkness, but will have the light of life'" (John 8:12 NIV).

B. *There are at least three ways in which Christ is the Light of the World.*
1. He is the light for the world's darkness.
2. He is the light for the world's disillusionment.
3. He is the light to give direction to the people of all the world.

Jesus points the way. His words are a map. He furnishes the light. We lose our way, and darkness envelops us. He is the brightest light that ever dawned on the world. We must follow him or walk in darkness.

III. God thought enough to send his best—to bring us together.

Because of God's best, "there is neither Jew nor Greek, slave nor free, male nor female, for you are all one in Christ Jesus" (Gal. 3:28 NIV).

Eternal life is a blessed state begun on earth and continued forever. Without the cross of Christ, people could not have eternal life. People are brought to God by him, and they are brought together by him.

Hymnwriter Edgar John Hopkins wrote:

The wise may bring their learning,
The rich may bring their wealth;
And some may bring their greatness,
And some bring strength and health;
We, too, would bring our treasures
To offer to the King;
We have no wealth or learning,
What shall we children bring?

We'll bring Him hearts that love Him,
We'll bring Him thankful praise,
And young souls meekly striving
To walk in holy ways;
And these shall be the treasures
We offer to the King
And these gifts that even
The poorest child may bring.

Conclusion

On that first Christmas, God thought enough of us to send his best—his only begotten Son, Jesus Christ! Without Christ life would be brutish. With Christ life can be blessed. Follow him now!

MESSAGE ON THE LORD'S SUPPER

Title: Communion

Text: "Where can I go from your Spirit? Where can I flee from your presence? If I go up to the heavens, you are there; if I make my bed in the depths, you are there. If I rise on the wings of the dawn, if I settle on the far side of the sea, even there your hand will guide me, your right hand will hold me fast" *(Ps. 139:7–10 NIV).*

Introduction

God is everywhere. There is no place where he is not present, except in hell. The essence of hell is the absence of God, separation of the soul from its maker.

The author of Psalm 139 wrote about escaping from God's omnipresence but discovered that he could not. Later another poet, Francis Thompson, described this inescapable divine presence as "the hound of heaven" with feet that "follow, follow after."

The divine presence that is everywhere is focused in our worship. John Calvin called this "Word and sacrament," Scripture and the ordinances. God encounters us, and we are never again the same. Consider three encounters with God recorded in the Scriptures.

I. Jacob.

Jacob and his mother, Rebekah, tricked his blind father, Isaac, and stole his elder brother, Esau's, inheritance. Then, en route to Haran to find a bride, Jacob unexpectedly encountered God. Listen to what happened. [Read Gen. 28:10–19.]

Using a stone for a pillow, Jacob dreamed of a ladder that reached from earth to heaven—with angels going up and down it. The ladder is a reminder of God's providential care through the ministry of his angels. It also foreshadows the incarnation—that night when God himself came down the ladder at Bethlehem with a baby in his arms.

Jacob's experience was awe-inspiring: He said, "Surely the LORD is in this place, and I was not aware of it. How awesome is this place! This is none other than the house of God; this is the gate of heaven" (Gen. 28:16–17 NIV). Jacob named the place Bethel, meaning "house of God." He set up a stone pillar and worshiped God there.

II. Isaiah.

Isaiah was a sensitive young man who was grieving at the death of his friend King Uzziah. At worship in the temple, he had a vision and heard the call of

God. Listen. [Read Isa. 6:1–8.] Isaiah felt unworthy. His lips were purified with a coal from the altar. He gave a ready answer to God's call, unlike Moses, who was hesitant.

III. Two at Emmaus.

Luke 24:13–35 helps us see this third cameo of encounter. The risen Christ walked beside the two disciples from Jerusalem to Emmaus (seven miles). They recognized him in the breaking of bread.

Notice these observations about the three encounters.

A. *They occurred to very different people.* Jacob was a crook, a trickster. He was a sinner unworthy of divine grace. (So are we all.) Isaiah was a young aristocrat, a courtier at the king's palace. The two at Emmaus were a couple of Jesus' disciples.

B. *They occurred at very different places.* Jacob met the Lord at a campsite. Isaiah encountered him at worship in the temple in Jerusalem. Those at Emmaus realized they were in the presence of Christ at their dinner table.

C. *The common denominator in these three encounters was crisis.* Jacob was fleeing the wrath of his brother, Esau. Isaiah was grieving the loss of his friend, King Uzziah. The two at Emmaus had experienced the death of their fondest dream. They said to Jesus, "We had hoped that he was the one who was going to redeem Israel" (Luke 24:21 NIV). Note the pathos of their crushed dream: all three encounters involved personal crisis. That is not the only way in which God comes to us, but it is one way. C. S. Lewis contended that God whispers in our pleasures but shouts in our pain.

Conclusion

The risen Christ is very much alive. We are apt to meet him in our worship at the table—a reminder of the crisis of the cross. Be sensitive to the divine presence.

1. Hear his *claim* on us: "Follow me and I will make you fishers of men" (Matt. 4:19).
2. Hear his *offer* to us: "If we confess our sins, he is faithful and just to forgive us our sins, and to cleanse us from all unrighteousness" (1 John 1:9).
3. Be aware of his *presence* with us: "I will not leave you comfortless; I will come to you" (John 14:18).

MESSAGES FOR CHILDREN AND YOUNG PEOPLE

Title: Keeping Our Appointments with God

Text: "Now the eleven disciples went to Galilee to the mountain to which Jesus had directed them" *(Matt. 28:16 RSV)*.

Introduction

One of the most exciting experiences in a young person's life is the first date. However, most young people have appointments of one sort or another long before they are old enough to have a date.

Have you ever had a date with the dentist? Most of us do not look forward to that. Have you ever had an appointment with your doctor? Of course you have. Have you ever had an appointment with one of your parents to make a trip or to go to a ball game or to do something else that was exciting?

You may be surprised to learn that Jesus made appointments with his disciples. He has also made appointments with us.

I. We have an appointment with our Lord in Bible study.

As we study the Bible, God wants to speak to us. He wants to assure us of his love. He wants to invite us to live a life of faith and faithfulness. He wants to warn us about dangers in life that could bring great harm to us.

He also wants to extend invitations to us that will make it possible for us to live an abundant life. He wants to assure us that spiritual resources are available for living a victorious life.

II. We have an appointment with our Lord in the closet of prayer.

"But when you pray, go to your room, and shut the door and pray to your Father who is in secret; and your Father who sees in secret will reward you" (Matt. 6:6 RSV).

The King James Version of the Bible speaks about the "closet" for prayer. It is really speaking about entering into a secret place with God where you can converse with him. It is much easier to do this in secret, but it is possible to talk with God while in a public place in the middle of a throng of people.

Jesus did encourage us to have the habit of keeping an appointment with God in prayer every day and even several times a day.

In our prayers we can thank God for his blessings. We can confess our sins and experience forgiveness.

III. We have an appointment with our Lord in worship.

Jesus encouraged his disciples with the promise to bless them with his presence when they came together for worship: "For where two or three are gathered in my name, there am I in the midst of them" (Matt. 18:20 RSV).

Who do you expect to be present during a worship service? You expect the pastor to be present. You expect the song leader to be present. Perhaps you would expect your parents and friends to be present. By faith you can even expect the living Lord to be present.

God communicates with you in a variety of ways. He will speak to you through the Scriptures if you are listening. He will speak to you through the hymns if you are listening. He will speak to you through your pastor's message if you are listening. He will speak to you through the presence of significant people if you are listening.

Some people are always dependable in keeping their appointments. Some people are always late for their appointments. Some people forget or ignore their appointments. The way they handle their appointments shows their priorities. If you want to live an abundant life, keep your appointments with God.

Title: The Best News

Text: "Be not afraid; for behold, I bring you good news of a great joy which shall come to all the people" *(Luke 2:10 RSV).*

Introduction

What is the best news you ever heard?

Can you remember responding joyfully to the good news that your grandparents were going to come to see you? Have you ever rejoiced over the news that some cousins were coming to visit?

How many of you have rejoiced over the good news of a new baby brother or sister?

Have you had the privilege of rejoicing over the news that you were going to receive a favorite toy for your birthday or at Christmas?

Have you ever heard good news about moving to a new home or new school?

Have you ever brought good news home to your parents when you receive a report card with high marks?

What is the best news you have ever heard? Would we all agree that the best news is that which the angel spoke to the shepherds concerning the birth of Christ? The coming of Christ brought the best news that can possibly be brought to human ears. But why is this such good news?

I. The good news that God is love.

Some people think of God only as being powerful and mighty and righteous and holy. They think of him as being a judge to whom we must all give an account someday.

Jesus came as the full disclosure of God's loving heart to all humankind (John 3:16). God always has loved us. God always will love us. God loves us not because we are good, but because he chooses to love us. This means he cares for us and wants the best for us.

II. The good news regarding forgiveness.

All of us are sinners. All of us are prone to mistakes. All of us fall short of the goal of what we ought to be and what we ought to do. We have been guilty of disobedience. We have even failed to live up to our own standards for ourselves. We stand in need of forgiveness.

God offers us the gift of forgiveness when we receive Jesus Christ through repentance and faith.

III. The good news concerning eternal life.

"For God so loved the world that he gave his only begotten Son, that whosoever believeth in him should not perish but have everlasting life" (John 3:16).

In the new birth, God gives us his kind of life. Eternal life is about more than quantity. It is about quality as well. The gift of eternal life enables us to love as God loves and causes us to want to live as Jesus lived.

As followers of Jesus, we need to live as citizens of heaven here on earth. This means that we should live for something more than material values. We should live for God and for others.

IV. Good news regarding the future.

Most of us worry about the future. Many worry about death and eternity. The angel spoke of good news through the birth of Christ, and that includes good news regarding death and eternity.

For the Christian, death is not destruction; it is going to be with God in his home, which the Bible calls heaven. It is very good news to know that the Father God is providing for us a home in heaven. How have you responded to this good news? Have you neglected to hear it? Have you been so busy listening to other things that you did not hear it?

Conclusion

You would be very wise to respond to the good news of God in and through Jesus Christ. Let him become your Savior and Lord. It's the best news you'll ever get.

Title: Learning to Have Faith in God

Text: "Without faith it is impossible to please him. For whoever would draw near to God must believe that he exists and that he rewards those who seek him" *(Heb. 11:6 RSV).*

Introduction

The Bible is a book about faith. The Bible encourages us to have faith in God. The words of our text define the nature of faith and emphasize its importance.

Faith is the sincere belief that God is and that he is the kind of God who rewards those who seek him.

Faith is an activity in which all of us participate at all points in our lives.

I. We begin life with faith in our parents.

Little children depend on their parents for caring concern that continues day by day. Infants may protest when they do not receive food immediately but don't worry about earning a living to buy that food. In a very real sense, children depend totally on their parents for nourishment, affection, and protection.

II. We enter school by faith.

We believe that we can trust teachers to give us an education. We depend on teachers to instruct us and assist us in the learning process. Without teachers we would be greatly handicapped at the point of developing our minds and our skills. We are fortunate if we can believe that our teachers will be helpful always.

III. We give expression to faith when we travel.

Every time we get in an automobile or a bus or an airplane, we demonstrate faith in the driver or the crew in charge. We believe not only that they exist but also that they will deliver us safely to the desired destination. If we did not believe this, we would hesitate to enter a vehicle to make a trip.

IV. We express faith when we go to a restaurant.

When we go to a restaurant, we assume there is a cook somewhere who prepares the food. We assume that the cook is a good cook. When we eat the food, we demonstrate faith that it has been prepared properly and that it does not contain anything that would harm our health.

V. Each of us needs to have faith in God.

While it may be easy to accept the faith of your parents, you must put faith in God for yourself. What is that type of faith?

A. *Real faith is believing that God is.*

B. *Real faith is believing that God is good.* The Bible gives evidence that God is good. Nature tells us that God has made good provisions for us. The coming of Jesus Christ and all that this implies is the supreme evidence that God is good.

C. *Real faith is deciding to depend on God with the same kind of faith that we use when we depend on parents, teachers, automobile drivers, and cooks.*

Conclusion

We must put faith in God for the forgiveness of our sin. We need to put faith in God to receive the gift of eternal life. We need to put faith in God for guidance and help each day. We can learn about God and be encouraged to trust him by reading the Bible and depending on him to do for us as he has promised.

FUNERAL MEDITATIONS

Title: Sorrow Not as the Hopeless

Text: "I would not have you to be ignorant, brethren, concerning them which are asleep, that ye sorrow not, even as others which have no hope" *(1 Thess. 4:13).*

Introduction

You are experiencing the pain of loss. Grief taps many emotions, including shock and disbelief. This came so suddenly, so unexpectedly, that it does not seem real. It is like a bad dream from which you expect to awaken. Sometimes when we lose someone in death, we have feelings of anger at the unfairness of our loss. We may even have feelings of guilt that we did not do everything we might have. We may have periods of depression. But the healing of time and grace will bring eventual acceptance.

I. Grief with hope.

Grief can be therapeutic for Christians, because at the bottom there is hope. A pagan's sorrow is without hope of a future resurrection. This can lead only to denial of the reality of death, or despair.

By contrast, a Christian's sorrow is anchored in the hope of the resurrection—Christ's and our own. Death for a believer is sleep in God's eternal now. At our resurrection we will awaken in the presence of Christ. He who lives in Christ and dies in Christ will rise in Christ at the last day.

II. Hope because of Jesus.

In his book *Creative Suffering*, Paul Tournier writes, "The Christian hope which inspires me is not a thing, but a Person—not that little thing . . . forgotten at the bottom of Pandora's box . . . no, a person. The person of Jesus . . . who is alive . . . and who is awaiting us beyond death, where he told us that he would prepare a place for us (John 14:2)."

III. A new view of death.

If only we could glimpse death through God's eyes, for then it would lose its terror. He has pulled its sting. Death is an end to tears, pain, and the limitations of this mortal body. Death is a continuation of life abundant in Christ's presence. You may watch a ship sail over the horizon. It is beyond your sight, but it is still steaming toward its destination—the harbor and home.

Death from God's point of view also marks a glad new beginning in fellowship with himself and all the saints who have gone on before us. Think of the glad reunion that awaits us on the other side.

"We know that if the earthly tent we live in is destroyed, we have a building from God, an eternal house in heaven, not built by human hands" (2 Cor. 5:1 NIV).

Conclusion

We find comfort in the Word of God and in the warm memory of our loved one. God the Holy Spirit stands with us even now to be our Comforter.

"May the God of hope fill you with all joy and peace in believing, so that you abound in hope by the power of the Holy Spirit" (Rom. 15:13 NASB).

Title: "Death Be Not Proud, Thou Too Shalt Die"

Text: "Lo, I tell you a mystery. We shall not all sleep, but we shall all be changed, in a moment, in the twinkling of an eye, at the last trumpet. For the trumpet will sound, and the dead will be raised imperishable, and we shall be changed.... Death is swallowed up in victory.... Thanks be to God" *(1 Cor. 15:51–52, 54, 57 RSV)*.

Introduction

Death wears a double face. From this side death appears to be destruction. We are cut off from the living. Death is tragic. But from the other side death is viewed not as destruction, but as departure; it is a new beginning with the Lord.

I. From the other side death is glorious.

Human beings have been called the great amphibians, for we are made for two worlds—earth and heaven. We should acknowledge the reality of both.

Death is real. We should not attempt to deny death. It is universal, the lot for us all. Jesus shrank from death in the agony of Gethsemane. His sheer humanity is nowhere more obvious than there. But death came even to Jesus.

II. The conquering of death.

Easter made the difference. It tore the mask from death and showed it to be merely a departure and not total destruction. By his resurrection Jesus brought immortality to light. He gave us bright hope; "Death is swallowed up in victory." John Donne wrote, "Death, be not proud. Death, thou too shalt die."

One day when Christ returns, we who have lived and died in Christ will be clothed with immortality. We will receive a new glorified resurrection body.

Conclusion

Fanny Crosby wrote this now familiar song:

> *One day the silver cord will break,*
> *And I no more as now shall sing.*
> *But, oh the joy when I shall wake*
> *Within the palace of the King.*
>
> *Then I shall see Him face to face*
> *And sing the story—saved by grace.*

Title: Salt of the Earth

Text: "Ye are the salt of the earth" *(Matt. 5:13).*

Hymn: "Saved by Grace," Crosby

Introduction

Salt is a common commodity today and is inexpensive. In ancient times salt was very costly. In Rome a main road is named Via Salaria or "The Way of Salt." That name is said to date from ancient times, when a Roman soldier could have been paid in salt. Even today we still have common expressions such as, "He is the salt of the earth." We also say that someone is "not worth his salt."

When Jesus called his followers the salt of the earth, he paid them a high compliment. Salt stands for character and integrity. Note that Jesus did not say, "You may become the salt of the earth." Saltiness is not our potential; it is our reality. Let's examine the attributes of salt to understand our reality better.

I. Salt flavors food.

Salt adds zest to life. Salt gives itself; it is not an extract. Jesus was a man for others, and so are his followers. Salt makes its presence quietly but effectively known. So does a person who is the salt of the earth.

II. Salt symbolizes purity.

We need purity of thought, word, and deed. Those who are pure of heart are pronounced blessed in the beatitudes of Jesus. A Danish sculptor, Thorwaldsen, produced a famous statue of Christ. The French government wanted to commission Thorwaldsen to make a statue of Venus. He refused, saying that the hands that carved the figure of Christ would never carve a pagan goddess.

III. Salt also preserves.

In much the same way, good men and women preserve society. Recall that God promised to spare Sodom if there were ten righteous people living there. Moreover, before he destroyed it, God made sure that Lot was out of the city.

Conclusion

Being the salt of the earth does not allow for hermit theology. Salt penetrates and preserves society. It gives itself and readily shares its faith and power. It is a high compliment to call someone "the salt of the earth."

Title: The Shepherd Psalm

Text: Psalm 23

Introduction

This favorite Old Testament passage is a simple and profound affirmation of personal faith. It is also timeless—three thousand years old.

Psalm 22 is a poem of anguish: "My God, my God, why hast thou forsaken me?" It was quoted by Jesus on the cross. Psalm 24 is a song of triumph: "The earth is the LORD's and the fullness thereof . . . lift up your heads. . . ." Psalm 23 is the bridge psalm between these two—a bridge over troubled waters. Imagine the campfire scene when the shepherd David sang Psalm 23 for the very first time.

I. God as our shepherd.

God is with us here and now as our shepherd who provides for our needs (vv. 1–4). Green pastures are "our daily bread." Still waters quench our thirst and provide peace. "I shall not want."

God leads us. "He leadeth me! O blessed thought! O words with heavenly comfort fraught!" Jesus said he knows his sheep and we know the sound of his voice.

God protects us from a thousand harms, and even in the valley of the shadow of death, we fear no evil, for God is with us. His rod and staff are our protection and comfort.

II. God as our host.

God will be with us hereafter as our host (vv. 5–6). We walk with our Shepherd. We will one day dwell with our Host. Notice the Father's gracious hospitality. He provides food, safety in the midst of enemies, and perfumed oil—necessities as well as life's extras.

God is generous toward his own, providing overflowing abundance. Think how extravagant grace is. It is far beyond anything we could have deserved. An unknown Scot said of this psalm, "The Lord is my Shepherd, aye, and he has two fine collie dogs, goodness and mercy. They will see my safely home."

Conclusion

The psalmist concludes with the bright hope of dwelling in the house of the Lord, in his divine presence forever. Jesus is both the Lamb of God who takes away our sins and the Good Shepherd who gives his life for his sheep. Let us look to Jesus and find comfort for our sorrow and bright hope for tomorrow.

WEDDINGS

Title: A Simple Marriage Ceremony

After making remarks emphasizing the divine origin of marriage, the minister may read Genesis 2:18–24. The Old Testament passage may be followed by a New Testament passage, specifically Ephesians 5:21–33.

The apostle Paul says, "For this cause shall a man leave his father and mother, and shall be joined unto his wife, and they two shall be one flesh" (Eph. 5:31).

Who gives this woman to this man in marriage? (The person replying may say, "I Do" or "Her mother and I do.")

If you, then, beloved,_____ and _____, after careful consideration, and in the fear of God, have deliberately chosen each other as partners in this holy estate, and know of no just cause why you should not be so united, in token thereof you will please join your right hands.

Groom's Vow

_____, will you have this woman to be your wedded wife, to live together after God's ordinance in the holy estate of matrimony? Will you love her, comfort her, honor and keep her, in sickness and in health, and forsaking all others keep yourself only for her so long as you both shall live?

Answer: I will.

Bride's Vow

_____, will you have this man to be your wedded husband, to live together after God's ordinance in the holy estate of matrimony? Will you love him, comfort him, honor and keep him, in sickness and in health, and forsaking all others keep yourself only for him so long as you both shall live?

Answer: I will.

Vows to Each Other

I,_____, take you,_____, to be my wedded wife, to have and to hold from this day forward, in prosperity or adversity, in sickness or in health, in advances or reverses, to love and to cherish till death do us part, according to God's holy ordinance, and thereto I pledge you my troth.

I,_____, take you,_____, to be my wedded husband, to have and to hold from this day forward, in prosperity or adversity, in sickness or in health, in advances or reverses, to love and to cherish till death do us part, according to God's holy ordinance, and thereto I pledge you my troth.

Therefore you are given to each other for richer or poorer, for better or worse, in sickness and in health, till death alone shall part you.

From time immemorial the ring has been used to seal important covenants. The golden circlet, most prized of jewels, has come to its loftiest meaning in the symbolic significance that it vouches at the marriage altar. The ring is made of untarnishable materials; it is of the purest gold. Even so may your love for each other be pure and may it grow brighter and brighter as time goes by. The ring is also a circle, thus having no end. Even so may there be no end to the happiness and success that come to you as you unite your lives together.

365

Do you,_____, give this ring to your wedded wife as a token of your love for her?

Will you,_____, receive this ring as a token of your wedded husband's love for you, and will you wear it as a token of your love for him?

Do you,_____, give this ring to your wedded husband as a token of your love for him?

Will you,_____, receive this ring as a token of your wedded wife's love for you, and will you wear it as a token of your love for her?

Since you have pledged your faith in and love to each other in the sight of God and these assembled witnesses and have sealed your solemn marital vows by giving and receiving the rings, I, therefore, acting in the authority vested in me as a minister of the gospel by this state and looking to heaven for divine sanction, pronounce you husband and wife.

Therefore, what God hath joined together, let no man put asunder.

(Prayer)

Title: A Marriage Ceremony

Weddings are a very special time for a family as well as for the bride and groom. There seem to be a thousand and one details that demand attention.

One matter to be decided is the type of wedding ceremony that will be used. Some couples write their own ceremony, memorize their vows, and recite them during the service. From my perspective as a pastor, this is fine, with two provisions: the ceremony should conform to good taste and to correct Christian theology. Frankly, most couples do well to repeat their vows after the minister.

Some interesting innovations are being introduced to the traditional wedding ceremony. Much of the archaic language has been omitted. As an example, a man no longer says to his bride, "And thereto I plight thee my troth." He probably wouldn't know what he was saying. Neither do most brides any longer promise to "obey him and serve him."

The ceremony that follows is based on the traditional one. However, the language has been modernized, and additional Scripture has been introduced along with new thoughts in the prayers. Perhaps it will prove useful to a prospective bride.

The Marriage Service

Dearly beloved: we are assembled here in the presence of God and these friends to celebrate the joining of this man and this woman in holy matrimony. The covenant of marriage was established by almighty God at creation. It was blessed by the presence of our Lord Jesus Christ as the wedding in Cana of Galilee. It is symbolic of the mystic union between Christ and his church. Marriage is commended in Scripture and is to be honored by all persons.

The uniting of husband and wife in heart, body, and spirit is intended by God for their mutual joy and well-being. Marriage is not to be entered into unadvisedly or lightly, but reverently and in accordance with the purpose for which it was instituted by God.

Into this holy marriage relationship_____ and _____come now to be united.

_____, will you have this woman to be your wife, to live together in the sacred covenant of marriage? Will you love her, comfort her, honor and keep her, in sickness and in health; and forsaking all others, be faithful to her as long as you both shall live?

The man shall answer: I will.

_____, will you have this man to be your husband; to live together in the sacred covenant of marriage? Will you love him, comfort him, honor and keep him, in sickness and in health; forsaking all others, be faithful to him as long as you both shall live?

The woman shall answer: I will.

Will those of you witnessing these promises do all in your power to uphold these two persons in their marriage? If you so agree, please answer, "We will."

The people shall answer: We will.

Who presents this woman to be married to this man?

Father of the bride shall answer: Her mother and I.

Hear the Bible's description of love:

> Love is patient; love is kind and envies no one. Love is never boastful, nor conceited, nor rude; never selfish, not quick to take offense. Love keeps no score of wrongs; does not gloat over the sins of others; but delights in the truth. There is nothing love cannot face; there is no limit to its faith, its hope, and its endurance.
>
> In a word, there are three things that last forever; faith, hope, and love; the greatest of them is love. (1 Cor. 13:4–7, 13 NEB)

_____, you will take _____'s hand and repeat to her after me:

In the name of God, I, _____, take you, _____, to be my wife, to have and to hold, from this day forward, for better or for worse, for richer or for poorer, in sickness and in health, to love and to cherish, as long as we both shall live.

_____, please repeat after me:

In the name of God, I, _____, take you, _____, to be my husband, to have and to hold, from this day forward, for better or for worse, for richer or for poorer, in sickness and in health, to love and to cherish, as long as we both shall live.

The minister shall bless the rings:

Bless, O Lord, these rings, that those who give them and wear them may see them as symbols of their vows and covenant here made. May they abide in your will and continue in your favor throughout all their life, through Jesus Christ our Lord. Amen.

The man shall repeat after the minister:

I give you this ring, as a symbol, of my love and devotion, in the name of the Father, and of the Son, and of the Holy Spirit.

The woman shall repeat after the minister:

I give you this ring, as a symbol, of my love and devotion, in the name of the Father, and of the Son, and of the Holy Spirit.

Let us pray.

Eternal God, creator and preserver of all humankind, the author of everlasting life and giver of all grace: Look with favor upon these your servants, _____ and _____, whom we bless in your name. May they keep the vows and covenant they have made here today. Grant that they may live according to your will with peace, joy, and love. Make their life together a sign of Christ's sacramental presence.

Grant that all married persons who have heard these vows may find their lives strengthened and their loyalties confirmed.

Now hear us as we pray together the model prayer our Lord taught us:

Our Father, who art in heaven, hallowed be thy name. Thy kingdom come, thy will be done, on earth as it is in heaven. Give us this day our daily bread. And forgive us our debts as we forgive our debtors. And lead us not into temptation, but deliver us from evil. For thine is the kingdom, and the power, and the glory forever. Amen.

Since _____ and _____ have consented together in holy matrimony before God and these friends and have exchanged vows and rings; therefore, by the ordinance of God, I pronounce them husband and wife, in the name of God the Father, the Son, and Holy Spirit. Amen.

Whom therefore God has joined together, let not man put asunder.

The couple may kneel.

Benediction: Now may God the Father, God the Son, God the Holy Spirit, bless, preserve, and keep you. The Lord mercifully with his favor look upon you and fill you with all spiritual benediction and grace, that you may faithfully live together in this life, and in the world to come have life everlasting. Amen.

The couple may remain kneeling as a prayer is sung. The couple will rise and light the unity candle.

"For this cause shall a man leave his father and his mother, and cleave to his wife. And they two shall be one."

Congratulations! The groom may kiss the bride.

Recessional

SENTENCE SERMONETTES

A kind word may be incomplete without action.

Life is like a grindstone—it either wears you down or polishes you up.

When we have nothing left but God, then we become aware that God is enough.

To learn the art of giving is to know the joys of living.

Each day is a gift from God wrapped in his love.

Indifference will find an excuse—love will find a way.

You can always tell a failure by the way he or she criticizes success.

A cheerful friend is like a sunny day.

A day that is wasted is gone forever.

Anyone can count the seeds in an apple, but only God can tell how many apples are in a seed.

Blessedness comes not by escape from trouble, but by victory over trouble.

Every little unfolding flower is a gentle reminder of God's great power.

The Light of the World gives a world of light.

Praise starts with grateful hearts.

God's decisions need no revisions.

Christian love goes the second mile with a God-given smile.

Jesus is the Light of the World; Christians are his shining examples.

Home is where you live your life and build your memories.

Sharing comes naturally to those who really care.

The Great Physician still makes house calls.

To watch a flower grow is to witness a little miracle.

America suffers from truth decay.

Faith believes in spite of what the eye can see.

Speak kind words and you will get kind echoes.

If you are a child of God, call home.

There is nothing so dark as a closed mind.

If God seems far away, who moved?

To know God's will is life's greatest treasure. To do God's will is life's greatest pleasure.

Marriage is the union of two good forgivers.

Worry never climbed a hill.

God's mercies are fresh with each new day.

Don't trouble trouble until trouble troubles you.

Daily prayers dissolve your cares.

Jesus is the best news we have to share.

There are no exits in hell.

Each day is a new beginning.

What was the good thing I noticed today?

Death is not an end but an entrance.

A smile is a curve that can set a lot of things straight.

To belittle is to be little.

Life at best is very brief—like the falling of a leaf.

Life is not measured by the years we live, but by what worthwhile things we accomplish during those years.

The greatest gift one person can give another is time.

God will supply, but we must apply.

You get to keep and enjoy only what you share and give away.

SUBJECT INDEX

Abraham, 163
anxiety, 224
"backsliders," 239
belief, 65
Bible, the, 32, 152
bitterness, 218
blessings, 59, 105
born again, 241
children, 147, 357, 358, 359
Christian life, 27, 115, 176, 247, 261, 317, 323, 333, 340, 357, 362
Christmas, 331, 333
church, the, 53, 215, 261, 275, 323; health of, 285; revival of, 84; unity of, 222, 228
church discipline, 234
commitment, 82
consistency, 178
conversion, 256, 330, 335, 342, 348
criticism of others, 200
cross, the, 73
death, 98, 124, 289, 301, 304, 361, 362
deliverance, 124
depression, 236
Devil, the, 55; deliverance from, 124
discipleship, 82, 157, 330, 335
discipline, 184
excellence, 191, 193
faith, 13, 133, 161, 163, 166, 169, 265, 359
faithfulness, 121, 129
family, the, 135, 147, 154, 161, 167, 173, 181, 346
fatherhood, 167
feeling lost, 16
forgiveness, 43, 67, 218
gender roles, 135
giving, 198, 210, 283, 286, 289, 294, 298

God, 188, 344; character of, 145, 350, 352, 364; encountering, 195, 355; knowledge of, 63, 195; promise of, 201; sovereignty of, 318; speech of, 102
Gospel, the, 254, 358
grace, 50, 270, 276, 281, 292
happiness, 18
heaven, 98, 308, 314, 320
hedonism, 193
Holy Spirit, the, 254
home, the, 181
hope, 13, 157
invitation, God's, 188, 208
Jesus, 34, 48, 73, 79, 106, 108, 119, 131, 143, 181, 241, 249, 262, 328, 331, 337, 352, 358
judgment, 55, 95
love, 13, 16, 43, 86, 89, 157, 251, 258; God's, 23, 63
mankind, 25
mercy, 89
Moses, 169
motherhood, 135
needs, 13
Nicodemus, 241
oaths, 226
obedience, 30, 161, 163
Old Testament, the, 137
partiality, 159
patience, 220
Paul, 256
peace, 201
plan, God's, 20
prayer, 36, 75, 133, 232, 291
preaching, 267
prejudice, 159
problems, dealing with, 52
religion, purpose of, 46

repentance, 95

Resurrection, the, 79, 117; challenge of, 129; necessity of, 100, 111: truth of, 93

resurrection of the body, 122

righteousness, 163

sacred things, 41

sacrifice, 163; Jesus', 149

salvation, 58, 59, 63, 65, 270, 312; assurance of, 244, 314, 320

Second Coming, the, 311

self-criticism, 39

serving, 276

sexuality, 297

sin, 71, 77; freedom from, 34, 124

sincerity, 210

sorrow, 304, 362

spiritual health, 280, 285

spiritual rewards, 91

stewardship, 105, 110, 121, 204, 273, 278, 289

suffering, 59, 127, 133, 262

temptation, 145

thanksgiving, 115, 312

trials, 127, 139

wealth, 206, 213, 298, 305, 325

wisdom, 133, 186

witnessing, 20, 141, 275, 348

women, 141

words, 172, 178, 226

world, the, 77

worry, 231

worship, 157

INDEX OF SCRIPTURE TEXTS

Exodus
35:21 278

2 Samuel
18:32–33 147

1 Kings
19:4 236

Psalms
1:1 18
8:4 25
17:15 97
19:7 32
19:12 39
23 364
24:1–2 318
37:21–22 46
40:1–3 58
46:10 63
65:3 71
85:6 84
115:16 77
121:1–2 52
126:5–6 91
139:7–9 355

Proverbs
22:28 41

Isaiah
1:18 188
6:8 195
26:3 201
55:1 208

Hosea
3:1 173

Zechariah
9:9 337

Matthew
1:23 344

5:13 363
6:34 231
7:24 30
7:24–25 160
8:11–12 314
10:7 20
12:19–20 48
12:45 154
13:39 55
13:44 23
18:21–22 67
21:1–11 106
25:13 95
28:16 357
28:19–20 53

Mark
1:29 181
11:11 339

Luke
1:64 311
2:3 346
2:7 333
2:10 358
7:41–43 43
8:15 50
10:25–29 89
11:9–10 74
14:23–24 61
14:27 82
15:7 16
16:1–2 325
16:9 298
16:10–11 104
16:13 305
17:10 218
18:14 36

John
1:40 329

1:47 335
3:1–2 341
3:3 241
3:16 352
4:7 348
4:13–14 249
8:12 327
14:1–2 308
20:15 262

Acts
9:4–6 256
16:30–31 65

Romans
15:15–16 276

1 Corinthians
1:2 215
1:10 222
1:22–24 73
3:10 228
4:2 120
5:7 234
13:13 13
13:4–7 86
15:3–4 93
15:14 79
15:17–18 100
15:23–24 117
15:32 111
15:49 122
15:58 129
15:51–52, 54, 57 . .362
16:2 283

2 Corinthians
8:2–3 294
8:3 204
8:7 . . . . . .191, 286
8:8 198

8:9 110
9:4 210
9:7 286
9:15 115
12:9 292

Galatians
3:28 135
4:4–5 331

Ephesians
2:8 270

1 Thessalonians
1:2 247
1:5 254
1:7 260
2:4 267
2:8 275
3:2 280
3:6 285
3:11 291
4:7 297
4:13 . . . . .304, 361
5:2 311
5:5 316
5:11 323

1 Timothy
6:11 167

2 Timothy
1:7 224

Hebrews
1:1–2 102
1:2 108
2:1 113
2:10 119
2:14–15 124
4:14 131
6:4–6 137
8:6 143
10:10 149
10:23 156
11:4 289
11:6 359
11:8 163
11:23 169
12:1 176
12:7 183

James
1:26–27 27
1:2–4 127
1:5–8 133
1:12 139
1:14 145
1:22 152
2:9 159
2:14 166
3:8 171
3:10 178
3:13 186
4:3 193

4:11 200
4:13, 15 206
5:3 213
5:8 220
5:12 226
5:16 232
5:20 239

1 Peter
1:3–5 59
1:4 301
3:1–2 141
4:10 273

2 Peter
3:18 281

1 John
5:4 350
5:13 244

2 John
5–6 251

3 John
2 258

Jude
3 265

Revelation
1:5–6 34
21:27 320

Preaching God's Word

A Hands-On Approach to Preparing, Developing, and Delivering Sermons
Preaching God's Word

Terry G. Carter, J. Scott Duvall, and J. Daniel Hays

Preaching God's Word is a homiletics textbook that promotes a strong connection between the process of exegesis and the process of developing a sermon. It ties together the science of biblical interpretation and the art of contemporary communication, resulting in expository preaching that connects with its audience. The book uses numerous examples to illustrate the central points and outlines helpful methodology for students to incorporate into their own sermon preparation. It shows students how to incorporate various aspects of the exegetical process into the biblical sermon. For example, the book demonstrates how students can use the historical cultural background material they have uncovered during exegesis when it comes time to craft their sermons. *Preaching God's Word* is also a valuable resource for today's busy pastor who wishes to communicate strong exegetical messages that will connect with their audience.

Preaching God's Word serves as a companion volume to *Grasping God's Word*, which deals with interpreting and applying the Bible, but it can also be used by itself.

Hardcover: 0-310-24887-6

Pick up a copy today at your favorite bookstore!

ZONDERVAN™

GRAND RAPIDS, MICHIGAN 49530 USA

WWW.ZONDERVAN.COM

The Bible in 90 Days

Ted Cooper Jr.

The Bible in 90 Days is both a Bible and a curriculum that allows individuals to complete what for many Christians is the goal of a lifetime—to read through the Bible completely, from "cover to cover," in a manageable time frame. The basic plan consists of reading 12 pages a day of this specially prepared large-print Bible—a task that usually takes between 45 minutes and an hour—to help readers achieve their goals. Many people spend more time than that commuting back and forth to work every day!

This Bible is part of a larger program, a 14-week curriculum kit designed to help people read through the entire text of the Bible with an opportunity to discuss their reading in a community setting. Developed, field-tested, and used by its creator, Ted Cooper, a Houston businessman, this curriculum has proven successful at many different churches with a wide range of denominational affiliations.

Curriculum Kit: 0-310-26688-2

Pick up a copy today at your favorite bookstore!

ZONDERVAN™

GRAND RAPIDS, MICHIGAN 49530 USA

WWW.ZONDERVAN.COM

Coaching Life-Changing Small Group Leaders

Bill Donahue and Greg Bowman

Leaders within a congregation oversee their members, but who helps coach and train the small-group leaders? Bill Donahue and Greg Bowman, staff members of Willow Creek Association, have developed a handbook for coaches-the people who minister to the needs of small group leaders. Coaches provide leadership development, pastoral care, ministry support and expansion, and meeting facilitation. Originally self-published by Willow Creek, this tested and proven resource has been revised and expanded. It includes new chapters on shepherding, training, and conducting assimilation events; revised charts and diagrams; and extensive theological and biblical support. Instructions and explanations of key concepts have been expanded, while references and content have been updated to align with *Leading Life-Changing Small Groups* and other Willow Creek small-group resources. This is the "go-to" resource for small-group coaches who want to lead and shepherd with excellence. It also features a section specifically for leaders who are responsible for setting up small-group structures in the church.

Softcover: 0-310-25179-6

Pick up a copy today at your favorite bookstore!

GRAND RAPIDS, MICHIGAN 49530 USA

WWW.ZONDERVAN.COM

Thriving through Ministry Conflict

James P. Osterhaus, Joseph M.
Jurkowski, and Todd A. Hahn

Two of the greatest challenges facing ministry leadership are expectations and conflict. Ironically, the more a pastor cares, the more he or she is set up to fail. The solution is not that the effective minister learns to care less, but that he or she cares within legitimate expectations. Using a fictional story of how personal conflict and unmet expectations are resolved into hope and restoration, this book guides pastors and leaders in ministry through three simple principles that are indispensable to successful ministry:

- Identify your own "red zone"—the source of unresolved conflict within yourself.
- Understand how you reinforce the "red zone" in others-unhealthy conflict.
- Learn skills for relating to others in the "blue zone"—where conflict is over ideas and values, not self.

The book includes implementation worksheets.

Hardcover: 0-310-26344-1

Pick up a copy today at your favorite bookstore!

ZONDERVAN™

GRAND RAPIDS, MICHIGAN 49530 USA

WWW.ZONDERVAN.COM

Seismic Shifts

Kevin G. Harney

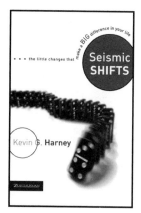

Is it possible for a person to experience dramatic and powerful transformation? Can an ordinary man or woman begin a season of forward movement and growth in areas that have stayed the same for many years? Can our dream of becoming more like Jesus and experiencing a life of health, growth, and joy become a reality? Not only is it possible, but this is exactly what God wants to happen. In the physical world, this kind of change is called a seismic shift. A small movement in the crust of the earth can send out shock waves that have radical and far-reaching effects, redefining an entire landscape. It is the same in the spiritual world. Small changes can transform our faith, hearts, relationships, personal habits, and finances, and even the world in which we live. If we are willing to make small, simple, biblically inspired "seismic shifts," God will enter the process and do amazing things, transforming our lives into ones of joy, victory, and purpose.

Softcover: 0-310-25945-2

Pick up a copy today at your favorite bookstore!

ZONDERVAN™

GRAND RAPIDS, MICHIGAN 49530 USA

W W W . Z O N D E R V A N . C O M

No Perfect People Allowed

John Burke

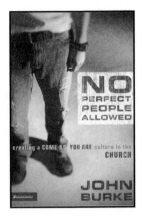

The age demographic of twelve-to-thirty-five-year-olds is America's most unchurched generation. But God is using innovative new churches to reach thousands of spiritually curious "imperfect people" for his kingdom. *No Perfect People Allowed* challenges Christian leaders to engage in the messy art of creating a culture that will reach our postmodern, post-Christian society. The book tells stories of God's perfect work in the lives of imperfect people, showing that the community of believers is what serves as the final apologetic in a post-Christian age. Although the missional leadership required for creating an authentic new "come-as-you-are" culture may feel uncomfortable at first, it holds hope and healing. This book also teaches leaders how to deconstruct five main barriers standing between emerging generations and Christian faith, revealing how the culture of a church can go from being the unseen enemy to becoming its greatest ally.

Hardcover: 0-310-25655-0

Pick up a copy today at your favorite bookstore!

ZONDERVAN™

GRAND RAPIDS, MICHIGAN 49530 USA

WWW.ZONDERVAN.COM

Membership Matters

Chuck Lawless

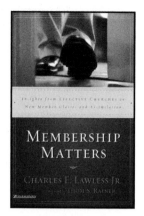

How do churches move members—both old and new—into ministry? Many church staff and lay leaders know they need to start new member classes as a point of entry into their churches but don't know how. This book is based on a national study of effective churches and shows how growing churches implement new member classes and motivate their members into ministry. *Membership Matters* is designed to be a guide for church leaders wanting to start or improve a membership class. It includes models for classes and examples of resources such as church covenants, class schedules, and lesson outlines. It also gives direction on motivating uninvolved members to participate in ministry. One chapter chronicles an ongoing discussion among pastors of growing churches that are effectively motivating members to do ministry.

Hardcover: 0-310-26286-0

Pick up a copy today at your favorite bookstore!

GRAND RAPIDS, MICHIGAN 49530 USA

WWW.ZONDERVAN.COM

God Is Closer Than You Think

John Ortberg

Someone who loves you is waiting to see you. The Bible is filled with examples of an intimate God. A God keenly interested in connecting with ordinary people.

He promises to be with us. He says he will personally guide us. Yet somehow, intimacy with God eludes us. Caught up in the mainstream of life, we know we're missing something vital. But how do we attain it?

God Is Closer Than You Think shows how you can enjoy a vibrant, moment-by-moment relationship with your heavenly Father. This is not about some abstract theological concept, but about the real deal—intimate connection with a deeply personal God.

Softcover: 0-310-25318-7

Pick up a copy today at your favorite bookstore!

ZONDERVAN™

GRAND RAPIDS, MICHIGAN 49530 USA

WWW.ZONDERVAN.COM

A behind-the-scenes analysis of 21 key essential leadership principals from the life of Billy Graham.

The Leadership Secrets of Billy Graham

Harold Myra and Marshall Shelley

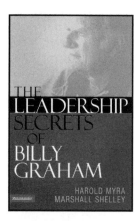

Billy Graham looms large as one of the twentieth century's most influential and innovative leaders. Most people are unaware of his remarkable effectiveness not only as preacher and pastor, but as a CEO and a global leader as well.

The Leadership Secrets of Billy Graham is full of transferable applications for leaders in the church, parachurch, academia, government, and business. Lively interviews with his closest associates illustrate 21 principles that have driven six decades of visionary impact. First-hand accounts reveal stories of courageous leadership and growth through painful lessons.

Graham's relentless application of his core beliefs and leadership principles have resulted in, among many honors, being listed in Gallup's ten "most admired men" thirty times, more than anyone else. *Time* magazine named him one of the top ten leaders of the twentieth century. This book asks: How did this happen? What are the essentials he embraced to achieve such extraordinary results? What can we learn from him and apply to our own leadership roles?

Hardcover: 0-310-25578-3

Pick up a copy today at your favorite bookstore!

GRAND RAPIDS, MICHIGAN 49530 USA

WWW.ZONDERVAN.COM

Exploring the Worship Spectrum

Paul E. Engle, Series Editor; Paul A. Basden, General Editor

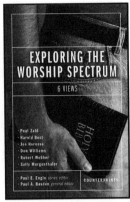

What does worship look like? Is there just one truly right way to worship? Are there any wrong ways? To what extent should our unity as believers manifest itself in unified public worship?

Sadly, disagreement over how we should worship our loving God has sparked some most unloving attitudes among Christians. Exploring the Worship Spectrum seeks to correct this. It provides a forum for presentation, critique, and defense of six prominent worship styles:

- Formal-Liturgical - Paul Zahl
- Traditional Hymn-Based - Harold Best
- Contemporary Music-Driven - Joe Horness
- Charismatic - Don Williams
- Blended - Robert Webber
- Emerging - Sally Morgenthaler

This unique format allows those with a heart for worship to compare different perspectives and draw their own conclusions on what the Bible teaches. It engages the critical thinking in a way that allows readers to understand the various approaches to worship, carefully evaluate their strengths and weaknesses, and make personal choices without adopting a judgmental spirit.

The Counterpoints series provides a forum for comparison and critique of different views on issues important to Christians. Counterpoints books address three categories: Church Life, Exploring Theology, and Engaging Culture. Complete your library with other books in the Counterpoints series.

Softcover: 0-310-24759-4

GRAND RAPIDS, MICHIGAN 49530 USA
WWW.ZONDERVAN.COM

The Art & Craft of Biblical Preaching

Haddon Robinson and Craig Brian Larson,
General Editors

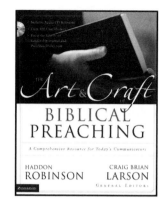

The most complete practical encyclopedia ever on the practice of preaching based on articles from a who's who of over a hundred respected communicators of Christian truth, using significant resources from the ministries of Christianity Today International. It includes an audio CD with examples of preaching technique drawn from the book.

Softcover: 0-310-25248-2

Effective First-Person Biblical Preaching

J. Kent Edwards

A practical text to help students and pastors understand why and how first-person sermons can be preached with biblical integrity. While following Haddon Robinson's "big idea" preaching methodology, the author walks the readers through the steps they can take to prepare an effective first-person message.

Softcover: 0-310-26309-3

Pick up a copy today at your favorite bookstore!

ZONDERVAN™

GRAND RAPIDS, MICHIGAN 49530 USA

WWW.ZONDERVAN.COM

More Movie-Based Illustrations for Preaching & Teaching

Craig Brian Larson and Lori Quicke

If you have used the original *Movie-Based Illustrations for Preaching and Teaching*, you already know why this sequel is a must-have. If not, you're about to discover why *More Movie-Based Illustrations for Preaching and Teaching* is one of the most effective people-reachers you can add to your tool kit. Movies have become the stories of our culture, and they can help you communicate God's Word with power-if you have exciting, movie-based illustrations at your fingertips.

The editors of PreachingToday.com have gathered the best movie-based illustrations, the scenes that convey biblical truth convincingly. This collection contains 101 complete illustrations straight from popular movies your listeners can relate to. Each illustration is easy to use-you don't even have to be familiar with the movie to share the truth it portrays.

- Complete indexes include multiple keywords, movie titles, and relevant Scripture passages for easy selection.
- Each illustration provides plot summary and detailed description of the scene-you can tell the story well even if you haven't seen the movie.
- Exact begin and end times are given for each illustration if you wish to show the video clip.
- Each illustration gives background information on the movie-year created, MPAA rating, and more.

Softcover: 0-310-24834-5

Pick up a copy today at your favorite bookstore!

ZONDERVAN™

GRAND RAPIDS, MICHIGAN 49530 USA

WWW.ZONDERVAN.COM

The Unchurched Next Door

Thom S. Rainer

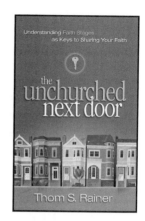

This Silver Medallion Award-winning book is based on a national interview survey of unchurched people and sheds insight on who the unchurched next door are, what objections they raise, and how to connect with them, taking into account their various faith stages. These stages are based on the Rainer scale with rankings from U5 (highly antagonistic) to U1 (highly receptive).

Hardcover: 0-310-24860-4

On Jordan's Stormy Banks

H. Beecher Hicks Jr.

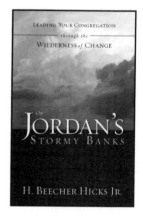

Using the metaphor of God's leading the Israelites through the wilderness by way of the tabernacle, H. Beecher Hicks offers insight based on his own experiences for how to help a congregation capture a vision, overcome obstacles, and see God at work through that vision.

Softcover: 0-310-24774-8

Pick up a copy today at your favorite bookstore!

ZONDERVAN™

GRAND RAPIDS, MICHIGAN 49530 USA

WWW.ZONDERVAN.COM

Mending the Soul

Steven R. Tracy

Biblically grounded and psychologically informed, *Mending the Soul* is a first-of-its-kind, comprehensive approach to understanding and treating every form of abuse for:

- Pastoral and ministry staff
- Small-group leaders and youth workers
- Educators and seminary students
- Pastoral and clinical counselors

It is time for the church to recognize the epidemic scale of abuse.

Abuse kills. In its different forms-physical, sexual, verbal, spiritual, or neglectful-abuse deadens the emotions, slays self-worth, cripples the mind, even destroys the body.

Its victims are legion. They live in your neighborhood, play with your children, and attend your church. In the United States:

- One in three women will be physically assaulted by an intimate partner.
- About 1.5 million children are abused or neglected annually.
- At least 25 percent of girls experience contact sexual abuse.

But there is hope.

God delights in mending shattered souls. However, healing doesn't come by ignoring the problem of abuse, minimizing its complexities, or downplaying its devastating impact. Healing comes by fully understanding the nature and ramifications of abuse, and by following a biblical path of restoration that allows God's grace to touch the heart's deep wounds.

Mending the Soul sounds the call and leads the charge. Thorough and accessible, this is a unique and powerful resource for understanding and healing victims of abuse.

Softcover: 0-310-24363-7

Pick up a copy today at your favorite bookstore!

ZONDERVAN™

GRAND RAPIDS, MICHIGAN 49530 USA

WWW.ZONDERVAN.COM

Lasso Them with Laughter

1002 Humorous Illustrations for Public Speaking

Michael Hodgin

One way to your listeners' hearts is through their funny bones. Want to grab their attention? Do it with humor. Need to drive home a point they'll remember? Nothing does it better than a rib-tickling anecdote-like the ones in this book. *1002 Humorous Illustrations for Public Speaking* is jam-packed with one-liners, jokes, humorous stories, and pithy proverbs for just about any subject or circumstance under the sun.

Pick your topic. Appearances, Communication, Opportunity, Prayer, Self-Image, Sports . . . these and plenty more come to you conveniently alphabetized, numbered, and indexed for instant referencing. There's even a space for you to log what you use, so fresh nuttiness doesn't become old chestnuts.

Tested by preachers and public speakers, this ensemble of humor is just the ticket to get your audience laughing-and listening.

Softcover: 0-310-25602-X

Pick up a copy today at your favorite bookstore!

ZONDERVAN™

GRAND RAPIDS, MICHIGAN 49530 USA

WWW.ZONDERVAN.COM

Cross the bridge between the church you are and the church you want to be

The Purpose-Driven® Church

Growth Without Compromising Your Message and Mission

Rick Warren

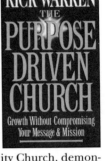

Read the groundbreaking half-million-copy bestseller that has influenced churches worldwide. This award-winning book offers a biblical and practical strategy to empower churches to minister to the 21st century. Rick Warren, pastor of Saddleback Valley Community Church, demonstrates that growing churches have a clear-cut identity and mission, precise in their purpose and knowing what God has called them to do.

Hardcover: 0-310-20106-3
Abridged Audio Pages® cassettes: 0-310-20518-2
Unabridged Audio Pages® cassettes: 0-310-22901-4

Transitioning

Leading Your Church Through Change

Dan Southerland

If you've been thinking about leading your traditional church toward becoming a purpose-driven church, *Transitioning* gives you the wisdom and guidance you need. Drawing from a wealth of experience, Pastor Dan Southerland takes you through the eight-step process of discovering and implementing God's unique mission for your congregation. With thought, prayer, planning, and patience, you and your church can discover the rich rewards of being purpose driven.

> "One of the most exciting and encouraging examples of transitioning from being program driven to purpose driven."
>
> —From the foreword by Rick Warren,
> Author of *The Purpose-Driven® Church*

Softcover: 0-310-24268-1

Pick up a copy today at your favorite bookstore!

GRAND RAPIDS, MICHIGAN 49530 USA

WWW.ZONDERVAN.COM

Zondervan Practical Ministry Guides

Paul E. Engle, General Editor

These practical ministry guides are designed as tools for lay teacher and training groups that serve in various ministries within the local church. Features of each book include:

Softcover

Serving by Safeguarding Your Church: 0-310-24105-7
Serving as a Church Greeter: 0-310-24764-0
Serving in Church Music Ministry: 0-310-24101-4
Serving in the Church Nursery: 0-310-24104-9
Serving as a Church Usher: 0-310-24763-2
Serving in Church Visitation: 0-310-24103-0
Serving in Your Church Prayer Ministry: 0-310-24758-6

Time-Saving Ideas for...

Your Church Sign
1001 Attention-Getting Sayings
Verlyn D. Verbrugge

Your Church Sign offers sound pointers on signage. You'll find tips on impactful sign placement, captions, themes, and how to write effective messages. And you'll get more than one thousand ready-made, eye-catching sayings. Some are humorous, some are encouraging, some are wise, some are convicting. All are designed to turn a scant second of drive-by time into active spiritual awareness.

Softcover: 0-310-22802-6

Pick up a copy today at your favorite bookstore!

GRAND RAPIDS, MICHIGAN 49530 USA

WWW.ZONDERVAN.COM

Preaching in Black and White
What We Can Learn from Each Other

E. K. Bailey and Warren W. Wiersbe

*P*reaching in Black and White offers a unique look at two distinct preaching traditions and the wisdom they have to offer each other. But this book goes much deeper than mere stylistic nuances, for authors E. K. Bailey and Warren Wiersbe are far more than prominent pastors and preachers. They are men with a penetrating understanding of history, culture, and church tradition—and they are friends who genuinely enjoy and respect each other. The warmth of their relationship shines in this book, matched by a depth of honesty and humility as they address topics of vital interest to pastors, speakers, and church leaders of all ethnic backgrounds.

In a winsome dialog format, Drs. Bailey and Wiersbe look at the preparation not only of the sermon but also of the preacher's heart. They discuss sermon content and delivery and how it all comes together in practice. Taking a well-known Bible story, the authors demonstrate and then discuss their distinctive preaching styles and what it takes to learn from others (sermon transcriptions included). A section containing brief biographies of black preachers concludes this engaging and illuminating book.

Includes CD of sermon by E. K. Bailey.

Softcover: 0-310-24099-9

A Hand Up Instead of a Handout
The Gathering Place
Empowering Your Community through Urban Church Education

James R. Love Sr.

*I*n order to break the urban cycle of poverty and oppression, our communities need the empowerment that comes from a practical education—one that combines biblical principles with real-world knowledge and application. Inner-city churches are ideal for providing such an education. *The Gathering Place* shows how your church can give needy people not only a handout, but also an essential hand up to successful lives.

"This book serves as a training manual . . . even for those who are ill-equipped for or overwhelmed by the task of urban church education," writes Dr. James R. Love Sr. From his years of experience with urban churches, Dr. Love shows how the church can bring people together and give them the spiritual and practical resources needed to put the life-changing power of the gospel in motion.

Softcover: 0-310-24140-5

ZONDERVAN™

GRAND RAPIDS, MICHIGAN 49530 USA

WWW.ZONDERVAN.COM

Counseling in African-American Communities

Biblical Perspectives on Tough Issues

Lee N. June Ph.D., and Sabrina D. Black, M.A., Editors;
Dr. Willie Richardson, Consulting Editor

The gospel brings liberty to men, women, and children bound by every conceivable sin and affliction. Psychology provides a tool for applying the power of the gospel in practical ways. Drawing on biblical truths and psychological principles, *Counseling in African-American Communities* helps Christian counselors, pastors, and church leaders to meet the deep needs of our communities with life-changing effect.

Marshaling the knowledge and experience of experts in the areas of addiction, family issues, mental health, and other critical issues, this no-nonsense handbook supplies distinctively African-American insights for the problems tearing lives and families apart all around us:

- Domestic Abuse
- Gambling Addiction
- Blended Families
- Sexual Addiction and the Internet
- Depression and Bipolar Disorder
- Divorce Recovery
- Unemployment
- Sexual Abuse and Incest
- Demonology
- Grief and Loss
- Schizophrenia
- Substance Abuse . . . and much more

Softcover: 0-310-24025-5

Pick up a copy today at your favorite bookstore!

ZONDERVAN™

GRAND RAPIDS, MICHIGAN 49530 USA

WWW.ZONDERVAN.COM

Preaching That Connects

Using the Techniques of Journalists to Add Impact to Your Sermons

Mark Galli and Craig Brian Larson

Master the craft of effective communication that grabs attention and wins hearts.

Like everyone else, preachers long to be understood. Unfortunately the rules first learned in seminary, if misapplied, can quickly turn homiletic precision into listener boredom.

To capture the heart and mind, Mark Galli and Craig Larson suggest preachers turn to the lessons of journalism. In preaching that connects they show how the same keys used to create effective, captivating communication in the media can transform a sermon.

Softcover: 0-310-38621-7

Preaching Through a Storm

Confirming the Power of Preaching in the Tempest of Church Conflict

H. Beecher Hicks Jr.

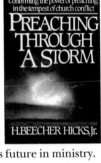

The context was a building program for an urban congregation. The beginning bore no omens of controversy. But before long, both the pastor (the author) and the congregation found themselves in a storm that threatened the church's very existence and the pastor's future in ministry.

Softcover: 0-310-20091-1

Preaching with Purpose

The Urgent Task of Homiletics

Jay E. Adams

Preaching needs to become purposeful, says Jay Adams, because purposeless preaching is deadly. This book was written to help ministers and students discover the purpose of preaching and the ways that the scriptures inform and direct the preaching task. *Preaching with Purpose,* like the many other books of Jay Adams, speaks clearly and forcefully to the issue. Having read this book, both students and experienced preachers will be unable to ignore the urgent task of purposeful preaching. And the people of God will be the better for it.

Softcover: 0-310-51091-0

Multicultural Ministry

David A. Anderson

In this groundbreaking book, David Anderson invites us all—African-American, Asian, Caucasian, and Latino—to learn how to dance the dance of multicultural ministry. We've all got different moves, but that's the beauty of diversity: the various gifts we bring, the wisdom of our heritages, the different creative ways we express the same Lord. Think it can't be done? Think again. As Anderson demonstrates, it is being done successfully by more and more churches.

Softcover: 0-310-25158-3

Lights, Drama, Worship!
Volumes 1-4
Karen F. Williams

Each book in this four-volume series offers a variety of performance materials, from short, easy-to-perform sketches and readings to longer, more structured plays. Whether your church drama ministry is brand new or has been established for years, there's something for everyone, from beginners with little or no experience to seasoned players who want a challenge.

This one-stop drama resource covers . . .

- Key aspects of Christian living—such as salvation, forgiveness, God's provision, love, persistence, and faith
- Special occasions—Christmas, Easter, Mother's Day, Black History Month, and more
- Each play includes—production tips for costuming, set design, props, and rehearsal notes, Scripture references , themes, summaries, and character lists

- The volume also includes blocking tips and helpful tips from other dramatists
- topical index

Softcover
Volume 1: 0-310-24245-2
Volume 2: 0-310-24249-5
Volume 3: 0-310-24263-0
Volume 4: 0-310-24264-9

How to Thrive as a Small-Church Pastor

A Guide to Spiritual and Emotional Well-Being

Steve R. Bierly

Steve Bierly knows firsthand the needs and concerns of small-church pastors. He also knows how to meet the needs, handle the concerns, and thrive as a pastor with a congregation of 150 or less.

Drawing on his many years of small-church experience, Bierly helps pastors reframe their perspective of God, ministry, relationships, their own needs, and more. He offers seasoned, fatherly counsel—assurance to small-church pastors that they're not alone; a fresh outlook on the successes of their ministries; and an upbeat, practical approach to spiritual, emotional, and physical well being.

Filled with good humor, here is help for small-church pastors to face the rigors of their vocation realistically and reclaim their first love of ministry.

Softcover: 0-310-21655-9

I'm More Than the Pastor's Wife

Lorna Dobson

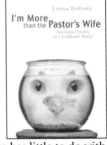

Lorna Dobson knows firsthand the struggles and joys of being married to a pastor—and the questions, not the least of which is, "What is a 'pastor's wife,' anyway?" As her poll of hundreds of women reveals, the wife of a minister rarely fits the piano-playing, committee-leading stereotype.

With humor, disarming genuineness, personal stories, and wisdom rooted in Scripture, Dobson cuts through the labels. "How I live has little to do with whether my husband is a pastor; rather, my life reflects my growth, or lack of it, as a Christian." In this revised edition of *I'm More Than the Pastor's Wife*, she includes new perspectives as a grandparent, soon-to-be empty-nester, and speaker. Here are frontline insights on

- Making friends and cultivating personal support outside the church
- Learning to handle expectations and pressures
- Balancing time and using your gifts

And more . . .
Softcover: 0-310-24728-4

GRAND RAPIDS, MICHIGAN 49530 USA

WWW.ZONDERVAN.COM

Zondervan 2006 Church and Nonprofit Tax and Financial Guide

Dan Busby, CPA

Coming in December

For 2005 Returns

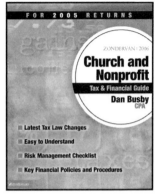

This annual reference guide continues to be one of the few resources offering tax and financial aid to churches and nonprofit organizations. The 2006 edition also contains a thorough description of tax laws affecting churches, including changes made in 2005, compliant with all regulations.

Softcover: 031026183x

Zondervan 2006 Minister's Tax and Financial Guide

Dan Busby, CPA

Coming In December

For 2005 Returns

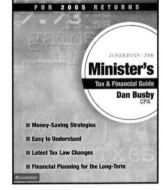

This easy-to-understand workbook simplifies the tax code and offers dozens of tips to reduce your tax bill. For 2006, the guide includes a line-by-line explanation of the 1040 Form, retirement tips, compensation planning guidance, and ways to maximize business expense reimbursements.

Softcover: 031026216x

Pick up a copy today at your favorite bookstore!

We want to hear from you. Please send your comments about this
book to us in care of zreview@zondervan.com. Thank you.

GRAND RAPIDS, MICHIGAN 49530 USA

WWW.ZONDERVAN.COM